Different Faces of Attachment

Cultural Variations on a Universal Human Need

Attachment between an infant and his or her parents is a major topic within developmental psychology. An increasing number of psychologists, evolutionary biologists, and anthropologists are articulating their doubts that attachment theory in its present form is applicable worldwide, without, however, denying that the development of attachment is a universal need. This book brings together leading scholars from psychology, anthropology, and related fields to reformulate attachment theory in order to fit the cultural realities of our world. Contributions are based on empirical research and observation in a variety of cultural contexts. They are complemented by careful evaluation and deconstruction of many of the underlying premises and assumptions of attachment theory and of conventional research on the role of infant–parent attachment in human development. The book creates a contextual cultural understanding of attachment that will provide the basis for a groundbreaking reconceptualization of attachment theory.

HILTRUD OTTO is a postdoctoral member of the Martin Buber Society of Fellows in the Humanities at the Hebrew University of Jerusalem, Israel.

HEIDI KELLER is Professor of Culture and Development in the Faculty of Human Sciences at the University of Osnabrück.

Different Faces of Attachment

Cultural Variations on a Universal Human Need

Edited by

Hiltrud Otto and Heidi Keller

CAMBRIDGE
UNIVERSITY PRESS

CAMBRIDGE
UNIVERSITY PRESS

University Printing House, Cambridge CB2 8BS, United Kingdom

Cambridge University Press is part of the University of Cambridge.

It furthers the University's mission by disseminating knowledge in the pursuit of education, learning and research at the highest international levels of excellence.

www.cambridge.org
Information on this title: www.cambridge.org/9781107027749

© Cambridge University Press 2014

First published 2014

Printed in the United Kingdom by Clays, St Ives plc

A catalogue record for this publication is available from the British Library

Library of Congress Cataloguing in Publication data
Different faces of attachment: cultural variations on a universal human need / edited by Hiltrud Otto and Heidi Keller.
    pages   cm
Includes bibliographical references and index.
ISBN 978-1-107-02774-9 (hardback)
1. Attachment behavior   2. Attachment behavior – Cross-cultural studies.
3. Attachment behavior in children – Cross-cultural studies.   4. Child psychology – Cross-cultural studies.   I. Otto, Hiltrud, 1977–   II. Keller, Heidi, 1945–
BF575.A86D54   2014
155.9'2 – dc23   2014007617

ISBN 978-1-107-02774-9 Hardback

Contents

Figures

Tables

Contributors

VIVIAN J. CARLSON, Ph.D., is an Associate Professor (tenured) of Human Development and Family Studies in the School of Graduate and Professional Studies at the University of Saint Joseph, West Hartford, Connecticut. She has served as Chair of the Department of Human Development and Family Studies since 2007. Dr. Carlson is also a developmental psychologist and a professional in special education who brings over thirty years of home-based early intervention experience to her research and teaching career. She completed her Ph.D. in Family Studies at the University of Connecticut. Her publications and presentations focus on the interface of culture and development and its impact on parenting, attachment, aggression among girls, and bullying among young urban children. Her research has challenged the cultural biases inherent in definitions of optimal parenting in attachment theory, and has provided concrete examples and applications of cultural knowledge for professionals from fields as diverse as early intervention, special education, marriage and family therapy, and law enforcement. Her current work includes an ethnographic study of women from urban, resource-poor backgrounds in Guyana, South America, and the USA who become transformative leaders in their communities. Dr. Carlson also works among the indigenous peoples of the interior rain forests and savannahs of Guyana, providing services for people with disabilities during biannual visits.

DANIEL L. EVERETT is Dean of Arts and Sciences at Bentley University in Waltham, Massachusetts. He has published more than 100 articles and 11 books on linguistics and Amazonian languages and has received many grants for his research in the Brazilian Amazon. A film about his life and work, *The Grammar of Happiness,* was released worldwide in 2012. He is currently writing "Dark Matter of the Mind: How Unseen Forces Shape Our Words and World" for the University of Chicago Press.

ALMA GOTTLIEB is Professor of Anthropology, African Studies, Global Studies, and Gender and Women's Studies at the University of Illinois at Urbana-Champaign. She has also taught and held research appointments at Princeton University, the École des Hautes Études en Sciences Sociales (Paris), the Katholieke University of Leuven, the Instituto Superior da Ciências Sociais e Políticais (Lisbon), and other institutions. Her teaching and research specializations include infants and children, feminism, religion, humanistic anthropology, and ethnographic writing. She has conducted fieldwork in Ivory Coast and, more recently, with Cape Verdeans on and off the islands (in Europe and the USA). She has authored or edited eight books, including *The Afterlife Is Where We Come From: The Culture of Infancy in West Africa* (University of Chicago Press, 2004) and *A World of Babies: Imagined Childcare Guides for Seven Societies* (Cambridge University Press, 2010) (with Judy DeLoache), and with her husband, the author Philip Graham, she has written two memoirs of their life with the Beng, *Parallel Worlds: An Anthropologist and a Writer Encounter Africa* (University of Chicago Press, 1993) and *Braided Worlds* (University of Chicago Press, 2012). Her work has been supported by the Guggenheim Foundation, the Social Science Research Council, the US National Endowment for the Humanities, and other agencies.

ROBIN L. HARWOOD, Ph.D., is a Health Scientist in the Division of Research in the Office of Epidemiology and Research (OER), the Maternal and Child Health Bureau (MCHB), and the Health Resources and Services Administration (HRSA). She is the federal liaison and project officer for the Home Visiting Research Network, and project officer for the MCHB Home Visiting Research Grants, an investigator-initiated program. In addition to home visiting, Robin's portfolio also includes research grants and networks from the Combating Autism Act Initiative, and the MCHB Research Program. Prior to joining the federal government, she was an Associate Professor (tenured) in the School of Family Studies at the University of Connecticut. During her years in academia, she was Principal Investigator for two separate National Institute of Child Health and Human Development (NICHD) grants examining culture, attachment, and parenting beliefs among mothers in Puerto Rico, Germany, and the USA. She has published numerous articles in peer-reviewed journals, as well as two books on child development, culture, and attachment. She received her Ph.D. from Yale University.

SEAN HAWKS is a Ph.D. student in cultural anthropology at Washington State University. He is interested in attachment theory from a human behavioral ecology perspective. He is interested in the world-views and relationships with neighboring groups of hunter-gatherers, and he uses both evolutionary and cultural theory to describe and explain the nature of these relationships.

JOHANNES JOHOW is a postdoctoral research fellow at the Institute of Philosophy, Justus Liebig University of Giessen, Germany. His research focuses on life-history theory and cooperative breeding in humans.

HEIDI KELLER is a Professor at the University of Osnabrück, Germany, and director of the research unit "Culture, Learning and Development" at the Lower Saxony Institute of Early Childhood Education and Development. She directs a multicultural research program of developmental pathways across infancy and childhood. She has been a visiting professor at, among other institutions, the NICHD (Washington, DC), the University of California, Los Angeles; the Universidad de Costa Rica, San José; and the MS University of Baroda, Vadodara, India. She was president of the International Association for Cross-Cultural Psychology from 2008 to 2010.

MICHAEL E. LAMB, Ph.D., is Professor and the Head of the Department of Social and Developmental Psychology at the University of Cambridge, UK. In 2003 Lamb was the recipient of the 2003–2004 James McKeen Cattell Fellow Award from the Association for Psychological Science. Lamb researches early family relationships, childcare, developmental science, and related public policy. This work has focused on divorce, child custody, child maltreatment, and the effects of childcare on children's social and emotional development. Lamb was the head of the section on social and emotional development of the NICHD in Washington, DC, for seventeen years.

DAVID F. LANCY, Emeritus Professor of Anthropology at Utah State University, earned degrees from Yale and the University of Pittsburgh. He has done fieldwork in Liberia, Papua New Guinea, Trinidad (Fulbright Fellowship), Sweden (Fulbright Fellowship), and the USA. His research interests include the study of cultural influences on children's literacy, ethnographic research methods, and the anthropology of childhood. He is the author of *The Anthropology of Childhood: Cherubs, Chattel, Changelings* (Cambridge University Press, 2008), and *Playing on the Mother-Ground: Cultural Routines for Children's Development* (Guilford Press, 1996), and is coeditor of *The Anthropology of Learning in Childhood* (Cambridge University Press, 2008).

ROBERT A. LEVINE is Roy E. Larsen Professor of Education and Human Development, Emeritus, Harvard University. He is an anthropologist who has devoted a long career to the cross-cultural study of parenting and child development, carrying out research in Africa, Asia, and Latin America with his wife Sarah LeVine. Their book (with Beatrice Schnell-Anzola, Meredith Rowe, and Emily Dexter), *Literacy and Mothering: How Women's Schooling Changes the Lives of the World's Children* (Oxford University Press, 2012), won the Eleanor E. Maccoby Book Award in Developmental Psychology of the American Psychological Association in 2013. His other books include *Anthropology and Child Development: A Cross-Cultural Reader* (Wiley-Blackwell, 2008) and *Child Care and Culture: Lessons from Africa* (Cambridge University Press, 1994).

COURTNEY L. MEEHAN is a faculty member in the Department of Anthropology at Washington State University. She is a human behavioral ecologist whose research focuses on early childhood environment and children's physical, social, and emotional development. Currently, she is the principal investigator on a longitudinal project, funded by the US National Science Foundation, on the effects of cooperative breeding on child development, maternal reproduction, and family health. She conducts her research in the Central African Republic among a forager population and several farming populations.

HILTRUD OTTO is a postdoctoral member of the Martin Buber Society of Fellows in the Humanities at the Hebrew University of Jerusalem, Israel. She is an early childhood scholar specializing in early socioemotional development, as well as culture and attachment. For her research on the development of attachment relationships among Cameroonian Nso children and their caregivers, she received her Ph.D. in 2009 from the University of Osnabrück, Germany, where she was a research associate at the Department of Culture and Development and a scientific staff member of the Lower Saxony Institute of Early Development and Learning. Dr. Otto is a junior investigator in the research project, "Development of Relationships During Infancy: Risk and Protective Factors in Minority and Majority Families in Germany and Israel" (supported by the State of Lower Saxony, Hannover, Germany), and she participates in various national and international research projects promoting context-informed research and training for children in need.

BIRGITT RÖTTGER-RÖSSLER is Professor of Social and Cultural Anthropology at the Freie Universität Berlin. She is head of the focus group "Anthropology of Emotions" at the faculty of Political and Social

Sciences and acts as associate director of the cluster of excellence "Languages of Emotion" at the Freie Universität Berlin. She studied cultural and social anthropology, Romance studies, and Malay languages and literatures, as well as European ethnology, at the universities of Göttingen, Zurich, Cologne, and Bonn. In recent years her research has focused on the emotions, primarily dealing with the cultural modeling of emotions in Southeast Asian societies. She has conducted long-term fieldwork in Indonesia. Her current projects deal with the socialization of emotions in cross-cultural comparison, with the connection of emotion and memory as well as with conflicting "feeling rules" in the context of migration.

NANCY SCHEPER-HUGHES is Professor of Medical Anthropology at the University of California, Berkeley, where she directs the doctoral program, "Critical Studies in Medicine, Science, and the Body." Scheper-Hughes' long-term work examines the violence of everyday life from a radical existentialist and politically engaged perspective. She has conducted research on, has written on, and has been politically engaged in topics ranging from AIDS and human rights in Cuba; death squads and the extermination of street children in Brazil; and the Catholic Church, clerical celibacy, and child sex abuse, to the repatriation of the brain of a famous Yahi Indian, Ishi (kept as a specimen in the Smithsonian Institution) to the Pit River people of northern California. Her most recent research is a multisited, ethnographic study of the global traffic in human organs, a shocking new triangular slave trade in which the poor are taken to distant cities by criminal syndicates and coerced into selling their organs for illegal transplants. Her next book, *The Ends of the Body: The Global Traffic in Organs*, is to be published by Farrar, Straus, and Giroux. She is cofounder and Director of Organs Watch, a medical human-rights project, and she is currently an adviser to the World Health Organization (Geneva) on issues related to global organ transplantation. Scheper-Hughes has lectured internationally and has been a research professor in residence at the École des Hautes Études en Sciences Sociales in Paris in 1993.

ECKART VOLAND is a Professor of the Philosophy of Biology at the Institute of Philosophy, Justus Liebig University of Giessen, Germany. He is mainly interested in human reproductive ecology, life-history theory, evolutionary ethics, and philosophy of mind.

THOMAS S. WEISNER, Ph.D., is Professor of Anthropology in the Departments of Psychiatry (Semel Institute, Center for Culture and Health) and Anthropology at the University of California, Los Angeles.

His research and teaching interests are in culture and human development; medical, psychological, and cultural studies of families and children at risk; mixed methods, and evidence-informed policy. He has done fieldwork with the Abaluyia of Kenya, native Hawaiians, countercultural US families, US families with children with disabilities, and US poor working families. He is the author or editor of *Higher Ground: New Hope for the Working Poor and Their Children* (with Greg Duncan and Aletha Huston) (Russell Sage Foundation, 2007); *Making It Work: Low-Wage Employment, Family Life and Child Development* (with Hiro Yoshikawa and Edward Lowe) (Russell Sage Foundation, 2006); *Discovering Successful Pathways in Children's Development: New Methods in the Study of Childhood and Family Life* (University of Chicago Press, 2005); and *African Families and the Crisis of Social Change* (with Candice Bradley and Phil Kilbride) (Greenwood, 1997).

Foreword

Attachment theory developed amidst the talented group of psychologists and clinicians who surrounded John Bowlby in London between the publication of his memorable report on maternal deprivation for the World Health Organization (*Maternal Care and Mental Health*) in 1951 (a more popular version was published by Pelican as *Child Care and the Growth of Love* in 1953) and the publication of his article on "The Nature of the Child's Tie to His Mother" in 1958. As subsequently elaborated in the trilogy Bowlby published between 1969 and 1980, attachment theory represented a synthesis of the available clinical evidence, sensitive observations of young children experiencing stressful separations, and comparative experimental research by scientists such as Harry Harlow, a psychologist, and Robert Hinde, a behavioral biologist, all viewed in the context of the integrative control systems theory then emerging. The tremendous power of that synthesis has been demonstrated conclusively over the course of the ensuing decades as attachment theory has come to be recognized as the most coherent and predictively useful theory describing human developmental processes.

The enduring success of attachment theory is surely attributable not only to its scientific coherence but also to its timeliness and cultural resonance, although proponents of attachment theory have long preferred to claim it as a purely scientific theory with implications for policy (e.g., on early childcare) and practice (with an emphasis on maternal responsibility and responsiveness) rather than as an ideologically compatible framework for understanding early development. A traumatic half-century of war and devastation had precipitated widespread doubts and questions about the essence of human nature by the time Bowlby began creating attachment theory. Bowlby's theory provided comforting reassurance that human babies were biologically designed to thrive when assured of the continued availability and responsiveness of their mothers, and this emphasis on maternal love and exclusive domesticity strongly complemented a widespread desire to reclaim a "traditional" way of life, with mothers focused on caring for their children and fathers focused on economic activity, rebuilding the shattered economies and societies around them. There is little doubt that the widespread embrace of attachment theory in Western developmental psychology was attributable, at least in part, to its resonance with cultural values then in ascendance. Less remarked upon is the extent to which the theory itself was surely created under the influence of clear cultural values and ideology as well.

The contributors to Otto and Keller's remarkable anthology have no doubt about the important role played by values and practices in shaping beliefs, practices, and early child–parent relationships. Writing in both German and English over the last 30 years, Keller (e.g., Keller, 2007; Keller, Miranda, and Gauda, 1984; Keller, Poortinga, and Schoelmerich, 2002) has argued and demonstrated that different cultural groups view infancy, parenthood, and developmental processes in distinctive ways and that these often profound differences shape infant–parent interactions and relationships significantly, thereby raising searching questions about many of the assumptions and conclusions held dear by attachment theorists and developmental scientists. Now, in this volume, Keller and her coeditor, Hiltrud Otto, are joined by a phalanx of distinguished psychologists and anthropologists who have conducted research in diverse cultures and settings designed to document the central importance of ecological variations in understanding the role, or possible roles, of infant–parent relationships in development. The case they offer is challenging and compelling, strengthened by the impressive way in which empirical research and observation in a variety of cultural contexts is complemented by careful evaluation and deconstruction of many of the underlying premises and assumptions of attachment theory and of conventional research on the role of infant–parent (though often only infant–mother) attachment in human development. Collectively, these scholars have constructed a remarkable argument for the central importance of the cultural context when striving to understand the place of attachment in human development. Their examination and critique of attachment theory is thus much more comprehensive and provocative than much earlier evaluations of the empirical foundations of attachment theory written by my colleagues and me (e.g., Lamb, Thompson, Gardner et al., 1985).

Specifically, the contributors to *Different Faces of Attachment* address, in sequence, the extent to which attachment theory is as well grounded in evolutionary theory as Bowlby believed, cultural differences in the perception of close child–parent relationships, differences in the early experiences and processes of relationship formation in differently organized societies, and descriptive accounts of parent–child interaction in several quite distinctive socioecological contexts. It ends with two chapters by culturally sensitive scholars who have long pondered the role of culture in shaping social relationships, and a concluding chapter written by the editors.

Different Faces of Attachment is a unique collection, rich in insights and provocative ideas. It should be required reading for all developmental scientists and theorists, as well as for practitioners with responsibility for translating the fruits of research (often conducted in a rather narrow and unrepresentative cultural context) into practical guidelines to be followed in other, quite different cultural settings. At a time when there is increasing focus on the extreme fragility and vulnerability of infants and young children, there is a special need for scholars to recognize not only the remarkable resilience of young humans, but also our species' incredible adaptability to diverse sociocultural demands and contexts. *Different Faces of Attachment* offers a compelling argument for humility and for recognition of the rather unusual circumstances to which attachment theory has been responsive.

MICHAEL E. LAMB
Cambridge University, UK

References

Bowlby, J. (1951). *Maternal care and mental health*. Geneva: World Health Organization.
    (1953). *Child care and the growth of love*. London: Pelican Books.
    (1958). The nature of the child's tie to his mother. *International Journal of Psycho-Analysis, 39,* 350–73.
    (1969). *Attachment*. London: Hogarth.
    (1980). *Loss*. London: Hogarth.
Keller, H. (2007). *Cultures of infancy*. Mahwah NJ: Erlbaum.
Keller, H., Miranda, D., and Gauda, G. (1984). The naïve theory of the infant and some maternal attitudes: a two-country study. *Journal of Cross-Cultural Psychology, 15,* 165–79.
Keller, H., Poortinga, Y. H., and Schoelmerich, A. (Eds.) (2002). *Between culture and biology*. Cambridge University Press.
Lamb, M. E., Thompson, R. A., Gardner, W. P., and Charnov, E. L. (1985). *Infant–mother attachment: the origins and developmental significance of individual differences in strange situation behaviour*. Hillsdale, NJ: Erlbaum.

Introduction: understanding relationships – what we would need to know to conceptualize attachment as the cultural solution of a universal developmental task

Heidi Keller

The definition of attachment as a primary bond between infants and caregivers emerging at around 1 year of age as an evolved adaptation for ensuring survival and development was the seminal contribution of the British psychiatrist and psychoanalyst John Bowlby and his (later) Canadian-American counterpart Mary Ainsworth (Ainsworth, Blehar, Waters *et al.*, 1978; Bowlby, 1969). Attachment theory has initiated a tremendous body of research over the last decades, particularly expanding its focus on neurophysiological regulations, and extending it to adulthood and clinical applications. Nevertheless, the theoretical and methodological foundations have remained amazingly unaffected, although the basis of knowledge concerning the infant's socioemotional development has increased substantially since the publication of Bowlby's well-known trilogy *Attachment and Loss* and Ainsworth and collaborators' summary of their empirical research on the emergence of attachment during the first year of life (1978). The first encompassing proposal for the refinement of conceptual and methodological issues of attachment theory and research was published by Michael Lamb and collaborators in 1984 in the renowned journal *Behavioral and Brain Sciences* – though without any observable notice by other attachment researchers.

Attachment theory is grounded in evolutionary theory with its basic tenet that every human characteristic is shaped through selection processes and represents an adaptation to contextual demands. Bowlby stressed explicitly the contextual nature of attachment in his early writings. Yet Bowlby focused mainly on the social environment, especially the mother, since he did not include information about other caregivers and the family and their living conditions in his World Health Organization (WHO) report (Bowlby, 1969; for a more detailed discussion, see Vicedo, 2013).

Thus, an important piece of information is lacking – that is, the contextual embeddedness of the child in his social environment (see Bronfenbrenner, 1977; Keller, 2007; Keller and Kärtner, 2013; Super and Harkness, 1986). Acknowledgment of the differential nature of contexts would necessitate also different behavioral and psychological solutions representing adaptations. Instead the human condition that the offspring can survive and thrive only when attachment relationships serve a protective function has been taken as a universal in every respect. The repeated claims of cultural psychologists and anthropologists, as well as evolutionary biologists, for decades to recognize contextual/cultural variation and systematically introduce it into attachment theory have been largely ignored, so that Sarah Hrdy (1999, p. 174), among others, concluded that "the usefulness of such ill-defined and culturally de-contextualized terms . . . as . . . bonding, attachment" must be questioned. In a historical analysis, Marga Vicedo (2013) historicizes the various features, assumptions, and modes of expression of attachment as a product of Cold War America (see also the review of the book by Harris, 2013).

Van IJzendoorn and Sagi-Schwartz (2008), the experts in discussing "culture and attachment" from a point of view within attachment research, acknowledge contextual variations when reviewing attachment studies done with non-Western samples and attest to the need for a radical change from a dyadic perspective to a network approach (which would also have radical consequences for the definition and assessment of attachment) (p. 900; see Heinicke, 1995, for similar arguments), but, surprisingly, they conclude that, "in fact, taken as a whole, the studies are remarkably consistent with the theory" (p. 901). Yet, there is an impressive documentation (although by far insufficient with respect to cultural variability) of diverse realities and thus contexts in the anthropological and psychological literature, as documented in this volume. Moreover, there is recognition that attachment and its formation vary substantially with the contexts in which children grow and develop (e.g., Gottlieb, 2004, see also Gottlieb in this volume; Harwood, Miller, and Lucca Irizarry, 1995, see also Carlson and Harwood in this volume; Keller and Harwood, 2009; Lancy, 2008, see also Lancy in this volume; Rothbaum, Weisz, Pott *et al.*, 2000; Weisner and Gallimore, 1977, see also Weisner in this volume). Unfortunately, this body of literature did not find its way into attachment theory and did not inform the further development of attachment theory and methodology. The argument being put forward here is that contextual variations need to be systematically incorporated into attachment theory to lead to a radical shift from the view of attachment as a universal human need that has the same shape and emerges the same way across cultures to the view of attachment as a universal human need that looks differently and has different developmental trajectories across contexts. In line with evolutionary (e.g., Draper and Belsky, 1990, see also Johow and Voland in this volume) as well as cultural accounts (Keller and Kärtner, 2013; Whiting, 1977), these contexts need to be specified as psychological and material resources that afford particular strategies of adaptation. We have defined contexts as patterns of socio-cultural parameters with level of formal education as an organizer of fertility patterns and conceptions of family (Keller, 2007, 2012; Whiting, 1977). People who live in similar sociodemographic contexts share the values and conceptions of behavior (Greenfield and Keller, 2004) that are the major constituents of cultural models. Therefore, different contexts represent different cultural models or cultural milieus at the same time.

Anthropologists and cultural psychologists have claimed that attachment research (like much of psychology in general) does not recognize the fundamental differences in cultural conceptions of the self and the implications for normal and deviant developmental pathways. Therefore, obvious behavioral differences have been underestimated and interpreted from the prevailing Western conception of the self, so that LeVine and Norman (2001) conclude that attachment theory is more a Western philosophy of child rearing than a scientific theory (see also LeVine in this volume and Vicedo (2013) for the historical imprint of attachment). It is therefore argued here that, in order to understand children's development of relationships on a global scale, the conceptualization of attachment as a biologically based – but culturally shaped – construct is necessary. This aim necessitates comparative studies, including nonhuman primates in order to demonstrate contextual variation in them as well (Bard, Myowa-Yamakoshi, Tomonaga et al., 2005). Moreover, the study of indigenous views of attachment (see especially Part II in this volume) is crucial. In order to assess the development of attachment(s) in different cultural contexts from different disciplinary perspectives (evolutionary theory, cultural/cross-cultural psychology, linguistics, anthropology, and neurophysiology), a multimethod approach that integrates qualitative and quantitative methods, as represented in this volume, is a necessary condition. Such a fresh look at attachment does imply the substantial revision of the following two important claims.

First, the evolutionary/ethological foundation does not justify the assumption that attachment has the same shape, emerges the same way, and has the same consequences across cultures (assumptions of equivalence, normativity, and competence; see Rothbaum et al., 2000).

Second, cultural studies of the caregiving context in which attachment develops have underestimated apparent differences and overestimated the functional similarity of different behaviors (e.g., Kermoian and Leiderman, 1986; True, Pisani, and Oumar, 2001). The conception of maternal sensitivity, as well as later embodiments of "optimal parenting" (e.g., mind-mindedness), rests on an assumption of Western, middle-class psychology that does not apply to much of the world. Mainstream psychology in general has recently been described as WEIRD (*w*hite, *e*ducated, *i*ndustrialized, *r*ich, *d*emocratic) psychology because of its apparent cultural bias for Western, middle-class samples and contexts (Henrich, Heine, and Norenzayan, 2010).

Both conclusions imply a radical shift from the prevailing view and necessitate the reconceptualization of attachment as an evolved universal developmental task that has to be performed context/culture sensitively in order to have adaptive value. In this introduction we suggest a reconceptualization that necessitates a systematically empirical research program including nonhuman primates as well as various non-Western cultural communities and normal as well as deviant developmental trajectories within these different cultural communities. The chapters in this volume substantiate these claims from different disciplinary backgrounds.

In the following six sections, the rationale for this claim will be summarized in six issues that are relevant to the development of attachment theory as a culturally sensitive tool. Each section ends with a statement of what is needed in order to reach the goal of a culturally sensitive attachment theory.

Defining attachment: the role of culture

Attachment has been defined by Bowlby and his followers as the emotional bond between an infant and his or her caregiver(s) that is expressed in attachment behaviors like crying, clinging, and following with the aim of establishing and maintaining proximity, particularly in stressful situations (e.g., Bretherton 1992). Although Bowlby believed that "instinctive behaviour [attachment] is not stereotyped movement but an idiosyncratic performance by a particular individual in a particular environment" (Bowlby, 1982, p. 39), the emotional bond has not been qualified with reference to contextual variation by his students and followers (Hrdy, 1999). However, anthropological and cultural psychological accounts leave doubt that relationships can be defined as emotional bonds – that is, in mentalistic terms in all cultural environments (e.g., Everett, 2009; Ochs, 1993; see also Everett in this volume). Moreover, the few empirical approaches to assessing the meaning of attachment (behaviors) across cultures do not reflect the underlying conception of culture. For example, Posada, Goa, Wu *et al.* (1995) compared experts and mothers from China, Colombia, Germany, Israel, Japan, and the USA in their definitions of security of attachment based on the attachment Q-sort descriptions (Vaughn and Waters, 1990). The results revealed that across "cultures" mothers' and experts' conceptions of secure attachment converged. Culture is put here in quotation marks because it was defined as country, but country cannot be equated with culture (see below). It can be assumed that the childcare specialists surveyed had undergone Western oriented training, which would explain why their views converged with attachment theory. The mothers belonged to samples with similar sociodemographic profiles with an average of 31 years of age, 12.5 mean years of formal education, and an average of 1.9 children. This sociodemographic profile exactly represents middle-class groups, who hold similar child-rearing goals and values across countries (Keller, 2007, 2012). Nevertheless, there were variations between the samples and variations in the results that led the authors to conclude "that it becomes relevant to identify the ecologies in which such clusters [homogeneous groups] emerge" (Posada *et al.*, 1995, p. 45). Yet, this conclusion has not found its way into the contextual study of attachment relationships. This and other studies suggest that context and culture are, if at all, mentioned in the discussion sections of publications, where differences in data are interpreted post hoc as cultural when no other explanation seems to hold. However, there is no coherent conception of culture that guides these studies. As argued before, we propose to define culture as values, norms, and beliefs (ideational part of culture) and as actions and behaviors (behavioral part of culture) (Greenfield and Keller, 2004) that are shared by people who live in the same ecosocial context consisting of the level of formal education, age at first birth, number of children, and household composition. These dimensions are to be understood not as independent variables that should be statistically controlled for; rather, they should be seen as constituting social milieus with particular norms, values, and behavioral conventions (cultural models) that define children's learning environments (Keller, Bork, Lamm *et al.*, 2011; LeVine, 1977; Whiting, 1977). Countries can thus – and obviously do – contain multiple cultural milieus. What is therefore needed is not the accumulation of further studies, because "the cross-cultural database is . . . absurdly small" (van IJzendoorn and Sagi-Schwartz, 2008, p. 901), but, rather, the selection of cultural contexts that show systematic variation in cultural beliefs and practices in order to understand indigenous conceptions of what attachment is and how it develops in its adaptive and nonadaptive forms.

One attachment or many

One central issue of attachment research is its definition of attachment as the result of a monotropic, dyadically organized relationship despite the acknowledgment of the existence of different care systems involving different caregivers that hold different responsibilities. And again, amazingly, attachment researchers conclude, after stating these differences, that, "in general, Bowlby and Ainsworth's original ideas [the primacy of the mother–child relationship] held up well" (Cassidy, 2008, p. 17). This view of monotropy as an evolved tendency of human infants and their mothers is based on the primate model of rhesus macaques, with the particular role of the mother in the upbringing of the offspring, that is used as the evolutionary basis (Suomi, 2008). There are, however, other primate models with different care arrangements such as those of cotton-top tamarins, who rely more on distributed caregiving (Blum, 2002), and capuchin monkeys, whose activities with their mothers are not different from those with siblings or unrelated adults. As Suomi (2008, p. 177) concludes, "One wonders how Bowlby's attachment theory would have looked if Hinde [the ethologist on whose work Bowlby heavily relied] had been studying capuchin rather than rhesus monkeys." Parenting in over 300 primate species can vary greatly (Fairbanks, 2003) in terms of social systems and parenting strategies; moreover, it varies contextually (Bard *et al.*, 2005), so that the assumption of one natural model cannot be maintained.

The monotropic understanding of relationships and its formation has also been questioned for many decades by sociobiological (e.g., Hrdy, 1999), anthropological (e.g., Lancy, 2008; Weisner and Gallimore, 1977), and psychological (e.g., Tronick, Winn, and Morelli, 1985) accounts. It is, however, the question not only of whether a child can form more than one meaningful relationship but also of how these relationships are defined and organized. Van IJzendoorn and Sagi-Schwartz (2008) stress the absence of a network perspective as compared to dyadic views, a claim that had been already made by Heinicke, who stated "that the study of attachment needs to be expanded . . . to include multiple relationships" (Heinicke, 1995, p. 307). Nevertheless, this is exactly what is still lacking, a new conceptual as well as methodological approach capturing a network perspective of relationships. Moreover, it is important to reconsider the evolutionary basis of attachment in studying different primate groups. Therefore, what is needed is the empirical analysis of relationship formation in different primate species, as well as in cultural contexts that differ systematically with respect to infant-care systems and arrangements – the cultural contexts should be based on indigenous assessments, which means developed out of the culture and not imposed from outside.

Measuring attachment quality: emotional regulation and emotional expressiveness

Attachment involves psychological well-being and the experience of security in a caregiving environment. Although Bowlby had already distinguished between secure and insecure attachment, the development of the tripartite classification system is mainly attributed to Ainsworth and her collaborators (Ainsworth and Bell, 1970). Secure attachment as the trust in the caregiver (mainly the mother) is expressed as seeking bodily proximity after experiencing strain and stress. The second qualification of secure attachment is the activation of exploration when there is no distress and the attachment system is not activated (attachment/exploration balance; see below). Insecure attachment is defined in two modes. The first mode, insecure resistant attachment (also ambivalent attachment), is expressed in ambivalence between approaching and avoiding behaviors following the separation stress. The second mode, insecure avoidant attachment, is expressed in seemingly content behavior in situations of stress, but there are neurophysiological indicators, especially cortisol changes, that reveal stress responses. Later, Main and Solomon (1986) added a fourth classification – disorganized attachment, which is defined as a mix of behaviors, including avoidance or resistance; here children are described as displaying dazed behavior, sometimes seeming either confused or apprehensive in the presence of a caregiver. These attachment qualities are assumed to be universal strategies, with cultural differences only in their (numerical) distribution. The "standard distribution" is based on Ainsworth's Baltimore study and replicated in meta-analysis with about 60–70% of secure, 20–25% of avoidant, and 10–15% of ambivalent attachment (van IJzendoorn and Kroonenberg, 1988). Recently, about 15% of disorganized attachment strategies have been described, with an especially high amount (up to 30–40%) found in sub-Saharan samples (van IJzendoorn, Schuengel, and Bakermans-Kranenburg, 1999). This distribution has been regarded as normative, although there are notable exceptions, especially in studies from Germany, Israel, and Japan. Moreover, here culture is introduced *ex post facto* as an explanatory principle, with sometimes highly speculative claims (e.g., Grossmann, Grossmann, and Kindler, 2005).

From an evolutionary perspective, it seems highly unlikely that only one strategy – secure attachment – should be the best predictor of well-being in the existing environmental diversity. Rates of secure attachments in meta-analyses of between 50% (van IJzendoorn, Goldberg, Kroonenberg *et al.*, 1992) and 67% (van IJzendoorn and Kroonenberg, 1988) leave a percentage of at-risk developments that would be too high to represent evolutionary adaptation. In the same vein, Belsky, Steinberg, and Draper (1991) argued that insecure attachment should also be regarded as an adaptation when reproductive success is taken as the outcome measure. They have proposed two different life strategies that are modulated by secure and insecure attachment quality respectively. The secure strategy is adaptive in resource-rich environments, where parental investment is high and few offspring lead to optimal reproductive success. The insecure strategy is adaptive in unpredictable and low-resources environments, where more effort is devoted to mating than to parental investment and many offspring result in optimal reproductive success.

Attachment quality is mainly assessed by the "strange situation" procedure (Ainsworth and Wittig, 1969) and the attachment Q-sort technique (van IJzendoorn, Vereijken, Bakermans-Kranenburg *et al.*, 2004), preferably with 1-year-old children. The strange situation procedure can be regarded as the major cultural adaptation in attachment research. Ainsworth developed this laboratory situation in Baltimore as a consequence of being unable to reproduce her observations of infants' distress among the Ganda people in Uganda following maternal separation in the home environment. The strange situation procedure consists of a series of short episodes of mother–child social situations, stranger confrontations, and separations from the mother in a laboratory setting in order to increase the stress level of the child. Although an adaptation to the Euro-American context, this standard procedure has since then been exported to study qualities of attachment security in cultural contexts from African or South Sea villagers to Western and non-Western capital populations without question of its validity in those diverse contexts.

The central question for the assessment of attachment quality is how the infant emotionally regulates and enacts stressful experiences. Open expression of distress and successful comforting by the attachment figure – that is, the mother – are considered to be universal indicators of a secure relationship. Moreover, the formulation of the Q-sort items centrally focuses on the evaluation of emotional regulation and its expression. Emotional expressiveness, however, varies substantially across cultures due to different display rules and social conventions (Matsumoto, Olide, and Willingham, 2009) as part of different "selfways" (Markus and Kitayama, 1991). In many traditional communities, the display of emotions is not supported and not allowed, especially during interactions between children and adults. Although the confrontation with a stranger can be regarded as a crucial situation to elicit attachment behaviors (Kondo-Ikemura and Waters, 1995), the majority of a sample of Cameroonian Nso farmer children did not show any emotional expression when faced by a stranger. These children, moreover, displayed decreases in cortisol concentration over the course of an interactional episode with the stranger (Keller and Otto, 2011, see also Chapter 8 by Otto in this volume). Similarly, Gottlieb has observed in the Beng people of the Ivory Coast that children are trained from early on to welcome strangers (Gottlieb, 2004; see also Chapter 7 by Gottlieb in this volume). These results indicate that attachment relationships may be differently regulated across cultural environments.

The assumption of the universal validity of the attachment–exploration balance has also been challenged from a cross-cultural point of view (e.g., Rothbaum et al., 2000; see also Miller and Harwood, 2001). Like attachment, exploration can certainly be assumed to be an evolved behavioral predisposition; nevertheless, it is enacted very differently in different cultural environments, ranging from very supportive attitudes to restraining to a large degree, if not completely suppressing, exploratory activities (e.g., Power, 2000). Moreover, exploration in the attachment literature is very broadly defined (e.g., in the strange situation procedure, as any playing with toys). It has long been claimed that exploration needs to be distinguished from play since different regulations of arousal are implied (exploration is assumed to increase arousal, whereas play is linked with decrease; Keller, Schölmerich, Miranda et al., 1987). What is therefore needed is to define qualities of attachment by indigenous conceptions of how security and insecurity are embodied behaviorally and neurophysiologically, and to ascertain what is regarded as an appropriate context to assess relational qualities.

The origins: sensitivity, mind-mindedness and physical availability

The rationale for the understanding of the development of attachment is based on Mary Ainsworth's field studies with indigenous families in Uganda and Euro-American families in Baltimore. From extensive home observations, different scales of maternal caregiving qualities have been developed, of which the sensitivity scale has become most common. In fact, Ainsworth et al. (1978) defined sensitivity as the essence of good parenting during the first year of life and the major precursor of attachment security. Parenting is understood and evaluated as an exclusively dyadic activity – that is, one caregiver directs undivided attention to the infant and responds immediately, adequately, and consistently to even the most

subtle signals of the baby. Empirical analyses, however, have proved only a
limited significance (i.e., correlations of around .30 (Pearson correlation
coefficient) between earlier assessments of sensitivity and later attachment security; van IJzendoorn, 1995) not different from other dyadic
measures. Recently, it has been proposed that mind-mindedness (Meins,
1997) or reflective functioning (Fonagy, Target, and Steele, 1998) – that
is, narrative conversational discourses (Oppenheim and Waters, 1995)
characterized by the (verbal) reflection of infants' inner states and feelings – might be a more powerful precursor of attachment security. These
conceptions are also based on exclusive dyadic attention between caregiver and child. Both conceptions, sensitivity and mind-mindedness, rest
on the picture of the baby as an independent agent with its own will
and the right to express its own preferences and wishes, and the expectation of their fulfillment based on children's rights (for example, compare
descriptions in the Ainsworth sensitivity and cooperation scales with the
interference scale). This interactional style is typical of Western, middle-
class families with a high degree of formal education, affluent life circumstances, and a reproductive style of late parenthood and few children. This style is not prevalent and not valued in other, diverse cultural
contexts with early parenthood and many children such as those of traditionally living farmers (like the Nso; Demuth, 2008; see also Chapter 8
by Otto in this volume), pastoral groups (like the Fulani; Yovsi, 2003),
or foraging groups (like the Pirahã; Everett, 2009; see also Chapter 6 by
Everett and Chapter 4 by Meehan and Hawks in this volume). Anthropological analyses have claimed that the "opacity doctrine" distinguishes the
human psyche as a "private place" (Duranti, 2008, p. 485) that includes
indifference to others' mental states (Ochs, 1988; see also Mead, 1934)
and focus on the immediacy of experiences (Everett, 2009). According
to these cultural models, physical availability and closeness (body contact
and body stimulation) without verbal elaboration and mentalization are
regarded as central to good infant care (Keller, 2007; Lancy, 2008) and a
sign of love (Otto, 2008). Cross-cultural analyses of early caregiver–infant
interactions have revealed two different strategies that are associated with
different sociocultural milieus: the distal socialization strategy, which is
characterized by exclusive attention, high amounts of face-to-face contact, contingent responsiveness to distal signals, verbal elaborateness and
object stimulation, and little body contact and body stimulation, is typical of Western, middle-class families and is in line with the conceptions
of sensitivity and mind-mindedness. Another strategy consists mainly
of childcare as a co-occurring activity with extensive body contact and
body stimulation, little face-to-face interaction, little verbal monitoring,
and little object stimulation. The child is never alone, but also never the

center of attention. This strategy, for example, is favored by rural farmers with low levels of formal education (Keller, 2003, 2007). Both strategies are associated with specific later developmental achievements, reflecting different cultural emphases (Keller, 2007; Keller and Kärtner, 2013; Keller, Yovsi, Borke *et al.*, 2004). Thus, radically different views exist on the definition of social relationships, so that it is highly unlikely that these different views could lead to the same understanding of attachment and its development. Especially with respect to the evolutionary foundation of attachment, it would be important to include cultural environments that may represent different patterns of hominid social organizations. We referred already to the necessity to integrate different primate models in the study of attachment. It is also important to include groups with different forms of social organization. John Bowlby coined the term "environment of evolutionary adaptedness" (EEA), which is supposed to be the environment in which most of the psychological adaptations, including social relationships and parenting, evolved. The subsistence mode during the Pleistocene epoch is assumed to have been hunting and gathering. Although groups living as hunters and gatherers today cannot possibly be compared to the Pleistocene epoch, hunter-gatherer groups are still relatively egalitarian in organization (Lee and DeVore, 1968), a fact which should have consequences for their socialization strategies (see Chapter 4 by Meehan and Hawks in this volume). The pastoral (nomadic) mode can be regarded as a later cultural form of subsistence organization with more gender segregation and often polygamous households (Yovsi, 2003), again forming a different social milieu for children's learning environment. Finally, subsistence-based farmers can be regarded as hierarchically organized families with strong cohesive bonds (Lancy, 2008). In order to understand attachment and its development, these different cultural milieus with different subsistence modes need to be carefully studied and contrasted with modern urban families, who are often migrants from traditional village contexts in much of the world (Kağitcibaşi, 2007). What is therefore needed are systematic field studies of infants' social experiences over the first year of life in cultural communities that differ with respect to their modes of subsistence and presumably their cultural models and their caregiving strategies.

Attachment disorders and risk

It is part of the success story of attachment theory that it has become a primary source of reference for developmental deviations and pathology – see, for example, the inclusion of reactive attachment disorder in the

International Statistical Classification of Diseases and Related Health Problems, 10th Revision (ICD-10; WHO). Attachment disorders are assumed to be a consequence of the failure to develop normal attachment relationships during the early childhood period (until about 3 years of age). Neglect, abuse, separations, frequent change of caregivers, and excessive numbers of caregivers, as well as lack of caregiver responsiveness, are discussed as possible causes. The case of Romanian orphans has therefore become a major target of attachment disorder research (e.g., Gunnar, Morison, Chisholm *et al.*, 2001). The assumptions of attachment theory are widely represented in counseling and intervention programs (e.g., transition to parenthood and family-support programs). As in attachment theory, the ideas about deviations and pathological appearances rest on the assumptions of monotropic relationships, exclusive attention, sensitive responsiveness, and mentalistic dialogues (for more details, see Keller, 2010, 2013; see also Chapter 11 by Carlson and Harwood in this volume). Studies conceptualizing and testing conceptions of risk and disorders from indigenous perspectives are widely lacking. Environments that are highly variable, with scarce and unpredictable resources, and with threat and inconsistent care, will be associated with caregiving and child abilities different from stable, rich, and low-threat environments (see Chapter 1 by Johow and Voland in this volume). Barring pathology or cases at the far ends of the distributions of parenting and child behaviors to be found around the world, we require contextual evidence to infer a disorder or that parents are "insensitive." It is therefore necessary to assess relational development in contexts of poverty and adversity, which are generally assumed to constitute environments of risk.

Summary and conclusion

There seems to be considerable evidence that attachment theory and research are based on the Western, middle-class conception of man and development with the pre-eminent goal of psychological autonomy. There is also evidence that cultural contexts differ widely in their models of autonomy and relatedness, socialization goals, and caregiving strategies. Our cross-cultural and cultural analyses (Keller, 2007; Keller and Kärtner, 2013) have allowed us to identify different cultural models that represent different contextual conditions – two prototypical models and one hybrid model that are instrumental in informing different definitions of attachment as well as different developmental trajectories to develop cultural adaptive patterns of attachment.

We define prototypical models as encompassing conceptions that reach a larger array of domains of life. In our conception, we define Western, middle-class psychology as one prototypical model that can be labeled as psychological autonomy. We can also define non-Western, traditional farmers as a prototypical model that can be labeled as hierarchical relatedness. Hybrid cultural models can be defined as combinations of the two prototypical models that by definition can take multiple forms of appearances and characterize multiple populations. One group that belongs to this model are educated, middle-class families in non-Western societies; moreover, migrant families coming from a hierarchical, relational cultural model into an environment where psychological autonomy dominates may develop a hybrid model, as may groups with other subsistence activities. In the following discussion, the different cultural models will be briefly characterized and the implications for attachment relationships will be outlined.

The model of psychological autonomy reflects the culture from which Bowlby/Ainsworth attachment theory emerged. Psychological autonomy describes the cultural emphasis on the unique individual and his needs, preferences, intentions, and choices based on the assumed rights of human beings. Thus, the inner world of the individual – the cognitions and emotions – is the focus of attention. Infants experience from their first day the exclusive dyadic attention of one of a few caregivers who try to read the infant's mind in order to be sensitive and responsive interactional partners. The focus is on face-to-face exchanges with an emphasis on the display of positive emotions. Interactional situations are framed by elaborative verbal discourses in which the caregiver explains the inner and outer world, the past, and the future to the infant. Thus, infants acquire attachment relationships as emotional bonds that are co-constructed during these early social encounters. The population in which this model is adaptive is Western, middle-class families, representing less than 5 percent of the world's population. Yet, there is also a historical placement of social theories in general and attachment theory in particular. Marga Vicedo is making a compelling case in interrogating attachment theory and its creators as a historical phenomenon of Cold War America (Vicedo, 2013).

The model of hierarchical relatedness embodies the cultural emphasis on the social community of which the individual is a part. Thus, the social affordances including the roles and hierarchies of the community, mainly the extended family, are the primary target of socialization strategies. Infants are born into multiple caregiving networks, with the community being responsible for the well-being of the child. Infants are in constant body contact with caregivers, who involve them in social actions that blow the individual ego boundaries. Socialization effort is directed towards early physical and motor independence with an

emphasis on action autonomy that must not be verbally reflected. Therefore, the sense of security is based on trust in the availability and reliability
of a caregiving environment rather than in individual attachment relationships. The population where this model is adaptive is rural farmer
families, representing around 30–40% of the world's population. The
present volume also presents much evidence of distributed caregiving
from other subsistence-based communities besides farmers.

The hybrid model of autonomous relatedness combines elements
of both prototypical models. Studies using the classical attachment
paradigm in Western, middle-class families of non-Western populations,
such as Posada *et al.*'s (1995) study of Chinese, Japanese, and Colombian
families, have demonstrated similarities with Western families. This may
be owing to their comparably high amount of formal education, which
increases verbalization and mentalization. On the other hand, hierarchical relatedness is also present in strong family bonds based on respect that
result in high family cohesion. How these different elements combine in
attachment patterns has not yet been studied.

Research is therefore needed that systematically conceptualizes and
empirically analyzes the cultures of attachment within these and other
possible cultural models. Hence, a research strategy is needed that, on
the one hand, links to the Bowlby/Ainsworth tradition, but, on the other
hand, starts from the present knowledge about evolutionary as well as
cultural conceptions of socialization, parenting, and children's development. The link to Bowlby's groundbreaking work is the definition of
attachment as an adaptive social construct that is necessary for survival
and development and that has to be conceptualized within an interdisciplinary framework. The link to Mary Ainsworth's work is in the
recurrence of fieldwork – a necessity that she repeatedly stressed when
expressing her disappointment "that so many attachment researchers
have gone on to do research with the Strange Situation rather than looking at what happens in the home or in other natural settings . . . it marks
a turning away from 'field work', and I don't think it's wise" (Ainsworth,
1995, p. 12).

In her stimulating analysis of attachment as a historical phenomenon,
the historian of science Marga Vicedo (2013) asks "how a scientific
theory can endure when its evidence and logic are persuasively refuted
by experts" (cited in Harris, 2013, p. 926). This is certainly one of
the miracles of the attraction of attachment theory over the last decades
across different disciplines. Related to this is the ignorance of suggestions
and criticism. As early as 1984 in a paper in *Behavioral and Brain Sciences*,
Michael Lamb and collaborators voiced some methodological criticisms
of the intention to make attachment theory stronger. Their criticism was

not very well received by the group of attachment researchers around Mary Ainsworth, as Robert Karen (1994) vividly describes.

However, there is a sense of change in the air, particularly in the accumulation of voices of scholars with particular knowledge of non-Western social life. Besides the present volume, another edited volume, containing anthropological criticism, *Attachment Reconsidered*, by Naomi Quinn and Jeanette Mageo, has been published (2013).

The aim of this volume is a proposal to reconceptualize attachment theory with three main objectives:

(1) Attachment theory needs to be grounded in modern evolutionary approaches that conceptualize contextual adaptation of behavior and development.
(2) Attachment theory needs to incorporate cultural variation. Fieldwork in many cultural communities should inform the reconceptualization of attachment theory as a culture-informed science
(3) Analysis of attachment theory needs to reconsider its basic assumptions on evolutionary and cultural premises such as distributed caregiving and allomothering, stranger anxiety, and conceptions of intimacy and agency.

Plan of the book

This volume presents a collection of perspectives from different disciplines related to the three aims of the book. The chapters are conceptual and empirical, representing cultural and cross-cultural evidence concerning the claims made in the previous sections.

The volume starts with a foreword by Michael E. Lamb. Following is this introductory chapter by Heidi Keller. The main text of the book comprises three parts presenting intriguing views of the different faces of attachment. The authors of these chapters represent multicultural expertise from cultural and cross-cultural psychology, cultural anthropology, ethnology, linguistics, and evolutionary science. The chapters are based on quantitative as well as qualitative analyses.

Part I, "Attachment as an Adaptation: Evolutionary, Cultural, and Historical Perspectives," comprises three chapters. Chapter 1 by the evolutionary anthropologists Johannes Johow and Eckart Voland discusses the need to ground attachment theory in evolutionary context beyond the general claim made by Bowlby and Ainsworth. Reviewing the sociobiological literature, they show that human families embody different interests resulting from asymmetries in genetic relatedness and differences in reproductive strategies between the sexes. Therefore, they argue that families can provide very different environments for a child's socioemotional development, and they delineate the necessity for a dual perspective on attachment as a functional system for survival as well as reproduction. They develop an evolutionary argument that social relationships, including that of mother and child, also have to be regarded within a contextual framework. With this, they establish the biological necessity of considering cultural differences in understanding caregiver–child relationships.

Chapter 2 by the anthropologist Robert A. LeVine highlights the philosophical, cultural, and ideological nature of classical attachment theory and its resistance to change by analyzing the historical context of Bowlby and Ainsworth's original claims. LeVine convincingly shows that "Bowlby's thinking was bound to a dichotomous medical model in which deviations from an idealized pattern of good mothering prevalent among the Anglo-American middle classes leads inevitably to psychopathology." His analysis demonstrates the closeness of the link between ideology and psychopathology, which is of particular importance regarding the widespread application of attachment theory in clinical practice.

In Chapter 3, the anthropologist David F. Lancy provides an impressive overview of parenting practices across history and geography and puts "attachment parenting" in historical and cross-cultural perspective. He also identifies classical attachment theory as arising from the contemporary Western, middle-class model of society as a neontocracy prioritizing the infant/child in every respect. He opposes this view to the much more common gerontocracy model, in which the conferral of personhood may be delayed, as infants are not seen as fully human.

Part II, the longest of the book, deals with "Multiple Attachments: Allomothering, Stranger Anxiety, and Intimacy," comprising six chapters. Anthropologists and cultural, as well as cross-cultural, psychologists have observed and analyzed the development of relationships in a multitude of cultural environments, so that we have a substantial documentation of different patterns of caregiver–infant/child relationships. What is fascinating is the variety of combinations of maternal and allomaternal care. In Chapter 4, the cultural anthropologists Courtney L. Meehan and Sean Hawks report relational patterns among the forager group of the Aka, who live in the Congo basin of central Africa. They demonstrate convincingly that, while the mother is often the primary caregiver in many contexts, she is not necessarily so. Moreover, they point out that this "should not negate the role that others play in children's attachment system or in the formation of the mother–child relationship." Consequently, based on quantitative naturalistic observations, they highlight the role of allomothers for children's development of attachment. A second aim of their analysis is to study the similarity/dissimilarity of caregiving patterns of mothers and allomothers. Finally, they address the implications of multiple caregiving for maternal caregiving as well as children's outcomes. They conclude that children's overall sense of felt security – i.e., attachment quality – results from the integration of multiple attachment relationships.

In Chapter 5, the ethnologist Birgitt Röttger-Rössler uses ethnographic data from the Makassar of Indonesia to demonstrate the cultural blindness of classical attachment theory. She carried out on-site field studies in a typical highland village in the Gowa district of South Sulawesi. She describes multiple caregiving arrangements and multiple attachments with a particular emphasis on the special role that grandparents play in this cultural group. She argues that these caregiving systems, which are notably different from those of Western, middle-class families, must lead to different partners of attachment that are not compatible with the Bowlby–Ainsworth view. Children grow up amidst a large, transgenerational network of relatives, "within which – and this is a decisive aspect – the persons from their surroundings who will become their central attachment figures are broadly negotiable and already decisively negotiable for young children as well." She shows that the strange situation procedure is largely inappropriate to study attachment patterns beyond WEIRD groups. Finally, she emphasizes the children's agency in forming their attachment patterns.

In Chapter 6, the linguist Daniel L. Everett describes the development of attachment relationships on the basis of his long-term linguistic field studies and ethnographic observations with the Pirahã Indians in the Brazilian Amazon. He argues that the symbiotic interrelationship of language and culture is also crucial for the development of attachment. He defines "concentric circles of attachment" that imply that children attach to various sets of individuals – mother, parents, family, village, larger Pirahã population – at each stage of development. Before weaning, the mother is the primary attachment figure, yet there is an openness to receive care from other Pirahã as well. Caregiving, such as nursing, on the other hand, is directed not only to the mothers' own offspring but also to other children and even animals. Everett positions the special bond between humans and animals as one learning arena for children's development of their cultural identity.

The anthropologist Alma Gottlieb has done long-term anthropological and ethnographic research with the Beng, a mostly farming group in Ivory Coast. She discusses in Chapter 7 another cornerstone of classical attachment theory as related to multiple caregiving arrangements – that is, stranger anxiety from the perspective of the Beng. She describes convincingly how Beng babies are introduced to the wider community starting right after birth through encountering numerous villagers who come to greet the baby, and who necessarily are strangers to the baby. Her assertion of Beng multiple caregiving arrangements is rooted not only in the necessities of the circumstances of life but also in an ideology that privileges rebirth from the afterlife. She concludes that "all relevant individuals in a child's social universe must be investigated inductively, so as to understand from the local perspective the meanings of 'attachment' in culturally relevant contexts."

In Chapter 8, the psychologist Hiltrud Otto describes her research on indigenous patterns of attachment relationships and children's regulation of emotions in attachment-arousing situations – i.e., confrontation by a stranger – among the Nso farmer families of northwest Cameroon. With a quasi-experimental methodology, she observed 1-year-old children's reactions to a female stranger in the home environment in the presence of the mother. In line with the cultural conceptions of a good child as being calm and easy to care for by multiple caregivers, the majority of Nso children did not show any fear of strangers in the encounters, thus demonstrating a conception of trust that substantially differs from the Western view on attachment. Otto's study also demonstrates that secure attachment relationships are understood differently in different cultural environments and therefore that classical attachment classifications also mirror cultural ideology.

In Chapter 9, the anthropologist Nancy Scheper-Hughes uses long-term ethnographic records in the shantytown of Alto do Cruzeiro, Brazil. The adverse life conditions there make it necessary to reflect also on the model of ethnography that is appropriate under these circumstances. She concludes that "there is simply no substitute for long-term immersion, many returns to the field, and the anthropologist's constant companion of critical thinking and self-critical reflection." The long-term engagement allowed her, moreover, to see social changes over time in the community and how these affected the relational networks. She describes a *bricolage* of family formation – that is, making up relationships in an improvised manner, often short term and linked to provision of resources. "On the Alto a mother and her surviving children formed the stable core of the household, while fragile infants, casual husbands and weekend fathers were best thought of detachable, exchangeable, and circulating units." These observations need a different conceptualization of attachment and its development during infancy.

The last part of the book, "Looking into the Future and Implications for Policy Development," comprises two chapters. In Chapter 10, the anthropologist Thomas S. Weisner describes the different perspectives that attachment theory and research should take in the future. His argument is that attachment is an "evolutionary prepared mechanism to recruit the child and the caregiver into the socialization of trust and security." Because of the evolutionary foundation, multiple pathways have to be acknowledged and studied with mixed-method designs of naturalistic as well as experimental, quantitative, and qualitative approaches. Central to his analysis is also the socially distributed nature of caregiving and thus attachment relationships. Attachment from his perspective is "a cultural and ecological problem with pluralistic solutions," as in the title of his paper published in the journal *Human Development* in 2005. Although he includes a broad set of cultural environments into his analysis, his own fieldwork in Kenya certainly plays a special role. The implications for future measurement studies are that using Western attachment scales as decontextualized outcome measures for assessing parenting or classroom "quality" may be inappropriate. From scientific, policymaking, and moral-evaluative perspectives, it appears to be unjustified to claim that linear scales show that some communities or kinds of families are more "sensitive" or promote and produce more "security," while other communities and families (indeed, most of the majority world) are located towards the "insensitive" or "insecure" end of such scales . For analytical reasons, it might be useful to imagine that we can measure attachment or sensitivity in a linear, additive, and decontextualized way; doing so can have value. But the world is multilinear, pluralistic and complex, and deeply contextual. Future research and applied applications should incorporate context into comparative measures of attachment, security, sensitivity, and trust.

In Chapter 11, the psychologists Vivian J. Carlson and Robin L. Harwood place the "systemic influences of the sociocultural context" at the center of their discussion of what would be needed to adapt attachment theory to different worldviews. They particularly concentrate on issues that are relevant to the application of attachment theory and child-rearing ideologies in general to health issues. They formulate a platform that should be taken into account by childcare professionals working with populations at risk. They discuss implications related to war, famine and social trauma, chronic health problems, children's disabilities, and gender issues. With respect to policymakers, they stress the dual nature of caregiving relationships and ask for "efforts to integrate caregiver–infant relationship support into programs that address family, health, and environmental risk reduction." This will "necessarily involve holistic, contextual strategies."

All of the chapters in this part of the book provide, cumulatively, an impressive range of ethnographic and cultural evidence of multiple attachments as the normative pattern. The chapters concur in concluding that it is about time to "detach from attachment theory," as Alma Gottlieb phrases it. They all report the prevalence of general patterns of alloparenting as different from the monotropic conception of attachment, but they all highlight different cultural conceptions or emphases of particular elements of these patterns. Thus, alloparenting is not just a divergent view of monotropic parenting; it needs further conceptual development and empirical evidence.

With this book we hope to contribute to the inclusion of culture into the seminal groundwork that John Bowlby and Mary Ainsworth have undoubtedly laid with their conception of attachment. We hope that fruitful discourses may emerge from the proposals made in this volume.

References

Ainsworth, M. D. S. (1995). On the shaping of attachment theory and research: an interview with Mary D. S. Ainsworth (Fall 1994). *Monographs of the Society for Research in Child Development, 60*(2–3), 3–24.

Ainsworth, M. D. S., and Bell, S. M. (1970). Attachment, exploration, and separation: illustrated by the behavior of one-year-olds in a strange situation. *Child Development, 41,* 49–67.

Ainsworth, M. D. S., Blehar, M. C., Waters, E., and Wall, S. (1978). *Patterns of attachment: a psychological study of the strange situation.* Hillsdale, NJ: Erlbaum.

Ainsworth, M. D. S., and Wittig, B. A. (1969). Attachment and exploratory behavior of one-year-olds in a strange situation. In B. M. Foss (Ed.), *Determinants of infant behavior* (vol. IV, pp. 113–36). London: Methuen.

Bard, K. A., Myowa-Yamakoshi, M., Tomonaga, M., Tanaka, M., Costall, A., Matsuzawa, T. (2005). Group differences in the mutual gaze of chimpanzees (*Pan troglodytes*). *Developmental Psychology, 41*(4), 616–24.

Belsky, J., Steinberg, L., and Draper, P. (1991). Childhood experience, interpersonal development, and reproductive strategy: an evolutionary theory of socialization. *Child Development, 62,* 647–70.

Blum, D. (2002). *Love at Goon Park: Harry Harlow and the science of affection.* Cambridge, MA: Perseus.

Bowlby, J. (1969). *Attachment and loss,* vol. I: *Attachment.* New York: Basic Books. (1982). *Attachment and loss,* vol. I: *Attachment* (2nd rev. edn.). New York: Basic Books.

Bretherton, I. (1992). The roots and growing points of attachment theory. In P. Marris and J. Stevenson-Hinde (Eds.), *Attachment across the life-cycle* (pp. 9–32). New York: Routledge.

Bronfenbrenner, U. (1977). Toward an ecology of human development. *American Psychologist, 32,* 513–31.

Cassidy, J. (2008). The nature of the child's ties. In J. Cassidy and P. R. Shaver (Eds.), *Handbook of attachment: theory, research, and clinical applications* (2nd edn., pp. 3–22). New York: Guilford Press.

Demuth, C. (2008). Talking to infants: how culture is instantiated in early mother–infant interactions. The case of Cameroonian farming Nso and

North German middle-class families. Doctoral thesis, University of Osnabrück, Faculty of Human Sciences, Department of Culture and Psychology.

Draper, P., and Belsky, J. (1990). The relevance of evolutionary thinking for issues in personality development. *Journal of Personality, 58,* 141–62.

Duranti, A. (2008). Further reflections on reading other minds. *Anthropological Quarterly, 18*(2), 483–94.

Everett, D. (2009). *Don't sleep, there are snakes: life and language in the Amazonian jungle.* New York: Vintage Books.

Fairbanks, L. A. (2003). *Parenting.* In D. Maestripieri (Ed.), *Primate psychology* (pp. 144–70). Cambridge, MA: Harvard University Press.

Fonagy, P., Target, M., and Steele, H. (1998). *Reflective-functioning manual, version 5.0, for application to Adult Attachment Interviews.* London: University College London.

Gottlieb, A. (2004). *The afterlife is where we come from.* Chicago University Press.

Greenfield, P. M., and Keller, H. (2004). Cultural psychology. In C. Spielberger (Ed.), *Encyclopedia of applied psychology* (pp. 545–53). Oxford: Elsevier.

Grossmann, K., Grossmann, K. E., and Kindler, H. (2005). Early care and the roots of attachment and partnership representations: the Bielefeld and Regensburg Longitudinal Studies. In K. E. Grossmann, K. Grossmann, and E. Waters (Eds.), *Attachment from infancy to adulthood* (pp. 98–136). New York: Guilford Press.

Gunnar, M. R., Morison, S. J., Chisholm, K., and Schuder, M. (2001). Salivary cortisol levels in children adopted from Romanian orphanages. *Development and Psychopathology, 13*(3), 611–28.

Harris, B. (2013). Mother, love. *Science, 340*(6135), 926. (www.sciencemag.org/content/340/6135/926.1.full.pdf).

Harwood, R. L., Miller, J. G., and Lucca Irizarry, N. (1995). *Culture and attachment. Perceptions of the child in context.* New York: Guilford Press.

Heinicke, C. M. (1995). Expanding the study of the formation of the child's relationships. *Monographs of the Society for Research in Child Development, 60*(2–3), 300–9.

Henrich, J., Heine, S. J., and Norenzayan, A. (2010). The weirdest people in the world? *Behavioral and Brain Sciences, 33,* 61–83.

Hrdy, S. B. (1999). *Mother nature: a history of mothers, infants, and natural selection.* New York: Pantheon.

Kağitcibaşi, C. (2007). *Family, self, and human development across countries: theory and applications* (2nd edn.). Mahwah, NJ: Erlbaum.

Karen, R. (1994). *Becoming attached: unfolding the mystery of the infant–mother bond and its impact on later life.* New York: Warner Books.

Keller, H. (Ed.) (2003). *Handbuch der Kleinkindforschung* (3rd edn.). Bern: Huber.

  (2007). *Cultures of infancy.* Mahwah, NJ: Erlbaum.

  (2010). Linkages between the Whiting model and contemporary evolutionary theory. *Special Issue of the Journal of Cross-Cultural Psychology, 41*(4), 563–77.

  (2012). Autonomy and relatedness revisited: cultural manifestations of universal human needs. *Child Development Perspectives, 6*(1), 12–18.

(2013). Attachment and culture. *Journal of Cross-Cultural Psychology, 44*(2), 175–94.

Keller, H., Borke, J., Lamm, B., Lohaus, A., and Yovsi, R. D. (2011). Developing patterns of parenting in two cultural communities. *International Journal of Behavioral Development, 35*(3), 233–45.

Keller, H., and Harwood, R. (2009). Culture and developmental pathways of relationship formation. In S. Bekman and A. Aksu-Koc (Eds.), *Perspectives on human development, family and culture* (pp. 157–77). New York: Cambridge University Press.

Keller, H., and Kärtner, J. (2013). Development – the culture-specific solution of universal developmental tasks. In M. L. Gelfand, C.-Y. Chiu, and Y. Y. Hong (Eds.), *Advances in culture and psychology.* Oxford University Press.

Keller, H., and Otto, H. (2011). Different faces of autonomy. In X. Chen and K. H. Rubin (Eds.), *Socioemotional development in cultural context* (pp. 164–85). New York: Guilford Press.

Keller, H., Schölmerich, A., Miranda, G., and Gauda, G. (1987). Exploratory behavior development in the first four years. In D. Görlitz and J. F. Wohlwill (Eds.), *Curiosity, imagination, and play* (pp. 127–50). Hillsdale, NJ: Erlbaum.

Keller, H., Yovsi, R. D., Borke, J., Kärtner, J., Jensen, H., and Papaligoura, Z. (2004). Developmental consequences of early parenting experiences: self-regulation and self-recognition in three cultural communities. *Child Development, 75*(6), 1745–60.

Kermoian, R., and Leiderman, P. H. (1986). Infant attachment to mother and child caretaker in an East African community. Special Issue: Cross-Cultural Human Development. *International Journal of Behavioral Development, 9*, 455–69.

Kondo-Ikemura, K., and Waters, E. (1995). Maternal behavior and infant security in old monkeys: conceptual issues and a methodological bridge between human and nonhuman primate research. *Monographs of the Society for Research in Child Development, 60*(2–3), 97–110.

Lamb, M. E., Thompson, R. A., Gardner, W., Charnov, E. L., and Estes, D. (1984). Security of infantile attachment as assessed in the Strange Situation: its study and biological interpretation. *Behavioral and Brain Sciences, 7*, 127–47.

Lancy, D. F. (2008). *The anthropology of childhood: cherubs, chattel, changelings.* New York: Cambridge University Press.

Lee, R. B., and DeVore, I. (1968). *Man the hunter.* Chicago: Aldine.

LeVine, R. A. (1977). Child rearing as cultural adaptation. In P. H. Leiderman, S. R. Tulkin, and A. Rosenfeld (Eds.), *Culture and infancy: variables in the human experience* (pp. 15–27). New York: Academic Press.

LeVine, R. A., and Norman, K. (2001). The infant's acquisition of culture: early attachment reexamined in anthropological perspective. In C. C. Moore and H. F. Mathews (Eds.), *The psychology of cultural experience* (pp. 83–104). Cambridge University Press.

Main, M., and Solomon, J. (1986). Discovery of an insecure-disorganized/disoriented attachment pattern. In T. B. Brazelton and M. Yogman (Eds.), *Affective development in infancy* (pp. 95–124). Norwood, NJ: Ablex.

Markus, H. R., and Kitayama, S. (1991). Culture and the self: implications for cognition, emotion and motivation. *Psychological Review, 98*, 224–53.

Matsumoto, D., Olide, A., and Willingham, B. (2009). Is there an ingroup advantage in recognizing spontaneously expressed emotions? *Journal of Nonverbal Behavior, 33*, 181–91.

Mead, M. (1934). *Mind, self, and society*. University of Chicago Press.

Meins, E. (1997). *Security of attachment and the social development of cognition.* Hove: Psychology Press.

Miller, A. M., and Harwood, R. L. (2001). Long-term socialization goals and the construction of infants' social networks among middle-class Anglo and Puerto Rican mothers. *International Journal of Behavioral Development, 25*(5), 450–7.

Ochs, E. (1988). *Culture and language development: language acquisition and socialization in a Samoan village.* Cambridge University Press.

(1993). Constructing social identity: a language socialization perspective. *Research on Language and Social Interaction, 26*(3), 287–306.

Oppenheim, D., and Waters, H. (1995). Narrative processes and attachment representations: issues of development and assessment. *Monographs of the Society for Research in Child Development, 60*(2–3), 197–215.

Otto, H. (2008). *Culture-specific attachment strategies in the Cameroonian Nso: cultural solutions to a universal developmental task.* Doctoral thesis. University of Osnabrueck, Germany.

Posada, G., Goa, Y., Wu, F., Posada, R., Tascon, M., Schoelmerich, A., Sagi, A. et al. (1995). The secure-base phenomenon across cultures: children's behavior, mothers' preferences, and experts' concepts. *Monographs of the Society for Research in the Child Development, 60*(2–3), 27–47.

Power, T. G. (2000). *Play and exploration in children and animals*. Mahwah, NJ: Erlbaum.

Quinn, N., and Mageo, J. (Eds.) (2013). *Attachment reconsidered.* New York: Palgrave.

Rothbaum, F., Weisz, J., Pott, M., Miyke, K., and Morelli, G. (2000). Attachment and culture: security in the United States and Japan. *American Psychologist, 55*(10), 1093–1104.

Suomi, S. J. (2008). Attachment in Rhesus monkeys. In J. Cassidy and P. R. Shaver (Eds.), *Handbook of attachment: theory, research, and clinical applications* (2nd edn., pp. 173–91). New York: Guilford Press.

Super, C. M., and Harkness, S. (1986). The developmental niche: a conceptualization at the interface of child and culture. *International Journal of Behavioral Development, 9*, 545–69.

Tronick, E. Z., Winn, S., and Morelli, G. A. (1985). Multiple caretaking in the context of human evolution: why don't the Efe know the Western prescription for child care? In M. Reite and T. Field (Eds.), *Psychobiology of attachment and separation* (pp. 292–322). New York: Academic Press.

True, M. M., Pisani, L., and Oumar, F. (2001). Infant–mother attachment among the Dogon of Mali. *Child Development, 72*(5), 1451–66.

van IJzendoorn, M. H. (1995). Adult attachment representations, parental responsiveness, and infant attachment: a meta-analysis on predictive validity of the Adult Attachment Interview. *Psychological Bulletin, 117*(3), 387–403.

van IJzendoorn, M. H., Goldberg, S., Kroonenberg, P. M., and Frenkel, O. J. (1992). The relative effects of maternal and child problems on the quality of attachment: a meta-analysis of attachment in clinical samples. *Child Development*, *63*, 840–58.

van IJzendoorn, M. H., and Kroonenberg, P. M. (1988). Cross-cultural patterns of attachment: a meta-analysis of the Strange Situation. *Child Development*, *59*, 147–56.

van IJzendoorn, M. H., and Sagi-Schwartz, A. (2008). Cross-cultural patterns of attachment: universal and contextual dimensions. In P. Shaver and J. Cassidy (Eds.), *Handbook of attachment* (2nd edn., pp. 880–905). New York: Guilford Press.

van IJzendoorn, M. H., Schuengel, C., and Bakermans-Kranenburg, M. J. (1999). Disorganized attachment in early childhood: meta-analysis of precursors, concomitants, and sequelae. *Development and Psychopathology*, *11*(2), 225–49.

van IJzendoorn, M. H., Vereijken, C. M. J. L., Bakermans-Kranenburg, M. J., and Riksen-Walraven, J. M. (2004). Assessing attachment security with the Attachment Q-sort: meta-analytic evidence for the validity of the observer AQS. *Child Development*, *75*(4), 1188–1213.

Vaughn, B. E., and Waters, E. (1990). Attachment behavior at home and in the laboratory: Q-sort observations and Strange Situation classifications of one-year-olds. *Child Development*, *61*(6), 1965–73.

Vicedo, M. (2013). *The nature and nurture of love: from imprinting to attachment in Cold War America*. University of Chicago Press.

Weisner, T., and Gallimore, R. (1977). My brother's keeper: child and sibling caretaking. *Current Anthropology*, *18*, 169–90.

Whiting, J. W. M. (1977). A model for psychocultural research. In P. Leiderman, S. Tulkin, and A. Rosenfeld (Eds.), *Culture and infancy* (pp. 29–47). New York: Academic Press.

Yovsi, R. D. (2003). Ethnotheories about breastfeeding and mother–infant interaction: the case of sedentary Nso farmers and nomadic Fulani pastorals with their infants 3–6 months of age in Mbven subdivision of the Northwest Province of Cameroon. Münster: LIT Verlag.

Part I

Attachment as an adaptation: evolutionary, cultural, and historical perspectives

1 Family relations among cooperative breeders: challenges and offerings to attachment theory from evolutionary anthropology

Johannes Johow and Eckart Voland

Introduction

The attachment theory formulated by John Bowlby more than fifty years ago revised the then prevailing assumptions of psychoanalysis concerning the genesis of the mother–child bond and stood Freud's theory on its head, so to speak (Grossmann, 1987, p. 211). Whereas Freud tended to understand the development of a child's attachment to the mother mainly as a concomitant phenomenon of the infant's pleasure in nursing during the "oral stage," Bowlby (1969) instead emphasized that the mutual motivation of the mother and the child to be near each other represented a behavioral system – that is, a biologically functional behavioral pattern for the purpose of survival and reproduction. The attachment theory of Bowlby and Ainsworth takes into account the insights gained at that time from developmental and comparative psychology (e.g., René Spitz, Harry Harlow) and ethology (e.g., Konrad Lorenz, Niko Tinbergen). It represented the fusion of several perspectives from biology, psychoanalysis, and systems theory and is an explicitly evolutionary theory. As Hrdy (1999) writes, Bowlby can, therefore, be described as the "first evolutionary psychologist," even if some of his assumptions appear to be in need of revision from today's perspective. Thus, Hrdy (1999, 2009) points out that many representatives of attachment research have barely taken into consideration significant developments achieved to date in the understanding of parental care and human reproduction ecology from the perspective of evolutionary theory. On the one hand, the genetic parent–offspring conflict described by Trivers (1974) has significant implications for the functional logic of mother–child relationships, yet the relationship

Part of this study was supported by a grant from the German Research Foundation (DFG, Grant VO 310/16–1). Parts of the paper were written while E.V. was a Senior Fellow at the Alfried-Krupp-Wissenschaftskolleg (Institute of Advanced Studies), Greifswald, Germany.

between mother and child from this perspective tends to be more of a tug of war between varying genetic interests than a harmonious community. On the other hand, mothers and their offspring are not independent of the support provided by others. Possible helpers may be related, more or less, to the mother and, accordingly, may pursue completely different investment strategies. This means that the development of the mother–child relationship does not occur "in a vacuum," but within families, and all of the parties involved are exposed to the influences of changing allies and adversaries.

In this chapter, we argue that current developments in sociobiology and in life-history theory are also relevant to attachment research, because, on the one hand, they help to explain some otherwise not well understood findings, and, on the other hand, they make room for new hypotheses. We begin our considerations with a concise overview of the evolution of human reproduction in the context of facultatively cooperative breeding systems. Starting from this perspective of sociobiology, we then explore the progress that has been made in understanding the ontogenetic processes of attachment behavior and focus specifically on the possible explanations offered by life-history theory for the ascertained variability. Finally, as an overview, we summarize our key arguments for the integration of newer concepts of evolutionary theory into attachment theory, and provide an outlook for the resulting research issues.

From nuclear families to cooperative breeding to family conflicts

Our idea of Bowlby's "environment of evolutionary adaptedness" has drastically changed in recent decades. The image of a prehistoric hunter who provides for a kind of "bourgeois, nuclear family" with the calories that he has bagged is increasingly being replaced by the scenario of expanded kin networks in which individuals from various lineages pursue partly conflicting genetic interests. However, many of the popular ideas concerning the "nuclear family" as a harmonious community of both parents and their joint children have already proved to be implausible with the change in paradigm in evolutionary biology away from Lorenz' "drive to preserve the species" (*Arterhaltungstrieb*) toward Dawkins' "selfish gene" (e.g., in contributions contained in Salmon and Shackelford, 2008). Since then, and from a sociobiology perspective, the family has tended to be similar to a partnership of convenience which more or less compels its members to join and thus frequently creates a dilemma for individual interests. Either family members can support the reproduction of their kin and run the risk of being exploited, or they can claim resources for their own reproduction and thus risk failure owing to the lack of support (Hrdy, 2009). The following sections are intended to demonstrate that a differentiated view of the varied interests of the family members who are related to one another in varying ways is helpful in achieving a deeper understanding of the evolutionary dynamics. Consequences for attachment research arise from the circumstance that care provided by multiple caregivers holds both opportunities and challenges for the mother and the child. In view of the socioemotional development of the child, not only the possibilities for mutual manipulation by mother and child but also possibly other attachment-relevant transactions within the expanded family become the focus of interest in the research.

The cooperative breeding model of human reproduction

If human reproduction is compared with that of other large primates, it is noticeable that human mothers (even in traditional hunter and gatherer societies) have many more births within a relatively short period of time, despite a much longer phase of childhood during which human offspring are dependent on the support of older persons. In contrast, mothers in chimpanzees and the other great apes achieve a noticeably lower fertility even though their offspring become independent more quickly after weaning (Hawkes, 2010). The question arises of why no species of great ape achieves a level of performance comparable to that of humans with regard to the speed and efficiency of reproduction. Why are only humans able to combine a longer phase of childhood with shorter interbirth intervals and care for multiple children of varying ages at the same time?

According to the cooperative breeding model, human mothers are able to produce a number of offspring within a shorter period of time because they are supported by other members of the family in their reproductive effort and thus are able to spread the investments in their children (Hrdy, 1999, 2005, 2009). In order to understand how kin support can maximize reproductive success under a regime of cooperative breeding, Hamilton's (1964a, 1964b) concept of inclusive fitness provides the theoretical basis. Accordingly, reproductive success can be achieved not only by the production of one's own offspring but also by increasing the reproductive success of genetically related individuals. The logic here is that all carriers of a certain allele influence the reproductive success of this common gene variant with their reproduction in the same way and produce individuals who are genetically similar. The children of one's siblings, parents, uncles, or aunts – that is, generally all genetic kin – are likely to be carriers of common alleles. As genetic similarity coincides with a common lineage, there is a selection pressure to develop a general interest in the reproductive success of close kin.

On the other hand, the possibility of mutual support also provides the opportunity for individuals to be supported in their own reproduction by their kin. In a cooperative breeding system, this can, therefore, lead to a trade-off for individuals between the utilization of reproductive resources for direct reproduction – that is, the production of one's own offspring – and the use thereof for indirect reproduction – that is, the support of kin. Individual interests to maximize reproductive success collide in a biological market in which the supply and demand for helper and breeder positions are negotiated. This is why cooperative reproductive strategies are particularly pursued in constellations in which individuals, for various reasons, do not have the opportunity for direct reproduction. From adolescents to (still) childless adults and back to grandparents, a series of candidates end up in a position of acquiring surpluses of resources without having to care for offspring of their own (Voland, 2007). For example, the "grandmother hypothesis" assumes that even postmenopausal longevity in women represents an adaptation to such indirect fitness advantages by virtue of their helper role as grandmothers (see contributions in Voland, Chasiotis, and Schievenhövel, 2005). As already mentioned, other human life-history traits – such as the comparatively short interbirth intervals as well as the relatively long phase of childhood – indicate the importance of cooperative breeding strategies, and therefore, the potential helper role of grandmothers (Hrdy, 1999, 2005, 2009). In human families, on the one hand, there are potential helpers who do not have the possibility of direct reproduction but are able to support their kin instead. On the other hand, there are mothers who are dependent on the help of others or at least enormously benefit, from a reproductive standpoint, from the support provided by helpers.

According to the cooperative breeding model, helpers can utilize numerous investment channels in order to support kin in their reproduction (see contributions in Bentley and Mace, 2009; Voland *et al.*, 2005). For example, they may foster the development opportunities of already existing offspring or push for the reproduction of additional offspring. Depending on the underlying conditions, both of these strategies promise varying success in the currency of increased inclusive fitness. Human reproduction is a joint venture; however, the mother can be "supported" or, better yet, "influenced" in her reproduction in completely different ways.

In a systematic overview of previous studies, Sear and Mace (2008) have summarized how the mortality of offspring is influenced by kin, and they have found a wide range of different effects. As expected, the

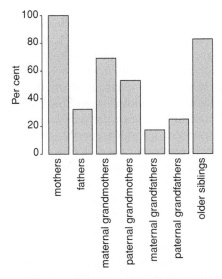

Figure 1.1 Proportion of studies showing a positive effect of kin on offspring survival (reproduced from Sear and Mace, 2008, Table 3).

mother has a positive effect on child survival in all studies (Figure 1.1). However, with regard to the influence of other kin on children's survival prospects, there is an uneven picture. Although a child's probability of survival, in the majority of the pertinent studies, is also increased by older siblings and grandmothers – especially maternal grandmothers – this is not always the case. And even when this increased probability does exist, the extent of improved survival varies. On the other hand, it is relatively rare for fathers and grandfathers to increase the survival prospects of their offspring. The fact that many of the child's kin have no (or sometimes even a negative) influence on the child's probability of survival definitely does not mean, however, that their behavior is not relevant to family reproductive events. As described in the following section, the fitness-maximizing influence of "helpers" does not always have to be in the mother's interests.

Family conflict theory

All mammals have in common that their offspring initially develop solely from the mother's resources. The embryo and the infant are physiologically dependent on the maternal organism to such an extent that comparison with the parasite–host relationship forces itself upon us. "From a gene's point of view," this analogy, according to Hamilton (1964a, 1964b) and Trivers (1974), is not completely absurd, because, ultimately, the child is only partly genetically related to the mother. Roughly half of the child's genome is foreign, from the mother's standpoint, because of its paternal origin. Hamilton (1964a, 1964b) has demonstrated that the cost–benefit ratio with regard to the decision of whether resources are to be made available to another individual or withheld, orients itself crucially to the genetic relationship between the parties involved. This perspective makes maternal investment – at least partly – plausible. After all, the genetic relationship between mother and child is substantial and (in contrast to the putative paternity) guaranteed. On the other hand, mothers have to distribute their available resources among all of their offspring somehow, so that the individual offspring competes for maternal resources with its (even future) siblings. Trivers (1974) argues that, as a matter of principle, offspring demand more resources from the mother than she is willing to give. Excessive demands on the part of the child *vis-à-vis* the parents are the evolutionary consequence of the child's genetic kinship being divided between both parents, so that, consequently, the reproductive interests of the parents and their offspring partly differ. Both parents are genetically represented in their offspring by only 50%, so that, with regard to the relationship between the offspring (which is related with itself by 100%) and its parents, selfish motives predominate over nepotistic – that is, "altruistic" – tendencies. The reasons for this lie in the fact that parents – in the simplest case – benefit from maximizing the reproductive success of all of their offspring, whereas siblings benefit more strongly from their own reproduction – once again in the simplest case – than that of their siblings. From an evolutionary perspective, therefore, the relationship between the mother and her offspring is characterized by an "arms race" between varying interests concerning the allocation of maternal resources.

However, whereas maternal alleles for "selfish" reasons are basically interested in preserving their gene copies in the maternal organism, paternal alleles can benefit from the ruthless exploitation of maternal resources (Crespi, 2010; Haig, 2010). Because child-development differences in growth and behavior cause different fitness costs for the maternal and the paternal genome respectively, the sexual conflict between the parents is also displayed within the genome in the form of epigenetic changes that influence the expression of the corresponding genes (such as certain growth factors) in contrary ways (see Úbeda and Gardner, 2010). Both parents will attempt to influence the development of offspring – e.g., by means of epigenetic mechanisms – at the expense of the other parent (see also Del Giudice and Belsky, 2011). If parents are able to manipulate the subsequent gene expression of their offspring by means of epigenetic mechanisms, the sexual conflict has the potential – in the case of asymmetrically inherited sex chromosomes – to cause an "evolutionary race" between maternal and paternal alleles, even within the genome. The resulting phenotype represents a "balance of power" between conflicting parental interests, as described by Frank and Crespi (2011), the contrary driving forces of which become clear only if there are disturbances within this balance. A series of complications during pregnancy (such as pre-eclampsia) appears to result from a unilateral disparity in this "balance of power" between maternal or paternal alleles. The high frequency of such alleles in view of the high fitness costs is unusual; however, these alleles are not lost due to "Mendel's laws" (Haig, 1993) or due to the "logic of the selfish gene."

Similar to the genetic conflicts between maternal and paternal alleles, which manipulate the intrauterine growth in different ways, the development of attachment behavior could also be influenced in varying ways through the expression of maternal or paternal alleles; after all, the conflict of interest between a child's demands and maternal restrictions concerning the investment being used up remains even after birth, especially during the phase of the "extrauterine year" and while breast-feeding (Trivers, 1974). In fact, Haig argues (2010) that genes of paternal origin can motivate the mother to make an increased investment, at least as far as the duration and frequency of infant breast-feeding is concerned. However, as frequent breast-feeding noticeably reduces the probability of renewed conception due to the ovulation-inhibiting effect of prolactin, mother–infant bonding could, theoretically, also serve the purpose of delaying the birth of siblings (i.e., potential rivals) for a certain period of time. This would then be a biological function of the attachment system, and it would be less in the mother's reproductive interest, but would tend to have fitness advantages for the child or the child's paternal alleles at the mother's expense. For example, as a possible expression of this conflict, Blurton Jones and Da Costa (1987) interpret the observation that about 20% of 1–3-year-olds often do not sleep all night, but wake up and cry so persistently that they wake their parents. Unless the child has acute illness, there are no recognizable reasons for it to wake up during the night; for all practical purposes, this action cannot be influenced by parental behavior, and it stops spontaneously at the age of about 3 years. At least under historical conditions, this has brought such children a survival benefit, because waking up at night leads to extended and more regular breast-feeding, and this delays the subsequent conception of the mother and increases the child's survival chances with the increase in the following interbirth interval.

Empirical findings that allegedly reinforce the theories of sexual conflict are derived in particular from studies on epigenetic diseases, which have ascertained an overexpression of paternal alleles (or an underexpression of maternal alleles), as in Angelman syndrome, or, vice versa, an over expression of maternal alleles, as in Prader–Willi syndrome (overview in Crespi, 2010; Haig, 2010). For example, children with Prader–Willi syndrome, which is characterized by the deletion of certain paternal alleles, hardly have any appetite during the first years of life (i.e., during the nursing period), but over the years – that is, typically after weaning and the use of allomothers – develop a ravenous appetite (Haig and Wharton, 2003). Accordingly, it appears that the overexpression of maternal alleles effectuates conservation of maternal resources, whereas, in contrast, the overepression of paternal alleles coincides with a stronger exploitation of maternal resources (Haig, 2010). Crespi (2010) also sees consequences for attachment research in this theory and argues that the intragenomic conflict between maternal and paternal alleles could help to explain the variance in different types of attachments. In particular, the clarification of the mechanisms of this intragenomic conflict should in the future contribute to a better understanding of the "deep-seated biological ambivalence" (Haig, 2011, p. 10884) in human kinships in general and the mother–child relationship in particular.

As Trivers (1972) describes, sex differences are ultimately rooted in the fact that the parental investment of mothers – as far as the obligate costs and opportunity costs are concerned – is noticeably higher than that of fathers. Thus, fathers could theoretically produce many offspring, whereas the maternal number of births is very strongly restricted by pregnancy, giving birth, and breast-feeding. In terms of evolutionary theory, varying optimums in reproductive output result from the varying costs of reproduction for both sexes. The more quantitatively oriented male reproductive strategy collides here with the more qualitatively oriented female reproductive strategy.

This view of family relationships oriented to evolutionary cost–benefit ratios brings the "classic" image of the father as a reliable male provider into doubt. Apart from the always present uncertainty about paternity, fathers also have high opportunity costs when making investments in their genetic offspring, if they waive further mating opportunities – that is, additional offspring – in favor of their role as a father. In fact, paternal investment (in contrast to maternal investment) is extremely rare among mammals as a whole, and even among humans it is to be regarded as extremely variable and optional (overview in Fernandez-Duque, Valeggia, and Mendoza, 2009). Thus, Hawkes, O'Connell, and Blurton-Jones (1991) have ascertained that in contemporary Tanzania, among the Hadza, who still follow their traditional ways for the most part, the man's contribution to providing food to his family is comparatively small. This is partly because the success of a hunt is frequently irregular and therefore unreliable, and partly because men – in contrast to women – distribute the outcomes of their work among the village community instead of among close kin. Finally, in the USA, it was reported for the year 2006 that only about one-third of the legal claims for child support that single mothers made against their child's father were completely paid, and more than one-third were completely unpaid (Anderson, 2011). Anderson (2011) also shows here that the paternal probability of additional children is significantly lowered by the making of child-support payments. This results in a divergence between maternal and paternal interests in parental investment, because both parents can attempt to shift the responsibility for the resources needed by their offspring to one another and instead use their own resources to support kin or to produce additional offspring (Houston, Székely, and McNamara, 2005). Hamilton (1964a, 1964b) has used the rule named for him to show that the probability of social discrimination between two individuals increases with decreased genetic relatedness. The contrary interests between the mother and the father regarding their relative share of parental investment also ensures that the paternal kinship is "on the other side" from the mother and her genetic kin as far as the costs and benefits of maternal effort are concerned. The interests of the matriline and the patriline are kept at a distance by the ditch dug by evolution. Owing to the asymmetric genetic relatedness of the parents to members of their two lineages, relationships by marriage are, therefore, more conflict-laden than relationships among biological kin (see also Leonetti, Nath, and Hemam, 2007).

These theoretically forecast differences between the influences of maternal and paternal kin on maternal biographies are also found in historical family data from Krummhörn, a region in Ostfriesland, Germany. Maternal and paternal grandmothers have different effects on infant mortality. Whereas maternal grandmothers decrease the early mortality rate of their grandchildren, paternal grandmothers tend to have the opposite effect and even lead to a slight increase in infant mortality (Voland and Beise, 2002). Jamison, Cornell, Jamison et al. (2002) report similar findings for a historical population in Japan. Moreover, Voland and Beise (2005) have described similar differences in the influences of the maternal or paternal grandmother, respectively, on stillbirths in the Krummhörn population. Obviously, the effects of grandmothers on maternal health or maternal stress correspond to the genetic relatedness between the mother and the grandmother. In the relationship between mother-in-law and daughter-in-law, there appear to be several fields of conflict, which can lead to social manipulation by the patriline. For example, this could be exploiting the work productivity of the genetically unrelated daughter-in-law and making her earnings available to one's own lineage (Voland and Beise, 2005).

Fox, Sear, Beise *et al.* (2010) have further differentiated the harmful influence of paternal grandmothers on the survival of their grandchildren in a meta-study based on the data of seven different populations. In all of the populations investigated, the paternal grandmother had a negative impact on the survival of her grandsons, whereas, in six out of seven cases, a positive impact on the survival of granddaughters was ascertainable. However, in the case of maternal grandmothers, there are no comparable differences related to the sex of the grandchildren. These data show that, at least as far as the survival prospects of the grandchildren are concerned, their sex, or, as Fox *et al.* (2010) argue, the X-chromosomal relationship to the paternal grandmother, obviously plays a special role. Due to the asymmetric inheritance of sex chromosomes, the paternal grandmother always passes one of her X chromosomes to her granddaughters, but never to her grandsons. Rice, Gavrilets, and Friberg (2010) show that the special situation in the case of the X chromosome has theoretically favored the evolution of "grandparental harm"; that is, harm to grandsons by their paternal grandmother can be advantageous to the reproductive success of the paternal X chromosome, because the share of "noncarriers" is reduced in the following generation as a result. In the data from the landless, worker families of the Krummhörn, which is the most numerous group of this population, an influence of the grandmother on the length of the interbirth intervals can be seen. Obviously, paternal grandmothers orient their investment strategy to the sex of the grandchild (Johow, Fox, Knapp *et al.*, 2011). Whereas in the group of children surviving the nursing period the presence of the paternal grandmother reduced the interbirth interval (as an indicator of the length of the nursing period) after a boy was born, her presence led to a longer interval until a subsequent birth after a girl was born (see Figure 1.2). It is probable that both counterstrategies from the maternal side, as well as antagonistic adaptations on the part of the autosomal genome of the paternal grandmother, counteract this effect, since X-chromosomal "grandparental harm," after all, causes relatively high fitness costs during the course of this intragenomic conflict (Rice *et al.*, 2010; Seki, 2012).

In this context, an interesting perspective emerges: Schlomer, Del Giudice, and Ellis (2011) describe to what extent varying attachment styles make varying demands on the mothers. Whereas insecure-avoidant children tend to develop a more distanced relationship with their mother

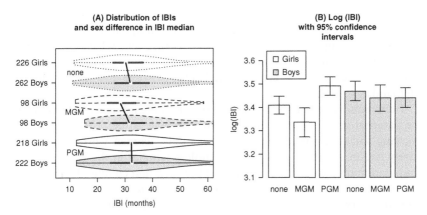

Figure 1.2 Panel A gives violin plots (a combination of box plot and kernel density distribution plot) for interbirth intervals (IBIs) following the birth of a girl or a boy, separated for families where the paternal grandmother (PGM) is present, where both grandmothers are absent, or where the maternal grandmother (MGM) is present. Panel B presents asymptotic tests with 95% confidence intervals (see Coeurjolly et al., 2009) to show differences in log-transformed IBI values. Reprinted with permission from Elsevier from Johow et al. (2011).

and develop relatively independently, frequently as a consequence of previous neglect experiences, secure children require much more attention from the mother later on as well. Children with secure attachments are used to a relatively large amount of maternal investment and will later demand this accordingly. However, according to Schlomer et al. (2011), from the mother's standpoint insecure/ambivalent children are even more expensive due to their attachment and their need for attention. Insecure/ambivalent children thus represent a special category, and it is noticeable that many more girls belong to this group, whereas, in contrast, insecure boys are much more frequently categorized as being avoidant (Del Giudice, 2008). Accordingly, boys claim less maternal effort, relatively speaking, if they develop into an insecure attachment type, but this would not apply to girls. It would be interesting to see whether X-chromosomal gene complexes also play a role in the development of this difference. After all, boys carry solely the maternal X chromosome and are, therefore, relatively "tamed" in view of X-chromosomally influenced features from the standpoint of the matriline. Thus, from a gene-selectionist perspective, the fact that differences in attachment styles are usually costly to the mother may also reflect the asymmetric inheritance of the paternal X chromosome, which could cause daughters to be more resistant to maternal demands than their brothers. Are boys with insecure attachments perhaps more frequently categorized as avoidant in comparison to insecure girls because they relieve the mother of effort in this way, as Schlomer *et al.* (2011) argue, but, in contrast to girls, are defenseless in terms of the X chromosome against matrilineal demands?

Furthermore, other studies have shown that the influences of maternal or paternal grandmothers on reproduction have to be differentiated by varying social groups. Whereas, for example, women who marry relatively late in economically limited, landless families in the Krummhörn population tend to marry and give birth to their first child in the presence of their own mothers, as opposed to in the presence of their mothers-in-law, this correlation is reversed among women who marry in prosperous farmer families. This variability shows that kin effects obviously react conditionally to socioecological conditions. On the whole, maternal kin appear to buffer ecological fluctuations better than paternal kin – at least, the fertility levels of women in the Krummhörn population who give birth to children near their own mother are relatively independent of socioeconomic conditions, whereas women without this support for their reproduction are more strongly affected by external circumstances (Johow and Voland, 2012). This is shown by the fact that the fertility differences that emerge between socioeconomically limited laborer families and prosperous farmer families are mitigated by the presence of the maternal grandmother, whereas this effect does not occur in the case of the paternal grandmother.

Therefore, as described, the influences of kin on maternal reproductive behavior can be extremely diverse and influence the relationship between mother and child in different ways. Maternal fertility, mortality among offspring, or the latter's specific reproductive prospects can all be affected by kin in varying ways. It is important to be cognizant of the fact that, within a family, genetic differences in interests exist between both parents, between parents and their children, and between siblings. Apart from the special case of monozygotic twins, theoretically, all family members can achieve individual reproductive advantages at the expense of the other family members. As soon as an alternative to a cooperative investment strategy arises, the (opportunity) costs of helping quickly exceed the reproductive benefit of an investment in kin. Therefore, from the standpoint of sociobiology, a "family" tends to result in a fragile alliance of individuals of varying kin relationships, whose reproductive interests only partly overlap. Which reproductive strategies may be pursued by family members obviously depends on the predominant ecological and socioeconomic conditions. Cultural differences, which are known in maternal behavior and the attachment behavior of children between different populations and subpopulations (Keller, 2007, 2008; see also Keller, this volume), are definitely to be expected from this point of view.

Evolution and ontogeny of attachment behavior

Individual conditions after birth and during childhood may drastically change between families, but also within one single family due to variable and dynamically changing family constellations. The diversity of varyingly motivated, intrafamilial transactions indicated in the foregoing discussion generates a wide spectrum of varying scenarios to which a child may be exposed. Therefore, an adaptive plasticity – that is, "if-then mechanisms" familiar from developmental psychology – is needed, through which child development can react to existing environmental conditions in biological and functional ways. As child development can adjust to the existing conditions, the child is able to cope with varying conditions and to orient its own life strategy accordingly. A very promising concept for understanding the individual development of attachment behavior, referred to by Bowlby (1951, p. 53, quoted in Crespi, 2010) as the "embryology of the mind," is offered by life-history theory. The idea here is that individual conditions during early development can influence the long-term development of certain features in accordance with a functional scheme.

Completely in the sense of the above-mentioned "if-then mechanisms," developmental "switches" can make alternative development options possible, through which the organism, depending on the existing conditions in childhood, can orient its later life in a secure or insecure environment. Long-term changes in the child's attachment system, which follow from early experiences with stress or perceived shortage situations, can then (at least partly) be understood as adaptive responses, the function of which is positioned in the development of an appropriate life strategy (overview in Del Giudice, 2009).

It is obvious that a child can benefit from a secure maternal attachment in a reproductive sense as well. But under insecure conditions, it is, presumably, especially modified concepts of security and attachment that promise optimal reproductive success (e.g., Del Giudice, 2009). This argument makes clear that varying attachment styles do not have to be failed attempts to achieve a secure attachment, but might possibly be adaptive-functional reactions in the service of varying reproductive life strategies. Such a standpoint allows a normative vocabulary, which is common in attachment research and operates with attributes, such as "suboptimal" and "maladaptive," to appear to be dubious. Ultimately, different types of attachments reflect an optimal result from a functional point of view – even if the ontogeny of the attachment system might have occurred under highly constrained suboptimal conditions.

Belsky (1997), with his "evolutionary theory of socialization," and Chisholm (1996), with his "ecological theory of attachment organization," have interpreted the known differences in the attachment behavior of children and the impact on their later development in the sense of an adaptive phenotypic plasticity. If the child has to cope with varying conditions, then conditional development strategies that are able to react to the respective ecological conditions are superior to an inflexible behavior pattern.

This is where attachment research meets evolutionary life-history theory. For example, a highly intrinsic mortality (or an environment that is perceived as being "insecure") could mean that an assumption of reproduction at the earliest date possible would be advantageous, because in view of the uncertain survival prospects, every day could be the last (Nettle, 2010). Under relatively stable conditions with more favorable survival prospects, it might, on the other hand, be more advantageous to initially accumulate more resources in order to be able to make one's offspring more competitive and more resistant. Belsky, Houts, and Pasco Fearon (2010) describe a correlation between an insecure attachment style and the early onset of puberty for American women of European descent. The authors interpret the accelerated sexual maturity in insecure girls completely within the sense of Belsky's original model of a functionally adaptive plasticity of the attachment system. This means that, depending on the conditions prevailing during early childhood, varying reproductive strategies would develop, whereby this can definitely be in the sense of "making the best of a bad job." By the way, a correlation between insecure living conditions and the accelerated commencement of reproduction are also found in the historical data from the Krummhörn, Quebec, and Finland, which show that men and women marry and reproduce earlier if they were exposed to the influence of increased mortality within their natal families (Störmer and Lummaa, 2014).

However, doubts have also been expressed as to whether the strong weighting of individual developmental plasticity might too much neglect the significance of genetic polymorphisms within a population (e.g., Penke, 2009). Even if many studies actually do report significant influences on reproductive behavior and attachment styles, such as different alleles for certain dopamine-receptors (Bakermans-Kranenburg and van IJzendoorn, 2008), both theoretical and empirical evidence suggests that mechanisms of adaptive plasticity via epigenetic imprinting play a significant role in individual development of attachment behavior.

Thus, studies on the heritability of the attachment style show that most of the variance is due to the nonshared environment, as consistent with the assumption of an experience-related, differential development of types of attachment (overview in Fearon, Bakerman-Kranenburg, and van IJzendoorn, 2010). Moreover, the concordance in the attachment style of monozygotic twins in comparison with dizygotic twins barely increases, although this would be expected if differences in attachment behavior were primarily due to genetic polymorphisms (O'Connor and Croft, 2001). On the other hand, it is seen that epigenetic differences between twins – that is, differences in the readability between certain genes – increase with age (Fraga, Ballestar, Paz *et al.*, 2005). Studies of rodents provide clear insights into the mechanisms of epigenetic modification of genes and thus coincide with the occurrence of long-term changes in reproductive strategy (overview in Zhang and Meaney, 2010). For example, different variations of maternal behavior can be distinguished in rats as well, and it is known from cross-breeding experiments what effect these individual differences in maternal behavior have on their offspring, specifically regarding the methylation of glucocorticoid receptor genes and estrogen receptor genes, respectively (Weaver, Cervoni, Champagne *et al.*, 2004). Such epigenetic changes have long-term consequences for individual stress reactions and later reproductive behavior. Experiments with rats have also shown that, due to social experiences, this "epigenetic programming" of later development is extremely flexible and can potentially be reversible. Thus, if the offspring of mothers who only relatively rarely engage in maternal care in the form of "licking and grooming" (LG) (low-LG mothers) are replaced soon after birth with the offspring of mothers who engage in such care to an above-average extent (high-LG mothers), the female offspring will later exhibit the maternal behavioral styles of their foster-mothers and not that of their genetic mothers (Francis, Diorio, Liu *et al.*, 1999). Through external influences on the interaction between mother and offspring, both stress-related "disorders" and "gains" (as a consequence of certain social structures) can establish transgenerational deviations from maternal behavior between mother and daughter generations (Champagne and Meaney, 2006; Curley, Davidson, Bateson *et al.*, 2009). Possibly, human development is influenced by comparable epigenetic mechanisms like the ones that have been described for rats. The influence of epigenetic structures through social experiences would explain the transgenerational transfer of parental styles, as already described by Main and Hesse (1990), and previously by Bowlby (1951), without this variability being an expression of genetic polymorphisms. Individual differences in attachment behavior are thus less a consequence of genotypic discrepancy and more the result of ontogenetic developmental plasticity.

The individual imprinting of the hypothalamic-anterior pituitary-adrenal (HPA) cortex could have an adaptive correlation with conditional strategies for coping with stress that are realized in the long run under conditions which are perceived to be more or less "secure" and which make the child either more susceptible to or more resistant to external influences (Belsky and Pluess, 2009; Flinn, 2006). Like a smoke detector, it is also expedient for the physiological stress system to register every possibly significant event without triggering a permanent alarm by being hypersensitive. Flinn and England (1995) describe to what extent stress reactions of the child's organism increase attention and responsiveness at the expense of the functionality of the immune system, but also cause long-term changes in the HPA axis. In particular, the noticeable increase in the cortisol level in children that occurs under the influence of step-parents is of particular interest here. This increase points to the initially described significance of cooperative breeding in humans, whereby it is difficult, according to Hamilton (1964a, 1964b), to motivate individuals who are unrelated to the child to provide "unpaid" investments; on the contrary, such persons represent a potential risk from the child's point of view.

Genetic polymorphisms clearly appear to contribute to the variance in attachment behavior within the population, at least to the extent that they make the phenotypic development of the organism more or less receptive to environmental influences. The theory of a differential susceptibility sees the genetic risk factors described by psychologists as genetic vulnerability (which are more frequent in insecure children, according to several studies) more as an indication of stronger susceptibility to environmental influences and therefore greater malleability (overview in Belsky *et al.*, 2007). In contrast to the theory to date (that of the "diathesis-stress model"), the theory of a differential susceptibility can explain the evolutionary persistence of apparently "disadvantageous" gene variants (overview in Belsky *et al.*, 2007). Thus, genes which are more commonly found in depressive, suicidal, or substance-dependent persons are also found more frequently among especially happy, successful, and creative persons, depending on the influences to which the child was exposed during its early development. As soon as the organism makes phenotypic adjustments to specific living conditions as a consequence of past experiences, there is a risk that, if these living conditions subsequently change, the selected development option will no longer have a functional impact. Precisely as described by Penke (2009), phenotypic plasticity is preserved in persons only if the change in the conditions primarily occurs in middle-term timescales. Whereas many changes within relatively short intervals can lead to the influences during early childhood losing their predictive value, conditions that remain stable over very long periods of time ensure that genetically fixed ("rigid") features are superior to plasticity mechanisms, which are relatively susceptible to errors.

Accordingly, there is an ontogenetic trade-off between the advantages of as high a plasticity as possible during development and the disadvantages of a lower phenotypic robustness. In other words, organisms that adjust to certain conditions in their development are disadvantaged, if the conditions subsequently either deteriorate or improve. Under fluctuating circumstances, it would be advantageous if the development were influenced as little as possible by early circumstances but were robustly (i.e., "rigidly") oriented to the optimal phenotype on average.

It needs to be borne in mind that fitness maximization – depending on the predictability of the environment – can be ensured either by a relatively uniform imprinting of features (which are, therefore, also relatively robust against temporary "disruptions") or by orientation to environmental cues, which on average provide early information on later living conditions quite reliably. In other words, two contradictory types of development strategies become manifest – namely, on the one hand, that of the comparatively inflexible, because uniformly imprinted, "generalist" under all circumstances, who runs the risk of being suitable "slightly for everything, but not for anything really," and, on the other hand, that of the versatile, but at the same error-susceptible, "specialist," whose development very strongly depends on the prevailing conditions. All of this leads to a conditional versatility of individual behavioral and attachment options, in which family conflicts about kin transactions and differential caregiver behavior – that is, those phenomena of special interest to an evolutionary attachment theory – play a role.

Cooperative breeding, kinship, and adaptive attachment behavior

Evolutionary concepts of family networks provide extremely variable roles for maternal and paternal kin in view of conflicts with in-laws and reproductive competition. As described at the beginning of this chapter, a family is not a harmonious community of absolute solidarity; rather, family ties are a dynamic system of mutual influence and are contingent on opportunity costs in the sense of Hamilton's rule against the background of ecological circumstances (see Emlen, 1995). From the child's standpoint, kinship asymmetries can have a context-dependent impact depending on the sex, age, and individual possibilities of the persons involved – and also on what support mothers receive from their kin. Viewed like this, childhood occurs within a field of tension of varying genetic interests, and the child inevitably has to establish relationships with different and possibly conflicting persons.

In a cooperative breeding model of attachment behavior, Bowlby's original model of a sole-child relationship with a maternal "secure base," which is frequently described as a "monotropic model," has been replaced by a web of relations in which the child, starting from an initial relationship with the mother, increasingly also incorporates ties with other caregivers into its concept of security. Therefore, it is possible for the child to develop multiple attachment bonds, and, as Keller (this volume) points out, the availability and reliability of a caregiving environment may be more important in many situations than individual attachment relationships, such as that between the child and the mother. In this context, it is interesting to note that the correlations between a secure attachment style and the children's developmental status noticeably increase, if, in addition to the bond with the mother, the ties to the child's other caregivers are also incorporated (van Ijzendoorn, Sagi, and Lambermon, 1992). The authors attribute differences in the degree of these correlations between an Israeli kibbutz population and a population from The Netherlands – at least in part – to the varying significance of double-income parents in both populations. As childcare was institutionalized by the community at a very early age and both parents usually worked in an Israeli kibbutz, Israeli children were much more reliant on ties to other caregivers and affected by the influences of such caregivers than in The Netherlands, where double-income parents were comparatively rare at the time of the study.

In our opinion, it becomes clear here what Keller (2008) meant by "the cultural nature of attachment" – namely, that cultural differences in parental behavior and the development of attachment by children cannot be regarded independently of the underlying ecological and socioeconomic conditions, and this dependence is regulated by biologically evolved mechanisms. Instead of one single universal solution in the socioemotional development between mother and child – or with other kin as well – there are instead varying local solutions adjusted to their respective context. Therefore, Keller and Otto (2009) argue that conventional tests to study mother–child attachment, which have mostly been developed solely in Western societies, are unsuitable for adequately grasping the adaptive value of the child–caregiver interaction in other cultures. In the traditional farming community of the Cameroonian Nso, for example, children are looked after by multiple caregivers at a very early age, and Nso mothers say that they prefer children who are as quiet as possible and able to control their emotions at an early age (Keller and Otto, 2009). Moreover, the authors report that most of the 1-year-old children studied in this population remained expressionless in the presence of a stranger, even in the case of physical contact, and did not show any emotions.

Whereas such behavior in Western societies would presumably be classified as disorganized, Keller and Otto (2009) propose instead that precisely this type of attachment behavior is especially desired and targeted by Nso mothers. As is common in West Africa, Nso mothers are very fertile, and, at the same time, they work in the fields. Therefore, it would be problematic if Nso children were strongly fixated on their mothers; after all, they are being cared for at an early age by extended kin networks, in which, traditionally, older siblings or male and female cousins assume the helper role.

This example shows that a uniformly optimal solution to the attachment problem for all socioeconomic living situations is very unlikely. This would contradict the functional logic of an adaptive system. Family constellations can have diverse influences and either enable a very close mother–child attachment and extended breast-feeding periods or open up productive or other reproductive opportunities for the mother, by having the offspring cared for by allomothers at an early age (Kushnick, 2012). By virtue of the described genetic asymmetries within families, the opportunity costs of maternal and paternal kin also differ, as do their investment strategies accordingly. Reproductive conflicts due to these asymmetric kin relationships can lastingly imprint the socioemotional development of the child.

All of the above evidence seems to indicate that an adaptive perspective in attachment research can help to lead the findings to date to promising functional explanations, such as life-history theory and family-conflict theory, and, at the same time, expand the focus from the prototype of the nuclear family to extended kin networks, as the model of cooperative breeding suggests.

References

Anderson, K. G. (2011). Does paying child support reduce men's subsequent marriage and fertility? *Evolution and Human Behavior, 32,* 90–6.

Bakermans-Kranenburg, M. J., and van IJzendoorn, M. H. (2008). Oxytocin receptor (OXTR) and serotonin transporter (5-HTT) genes associated with observed parenting. *Social Cognitive and Affective Neurosciences, 3,* 128–34.

Belsky, J. (1997). Attachment, mating, and parenting: an evolutionary interpretation. *Human Nature, 8,* 361–81.

Belsky, J., Bakermans-Kranenbug, M. J., and van IJzendoorn, M. H. (2007). For better and for worse: differential susceptibility to environmental influences. *Current Directions in Psychological Science, 16,* 300–4.

Belsky, J., Houts, R. M., and Pasco Fearon, R. M. (2010). Infant attachment security and the timing of puberty: testing an evolutionary hypothesis. *Psychological Science, 21,* 1195–1203.

Belsky, J., and Pluess, M. (2009). Beyond diathesis-stress: differential susceptibility to environmental influence. *Psychological Bulletin, 135,* 885–908.

Bentley, G. R., and Mace, R. (Eds.) (2009). *Substitute parents – biological and social perspectives on alloparenting in human societies.* New York and Oxford: Berghahn.

Blurton Jones, N. G., and Da Costa, E. (1987). A suggested adaptive value of toddler night waking: delaying the birth of the next sibling. *Ethology and Sociobiology, 8,* 135–42.

Bowlby, J. (1951). *Maternal care and mental health.* New York: Schocken Press. (1969). *Attachment and loss,* vol. I: *Attachment.* New York: Basic Books.

Champagne, F. A., and Meaney, M. (2006). Stress during gestation alters postpartum maternal care and the development of the offspring in a rodent model. *Biological Psychiatry, 59,* 1227–35.

Chisholm, J. S (1996). The evolutionary ecology of attachment organization. *Human Nature, 1,* 1–38.

Coeurjolly, J.-F., Drouilhet, R., Lafaye De Micheaux, P., and Robineau, J.-F. (2009). asympTest: a simple R package for classical parametric statistical tests and confidence intervals in large samples. *R Journal, 1/2,* 26–30.

Crespi, B. J. (2010). The strategies of the genes: genomic conflicts, attachment theory and development of the social brain. In A. Petronis and J. Mill (Eds.), *Brain and behavior: an epigenetic perspective* (pp. 143–68). Berlin: Springer.

Curley, J. P., Davidson, S., Bateson, P., and Champagne, F. A. (2009). Social enrichment during postnatal development induces transgenerational effects on emotional and reproductive behavior in mice. *Frontiers in Behavioral Neuroscience, 3(25),* 1–14.

Del Giudice, M. (2008). Sex-biased ratio of avoidant/ambivalent attachment in middle childhood. *British Journal of Developmental Psychology, 26,* 369–79. (2009). Sex, attachment, and the development of reproductive strategies. *Behavioral and Brain Sciences, 32,* 1–67.

Del Giudice, M., and Belsky, J. (2011). Parent–child relationships. In C. Salmon and T. Shackelford (Eds.), *The Oxford handbook of evolutionary family psychology* (pp. 65–82). New York: Oxford University Press.

Emlen, S. T. (1995). An evolutionary theory of the family. *Proceedings of the National Academy of Sciences of the United States of America, 92,* 8092–9.

Fearon, P. R. M., Bakermans-Kranenburg, M. J., and van IJzendoorn, M. H. (2010). Jealousy and attachment. In S. L. Hart and M. Legerstee (Eds.), *Handbook of jealousy: theory, research, and multidisciplinary Approaches* (pp. 362–86). Oxford: Blackwell.

Fernandez-Duque, E., Valeggia, C. R., and Mendoza, S. P. (2009). The biology of paternal care in human and nonhuman primates. *Annual Review of Anthropology, 38,* 115–30.

Flinn, M. V. (2006). Evolution and ontogeny of stress response to social challenge in the human child. *Developmental Review, 26,* 138–74.

Flinn, M. V., and England, B. (1995). Childhood stress and family environment. *Current Anthropology, 36*, 854–66.

Fox, M., Sear, R., Beise, J., Ragsdale, G., Voland, E., and Knapp, L. A. (2010). Grandma plays favourites. X-chromosome relatedness and sex-specific childhood mortality. *Proceedings of the Royal Society of London: Series B, Biological Sciences, 277*, 567–73.

Fraga, M. F., Ballestar, E., Paz, M. F., Ropero, S., Setien, F., Ballestar, M. L., Heine-Suñer, D., *et al.* (2005). Epigenetic differences arise during the lifetime of monozygotic twins. *Proceedings of the National Academy of Sciences of the United States of America, 102*, 10604–9.

Francis, D., Diorio, J., Liu, D., and Meaney, M. J. (1999). Nongenomic transmission across generations of maternal behavior and stress responses in the rat. *Science, 286*, 1155–8.

Frank, S. A., and Crespi, B. J. (2011). Pathology from evolutionary conflict, with a theory of X chromosome versus autosome conflict over sexually antagonistic traits. *Proceedings of the National Academy of Sciences of the United States of America, 108*(suppl. 2), 10886–93.

Grossmann, K. E. (1987). Die natürlichen Grundlagen zwischenmenschlicher Bindungen. Anthropologische und biologische Überlegungen. In C. Niemitz (Ed.), *Erbe und Umwelt. Zur Natur von Anlage und Selbstbestimmung des Menschen* (pp. 200–35). Frankfurt/M.: Suhrkamp.

Haig, D. (1993). Genetic conflicts in human pregnancy. *Quarterly Review of Biology, 68*, 495–532.

(2010). Transfers and transitions: parent–offspring conflict, genomic imprinting, and the evolution of human life history. *Proceedings of the National Academy of Sciences of the United States of America, 107*(suppl. 1), 1731–5.

(2011). Genomic imprinting and the evolutionary psychology of human kinship. *Proceedings of the National Academy of Sciences of the United States of America, 108*(suppl. 2), 10878–85.

Haig, D., and Wharton, R. (2003). Prader–Willi syndrome and the evolution of human childhood. *American Journal of Human Biology, 15*, 320–9.

Hamilton, W. D. (1964a). The genetical evolution of social behavior. I. *Journal of Theoretical Biology, 7*, 1–16.

(1964b). The genetical evolution of social behavior. II. *Journal of Theoretical Biology, 7*, 17–52.

Hawkes, K. (2010). How grandmother effects plus individual variation in frailty shape fertility and mortality: guidance from human–chimpanzee comparisons. *Proceedings of the National Academy of Sciences of the United States of America, 107*(suppl. 2), 8977–84.

Hawkes, K., O'Connell, J. F., Blurton Jones, N. G. (1991). Hunting income patterns among the Hadza: big game, common goods, foraging goals and the evolution of the human diet. *Philosophical Transactions of the Royal Society of London: Series B, Biological Sciences, 334*, 243–51.

Houston, A. I., Székely, T., and McNamara, J. M. (2005). Conflict between parents over care. *Trends in Ecology and Evolution, 20*, 33–8.

Hrdy, S. B. (1999). *Mother nature: a history of mothers, infants, and natural selection.* New York: Pantheon.

48   *Johannes Johow and Eckart Voland*

(2005). Cooperative breeders with an ace in the hole. In E. Voland, A. Chasiotis, and W. Schiefenhövel (Eds.), *Grandmotherhood – the evolutionary significance of the second half of female life* (pp. 295–317). New Brunswick, NJ and London: Rutgers University Press.

(2009). *Mother and others: the evolutionary origins of mutual understanding.* Cambridge, MA: Harvard University Press.

Jamison, C. S., Cornell, L. L., Jamison, P. L., and Nakazato, H. (2002). Are all grandmothers equal? A review and a preliminary test of the "grandmother hypothesis" in Tokugawa Japan. *American Journal of Physical Anthropology, 119,* 67–76.

Johow, J., Fox, M., Knapp, L. A., and Voland, E. (2011). The presence of a paternal grandmother lengthens interbirth interval following the birth of a granddaughter in Krummhörn (18th and 19th centuries). *Evolution and Human Behavior, 32,* 315–25.

Johow, J., and Voland, E. (2012). Conditional grandmother effects on age at marriage, age at first birth, and completed fertility of daughters and daughters-in-law in historical Krummhörn. *Human Nature, 23,* 341–59.

Keller, H. (2007). *Cultures of infancy.* Mahwah, NJ and London: Lawrence Erlbaum.

(2008). Attachment – past and present: but what about the future? *Integrative Psychological and Behavioral Science, 42,* 406–15.

Keller, H., and Otto, H. (2009). The cultural socialization of emotion regulation during infancy. *Journal of Cross-Cultural Psychology, 40,* 996–1011.

Kushnick, G. (2012). Helper effects on breeder allocations to direct care. *American Journal of Human Biology, 24,* 545–50.

Leonetti, D. L., Nath, D. C., and Hemam, N. S. (2007). In-law conflict: women's reproductive lives and the roles of their mothers and husbands among the matrilineal Khasi. *Current Anthropology, 48,* 861–90.

Main, M., and Hesse, E. (1990). Parents' unresolved traumatic experiences are related to infant disorganized attachment status: is frightened and/or frightening parental behavior the linking mechanism? In M. T. Greenberg, D. Cicchetti, and E. M. Cummings (Eds.), *Attachment in the preschool years: theory, research, and intervention* (pp. 162–82). University of Chicago Press.

Nettle, D. (2010). Dying young and living fast: variation in life history across English neighborhoods. *Behavioral Ecology, 21,* 387–95.

O'Connor, T. G., and Croft, C. M. (2001). A twin study of attachment in preschool children. *Child Development, 72,* 1501–11.

Penke, L. (2009). Adaptive developmental plasticity might not contribute much to the adaptiveness of reproductive strategies: a commentary on M. Del Giudice. *Behavioral and Brain Sciences, 32,* 38–9.

Rice, W. R., Gavrilets, S., and Friberg, U. (2010). The evolution of sex-specific grandparental harm. *Proceedings of the Royal Society of London: Series B, Biological Sciences, 277,* 2727–35.

Salmon, C. A., and Shackelford, T. K. (Eds.) (2008). *Family relations: an evolutionary perspective.* Oxford University Press.

Schlomer, G. L., Del Giudice, M., and Ellis, B. J. (2011). Parent–offspring conflict theory: an evolutionary framework for understanding conflict within human families. *Psychological Review, 118,* 496–521.

Sear, R., and Mace, R. (2008). Who keeps children alive? A review of the effects of kin on child survival. *Evolution and Human Behavior, 29*, 1–18.

Seki, M. (2012). Intra-individual conflicts between autosomal and X-linked altruistic genes: evolutionary perspectives of sex-specific grandmothering. *Journal of Theoretical Biology, 304*, 273–85.

Störmer, C., and Lummaa, V. (2014). Increased mortality exposure within the family rather than individual mortality experiences triggers faster life history strategies in historic human populations. *PLoS ONE*, doi: 10.1371/journal.pone.0083633.

Trivers, R. L. (1972). Parental investment and sexual selection. In B. Campbell (Ed.), *Sexual selection and the descent of man 1871–1971* (pp. 136–79). Chicago: Aldine.

(1974). Parent–offspring conflict. *American Zoologist, 14*, 249–64.

Úbeda, F., and Gardner, A. (2010). A model for genomic imprinting in the social brain: juveniles. *Evolution, 64*, 2587–2600.

van IJzendoorn, M., Sagi, A., and Lambermon, M. W. E. (1992). The multiple caretaker paradox: data from Holland and Israel. *New Directions for Child and Adolescent Development, 57*, 5–24.

Voland, E. (2007). Evolutionary psychology meets history: insights into human nature through family reconstruction studies. In R. Dunbar and L. Barrett (Eds.), *The Oxford handbook of evolutionary psychology* (pp. 415–32). Oxford University Press.

Voland, E., and Beise, J. (2002). Opposite effects of maternal and paternal grandmothers on infant survival in historical Krummhörn. *Behavioral Ecology and Sociobiology, 52*, 435–43.

(2005). 'The husband's mother is the devil in house' – data on the impact of the mother-in-law on stillbirth mortality in historical Krummhörn (C18–C19 Germany) and some thoughts on the evolution of postgenerative female life. In Voland et al., *Grandmotherhood*, pp. 237–55.

Voland, E., Chasiotis, A., and Schievenhövel, W. (Eds.) (2005). *Grandmotherhood: the evolutionary significance of the second half of female life.* New Brunswick, NJ, and London: Rutgers University Press.

Weaver, I. C. G., Cervoni, N., Champagne, F. A., D'Alessio, A. C., Sharma, S., Seckl, J. R., Dymov, S., et al. (2004). Epigenetic programming by maternal behavior. *Nature Neuroscience, 7*, 847–54.

Zhang, T. Y., and Meaney, M. (2010). Epigenetics and the environmental regulation of the genome and its function. *Annual Review of Psychology, 61*, 439–66.

2   Attachment theory as cultural ideology

Robert A. LeVine

During the nineteenth century, the treatment of children in Great Britain and the USA changed radically, not only through legislation making school attendance compulsory and abolishing child labor, but also by the rise of a sentimental view of children as innocent and lovable creatures needing both protection from harsh conditions and loving care from their mothers. By the time scientific approaches to child development emerged in the 1880s, this view of childhood was already well established in the literature popular among the middle and upper classes, from Dickens' *Oliver Twist* (1838) to Mayhew's *London Labour and the London Poor* (1861) and had been translated into action by social reformers of mid-nineteenth-century Britain and the USA (e.g., societies for "the prevention of cruelty to children" of the 1870s). Romantic literature and the "child-saving" movements were based not on science but on morality – a Christian morality derived in part from images of the innocent Christ Child – but these movements were also secular in their Romantic forms and applications to social problems. Moral outrage about the neglect and abandonment of children in the expanding cities and their exploitation in factories did not require scientific research; the rise in emotional concern for child victims and their suffering was an ideological response to the new conditions vividly portrayed in newspapers and books. In the century that followed, however, many treatises on children would combine science with moral ideology and advocacy of reform, and the works of John Bowlby provide a case in point.

Bowlby was both a reformer and a scientist. He played a major role in the post-World War II reform of childcare institutions in Britain and the USA, especially during the 1950s, and later contributed a theoretical model that influenced empirical research on infant social development. As a reformer, Bowlby was an unabashed advocate of what he regarded as the humane treatment of children; as a scientist, he assumed a posture of empirical inquiry without recognizing the ways in which his ideological advocacy influenced its assumptions.

This chapter presents a historical perspective on the psychology of attachment that Mary Ainsworth and her students based on Bowlby's model. I call into question its claimed status as an objective perspective based on empirical evidence concerning infancy and early childhood in the human species, and I argue that it should be seen as part of a twentieth-century moral campaign to change childcare in Britain and America. Attachment research, implicitly and sometimes explicitly, identified *bad mothers*, recasting moral judgments specific to middle-class Anglo-American culture of the middle and late twentieth century into a psychiatric model of early development in which the infant's need for "mother-love" leads to psychopathology when not satisfied by particular maternal behaviors. Defending Bowlby's claims that this model applies to all humans as a genetically transmitted precipitate of natural selection, attachment researchers have ignored, dismissed, and distorted cross-cultural evidence indicating greater diversity in both maternal behavior and infant emotional resilience that might refute the model.

Bowlby: the reformer as scientist

Bowlby is best known in developmental psychology for his theory-building trilogy *Attachment and Loss*, published between 1969 and 1980, but the basic features of his approach to child development were already present in his famous World Health Organization (WHO) monograph *Maternal Care and Mental Health* (1951), and its abridged form as a book, *Child Care and the Growth of Love* (1953), which sold 450,000 copies in the English-language edition and was translated into ten languages (Holmes, 1993, p. 27).

Bowlby's approach was focused on pathology in medical, specifically psychiatric, terms and how to prevent it, and on the environmental factors responsible for behavioral or psychological pathologies. He saw maternal care as similar to nutrition – necessary for normal development, an insufficiency, "maternal deprivation," causing psychopathology.

[T]he evidence is now such that it leaves no room for doubt . . . that the prolonged deprivation of a young child of maternal care may have grave and far reaching effects on his character and so on the whole of his future life. It is a proposition exactly similar in form to those regarding the evil after-effects of German measles before birth or deprivation of Vitamin D in infancy. (Bowlby, 1953, p. 50)

This need for maternal care was said to be supported by a consensus of childcare workers, in addition to suggestive evidence from research. As Bowlby explained in the preface to the first edition of his WHO report, he visited childcare and child guidance workers in the USA and Western Europe in 1950, finding "a very high degree of agreement existing both in regard to the principles underlying the mental health of children and the practices by which it may be safeguarded" (Bowlby, 1952, p. 6). It is doubtful, however, that this agreement in 1950 could have reflected simply the empirical evidence available at that time; it was based on shared moral views concerning how children should be treated.

Bowlby (1953, p. 182) presented as urgent the need to reform the treatment of children, to take action "against these evils," in terms derived from the humanitarian reform movements and Romantic ideologies of the nineteenth century. Jeremy Holmes, a British psychiatrist and largely sympathetic critic, notes in his *John Bowlby and Attachment Theory*:

Bowlby's tenderness towards little children carries echoes of Blake and Wordsworth, Dickens and Kingsley. There had to be a safe place from the violence of the modern world, and the Christian imagery of mother and child reappears, in his work, as an icon for a secular society. (1993, p. 46)

It is clear that Bowlby's convictions about mother-love came first, and the empirical evidence was assembled, in the 1950s and later, to support them. That is not in itself inconsistent with empirical inquiry, but he also excluded from consideration evidence of nonpathological alternatives at the level of individual differences and cultural variations, evidence that might have challenged the universality of the infant's needs and developmental (especially pathological) outcomes posited by his mother-love model. In other words, what if Western-style mother-love was not as necessary as vitamin D, but only – like peanut butter or spinach – one of several equally healthy alternatives for the child's needs? Bowlby's thinking was bound to a *dichotomous* medical model in which deviations from an idealized pattern of good mothering prevalent among the Anglo-American middle classes lead inevitably to psychopathology.

Bowlby was hardly alone in this line of thought, in 1950 or later. In fact, though a full history has yet to be written, a sweeping change of popular and professional opinion about the treatment of children in the USA and Britain after World War II was well underway by 1950, when the psychologist Celia Stendler (1950) referred to it as a "revolution." A generation of young parents was reacting against the way in which their parents had raised them in the 1920s and 1930s, under the influence of pediatricians for whom cleanliness, discipline, and strict scheduling were dictated by "medical science." But now a new breed of medical experts advocated empathy for children and freedom from excessive discipline, while putting a novel burden of responsibility on parents – not only for their children's conduct but also for their mental ills. Child rearing in ordinary families was now to be seen in psychiatric terms, with risks of psychopathology that had previously been overlooked. Stendler concluded from her review of these drastic changes in advice to parents "that the reasons for the revolution lie outside the realm of scientific fact" (1950, p. 122).

It may come as no surprise that these new experts, including the pediatrician Benjamin Spock (1946), had been trained in psychoanalysis, but, like Bowlby, they had rebelled against the orthodox Freudian model of childhood and were focused on the *emotional security* of the child rather than the gratification of libidinal needs. An early voice in this movement was that of Karen Horney, once a senior faculty member at the Berlin Psychoanalytic Institute, whose best-selling book of 1937, *The Neurotic Personality of Our Time*, claimed that neuroses seen in adult psychoanalysis stem from a lack of parental attention to a child's emotional needs and the consequent development of a *basic insecurity* – a claim that, in different versions, would be made by her and others writing in the 1950s and 1960s. Thus, it is no wonder that Bowlby – who seemed to be alienated from his own upbringing by a distant mother and a nanny who left when he was 4 years old – found on his arrival in the USA in 1950 many kindred spirits and a consensus that confirmed his own ideas.

This mental health movement, with its own echoes of the Romantic view of childhood and nineteenth-century "child-saving," was promoting new standards for parental behavior. Bowlby helped give that movement a focus on policies concerning children separated from parents and their treatment in institutions. His WHO monograph and popular book, received with enthusiasm by those predisposed to share his position, had an important impact on childcare policy. Bowlby also advised ordinary parents, giving voice to a generation deeply critical of the "distant" parental care they had received in the 1920s and 1930s. He admonished their cold and unresponsive mothers and called for warmth, love, and proximity. He constantly sought to support his case with empirical evidence, but he was always an advocate for a generation that felt itself neglected.

Thus, Bowlby's emphasis on mother-love was part of a larger ideological turn that highlighted the emotional security of young children and the risks of parents' behavior to their offspring's mental health. This ideological movement had preceded Bowlby's contribution, but his success as a reformer strengthened it. The movement itself, like Bowlby's own formulations, combined moral ideology with clinical observation and empirical research in an expansive effort to redefine parenting in psychiatric terms.

Bowlby was committed to empirical research, but also to generating universal generalizations from a combination of primate evidence and Western data, and he did not seek or take serious account of evidence from culturally varying human populations – a point Sarah LeVine and

I confirmed personally when we visited him in 1976 to report some pre-liminary findings from our Gusii Infant Study in Kenya. In 1986, he gave a lecture to the American Psychiatric Association, "Developmental Psychiatry Comes of Age," in which he expounded Ainsworth's categories of attachment in the strange situation (SS) as follows:

Three principal patterns of attachment present during the early years are now reliably identified, together with the family conditions that promote them. One of these patterns is consistent with the child's developing healthily, and two are predictive of disturbed development . . .

A third pattern is that of anxious avoidant attachment . . . Clinical evidence suggests that, if it persists, this pattern leads to a variety of personality disorders from compulsive self-sufficiency to persistent delinquency. (Bowlby, 1988, pp. 166–7)

In these very paragraphs, Bowlby cited the Grossmanns' study in Bielefeld, northern Germany, as if it confirmed the patterns he was presenting. In fact, however, the Grossmanns' (Grossmann, Grossmann, Spangler *et al.*, 1985) careful replication of Ainsworth's early work showed that 49% of the Bielefeld infants were anxious-avoidant, and fully two-thirds were not securely attached and, therefore, in Bowlby's terms, not "developing healthily" but on a course of "disturbed development." In the American sample (Ainsworth, Blehar, Waters *et al.*, 1978), only 35% were not securely attached. Does that mean that two-thirds of the Germans but only a bit more than one-third of the American infants were likely to be disturbed? Bowlby did not consider this question; nor, for the most part, did other attachment researchers, who were reluctant to confront such unsettling epidemiological implications. The Grossmanns (Grossmann and Grossmann, 1990) replicated their own study in Regensburg, in southern Germany, and their findings there were closer to those of the USA, but a study by Ahnert, Meischner, and Schmidt (2000) in East Berlin (also in the north of Germany) classified 42% of the infants as anxious-avoidant. These findings pose a challenge to Bowlby's developmental psychiatry that has yet to be fully confronted within the attachment research community, though the questions of cultural norms and meanings raised by the Bielefeld data were long ago discussed at length by leading child psychologists outside the attachment circle (Lamb, Thompson, Gardner *et al.*, 1985).

Bowlby's early analysis of maternal deprivation was criticized, partly confirmed, and substantially revised, notably by Michael Rutter (1979, 1981), though in a Western context. It was through Ainsworth's research on attachment, however, that Bowlby exerted his strongest influence on developmental psychology.

Ainsworth: the scientist as moralist

Mary D. S. Ainsworth was neither a psychiatrist nor an ideological advocate of reform but a rigorous scientist of child development. In translating Bowlby's attachment theory into the study of "normal" children (those not identified by a diagnostic category or particular experience), however, she retained the morally freighted and culture-specific dichotomies of emotional security/insecurity and maternal sensitivity/insensitivity. She found that 35% of the American children studied were in the "insecurely attached" categories that Bowlby claimed were prognostic of psychological disturbance resulting from experience of maternal behavior that was insensitive to their needs. (Later studies found slightly higher proportions; in the NICHD national study (1997), it was 38.8%.)

Those of us who have followed attachment research over the years are so well acquainted with these figures that we may have become immune to their implications: If testing American children at 11–15 months after birth finds 35–40% of them insecurely attached, indicating "disturbed development" due to "insensitive" mothering and at risk of personality disorders, does that mean we are undergoing an epidemic of parent-caused mental illness in the USA, or is there something wrong with the diagnostic concepts? Ainsworth and other attachment researchers in psychology have simply ignored this question, sidestepping what they may view as Bowlby's hyperbole about psychopathology while nevertheless using the categories of "insensitive" maternal care and "insecure attachment." Yet, "insecure attachment" in Bowlby's mature theoretical model unquestionably implies that mental health is at risk, and "insensitive" maternal care carries serious moral as well as psychiatric implications. If you were a mother, and you were insensitive to your infant's attempts to elicit the kind of care all humans can and should provide, you were at least an inadequate mother, responsible for the mental ills and emotional suffering that might befall him in the future. Can it be that such a large proportion of US mothers fall so short of the mark in evolutionary terms, and that an even larger proportion (twice as many) of German mothers in Bielefeld in 1977 were so culpable? Or is this psychiatric interpretation of child development an instance of diagnostic inflation by twentieth-century theorists viewing all psychological development in terms of mental health? As Lamb, Thompson, Gardner et al. (1985) said of the Bielefeld study:

These findings raise questions about the appropriateness of value-laden terms like "insensitivity" when we may be observing cultural variations in the goals and practices of parents. (p. 73)

The importation of this mental-health approach in empirical research on children and parents in the general population opened the door to the use of psychiatric categories to describe individual differences among infants and children – and to the blaming of mothers whose children (at 1 year of age) deviated from the norm. It gave tacit support to the growing tendency of mental-health professionals in the second half of the twentieth century to write popular books and articles in women's magazines warning of dangers in parenting and blaming mothers for their children's mental disorders, ranging from neuroses and narcissism to autism and schizophrenia.

Ainsworth's research endowed this tendency with a scientific legitimacy it had not had. By the 1980s, the SS was being used as a screening instrument in clinical assessments of child psychopathology, and attachment researchers were warning about the deleterious effects of infant day care. Later, books on "attachment parenting" gave advice to mothers, and "attachment therapy" offered help to adults damaged in infancy. The pathogenic potential of mothers, once the speculation of a few psychiatrists, became part of the common culture in America and Britain.

These unfortunate *sequelae* of attachment research could have been prevented by taking the findings from cross-cultural studies more seriously. Ainsworth, whose first full observational study was in Uganda, frankly revealed in her book on the SS (Ainsworth *et al.*, 1978, p. vii) that the method was constructed for the routine environments of American infants and had not been necessary in Uganda, yet it became established as the universal instrument for assessing "security" – as if that English word designated an emotional experience common to all cultures. She also revealed that the routine environments of infants among the !Kung San of Botswana, as studied by Konner (1972), and the Japanese, as reported to her by Keiko Takahashi, differed dramatically from those of the USA and Uganda (Ainsworth *et al.*, 1978, p. xiv).

The Grossmanns' replication of Ainsworth's Baltimore study, published in English in 1985, was a powerful warning that all was not well with the Bowlby–Ainsworth model – not merely because it showed Bielefeld infants to be almost twice as likely as Americans to be insecurely attached but also because Grossmann *et al.* (1985) provided a convincing cultural explanation for the large proportion of infants classified as avoidant (49%) – that is, that their German mothers by being less responsive ("insensitive" in Ainsworth terms) were deliberately fostering self-reliance (*Selbständigkeit*) and attempting to prevent their babies from becoming "spoiled" (*verwöhnt*). In their words,

We interpret this part of our findings with respect to the cultural values that we believe to be dominant in North Germany, where people tend to keep a larger interpersonal distance. As soon as infants become mobile, most mothers feel that they should now be weaned from close bodily contact. To carry a baby who can move on its own or to respond to its every cry by picking it up would be considered spoiling. The ideal is an independent, nonclinging infant who does not make demands on the parents but rather unquestioningly obeys their commands (Grossmann *et al.*, 1985, p. 253).

These mothers were, in other words, successful in achieving *their* cultural goal for infant development (LeVine and Norman, 2001), though they would count as failures in terms of the Anglo-American "security" goal. This comparison alone exposes the "universal" standard for attachment – security – as a culture-specific developmental priority not shared even with north Germans of the 1970s. I would add that it was also not shared with earlier generations of Anglo-Americans before the mid twentieth century, when emotional security became a widespread ideal. American middle-class mothers as late as the early 1930s (when I was an infant) were probably much more like the Bielefeld mothers of 1977 in their responsiveness than they were like their granddaughters in the era of Ainsworth's Baltimore study.

From an anthropological point of view, the Bielefeld study's findings should have initiated a wider search for comparative data on human attachment, as proposed more than twenty-five years ago by Lamb *et al.* (1985, pp. 280–1). If a group of German parents and infants deviated as much from the universal model of attachment (based on American data) as did the Bielefeld sample, then what about parents and infants in China, India, New Guinea, or the Amazon basin? And what about the possibility that attachment, like language, is a product of evolution that is realized differently in diverse human contexts? This wider search was not launched for several reasons:

(1) developmental researchers took Bowlby's universal model as a paradigm to work within rather than seeking ways to refute it;
(2) psychologists were more inclined by virtue of their training and ideals to conduct laboratory research than engage in fieldwork abroad;
(3) developmental psychologists took Ainsworth's Uganda study as having already demonstrated that infant–mother attachment is universal;
(4) psychologists who do conduct fieldwork abroad are often less attentive than anthropologists to contextual factors critical for understanding parental and infant behavior;
(5) some psychologists (e.g., van IJzendoorn and Sagi-Schwartz, 2008) believe it is possible to study human infant–mother attachment

through an *etic* approach, not recognizing that the human capacities involved can only be realized in behavior *through* the *emic* categories of a particular culture.

This last point can be illustrated from Ainsworth's (1967, 1977) Uganda study. Finding herself in Uganda by virtue of her husband's employment at the East African Institute for Social Research, and just after she had been working with Bowlby in London, Ainsworth decided to study infant care among the Ganda people, who live in and around the city of Kampala, where the institute is located. Old ethnographic accounts reported that Ganda children are sent away to their grandmothers after abrupt weaning from the breast. Ainsworth hoped to use this custom to study the impact of mother–child separation on the young children, but she found that, in 1954, weaning was not abrupt and only a few children were being sent away. To her credit, she did not give up but conducted a pioneering observational study of the emergence of attachment and its determinants in a sample of Ganda infants.

Her work is a classic, for its longitudinal observation of infant social behavior as it develops over the first year of life, and for its proof that – contrary to Freud and Spitz – babies become socially (i.e., visibly) attached to adults who do not feed them as well as those who do. For all the detail of her published observations, however, Ainsworth provides little evidence of the Ganda mothers' cultural ideals for infant development (unlike the Grossmanns' report on Bielefeld quoted above), focusing instead on variables she had already studied in the Baltimore sample by the time the Ganda book was published. Thus, there is a lack of contextual material that would give us a sense of how Ganda mothers were guiding infant behavioral development in culturally distinctive directions.

Ainsworth showed that, in a sample of 28 infants, those she classified as "securely attached" had mothers who were more "sensitive" to their "signals" – a finding that would be central in attachment research thereafter. Indeed, this finding's replication in the Bielefeld data is a major reason that that study is counted by attachment researchers as *confirming* the basic premises of the Bowlby–Ainsworth model rather than challenging it with a larger proportion of insecurely attached infants. (This interpretation assumes the primacy of individual differences within a group as an arena for demonstrating environmental influence, putting group differences and population variations on the side or not counting them at all.) So even though the Ganda mothers behaved differently from their American counterparts in many ways, and their children had different experiences, maternal sensitivity was correlated with infants' secure attachment – as it would prove to be in Baltimore and Minneapolis,

Bielefeld and Regensburg, and elsewhere in the world. With these replications of what van IJzendoorn and Sagi (1999, 2008) called the sensitivity hypothesis as well as the universality and competence hypotheses, the latter two researchers declared a victory for the Bowlby–Ainsworth model over cross-cultural challenges to its validity. But this declaration may be not only premature in terms of future comparisons of results from applications of the SS, but also in terms of a deeper critique of the Bowlby–Ainsworth model as science.

Problems with attachment theory as science

The defenders of attachment theory "against" cross-cultural research seek to preserve in its entirety the Bowlby–Ainsworth model of fifty years ago, but science does not stand still. Lamb *et al.* (1985) provided a sound and comprehensive critique of the model decades ago that was overlooked by attachment researchers at the time. Further doubts have accumulated about the assumptions, method, and evidence of attachment research during the past half-century. With more and better evidence from the USA, even those who previously defended the model have reduced their claims – for example, Alan Sroufe's claim of infant attachment's long-term influence (Sroufe, Coffino, and Carlson, 2010) and Jay Belsky's claim of maternal sensitivity as a predictor of attachment security (Belsky and Pasco Fearon, 2008). The hypothesis that infant day care leads to insecure attachment was refuted at the national level (NICHD, 1997). As mentioned earlier, developmental researchers had rarely endorsed Bowlby's conflation of the pathological consequences of extreme mother–child separation with insecure attachment in the SS, even while this line of thought spread in the more "applied" fields of psychotherapy and parental advising.

Strangely, cross-cultural data played little role in the decline of attachment theory as a credible framework for infant psychology. This is partly because – as Rothbaum *et al.* pointed out in 2000 – few investigations had been launched to explore attachment around the world in varying human populations, and partly because many of those that were conducted were inadequate attempts to replicate the SS, yielding ambiguous results that were interpreted as confirming rather than challenging the Bowlby–Ainsworth model, including its implications for health and pathology. The chapters of this volume help to fill this void and point in a different direction.

As principal investigator of two (Hausa and Gusii) of the fourteen studies cited by van IJzendoorn and Sagi in their 1999 review, I can testify that neither used the SS in a form likely to expose its methodological

problems. The Hausa observations by Sarah LeVine (Marvin, VanDevender, Iwanaga *et al.*, 1977) did not include the SS at all, and the
Gusii infants were assessed in the SS by P. Herbert Leiderman only at
home, a completely familiar, rather than strange, situation (Kermoian
and Leiderman, 1986). There are similar problems with many of the
non-Western studies reviewed in 1999, which were not true replications.
We need research like the Bielefeld study of the 1970s (which included
systematic home observations of maternal routines and separations) for
valid comparisons of SS results, and when the investigator deems the
standard procedure impossible to apply, we need extensive exploration
of the infant care parameters leading to this judgment. This should lead
to new insights into the mother–child relationship beyond what is accessible through the SS.

But there is more fundamental rethinking and basic research to be
done. The basic differentiating concepts of attachment research – *secure
versus insecure attachment* and *maternal sensitivity versus insensitivity* to
infant signals – involve moral judgments specific to the Anglo-American
cultural ideology of parent–child interaction that became influential in
the mid twentieth century and has remained so. Bowlby's leadership in
the campaign leading to the dominance of this ideological influence is
obvious, but his later construction of a scientific theory, and Ainsworth's
operationalizing parts of that theory in her empirical research, have dis-
guised the moral ideology at the core of their mental-health approach.
Creating categories of pathology or mental-health risk out of normal individual differences in infant and maternal behavior, they have perpetuated
the blaming of mothers characteristic of mid-twentieth-century pop psychology. The time has come to break the mold of attachment theory and
reconsider the relationships of infant, mother, and others with a renewed
and expanded search for universals as well as variations across a fuller
range of the world's cultures.

This is being done by many of the contributors to this volume who
report ethnographic work on mothers and infants in several non-Western
societies, including Daniel Everett, Alma Gottlieb, and Hiltrud Otto.
This research raises new questions about, as well as providing new
insights into, the mother–infant relationship. I shall end with evidence
from the Hausa and Gusii studies that has not been discussed in the
attachment literature.

Hausa

The Hausa babies were reported to interact with at least four adults, but
Marvin *et al.* (1977) left out the cultural context for these interactions.
The Hausa mothers were practicing a custom of avoidance with their

first- and second-born infants – not looking at or talking to their babies – in accordance with a kin-avoidance code focused on their husbands, whose names they are forbidden to speak, and which is applied also to their first offspring with him. The avoidance, known as *kunya*, which means embarrassment or shame but also moral control, dictates that mothers must not utter the names of their first or second children as well as avoiding the most immediate kinds of distal contact, even in infancy. The Hausa mothers obeyed these rules, even while holding, cleaning, and breast-feeding their babies. The older women in the compound, who gave the babies the kinds of interaction their mothers withheld, seemed to be compensating for the missing elements of care. Sarah LeVine also noted, however, that when mothers were alone with their babies, they broke the rules and interacted more freely.

The questions raised by this remarkable cultural pattern – what is it like to be raised by a mother who avoids you in public, what kinds of relationships develop with the more attentive grandmothers and other older women, etc.? – would have been pursued had we been able to continue the project the following year. This is a case where the unusual complexity of early social interaction poses a problem worth examining intensively.

Gusii

In the Gusii infant study, we were able to collect data on a sample of twenty-eight infants and toddlers over a 17-month period, and to analyze the data in detail (LeVine, 2004; LeVine, Dixon, LeVine *et al.*, 1994). These children slept with their mothers, were carried on their backs, and were rarely off the body of a mother or a sibling caregiver during the first year. They had, in other words, far more tactile contact with their mothers and others than babies in Europe or North America typically do. How does an infant experience this daily and prolonged body contact in psychological terms, and what are its effects on development? Does this practice, found in many parts of sub-Saharan Africa and elsewhere in the world, bear on the infant's sense of security or related psychological dispositions as much as maternal sensitivity to signals, and what are the psychophysiological mechanisms involved? By focusing on responsiveness to signals, does the Bowlby–Ainsworth paradigm overlook background parameters like tactile experience that could be crucial to mother–infant adaptation?

We found that Gusii caregivers responded frequently and rapidly to infants' cries, with breast-feeding or gentle jiggling, but infrequently to their babbling or efforts to make eye contact, as compared with a sample of American, middle-class mothers at 9 months. Mothers were thus "sensitive" to distress signals but not to nondistress signals. Does their sensitivity count as high (using Gusii standards of care), medium (if averaged across the two kinds of signals), or low (if responsiveness to nondistress signals is given priority, as American or German standards might)? This question raised by the Gusii pattern is unanswered in the attachment literature.

Gusii infants at 3–4 months cry less than half the time that American, middle-class infants do (LeVine et al., 1994, pp. 200–1). This is partly because the Gusii babies are promptly soothed when they begin to cry, but also perhaps because their body contact with the caregiver may prevent the distress that leads to crying. Gusii mothers are behaving adaptively in reducing both the amount of time their babies experience distress and the energy expenditure of crying. Does their style of maternal care prevent distress episodes from occurring and therefore afford the infant more "security" than a sensitivity in which the mother waits for infant signals before providing comfort? The answers to such questions cannot be found within the Bowlby–Ainsworth attachment paradigm, and will be found only when researchers are willing to move beyond it.

Gusii mothers, like the Bielefeld mothers mentioned above, are consciously pursuing culture-specific goals in infant care. In addition to minimizing distress, they seek to maximize growth through feeding, and to foster the infant's compliance. Their success in achieving the last goal was shown in Suzanne Dixon's video study (Dixon, LeVine, Richman et al., 1984; LeVine et al., 1994, pp. 213–16). Gusii infants and toddlers showed greater compliance and significantly less distress in a mother–child teaching situation than their American, middle-class counterparts. The American children tried to perform the task by themselves, shaking off their mothers' attempts to guide their hands, while the Gusii babies never did so. The Gusii mothers never praised their infants' performance, while the American mothers did so profusely. Keeping babies calm and compliant, Gusii mothers believe they are fostering growth and motor development, while preparing infants to join the domestic work team as they become toddlers; language development is not a priority for maternal behavior, as Gusii mothers see it as happening naturally when the toddler becomes part of a sibling group. Their different goals for infant behavioral development give them a different perspective on what is happening and should happen during infancy.

Hausa and Gusii

In both Hausa and Gusii studies, observations by Sarah LeVine (as well as others in the Gusii case) showed that infants were kept from crawling

and other motoric exploration (secure-base exploration, in the Bowlby–
Ainsworth framework) throughout the first year and beyond. All the Gusii
children could walk by 9–10 months but were still being held in more than
half of the daytime episodes during the 12–15-month period (LeVine
et al., 1994, p. 161). This is probably true of many other populations in
Africa and elsewhere, yet its implications for the validity of the Bowlby–
Ainsworth framework have rarely been mentioned, and its impact on the
child's psychological development remains a matter of speculation.

These brief reflections on the Hausa and Gusii studies indicate some of
the questions about attachment and the mother–child relationship that
have been raised by previous cross-cultural research but have not yet
been explored. Many others remain to be discovered in fieldwork not yet
done. We need to pursue the comparative study of infancy and maternal behavior in context, unencumbered by the strictures and ideological
biases of previous doctrines like the Bowlby–Ainsworth model, and this
volume provides illustrations and theoretical arguments to inform future
research.

References

Ahnert, L., Meischner, T., and Schmidt, A. (2000). *Maternal sensitivity and
attachment in East German and Russian family networks*. In P. Crittenden and
A. H. Claussen (Eds.), *The organization of attachment relationships: maturation,
culture, and context* (pp. 61–74). New York: Cambridge University Press.

Ainsworth, M. D. S. (1967). *Infancy in Uganda*. Baltimore, MD: Johns Hopkins
University Press.

(1977). Attachment theory and its utility in cross-cultural research. In P. H.
Leiderman, S. R. Tulkin, and A. Rosenfeld (Eds.), *Culture and infancy:
variations in the human experience* (pp. 49–67). New York: Academic Press.

Ainsworth, M. D. S., Blehar, M. C., Waters, E., and Wall, S. (1978). *Patterns
of attachment: a psychological study of the Strange Situation*. Hillsdale, NJ:
Erlbaum.

Belsky, J., and Pasco Fearon, R. M. (2008). Precursors of attachment security. In
J. Cassidy and P. R. Shaver (Eds.), *Handbook of attachment: theory, research,
and clinical applications* (2nd edn., pp. 295–316). New York: Guilford Press.

Bowlby, J. (1951/1952). *Maternal care and mental health*. Geneva: World Health
Organization.

(1953). *Child care and the growth of love*. London: Penguin.

(1988). *A secure base: parent–child attachment and healthy human development*.
New York: Basic Books.

Dickens, C. (1838). *Oliver Twist*. London: Richard Bentley.

Dixon, S. D, LeVine, R. A., Richman, A. L., and Brazelton, T. B. (1984).
Mother–child interaction around a teaching task: an African-American comparison. *Child Development, 55*, 1252–64.

Grossmann, K., Grossmann, K. E., Spangler, G., Suess, G., and Unzner,
L. (1985). Maternal sensitivity and newborns' orientation responses as

64   *Robert A. LeVine*

related to quality of attachment in northern Germany. In I. Bretherton and E. Waters (Eds.), *Growing points of attachment: theory and research. Monographs of the Society for Research on Child Development, 50*(1–2), 233–65. University of Chicago Press.

Grossmann, K. E., and Grossmann, K. (1990). The wider concept of attachment in cross-cultural research. *Human Development, 33,* 31–47.

Holmes, J. (1993). *John Bowlby and attachment theory.* London: Routledge.

Horney, K. (1937). *The neurotic personality of our time.* New York: Norton.

Kermoian, R., and Leiderman, P. H. (1986). Infant attachment to mother and child caretaker in an East African community. Special Issue: Cross-Cultural Human Development. *International Journal of Behavioral Development, 9,* 455–69.

Konner, M. (1972). Aspects of developmental ethology of a foraging people. In N. Blurton-Jones (Ed.), *Ethological studies of child behaviour* (pp. 285–304). Cambridge University Press.

Lamb, M. E., Thompson, R. A., Gardner, G., and Charnov, E. L. (1985). *Infant–mother attachment: the origins and developmental significance of individual differences in Strange Situation behavior.* Hillsdale, NJ: Lawrence Erlbaum.

LeVine, R. A. (2004). Challenging expert knowledge: findings from an African study of infant care and development. In U. P. Gielen and J. L. Roopnarine (Eds.), *Childhood and adolescence: cross-cultural perspectives and applications* (pp. 149–65). Westport, CT: Greenwood Publishing.

LeVine, R. A., Dixon, S., LeVine, S., Richman, A., Keefer, C., Liederman, P. H., and Brazelton, T. B. (1994). *Child care and culture: lessons from Africa.* New York: Cambridge University Press.

LeVine, R. A., and Norman, K. (2001). The infant's acquisition of culture: early attachment re-examined in anthropological perspective. In H. Mathews and C. Moore (Eds.), *The psychology of cultural experience* (pp. 83–104). New York: Cambridge University Press.

Marvin, R., VanDevender, T., Iwanaga, M., LeVine, S., and LeVine, R. A. (1977). Infant–caregiver attachment among the Hausa of Nigeria. In H. McGurk (Ed.), *Ecological factors in human development* (pp. 247–59). Amsterdam: North-Holland Publishing.

Mayhew, H. (1861). *London labour and the London poor.* London: C. Griffin and Co.

NICHD Early Child Care Research Network (1997). The effects of infant child care on infant–mother attachment security: results of the NICHD study of early child care. *Child Development, 68,* 860–79.

Rothbaum, F., Weisz, J., Pott, M., Miyke, K., and Morelli, G. (2000). Attachment and culture: security in the United States and Japan. *American Psychologist, 55*(10), 1093–1104.

Rutter, M. (1979). Maternal deprivation, 1972–1978: new findings, new concepts, new approaches. *Child Development, 50,* 283–305.

  (1981). *Maternal deprivation reassessed* (2nd edn.). Harmondsworth: Penguin.

Spock, B. (1946). *The common-sense book of baby and child care.* New York: Duell, Sloan and Pearce.

Sroufe, L. A., Coffino, B., and Carlson, E. A. (2010). Conceptualizing the role of early experience: lessons from the Minnesota longitudinal study. *Developmental Review, 30*, 36–51.

Stendler, C. (1950). Sixty years of child training practices: revolution in the nursery. *Journal of Paediatrics, 36*(1), 122–34.

van IJzendoorn, M. H., and Sagi, A. (1999). Cross-cultural patterns of attachment: universal and contextual dimensions. In J. Cassidy and P. R. Shaver (Eds.), *Handbook of attachment: theory, research and clinical applications* (pp. 713–34). New York: Guilford Press.

van IJzendoorn, M., and Sagi-Schwartz, A. (2008). Cross-cultural patterns of attachment: universal and contextual dimensions. In J. Cassidy and P. R. Shaver (Eds.), *Handbook of attachment: theory, research and clinical applications* (2nd edn., pp. 880–905). New York: Guilford Press.

3   "Babies aren't persons": a survey of
     delayed personhood

David F. Lancy

Introduction

To better understand attachment from a cross-cultural and historical perspective, I have amassed over 200 cases from the ethnographic and archeological records that reveal cultural models (D'Andrade and Strauss, 1992) of infancy. The 200 cases represent all areas of the world, historical epochs from the Mesolithic to the present, and all types of subsistence patterns (Appendix 3.1). The approach is inductive where cases with similar models of infancy are clustered into archetypes, demonstrating that most societies view infants and even children as not-yet-persons. Infants are born into a state of liminality or incompleteness. Among the Wari, a baby is compared to unripe fruit as it is "still being made" (Conklin and Morgan, 1996, p. 672), and the Nankani reserve judgment on the infant's humanity until they can be certain it is not a spirit or bush child (Denham, Adongo, Freydberg *et al.*, 2010, p. 608). In this chapter, I will identify first the main factors that give rise to delaying personhood and, second, the cultural models that justify and guide the transformation of babies into persons.

Attachment and attachment parenting

In the middle of the last century, John Bowlby (1953), a British psychotherapist, advanced a set of ideas about the emotional ties between a mother and her infant and the deleterious effects of maternal deprivation. These propositions are now widely known as "attachment theory." A critical component of the theory was its universality; *all*

I am grateful to Amanda Davis Arthur, Tanya Collings, James Young, M. Annette Grove, and Elizabeth Payne for their contributions to this research project. Annette Grove also assisted with editing. I thank the volume editors Keller and Otto for their helpful critique of an earlier draft and Suzanne Gaskins for her valuable feedback.

mother–child dyads must engage in behaviors that build and strengthen mutual bonds during a critical period from 6 to 18 months. The theory has, since then, gathered adherents across a broad spectrum, from developmental psychologists testing for evidence of "secure" versus "avoidant" or "ambivalent/resistant" attachment (Ainsworth, Blehar, Waters et al., 1978) to social workers who point to attachment failure as the root of criminal behavior. Numerous empirical studies have extended attachment to nonindustrialized societies with mixed results, but, overall, they suggest considerable cross-cultural variability (Keller, 2007; Tomlinson, Murray, and Cooper, 2010; van IJzendoorn and Sagi-Schwartz, 2008).

There has, nevertheless, been a steady escalation in the expectation for adequate parenting to prevent attachment failure (Karen, 1998; Newton and Schore, 2008). Recently, attachment theory can be regarded as having morphed into a kind of secular religion where mothers worship at the altar of "attachment parenting."[1] That is, among the social elite in the USA, "attachment" has become synonymous with good, correct child rearing. This "movement" is supported by many quasi-scientific parenting volumes as well as by web-based organizations. The goal of "Attachment.org" is to provide help for "each wounded child with attachment disorder," which is caused by, for example, "caring for baby on a timed schedule or other self-centered parenting."[2] Much of the advice-to-parents literature suggests that full-scale attachment parenting is supported by anthropological research (especially on topics like the frequency of nursing and physical contact between mother and infant) and is, therefore "natural." Failure to embrace the whole suite of prescribed parenting practices is, therefore, unnatural. One confirmed apostate in the new attachment parenting faith is noted US media personality Erica Jong. She characterizes attachment parenting as follows: "You wear your baby, sleep with her and attune yourself totally to her needs [but how can you] do this and also earn the money to keep her."[3] Another, more credible, dissenting perspective is provided by a study of attachment in Germany. In spite of the fact that, by standardized measures, two-thirds of the Bielefeld children were classified as "insecurely attached," the authors reject the possibility that these children are at risk of developing personality disorders (LeVine and Norman, 2001, p. 97). And they suggest that the behavior of German mothers is guided by

---

[1] www.attachmentparenting.org/   [2] www.attachment.org/
[3] *Ibid.* Another variation in the intensive mothering movement is the "naturalist" approach, which has also attracted the attention of social critics (Badinter, 2012).

a cultural model of child development that cautions against excessive attention being paid to the infant:

They view the infant's needs for physical and social care as important but emphasize attention to satisfying those needs without disturbing family routines too much, and they are also concerned about the danger that a young child will become "spoiled," *verwöhnt*, by excessive attention and too much accommodation to its needs and demands. (LeVine and Norman, 2001, pp. 91–2)

Attachment and anthropology

Anthropologists studying mother–infant relations provide ethnographic descriptions that do not square with "attachment parenting" orthodoxy. Researchers who have directly addressed attachment theory have expressed considerable skepticism of the theory based on the evidence from their own ethnographic research; Gottlieb's study of the Beng (1995), Scheper-Hughes' (1987) study of Alto do Cruzeiro, and LeVine's (2004) work with the Gusii are notable. For example, consider the Kpelle in rural Liberia, where babies experience "casual nurturance by mothers who carry their babies on their backs and nurse them frequently but do so without really paying much direct attention to them; they continue working or . . . socializing" (Erchak, 1992, p. 50). Paradise records, "When a [Mazahua] mother holds a nursing baby in her arms she frequently has a distracted air and pays almost no attention to the baby" (1996, p. 382). "Gusii mothers rarely looked at or spoke to their infants and toddlers, even when they were holding and breast-feeding them" (LeVine, 2004, p. 154). In none of these cases did the anthropologists observe any decrement in the mental health of individuals subjected to – in attachment-parenting orthodoxy – maternal deprivation.

These studies represent robust illustrations of what LeVine has called the "anthropologist's veto" (2007, p. 250). That is, anthropologists have a history of undermining the claims of universality made by developmental psychologists. Two further examples include the practice of talking to nonverbal infants in a special speech register (baby talk or motherese). Usually assumed to be both universal and essential to the development of speech in children, it is neither (Ochs and Schieffelin, 1984). "Parenting style" theory (Baumrind, 1971) cannot withstand cross-cultural scrutiny. Central African Bofi farmers fit the so-called authoritarian parenting style in valuing respect and obedience and exercising coercive control over their children. Bofi children should, according to theory, be withdrawn, nonempathetic, aggressive, and lacking in initiative. On the contrary, they display precisely the opposite traits, leading Fouts to conclude that the theory "has very little explanatory power among the Bofi"

(2005, p. 361). More recently, Henrich, Heine, and Norenzayan (2010) have crafted a sophisticated literature review illustrating the ethnocentric bias and distortion that is found in leading research paradigms. Because of biased population samples and the inherent ethnocentrism of investigators, the views on child development found in WEIRD (*W*estern, *E*ducated, *I*ndustrialized, *R*ich, and *D*emocratic) society are taken as the norm and, hence, nurture is turned into nature (Lancy, 2010). A historical perspective on the same phenomenon argues that "the attachment model of early child development belongs to the ideological camp of child-centered freedom and equality against old-fashioned parentally imposed order and discipline" (LeVine and Norman, 2001, p. 100).

The basic argument underlying attachment theory is that each individual's mental health is at risk during the first two years of life. The child's psyche can be damaged if it is unable to establish a firm emotional tie to its mother (or appropriate substitute). The mother, in this theory, is expected to behave in ways that ensure attachment (Bowlby, 1953). In contemporary application of the theory (e.g., "attachment parenting"), the mother is challenged to take care of the infant's needs in a supportive and emotionally warm manner, leading to a strong emotional bond. Among maternal behaviors commonly assumed to play a critical role in this process are the following: being available at all times to tend the infant; breast-feeding; holding the infant *en face*; speaking to it in baby talk or motherese; cuddling, kissing, and otherwise demonstrating the strong positive affect the mother feels towards the infant and; playing with it. A mother's failure to actively promote her infant's emotional "high" leads to attachment failure, which leads to prison or worse.

From my survey of the literature on infancy outside contemporary bourgeois society, I can assert that the anthropological cases just mentioned are not atypical. The ethnographic record is quite consistent in showing mothers frequently nursing infants but, otherwise, paying them relatively little attention (Ainsworth, 1967; Lancy, 2007; Reichel-Dolmatoff, 1976). Indeed, LeVine (2004) and others (True, Pisani, and Oumar, 2001) are probably correct in arguing that any baby that is – minimally – given regular and predictable nourishment while in close contact with another human being will be protected from the orphan warehouse syndrome or what Spitz (1945) called "hospitalism" and any lasting emotional damage. But I want to do more than pile on further cases that cast the theory of attachment – or at least the extreme position represented by the attachment-parenting movement – into doubt. My goal here is to inductively construct a cultural model (D'Andrade and Strauss, 1992) or models of infancy that help us to understand why the contemporary preoccupation with attachment has more to do with fashion than child welfare. The survey suggests not only a very "light" version of attachment parenting but also that, in most societies, the greatest challenge facing families with newborns is to avoid forming a premature attachment. The infant's needs are obvious; less obvious are the needs of its mother and family and of the wider circumstances attendant on its birth. I identify the factors that may be present and that constitute the ecology of infancy. These factors all signal the need for caregivers to maintain a degree of emotional distance from the child. Six factors emerged from the survey that militate against or temper the attention paid to infants. These are as follows: high infant mortality rate and chronic illness; the mother's vulnerability; alloparenting and fostering; dysfunctional families; neglect because the infant is unwanted or on probation; abandonment and infanticide; and a utilitarian view of offspring. I take up each in turn.

Factors influencing cultural models of infancy

High infant mortality and chronic illness

Infant-mortality data are available for a range of societies from prehistoric settlements, nomadic foragers, and farmers to complex societies in Europe and Asia. These data suggest that from one-fifth to one-half of babies did not survive until the age of 5 years (Dentan, 1978; Kramer and Greaves, 2007; Lancy, 2008; Le Mort, 2008). We can extrapolate from these figures to conclude that miscarriages and stillbirths were also common by comparison to current levels. Likewise, we can expect that if half the children died, then somewhat more than half were seriously ill in childhood. Indeed, in many contemporary villages studied by anthropologists, the level of clinical malnutrition is 100 percent, as is the level of chronic parasite infestation and diarrhea. There are, then, ample reasons for withholding investment in the infant and maintaining a degree of emotional distance.

It was a Roman writer, Epictetus, who noted, "when you kiss your child, say to yourself, it may be dead in the morning." (Stearns, 2010, p. 168)

Childhood, according to the seventeenth-century French cleric Pierre de Bérulle, "is the most vile and abject state of human nature, after that of death." (cited in Heywood, 2001, p. 9)

The infant mortality rate [among the Bajau] is extremely high, and it is not uncommon to encounter a family with more deceased than living children. In fact, infant mortality is so high that some parents cannot even recall the number of their deceased children. (Nimmo, 1970, p. 261)

In the 1760's Lomonosov estimated that fully one-half of Russia's children died by the age of three. (Dunn, 1974, p. 385)

Of 15,000 babies left at the Ospidale Innocenti between 1755 and 1773, two-thirds died before reaching their first birthday. (Kertzer, 1993, p. 299)

The [Neolithic era] skeletal sample consists of 109 infants less than one year old, twenty-five juveniles, and 106 adults... [T]he age distribution of juveniles... reveals a high proportion of infants less than one year old, most of them (ninety-one per cent) deceased perinatally. (Le Mort, 2008, p. 25)

The relatively low reproductive rates of hunter-gatherer populations have been attributed to high natural mortality, low fertility, and cultural practices such as infanticide and sexual abstention. (Spielmann, 1989, p. 321)

These grim statistics provoke a "wait-and-see" attitude towards the newborn, and the narratives or parental ethnotheories (Harkness and Super, 1995) constructed about infancy reflect this uncertainty.

The mother's vulnerability

Another inexorable factor affecting the newborn is the threat it represents to its mother. Throughout much of human history, pregnancy has been treated as a serious illness. Childbirth was, until recently, extremely risky and even if the mother survived she might become the target of jealousy and witchcraft on the part of human and nonhuman adversaries. She and the babe are both contaminated by the process of birth and the spilling of puerperal blood. Women are also made vulnerable by the need to observe food taboos at critical junctures such as menstruation and pregnancy. These taboos often involve restricting their intake of high-quality fat and protein-rich foods (Spielmann, 1989). Most critical is the fact that the new mother is also likely to be responsible for maintaining a household; caring for a husband, older children, parents, or parents-in-law; and making a major contribution to subsistence or the domestic economy through (for example) craftwork (Boserup, 1970). The health and recovery of the mother are seen as far more urgent than the emotional health of the infant.

Childbirth is by far the greatest peril faced by [Semai] women in their reproductive years, accounting for thirteen of twenty-nine deaths (forty-five per cent), and half of all deaths from known causes. (Dentan, 1978, p. 111)

"A pregnant woman has one foot in the grave" according to a proverb from Gascony. (Heywood, 2001, p. 58)

Pregnant [Masai] women attempt to become as emaciated as possible in order that the birth may proceed more easily. During the last 3 or 4 months of pregnancy the woman abandons her normal diet and exists on a near starvation diet . . . The last month, she drinks only milk. (DeVries, 1987, p. 170)

A *budda* may "eat" the blood of the [Macha-Galla] child or the mother, causing illness or even death. A *tolca* may harm them by some malevolent action. (Batels, 1969, p. 408)

The [new Ladakh] mother is plied with foods [to] regain her strength. Her health is paramount – to care for the baby and to get back to the routine household and agricultural tasks upon which the success of the household depends – while household members simply hope for the best with regard to the newborn. (Wiley, 2004, p. 132)

Behavioral scan data also provide evidence for male dominance: women spent twenty-one per cent more time working than men . . . and men spent twenty-nine per cent more time resting than women. (Strassmann, 1997, p. 688)

Given the threats to its survival and low value relative to the mother (and older, living siblings), it is not surprising that the infant is, at least initially, in a marginal state.

Alloparenting and fostering

At the peak of her childbearing years, the young mother is also a critical contributor to the household economy. Hence, most societies embrace alloparenting as the means to lighten the mother's burden and thereby increase her fertility and her productivity. In a comprehensive survey of the ethnographic record, "forty per cent of infants were rated as being cared for by others . . . or cared for more than half the time by others. After infancy . . . less than twenty per cent of the societies had mothers as principal caretakers" (Weisner and Gallimore, 1977, p. 170). Numerous studies underscore that infants are tended as often by a grandmother or older sibling as by the mother (Hrdy, 1999). Furthermore, the widespread prevalence of wet-nursing (Sussman, 1982), adoption and fostering (Alexandre-Bidon and Lett, 1999), and, less commonly, the sale of infants (MacGinnis, 2011) suggests that the bond between mother and child should be, preferentially, weak.

Despite the fact that Aka [forager] and Ngandu [farmer] mothers carry their infants with them during subsistence activities, the frequency of maternal caregiving and maternal intimacy is negatively associated with work activities . . . [W]hen high-quality allomaternal care is available, Aka mothers reduce caregiving and spend more time in subsistence-economic activities. (Meehan, 2009, p. 389)

While awake, Hausa infants are almost always in close physical proximity to one or more adult caregivers . . . infant signals, such as crying, are responded to promptly by adults or older children . . . Although Hausa infants appear to be attached to three or four different figures (including fathers), most are primarily attached to one. Importantly, the principal figure is not necessarily the mother, who is solely responsible for feeding, but rather the person who holds and otherwise interacts with the infant the most. (Tomlinson *et al.*, 2010, p. 185)

[Beng mothers have several strategies] to bind the infant to potential caretakers. When a visitor calls, the baby is to be awakened and displayed proudly . . . "You want to teach your baby how to be sociable, too, and to get to know all her relatives . . . make sure the baby looks beautiful! Every morning after you give the baby her bath, make sure you put herbal makeup on her face . . . the baby will be so irresistibly beautiful that someone will feel compelled to carry her around for a while that day." (Gottlieb, 1995, pp. 23–4)

There are numerous taboos and rules of avoidance between [Baatombu] biological parents and children [who have been given in adoption]. They are forbidden to call the children by their first name. Instead, they have to use nicknames or paraphrases. Even in the first hours after birth I observed mothers expressing distance towards their newborn child in the presence of a watching crowd of friends and relatives. (Alber, 2004, p. 40)

To the extent that attachment theory focuses attention on the mother's behavior, we can see that her responsibilities as caregiver may be attenuated by cultural patterns that elevate other aspects of her multifaceted role and that cast others in the role of caregiver. If the child has not already been under the care of others, certainly at weaning it will be. "Toddler rejection" (Weisner and Gallimore, 1977, p. 176) is a widely reported phenomenon in which the infant is weaned early, separated from its (likely pregnant) mother, placed in the care of a grandmother or sib-caregivers, and, generally, ignored (Lancy and Grove, 2010).

Dysfunctional families

The flip side of the alloparenting, "It takes a village" childcare pattern is that, in some societies,[4] strife within the extended family is endemic – leading to chronically dysfunctional families. By dysfunctional, I mean that strife between the generations, between spouses, and between cowives is so common it is *expected*. Indeed, conflict is so much a part of daily life that it is reflected in the cultural model of infancy. The Dogon

---

[4] I must stress that this level of conflict within families is by no means universal or even widespread. On the contrary, I have to agree with Hrdy's (2006) characterization of humans as cooperative breeders, a corollary of which is that immediate and extended family members, including cowives, do contribute in positive ways to the child's survival. A key factor differentiating among these cases is the closeness of kin ties. In situations of chronic family conflict, the household consists of a mixture of people who are not all closely related. The women are living patrilocally, with little contact with their natal families, and the child may be exposed to the questionable care of stepfamily members.

case has been most thoroughly studied and reflects the rivalry that may exist among unrelated cowives.[5] Other examples of the child being the center of rivalry among women from West Africa follow.

The indigenous Dogon explanation is that poor survivorship under polygyny reflects competition among cowives. Cowives are not related, and the rivalry among them extends to their sons, who, upon the death of their father, almost invariably stop farming together ... [I]t was widely assumed that cowives often fatally poisoned each other's children. I witnessed special masked dance rituals intended by husbands to deter this behavior. Cowife aggression is documented in Malian court cases with confessions and convictions for poisoning. These cases raise the possibility that Dogon sorcery might have a measurable demographic impact – a view that is consistent with the extraordinarily high mortality of males compared with females. Males are said to be the preferred targets because daughters marry out of the patrilineage whereas sons remain to compete for land. Even if women do not poison each other's children, widespread hostility of the mother's cowife must be a source of stress. (Strassmann, 1997, p. 693)

Sorcery is considered to be the most important reason for a [Papel] child's death. It is seen as a serious ... problem. Because of envy, hatred, vindictiveness, or simply bad intentions some people decide to use sorcery to hurt a rival or someone they dislike. A child is often the chosen victim. (Einarsdottir, 2004, pp. 116–17)

[Hausa] babies can be stolen by witches or child-seeking spirits. To avoid the attention of these entities, it is best not to openly praise children. "Rolling your child in cow dung is also a good way to fool greedy spirits into thinking that your child is not worth taking." Occasionally, remark to a friend, "Have you ever seen such an ugly baby?" (Johnson, 2000, p. 187)

The source of conflict may be the adulterous liaisons of a parent. "Divorce and remarriage ... increase a child's risk of dying" (Sear and Mace, 2008, p. 9), and children exposed to interparental conflict show heightened levels of cortisol and long-term negative health outcomes (Flinn and England, 2002).

[Phiringaniso is an] illness attributed to violation of the norms of sexual behavior by a [Tsonga] parent of the sick child. It is usually provoked by a man's having extramarital intercourse while his child is still breastfeeding ... The child becomes "contaminated" and soon after exhibits watery diarrhea. The mother might also cause this diarrhea in her child by having "outside" sexual relations. (Green, Jurg, and Djedje, 1994, p. 11)

A woman in San Gabriel sometimes said that her second child had died of colerin, caused by drinking her breast milk when she was consumed by jealousy, rage, and

---

[5] Anecdotally, cowives are described as assisting each other with domestic duties, including childcare. However, the only studies to attempt to document a positive effect on child outcomes in a polygynous household found such effects only for high-ranking wives with negative outcomes for the children of low-ranking wives (Isaac and Feinberg, 1982).

pain from learning that her husband was having an affair. Colerin is incurable; it strikes and kills vulnerable infants quickly and surely. Children are thus killed by their fathers' selfish, irresponsible actions, which poison their mothers' milk. (Morgan, 1998, p. 70)

The conflict could arise from the jealousy of an older sibling who has been (or is about to be) displaced from the breast or the mother's full attention.

If [an Ijaw] woman with a living child has experienced one or more unsuccessful pregnancies, or if she has not apparently conceived for a long period after having a child, a diviner might tell her that the living child wishes to be the last child, that it wants no younger rivals, and that it is killing her unborn babies. (Leis, 1982, p. 163)

In at least some societies, conflict within the family is endemic or to be expected. Under these circumstances, the threats to the child's survival are magnified, casting in the shadow any concerns over attachment and the child's long-term emotional health. On the contrary, conspicuous displays of affection or emotional bonding could attract the attention of harmful forces or individuals.

Infant unwanted or on probation, leading to neglect, abandonment, and infanticide

Only a tiny fraction of the world's societies has accorded an unconditional welcome to every new member (Meskell, 1994). In societies where well-formed, full-term newborns may not survive to become helpful and able to pay back the investment made in them, the actuarial odds dictate a very careful evaluation of the newborn. Is it completely whole? Does it behave normally, crying neither too little nor too much? Is it a girl when a boy is infinitely preferred? Did it arrive "too soon" before its older and, hence more valuable, sibling had been weaned? Is it unquestionably the offspring of its mother's husband (Schiefenhovel, 1989)? Does the mother have a husband?

Illegitimate [Mundurucu] children are usually killed at birth, along with twins and children with birth defects. If the child does survive it is referred to as "tun" which means excrement. They are not abused, but they cannot marry due to their indefinite status. (Murphy and Murphy, 1985, p. 127)

It was an ironclad rule that no [Tapirapé] woman should have more than three living children . . . A fourth child, or a third child if it were of the wrong sex, was buried immediately after its birth . . . "We do not want to see hunger in their eyes." They pointed out to me the difficulty of providing food, especially meat, for more than three children. (Wagley, 1977, p. 135)

Children delivered in breech births were sometimes exposed. In a Han-dynasty lexicon, the word for *breech* is equated with (*wu*), meaning "obstinate", disobedient, or unfilial. Thus it is possible that the child's ability to physically torment its mother on its first day of life may have been interpreted as foreshadowing its future unfilial behavior. (Kinney, 1995, p. 25)

The Bakairí selectively practice infanticide . . . Most of such cases occur when the mother is still nursing an older infant and cannot properly care for another baby. (Picchi, 2000, p. 64)

You take them out into the bush and you leave them . . . they turn into snakes and slither away . . . You go back the next day, and they aren't there. Then you know for a sure that they weren't really [Dogon] children at all, but evil spirits. (Dettwyler, 1994, pp. 85–6)

Among the Songye, those defined as "bad" or "faulty" children, including albino, dwarf, and hydrocephalic children, are considered supernaturals who have been in contact with sorcerers in the anti-world; they are not believed to be human beings, and they are expected to die. (Devleiger, 1995, p. 96)

Previous surveys of ethnographic and historical records affirm that the elimination of infants by abortion (Devereux, 1955) and infanticide (Daly and Wilson, 1984) is nearly a cultural universal. Dickeman claims that "This capacity for selective removal in response to qualities both of offspring and of ecological and social environments may well be a significant part of the biobehavioral definition of *Homo sapiens*" (Dickeman, 1975, p. 108) Again, the reasons for "not becoming too attached" predominate.

Utilitarian view of offspring

The society that spawned and embraces attachment parenting is, comparatively, wealthy and well educated and enjoys both low infant and maternal mortality and a low birthrate. As documented in the Value of Children (VOC) surveys, there has been an ongoing transition – driven by economic development – from valuing children for their economic contributions to valuing them for the psychological rewards they bestow (Kağitcibaşi and Ataca, 2005; see also Zelizer, 1985). Theoretically, each newborn is or was subjected to a cost/benefit calculation (Trivers, 1972). The costs are considered to be high, even for wanted, healthy offspring while the benefits lie in the future. In many societies, it is not until middle childhood that the individual can make a significant contribution to the household economy and is "noticed" (Lancy and Grove, 2011a).

Individual infants are devalued if they are unlikely to provide a future return on the investment that will, perforce, be made in them.

In [the Beng] language, one word for "child" really means "little slave". "As soon as the little one can walk confidently, don't hesitate to send your child on errands in your village or neighborhood." (Gottlieb, 2000, p. 87)

A[n Amish] baby is never spoken of as "a little stranger" but is welcomed as a "new woodchopper" or a "little dishwasher." (Hostetler and Huntington, 1971, p. 22)

In the Chinese language, "good" children are literally contrasted with "useless" or "unusable" children. (Wee, 1992, pp. 192–3)

In Salic law [of the sixth-century CE]... one who killed a free young woman of childbearing age had to pay 600 sous... [I]t is astonishing how small a case is made for the newborn, since the one who killed a male baby only had to pay sixty sous (thirty sous if it was a girl). (Alexandre-Bidon and Lett, 1999, p. 13)

I have earlier contrasted our culture as a neontocracy, in which infants are treated as cherubs, with the premodern world, which exhibits characteristics of a gerontocracy where children are viewed as chattel (Lancy, 2008). This contrast allows us to see that the culture that gave birth to "attachment parenting" is rather unique in human annals. Most humans would ask why we should be excessively concerned about the feelings of an individual of such low value/status?

Delayed personhood and cultural models of infancy

Although I have argued that there are at least six overarching issues militating against attachment, these constitute only the raw material from which cultural models can be constructed. These raw facts serve as the foundation for culturally constituted theories of child development. The single most common element in non-Western cultural models of infancy is delayed recognition of the infant's personhood or humanity. By treating infants as existing in a liminal state and not being fully human, the community erects a large shelter or cognitive comfort zone within which several problems can be worked out. First of all, infants really are different. Contemporary bourgeois society, almost uniquely, has chosen to construe those differences in a positive way (Lancy, 2008). Gurgling and babbling are evidence of cuteness, not limited mental capacity. Because we enjoy the luxury of diapers, fresh water from a faucet, soap, and lotions, our babies smell sweet, not poopy. Our mothers can take pleasure in playing peek-a-boo with their baby rather than having to lug it like a heavy bookbag for miles to and from the fields. If one is not inclined to view the baby as an adorable cherub, then many infant characteristics, such as its lack of speech, softness, lack of motor control, crying and screaming, constant runny nose, diarrhea, lack of teeth and hair, and lack of mobility, might be seen as anomalous, bestial, or frightening. The Lepcha (among others) think of the infant as still being in the womb (Gorer, 1938) and not yet fully born. Indeed, most societies subscribe to some version of the idea that the infant is not just a really pathetic human being – it is *not* a human being. Nor is it clear at the outset that it will necessarily become human, perhaps it is just a messenger or a vehicle being used by supernaturals.

A decision had to be made within four days after parturition, for by that time an [Inuit] infant had to be named. And, once named, the disposal of a child would be an act of murder because a named infant was regarded as a social person. (Balikci, 1970, p. 148)

During this period no one is very certain whether the [Ashanti] infant is going to turn out a human child or prove, by dying before this period has elapsed, that it was never anything more than some wandering ghost. (Rattray, 1927, p. 187)

Two [Fulani] folk illnesses regarded as supernaturally caused, *foondu* and *heendu*, were important final diagnoses of the cause of death [which, when applied] to a dead child's last illness shifts accountability for the death to the community as a whole, rather than leaving the individual mother personally responsible. (Castle, 1994, p. 330)

The dead child is thought to have been the soul of someone to whom the [Hong Kong] parents owed a debt. When the debt is paid in terms of care invested in the child, it dies. (Martin, 2001, p. 162)

Delayed personhood can serve as a firm foundation for building cultural models of infancy that are responsive to the six issues noted earlier. For example, infanticide is excused on the basis that one is not disposing of a person. Chronic illness and failure to thrive can be explained away as the failure of body and spirit to fuse, with the spirit drawn back to the other world (Teixeira, 2007). Infants still have one foot in the spirit world, rendering them vulnerable to supernatural forces.

The "not yet ripe" model

The delay in conferring personhood or outright denial serves as explicit or implicit foundation for several overarching cultural models of infancy. These models share one characteristic: most societies place the infant in a dynamic between two poles, expressed by concepts like hard versus soft. The infant's movement between these poles is closely monitored and carefully orchestrated.

We start with the "not yet ripe" model. The denial of personhood is based on the patent deficiencies of the infant as a social being. Various attributes are singled out, including, for example, the infant's softness and lack of motor control. Significantly, these models are used to explain the basis of nonpersonhood but also include prescriptions for turning the baby into a person (Bonnet, 2007) – they have "directive force" (Harkness, Super, and Keefer, 1992). For example, the extremely widespread use of swaddling or cradleboard to restrain the infant is seen as compensating for and minimizing the long-term effects of the infant's softness and lack of motor control.

[Navajo] babies are kept . . . in the cradle to make them straight and strong. Some women let their children lie on sheepskins and roll about, but they are always weak, sick children. (Leighton and Kluckhohn, 1948, p. 23)

Asked why infants are swaddled, [Nurzay] women explained that the newborn baby's flesh is *oma* (lit. unripe) like uncooked meat, and that only by swaddling will it become strong (*chakahosi*) and solid like cooked (*pokh*) meat. (Casimir, 2010, p. 16)

Food taboos are aimed at "hardening" the [baby's] body . . . The goal is to make the baby vigorous and strong, so it can grow fast and develop into an independent member of the longhouse. [Huaorani] men I interviewed insisted that both parents were . . . assisting in its fast growth through [their] fasting. (Rival, 1998, p. 623)

New-born [Amele] infants (*momodo*) are cold and soft . . . and must be strengthened by the application of warm hands heated over a fire. Only liquids, preferably lukewarm, may be given to *momodo*. As strength develops and the infant can hold up its head, it is known as *momo memen*, literally "infant becomes stone". (Jenkins, Orr-Ewing, and Heywood, 1985, p. 39)

[A]mong the Bororo . . . the naming process takes place only when it is detected that the baby is "hardened" enough (usually some five–six months after birth). It is only through the naming ceremony that the child becomes "socially born" and recognized. (Fabian, 1992, p. 66)

Other areas singled out as needing ripening to transform the infant into a human being are speech (Bird-David, 2005; Kleijueqgt, 2009), self-locomotion (Bugos and McCarthy, 1984; Remorini, 2011), acquisition of social knowledge and skill (Montague, 1985; Musharbash, 2011), and intelligence (Geertz, 1961; Riesman, 1992; Woolf, 1997).

But not until the *kulio* (from *kungh* + *li*, lit: head shaving), on the eighth day after birth, does the [Mandinka] infant move into the status of a fully recognized member of the family. (Whittemore, 1989, p. 87)

A [Ovimbundu] baby is born pink and it is only when he turns dark at the sixth or eighth day that he shows the first indication of becoming a person (*omunu*).

He shows further promise in that direction with his first show of sense, but all through childhood he is, in a sense, only a potential person. (Childs, 1949, pp. 120–1)

Before children can be treated . . . as individual persons or "selves", they have to become Ambonwari . . . the main concern of initiation is to bring a "non-being" into Ambonwari being . . . Until boys are initiated at six or seven, they are "not Ambonwari". (Telban, 1997, p. 316)

For a [Gusii] mother to engage a small child, let alone an infant, "in conversation" would . . . seem eccentric behavior . . . since . . . a child is not a valid human being until he reaches the age of "sense" . . . six or seven years old. (LeVine and LeVine, 1981, pp. 43–4)

There seem to be progressive phases of recognition of the [Bariba] child as a permanent member of society, key among which is the appearance of teeth. Both mothers and fathers state that they await the appearance of teeth anxiously to determine the future of the child and, in fact, to identify the child's essence – human or witch substance. (Sargent, 1988, p. 82)

Interestingly, there is relatively little consensus in the "not-yet-ripe" model or the remaining two to be discussed ("unconnected" and "two worlds") regarding the age at which personhood is achieved. In fact, of 200 cases in which there is an evident delay in granting personhood, only in forty-three has the investigator indicated a likely stage or transition point after which personhood is acknowledged. Of these, in roughly fifteen cases, the point falls within the first year with a second cluster (sixteen) at ages 5–9 – the age of "sense."

The "unconnected" model

A second, but obviously parallel, model highlights the view that an infant, because it is kept in seclusion or largely hidden in the voluminous layers of its mother's clothing (Tronick, Thomas, and Daltabuit, 1994), is still in a womb-like state (Cerulli, 1959). To become fully human, the infant must exit from this metaphorical womb and enjoy a second birth where it is joined to its father, his clan, and the extended family (Blanchy, 2007). To achieve this requires survival and maturation on the part of the newborn, but, as well, various rites of separation and attachment are mandated. Soninké rites of separation involve proper treatment of the umbilical cord and placenta, while attachment rites include a ceremony with singing by a *griot* (storyteller and praise singer), the exchange of gifts, and acknowledgment of the child by ritual leaders (Razy, 2007).

For the first three days of life the [Lepcha] baby is considered to be still in the womb and all the pre-natal precautions have to be observed. It is not even referred to as a human child; it is called a rat-child. (Gorer, 1938, p. 289)

The new-born [Vlach] child sleeps tightly swaddled in a wooden rocking cradle which is enveloped from end to end in a blanket, so that he lies in a kind of dark airless tent. (Campbell, 1964, p. 154)

The post-partum [Japanese] child remains, inseparably, a part of its mother. The infant continues to develop within the protective, womb-like environment of its mother's presence, excluding others. (Lebra, 1994, p. 261)

In a sense, a [Tamang] baby enters the world without a clan since it can only become part of the partriline after three days; to underscore this, male members of the household usually remain away from the child. (Fricke, 1994, p. 133)

Many . . . post-natal practices [involve the] gradual shedding of the symbols for maternal ties, e.g. for a [Hubeer] child that has not yet passed through the first ceremonies (e.g. the *banaan bixin*) that declare his agnatic links, it can be said that "his bones are not yet hard". (Helander, 1988, p. 150)

This set of cases suggests that *social* attachment, including attachment to collectives like the extended family and clan, is of far more importance in cultural models of human development than psychological attachment.

The "two worlds" model

In a strictly statistical sense, the most common rationale for withholding personhood is that the infant has not yet committed itself to being human. It is suspended between two worlds, the human world and the "other" world of spirits, ghosts, ancestors, and gods. There are several variations on this part-spirit/part-human theme, including characterizations of the child that emphasize its purity and innocence (see the section "Little angels," below), other views that see the child as a conduit of evil forces (see "Little devils," below), and, lastly, the notion that the spirit child has no intention of becoming fully human (see "Tricksters," below). First, I will discuss cases where there is a distinct tension between the spirit or soul and the body.

Having just come out of the Dreaming, the soul or spirit (*kurunpa*) of Anangu infants is still closely linked up and in communication with the Ancestors. (Eickelkamp, 2011, p. 109)

When the [Azande] child is born the soul has not become completely and permanently attached to its abode. Hence it is feared that the soul may flit away and this is one of the reasons for confining infant and mother to a hut for several days after birth lest "The child's soul might get lost". (Evans-Pritchard, 1932, p. 404)

The perceived relationship of [Mende] infants with the world of spirits generates loyalties in conflict with the world of the living... infants are presumed to develop unusual powers of vision and the powers to move across different sensory domains. (Fermé, 2001, p. 198)

Once people die, their souls ... are said to become ... spirits, that travel to *wrugbe*, the land of the dead ... Eventually, the ancestors are reincarnated into this life. All newborns are seen as having just emerged from *wrugbe* [but if they die they're seen as still residing there]. [S]ometimes their ancestral identities are revealed early in childhood. (Gottlieb, 2000, p. 59)

A newborn [Yukui] has been contaminated by [puerperal] blood and is also more likely to succumb to disease or birth defects during these first few weeks of life. The baby was therefore regarded as not yet belonging fully to the world but lay somewhere between the spirit domain and that of the living. (Stearman, 1989, p. 89)

In the following section, I will discuss the practices that are followed in order to ensure that the child's spirit and body are permanently joined.

How cultural models influence behavior

Uniting spirit and body

The "two worlds" cultural model not only explains observed phenomena but also prescribes actions to be taken by the infant's caregivers. Among the Nzebi in Gabon, twins are seen as spirits who choose to live among humans. It is important not to offend them so they do not engage in reprisals, such as the communication of various diseases and bad dreams, or simply return to where they came from. Ritual activity persisting to adolescence controls the malevolence and eventually, makes the child fully human (Dupuis, 2007). In the Bolivian Andes, a precise and elaborate swaddling procedure guards the infant against *susto*, an illness that results in the separation of body and soul (de Suremain, 2007). A caregiving style that emphasizes keeping the infant in a coma-like state – always quiet and sheltered – is also often justified on the basis of ensuring that the spirit does not flee (Broch, 1990; Howrigan, 1988; Reichel-Dolmatoff, 1976). Of course, this policy (along with using swaddling and cradleboards) also reduces the amount of attention that the mother must devote to the infant.

A [Mandok] newborn's inner self (*anunu*) was not yet firmly anchored inside its body... and for this reason both new parents observed many food and behavioral taboos after the birth ... New fathers were prohibited from going fishing in channels and in deep water, nor could they hull out canoes, carve, or chop down trees ... If the child cried inexplicably, the Mandok believed that one of the parents had violated a taboo that caused its *anunu* to leave. A ritual specialist was then called in to "call the baby back" ... As the child grew, the Mandok believed that the *anunu* gradually moved from "the surface of the skin" to the inside of the body, a common belief in other areas of Melanesia as well. (Pomponio, 1992, p. 77)

A new-born [Punan Bah] child is considered little more than a mere body of blood, bones and flesh. Only gradually as the soul ... takes up residence in the child, does it become human ... The souls of children ... can easily be scared away, and children must be handled with the greatest care at least till they are about four years old when they become more secure – [for example, they are] never punished physically so as not to scare off their souls. (Nicolaisen, 1988, pp. 198–9)

General or prolonged fussiness, a refusal to eat or outright sickness – all these may be diagnosed as symptomatic of the spirit's withdrawal from the body. To secure its permanent integration with the body, the [Qiqiktamiut] family and others make every effort to encourage it to remain [including] the maintenance of a congenial atmosphere ... and the creation of important ritual ties to members of the community outside the natal household. (Guemple, 1979, pp. 41–2)

In the earlier discussion of the ecology of child health and survival, I noted that illness and death are likely among children in many of the societies studied. Hence, even if correct preventative practices are followed, parents must confront the reality of sick children. In the next section, I show how folk medical theory and practice is also informed by "two worlds" thinking.

Illness and cure

A great deal of the ethnographic literature in infancy records strategies for diagnosing illness or discomfort and corresponding remedies. You will note that an underlying theory in these prescriptions is that the child's well-being is compromised when it appears excited or agitated. Caregivers seek to remove the source of agitation – which may be spirit forces – and return the child to a "healthy," quiescent state. If these remedies fail, the cause is sought in malevolent or supernatural forces, not the mother or the family.

[In rural Iran] *Djenn* are said to be after the mother's liver (*jigar*). They are also jealous of the baby, especially during the first ten, or better, forty, days; they might steal the baby or exchange it for their own, sickly one. A baby indicates that it might be a changeling by fussiness, weakness, or lack of growth. (Friedl, 1997, p. 69)

If an infant gets sick frequently, parents might give the child a new name – that of a blacksmith, for instance, or others who Tibetans consider to be of low birth – as a way of tricking malevolent forces into leaving the child alone... This act not only grounds the infant in this world, but also ties the child to his home and lineage. (Craig, 2009, p. 155)

During its first... months the babe is considered highly vulnerable to danger from local spirits. Infant mortality among rural Javanese is in fact high... *slametan* [communal feasts] follow at regular intervals during childhood, each accompanying a ritual event that introduces the child to a new, more secure stage in life. (Jay, 1969, p. 99)

[In rural Japan] the *Ubugoya* was a place where the mother and the baby could hide themselves from ghosts and evil spirits... A baby was considered to be transferred into the human world by a god. A midwife... played a religious role in guiding the baby from the gods' world to the human world and giving social recognition to the baby as a member of the community. (Yanagisawa, 2009, p. 88)

[Aborigine] babies... were vulnerable to attacks by *mamu*... evil spirits that live in the bush. When an infant was bitten, his soul would fall ill and the baby got unwell. (Tjitayi and Lewis, 2011, pp. 58–9)

The "two worlds" model underscores the child's vulnerability; its slender hold on life. But this impermanence may be construed in a more positive light. Quite a few societies, especially in ancient times, saw opportunity in the child's indeterminate – part spirit, part human – state. Because the child was not considered fully human, it was assumed to have extra-human capacities.

Little angels

These innocent and pure spirits could be utilized to appease or otherwise communicate with the other world of ancestors and gods (Hearn, 2007; Klaus, Centurion, and Curo, 2010). Child sacrifice is not uncommon. Infant and child remains are often recovered from "foundation deposits" at the base of important buildings (Colón with Colón, 2001; Moses, 2008; Sachs and Vu, 2005; Scott, 1999). In an example from the ethnographic record, the Bolobo believe that exchanging his or her soul with the uncontaminated soul of an infant can save a bewitched adult. As the adult gradually recovers health, the infant sickens and dies (Viccars, 1949, p. 223). Other examples from antiquity are as follows:

Children were seen to possess this particular gift and were considered to have a position intermediate between the human world and that of the gods... Children were considered suitable for the task of prophesy, functioning as intermediaries between the divine and human worlds in Greco-Roman society. (Horn and Martens, 2009, p. 179)

[A Japanese] saying [was] "one of the gods until the age of seven"... Before seven, children were weak, and could die easily from sickness... [T]hey could instantly return to the world of the gods and Buddhas at any time... possess[ed] the power to transmit the will of the [deities] and often played the role of medium between gods and people. (Kuroda, 1998, p. 10)

[Aymara] children who die before being named and gaining godparents are buried in a place far from the household and the community cemetery where they are "eaten" by the mountain spirits... because these unnamed and un-baptized children still belong to the world of the mountain deities and have not yet been socialized into the human world. Children only become truly human when they begin to walk and talk. (Sillar, 1994, p. 51)

The classical and biblical texts, as well as the archaeology, all indicate that healthy living children were sacrificed to the gods in the Tophet... The burned bones found inside jars from the Carthage Tophet provide conclusive evidence for Phoenician child sacrifice. (Stager and Greene, 2000, p. 31).

[Roman] children had long been used in religious and propitiatory ceremonies, because of the quality of purity often associated with children. (Rawson, 2003, p. 315)

The greatest number of... sacrificial offerings [in Mayan cenotes to the water god Chac] were between four and ten years of age – precisely the period of greatest potential and liminality, given current understandings of ancient Mesoamerican conceptualizations of childhood. These children... still embodied the purity and connection to the spirit world that would erode gradually until they were approximately ten. (Arden, 2011, p. 142)

These examples underscore that the child is in a liminal state – not yet fully human and not yet completely attached to the mother. These incomplete emotional bonds may enable the child's family more easily to relinquish the child to serve ritual ends.

Little devils

Alternatively, the infant may be viewed as threatening, either in its own right or as a vessel or avatar for ghosts and evil spirits (Nath, 1960). In practical terms, this view may lead to caregiving behaviors that are similar to those deployed when children are seen as transient spirits with special powers. Whether children were seen as pure and innocent or as threatening, the effect on childcare practices might be the same.

Protestant and Catholic dogma influenced the inclusion of infants within cemeteries. Newborns were considered to be corrupted by the original sin of their conception, and unbaptized or stillborn infants were not permitted burial in consecrated ground. (Lewis, 2007, p. 33)

[Certain] births coincide with the intensely active and aggressive phase of the yearly yin/yang cycle, thereby imbuing the nature of such neonates with these dangerous traits . . . Han histories suggest that parents who believed these predictions typically abandoned or killed ill-omened children rather than attempting to "transform" them. (Kinney, 1995, p. 24)

They did not consider infanticide itself an immoral act. The basic reason for this was that newborns are categorized as inhuman. Consistent with the perception that birth processes are repulsive and dangerous, Korowai say that a newborn is "demonic" (*laleo*) rather than "human" (*yanop*). People explain this categorization by noting that a newborn's skin is uncannily pale, that newborns are torpid, and that their bodies are generally freakish. (Stasch, 2009, p. 151)

When a [Pamiri] child is born and fidgets and cries [a lot] and he has a black circle around his mouth and eyes, it means that he may have *jinn* [genies or spirits]. To solve the problem, one has to open the child's mouth and look at the roof of his mouth. If you observe black veins, you need to make a hole in the veins with a needle and mop up the blood with a swab. The child gets better and does not cry again. (Keshavjee, 2006, p. 75)

The belief that infants were felt to be on the verge of turning into totally evil beings is one of the reasons why they were tied up, or swaddled, so long and so tightly. (Haffter, 1968, p. 61)

Because the very young are seen as a potential conduit allowing the transmission of dangerous forces into the family or community, steps have to be taken to guard against this possibility. These steps include practices like baptism, swaddling, avoiding eye contact with the infant, or bloodletting. However, one of the greatest threats posed by the spirit child is to thwart a mother's ardent desire for offspring. To counter this threat, truly drastic measures are required.

Tricksters

Across Nigeria, the cultural model of infancy includes the notion that the spirit intends to trick its parents by continually being reborn but then returning to its true abode. The remedies for breaking this endless cycle of rebirth are severe.

If [Ijaw] parents have experienced several infant deaths, one after another, they usually suspect that the same child is coming to them each time. (Leis, 1982, pp. 156–7)

Abiku children are "born to die"; after living with their parents for only a little while, they leave to rejoin the spirit companions who have always been tempting them to return. Sometimes, [the Yoruba] believe, the same *abiku* child will come back time and again to torment the parents with its temporary presence, only to die in due course... This belief in *abiku* children may be operating as a necessary and ingenious explanation for the high rate of infant deaths, providing a satisfactory framework within which such distressing episodes may be accepted. (Maclean, 1994, p. 161)

[The deceased child of an Ibo mother who has lost several in succession] is deemed unlucky, and cannot live in this world. The faster it is blotted out of existence the better... Dismembering the body before it is burned is also very common. The ashes are usually scattered to the four winds... Hanging the body from a tree and letting it rot... is another common disposal method for the child. (Basden, 1966, p. 282)

Another version of the infant as trickster is found among the Toradja of Sulawesi.

[Such] children were... put away in a hole that was made in a large, living tree... The body was placed... on end, with the head downward... after which the hole was nailed shut with a small board. This was done so that the child's *tanoana* would not return to earth and call the *tanoana* of other children, so that the latter would also be stillborn or die soon after birth. (Adriani and Kruijt, 1950, pp. 708–9)

Our data are not limited to the accounts of ethnographers or historians. Archeological excavations and analyses of postmortem treatment of the young offer very strong support for the claim that personhood is delayed.

Postmortem treatment and delayed personhood

Several lines of evidence drawn from the way in which infants and children are treated in death strongly reinforce the delayed personhood argument (Senior, 1994) and, in turn, signal the need to resist attachment. First of all, burial rites and mourning may be minimal or actively discouraged in the case of a child younger than 5 years (Fricke, 1994; Ndege, 2007) or even as late as 10 (Rawson, 2003). The variability is consistent with the variability in marking the age at which the child is considered a person. The attention of the family and community should be on the next child, not on the one that has died. For example, "the average duration of a birth interval is substantially shorter following an infant death than when an infant survives" (Kramer and Greaves, 2007, p. 720).

It is not unusual for the [Ayoreo] newborn to remain unnamed for several weeks or months, particularly if the infant is sickly. The reason given is that should the child die, the loss will not be so deeply felt." (Bugos and McCarthy, 1984, p. 508)

[Bagesu] children often died at birth or in infancy, and the bodies were thrown out into the bush." (Roscoe, 1924, p. 25)

[When a Chippewa infant died,] weeping was frowned upon for the fear that the sorrow would be passed on to the next child. (Hilger, 1951, p. 79)

When a [Tonga] child died before it was named, there was no mourning for no shades were involved . . . the old women will tell the mother to hush her wailing, saying this is only a ghost (*cello*). (Reynolds, 1991, p. 97)

When we turn to the archeological record, excavators find that, save for a few societies such as ancient Egypt (Meskell, 1994), and during the city-state period in Athens (Houby-Nielsen, 2000), infants and children were buried apart from older children and adults (King, 2006).

Children's remains located outside the confines of communal burial grounds are a common finding throughout the world, and during all time periods. (Lewis, 2007, p. 31)

In Xaltocan . . . burials of infants and young children less than four years of age were recovered . . . under room floors and . . . also incorporated into house walls. (De Lucia, 2010, pp. 612–13)

[Mapuche] infants are not buried in the cemetery, but are buried in the old family plot or somewhere near the house; it is believed that it would be harder for the child to be turned into a demon if it is closer to the house. (Faron, 1964, p. 91)

In Early Mycenaean Greece, infants of less than one year of age were differentiated by their total exclusion from organized extramural cemetery areas and by the absence of complete vases in their graves . . . Children of between 1–2 and 5–6 years of age were still only included in formal extramural cemeteries in exceptional cases. (Lebegyiv, 2009, p. 27)

An analysis of Etruscan child burials in Tarquinia enables one to conclude that the absence of children below the age of five and a half years from the principal cemeteries was suggestive of a major shift at that age. (Becker, 2007, p. 292)

A review of postmortem practices, including any funerary and internment rites, complements the ethnographic record. The data underscore the child's liminality and lack of integration into the social world of the community. At death, it is mourned privately or not at all, and it is interred discreetly, without ceremony.

Discussion

The goal of this chapter has been to use the archives of anthropology and history to interrogate or critique many of the claims made by Bowlby and his successors. For example, Bowlby argued that it was "essential for mental health that the infant and young child should experience a warm, intimate and continuous relationship with his mother . . . in which both find satisfaction and enjoyment" (Bowlby, 1953, p. 11). These arguments – particularly regarding the nature and effect of "maternal deprivation" – have not gone unchallenged by child-development scholars (Clarke and Clarke, 2000; Tizard and Tizard, 1974) and cultural anthropologists (LeVine, 2004). Moreover, many of Bowlby's more extreme arguments are sustained and expanded upon in the writing of his successors (Karen, 1998; Newton and Schore, 2008) who espouse "attachment parenting." The advocates operate from an assumption of universality – that the dictates of attachment parenting should be immune from significant cross-cultural variation.

In the survey reported here, the intent has been to go beyond merely identifying societies that do not seem congenial to attachment theory (e.g., Erchak, 1992; Paradise, 1996). With an extremely large and diverse database of cases, I have been able to find common patterns within the cross-cultural variability and construct both general and more specific models of infancy. These models can be used as lenses to examine claims made regarding the essential components of psychologically healthy infancy. "Attachment theory" and its descendants have created a narrative of infants "at risk" of emotional maladjustment. In this survey of sources from cultural anthropology, history, and archeology this perceived risk is absent. It is to be presumed that infants' emotional needs are met simultaneously with their need for sustenance, and nothing further need be done. The survey also reveals that an alternate narrative identifies attachment rather than attachment failure as the risk. A strong, emotional bond is seen as impeding a process whereby infants are pragmatically sorted into categories of wanted versus unwanted, timely versus untimely, legitimate versus illegitimate, strong fighters versus sickly ghosts, and innocent versus demonized, leading to sustained nurturance or extinction. The risk of inopportune attachment is met by an overarching cultural model that denies the newborn personhood – often until it is several months, if not years, old. Personhood is delayed until the child's spirit and body become firmly united, and the individual "ripens" into an independent and unique being capable of social interaction.

A very thorough survey has failed to provide either much evidence for maternal concern for the infant's emotional security or evidence of such concern in the cultural models of the infancy and early childhood period – just the contrary. We might then ask what are the cultural and historical forces shaping attachment theory or attachment parenting in the modern era? With the decline in infant mortality and beliefs concerning changelings and other malevolent incarnations of the infant, we should expect that restraints on attachment will be relaxed. Improved access to resources has reduced the need for infanticide and child labor. Various forces have combined, leading to lower birthrates. Contemporary parents now see their (fewer) offspring not as investments for the future but as providing emotional rewards in the present. Where much of the world can be considered a "gerontocracy" with ancestors and elders on top and children at the bottom, the society that has embraced attachment parenting is clearly a "neontocracy" with children at the apex of the value scale (Lancy, 2008, pp. 25–6). Caring for infants has become a pleasure rather than a burden. Adults' dignity is not impaired when they play with their children. Frequent gestures and words of affection exchanged between parents and children have become the norm. However, while genuine threats to the child's safety, health, and nutrition have declined dramatically in the last century, parental anxiety, seemingly, has not. The list of fears – sometimes quite irrational – such as fear of the child's abduction (Tulloch, 2004), has grown quite long. These include concern for the child's happiness, which historians trace to the early twentieth century Stearns (2010); exaggerated and misguided concern for the child's self-esteem (Baumeister, Campbell, Krueger *et al.*, 2005); and, quite recently, the curtailment of children's free play as exposing the child to unacceptable risks (Lancy and Grove, 2011b), to name just a few. I suggest that the fear that a normal child growing up in an average, middle-class home is at risk of reactive attachment disorder (RAS) flows from the same thinking. Collectively, these concerns have the effect of constantly raising the bar for what is considered adequate parenting. However, there is increasing resistance to these ever-rising expectations for parents, leading to what is referred to in the mass media as the "mommy wars." On one side are those who argue that raising a healthy and successful child requires the full-time attention of the mother, while on the other side are those who feel that children require less care and that it can be delivered by a range of caregivers (Steiner, 2007).

Given the many threats to the child's viability as outlined in this chapter, it is not at all certain that evolution would have favored the formation of strong bonds of attachment between children and their caregivers. I believe my findings are consistent with arguments made elsewhere in this volume (e.g., chapters by Johow and Voland, Keller, and Weisner) that suggest numerous fitness benefits of weak attachment. Among these, we would include a mother's motivation to become pregnant soon after loosing or disposing of a child whose viability was uncertain. Prolonged mourning or depression would undermine fecundity. In fact, we should ask several questions of attachment-theory adherents. First, why would a creature who is utterly dependent on others for its care and feeding *not* automatically (no further evolved mechanism needed) cling to its saviors? Second, why would a sentient human that has made and continues to make a huge investment to replicate itself genetically, not automatically take steps to protect that investment (no further evolved mechanism needed)? Third, why do we need to posit a special sort of emotional bond only experienced by the very young when we expect and take for granted the emotional bonds that form whenever human beings live in proximity and behave prosocially towards one another? The challenge is actually to resist forming an emotional bond given the inherent risks, and delaying personhood is the rationale that most societies offer to the infant's close kin to help them respond to that challenge. Hence, I would argue that much of attachment theory in both original and attachment parenting versions reflects not universal, species-wide adaptations but, rather, adaptations to a very recent and culture-specific model of infancy. And, unlike the widely accepted "delayed personhood," view, in this contemporary model, personhood now begins with conception, if not before.

Appendix 3.1 Geographic distribution of sample

Europe

(Mesolithic – Georgiadis, 2011) (Middle Ages – Alexandre-Bidon and Lett, 1999) (Etruscans – Becker, 2007) (Sicilian – Chapman, 1971) (seventeenth–nineteenth-century Europe – Cunningham, 1995) (Venice – Ferraro, 2008) (Athens – Houby-Nielsen, 2000) (Greece – Kleijueqgt, 2009) (Western Europe – Morel, 2007) (Mycenaean Greece – Lebegyiv, 2009) (Early Modern – Lewis, 2007) (medieval England – Orme, 2003) (Rome – Rawson, 2003) (Middle Ages – Hanawalt, 2003) (Vlach – Campbell, 1964) (Iron Age – Woolf, 1997) (Rome – Wileman, 2005) (Neolithic – Scott, 1999) (Neolithic – Le Mort, 2008) (Early Bronze Age – Rega, 1997) (Rome – Wiedemann, 1989) (medieval – Goodich, 1989) (Early Modern – Gillis, 2003) (Middle Ages – Haffter, 1986) (Roma – Fonseca, 1995) (Hungary – Bereczkei, 2001) (eighteenth-century Russia – Dunn, 1974) (contemporary Germany – LeVine and Norman, 2001)

North Africa

(ancient Carthage, Rome – Lee, 1994) (ancient Egypt – Meskell, 1994) (ancient Carthage – Stager and Greene, 2000) (Kerkenneh – Platt, 1988)

East Africa

(northern Somalia – Cerulli, 1959) (southern Somalia – Helander, 1988) (Anyi – Pourchez, 2007) (Nuer – Scheer and Groce, 1988) (Gusii – LeVine, 2004) (Lugbara – Middleton, 1965) (Datoga – Sellen, 1998) (Gogo – Mabilia, 2000) (Masai– DeVries, 1987)

Central Africa

(Nzebi – Dupuis, 2007) (Azande – Evans-Pritchard, 1932) (Songye – Devleiger, 1995) (Bagesu – Roscoe, 1924) (Bobangi – Viccars, 1949) (Macha Galla – Batels, 1969) (Azande – Baxter, 1953) (Bofi – Fouts, 2005)

West Africa

(Manjak – Teixeira, 2007) (Gouro – Haxaire, 2007) (Soninké – Razy, 2007) (Ibo – Basden, 1966) (Fulani – Castle, 1994) (Akan – Rattray, 1927) (Nankani – Denham et al., 2010) (Kpelle – Erchak, 1976) (Hausa – Faulkingham, 1970) (Anyi – Duchesne, 2007) (Ibo – Henderson, 1972) (Nso – Keller, 2007) (Mossi – Bonnet, 2007) (Dogon – Scheer and Groce, 1988) (Ijaw – Leis, 1982) (Mossi – Mangin, 1921) (Bariba – Sargent, 1988) (Papel – Einarsdottir, 2004) (Sisala – Grindal, 1972) (Mende – Fermé, 2001) (Beng – Gottlieb, 2000) (Mandinka – Whittemore, 1989) (Songhay – Stoller, 1989) (Dogon – Dettwyler, 1994) (Dogon – Strassmann, 1997) (Yoruba – Maclean, 1994) (Talensi – Fortes, 1970) (Kpelle – Erchak, 1992) (Fulani – Johnson, 2000) (Fulani – Riesman, 1992) (Hausa – Tomlinson et al., 2010) (Yoruba – Zeitlin, 1996) (Fulani – Hampshire, 2001)

Southern Africa

(Madagascar – Blanchy, 2007) (Umbundu – Childs, 1949) (Tsonga – Green et al., 1994) (Mozambique – Ndege, 2007) (Ngoni – Read, 1960) (!Kung – Shostak, 1981) (!Kung – Howell, 1979) (Tonga – Reynolds, 1991)

North America

(Netsilik "Eskimo" – Balikci, 1970) (Qiqiktamiut Inuit – Guemple, 1979) (Inupiaq – Sprott, 2002) (Chippewa – Hilger, 1951) (Puritans – Mintz, 2004) (Victorian era – Calvert, 2003) (Tlingit – De Laguna, 1965)

(Inuit – Wileman, 2005) (Klamath – Pearsall, 1950) (Navajo – Leighton and Kluckhohn, 1948) (Tlingit – Colón with Colón, 2001) (Netsilik – Riches, 1974) (contemporary bourgeois – Baumrind, 1971)

Highland South America

(Bolivian Andes – de Suremain, 2007) (Aymara – Buechler and Buechler, 1971) (Mapuche – Faron, 1964) (Muchik – Roach, 2010) (Aymara – Arnold, 2006) (Inka – Shein, 1992) (Inka – Sillar, 1994) (Quechua – Sillar, 1994) (Inka – Besom, 2009) (Barrio – Morgan, 1998) (Quechua – Tronick *et al.*, 1994)

Lowland South America

(Mbya – Remorini, 2011) (Ayoreo – Bugos and McCarthy, 1984) (Yanomano – Chagnon, 1968) (Wari – Conklin and Morgan, 1996) (Cubeo – Goldman, 1963) (Mehinacu – Gregor, 1970) (Mundurucu – Murphy and Murphy, 1985) (Bakairí – Picchi, 2000) (Huaorani – Rival, 1998) (Yanomamo – Chagnon, 1968) (Ayoreo – Bugos and McCarthy, 1984) (Yukui – Stearman, 1989) (Tapirapé – Wagley, 1977) (Bororo – Fabian, 1992) (Barrio – Scheper-Hughes, 1987) (Ache – Hill and Hurtado, 1996) (Airo-Pai – Belaunde, 2001)

Mesoamerica

(Mixtec – Katz, 2007) (Pre-Hispanic Maya – Tiesler, 2011) (Pre-Hispanic Maya – Arden, 2011) (Tlatelolco and Tenochtitlan – Berrelleza and Balderas, 2006) (Toltec – Hearn, 2007) (Aztec – Heilbrunn Timeline of Art History, n.d.) (coastal Oaxaca – King, 2006) (early colonial Chile and Peru – Allison, 1984) (Zincantec Maya – de León, 2013) (Tarahumara – Mull and Mull, 1987) (precolonial Maya – Sharer, 1994) (Yucatec Maya – Howrigan, 1988) (Kogi – Reichel-Dolmatoff, 1976)

Melanesia

(Anangu – Eickelkamp, 2011) (Warungka – Musharbash, 2011) (Aboriginal central Australia – Tjitayi and Lewis, 2011) (Bumbita Arapesh – Leavitt, 1989) (Baining – Fajans, 1997) (Drysdale River Tribes, northwest Australia – Hernandez, 1941) (Sepik Region, Papua New Guinea – Kulick and Stroud, 1993) (Ambonwari – Telban, 1997) (Mandok – Pomponio, 1992) (Vanatinai – Lepowsky, 1987) (Korowai – Stasch, 2009) (Kaliai – Counts, 1985) (Gapun – Kulick, 1992) (Amele – Jenkins *et al.*, 1985) (Trobriands – Montague, 1985) (Bena-Bena – Langness, 1981) (Eipo – Schiefenhovel, 1989) (Asabano – Little, 2008).

Polynesia/Micronesia

(Maori – Best, 1924) (Truk – Fisher, 1963) (Hawaiian-American – Howard, 1973) (prehistoric – Kinaston, Buckley, Halcrow *et al.*, 2009) (Ulithi, Micronesian – Lessa, 1966) (Tonga – Morton, 1996)

East Asia

(Edo period Japan – Kuroda, 1998) (Ainu – Batchelor, 1927) (Ch'ing Dynasty China – Furth, 1987) (Miao – Graham, 1937) (Yami – Arnaud, 2007) (Hong Kong – Martin, 2001) (contemporary Japan – Lebra, 1994) (Korean – Kim and Choi, 1994) (Japan – Yanagisawa, 2009) (China – Harvey and Buckley, 2009) (historical China – Kinney, 1995) (Japan – Kojima, 2003) (Hokkien – Wolf, 1972)

West Asia

(Neo-Babylonian and Neo-Assyrian – MacGinnis, 2011) (fourth-century CE Constantinople – Alberici and Harlow, 2007) (Neolithic – Wileman, 2005) (pottery Neolithic – Scott, 1999) (Neolithic – Moses, 2008) (Bedouin – Karplus and Karplus, 1989) (Byzantium – Smith and Kahila, 1992) (Turkey – Kağitcibaşi and Ataca, 2005)

Central Asia

(Tamang – Fricke, 1994) (Lepchas – Gorer, 1938) (Pamiri – Keshavjee, 2006) (Tibet – Craig, 2009) (Nurzay – Casimir, 2010) (Tibet – Maiden and Farwell, 1997) (Ladakh – Wiley, 2004) (Tamang – Fricke, 1994) (Bakkarwal – Rao, 1998) (Yomut – Irons, 2000) (Punjab – Miller, 1987)

Southeast Asia

(Nayaka – Bird-David, 2005) (Bonerate – Broch, 1990) (Javanese – Geertz, 1961) (Nso – Keller, 2007) (India – Kopp, Khoka, and Sigman, 1977) (Mentawai Islands – Loeb, 1962) (Bali – Covarrubias, 1937) (southern India – Nichter and Nichter, 1987) (Hmong – Liamputtong, 2009) (Javanese – Jay, 1969) (Bils – Nath, 1960) (Barrio – Jocano, 1969) (Dongria – Hardenberg, 2006) (Punan Bah – Nicolaisen, 1988) (Tamil – McGilvray, 1994) (Bengali – Bhattacharyya, 1981) (Bajau – Nimmo,

1970) (Semai – Dentan, 1978) (eleventh-century Hanoi – Sachs and Vu, 2005) (Chewong – Howell, 1988)

References

Adriani, N., and Kruijt, A. C. (1950). *The bare'e-speaking Toradja of Central Celebes*. Amsterdam: Noord-Hollandsche Uitgevers Maatschapp ij.

Ainsworth, M. D. (1967). *Infancy in Uganda: infant care and the growth of love*. Baltimore, MD: Johns Hopkins University Press.

Ainsworth, M. D. S., Blehar, M. C., Waters, E., and Wall, S. (1978). *Patterns of attachment: a psychological study of the Strange Situation*. Hillsdale, NJ: Erlbaum.

Alber, E. (2004). "The real parents are the foster parents": social parenthood among the Baatombu in Northern Benin. In F. Bowie (Ed.), *Cross-cultural approaches to adoption* (pp. 33–47). London: Routledge.

Alberici, L. A., and Harlow, M. (2007). Age and innocence: female transitions to adulthood in late antiquity. In A. Cohen and J. B. Rutter (Eds.), *Constructions of childhood in ancient Greece and Italy* (pp. 193–203). Princeton, NJ: American School of Classical Studies at Athens.

Alexandre-Bidon, D., and Lett, D. (1999). *Children in the Middle Ages: fifth–fifteen centuries*. Notre Dame, IN: University of Notre Dame Press.

Allison, M. J. (1984). Paleopathology in Peruvian and Chilean populations. In M. N. Cohen and G. J. Armelagos (Eds.), *Paleopathology at the origins of agriculture* (pp. 531–58). Orlando, FL: Academic Press.

Arden, T. (2011). Empowered children in classic Maya sacrificial rites. *Childhood in the Past, 4*, 133–45.

Arnaud, V. (2007). "La souillure des exocets s'envole à jamais!" Rite prophylactiques relatifs aux enfants Yami (Botel Tobal, Taïwan). In D. Bonnet and L. Pourchez (Eds.), *Du soin au rite dans l'enfance* (pp. 183–209). Paris: IRD.

Arnold, D. Y. (2006). *The metamorphosis of heads: textual struggles, education, and land in the Andes*. University of Pittsburgh Press.

Badinter, E. (2012). *The conflict: how modern motherhood undermines the status of women*. New York: Metropolitan Books.

Balikci, A. (1970). *The Netsilik Eskimo*. Garden City, NY: Natural History Press.

Basden, G. T. (1966). *Niger Ibos: a description of the primitive life, customs and animistic beliefs, etc., of the Ibo people of Nigeria*. London: Frank Cass.

Batchelor, J. (1927). *Ainu life and lore: echoes of a departing race*. Tokyo: Kyobunkwan.

Batels, L. (1969). Birth customs and birth songs of the Macha Galla. *Ethnology, 8*, 406–22.

Baumeister, R. F., Campbell, J. D., Krueger, J. I., and Vohs, K. (2005). Exploding the self-esteem myth. *Scientific American Mind, 16*(4), 50–7.

Baumrind, D. (1971). Current patterns of parental authority. *Developmental Psychology Monographs, 4*(1, Part 2), 1–103.

Baxter, P. T. W. (1953). *The Azande, and related peoples of the Anglo-Egyptian Sudan and Belgian Congo*. London: International African Institute.

Becker, M. J. (2007). Childhood among the Etruscans: mortuary programs at Tarquinia as indicators of the transition to adult status. In A. Cohen and J. B. Rutter (Eds.), *Constructions of childhood in ancient Greece and Italy.* (Hesperia Supplement 410; pp. 281–92). Athens: American School of Classical Studies at Athens.

Belaunde, L. E. (2001). Menstruation, birth observances and the couple's love amongst the Airo-Pai of Amazonian Peru. In S. Tremayne (Ed.), *Managing reproductive life: cross-cultural themes in sexuality and fertility* (pp. 127–39). Oxford: Berghahn Books.

Bereczkei, T. (2001). Maternal trade-off in treating high-risk children. *Evolution and Human Behavior, 22,* 197–212.

Berrelleza, J. A. R., and Balderas, X. C. (2006). The role of children in the ritual practices of the Great Temple of Tenochtitlan and the Great Temple of Tlatelolco. In T. Adren and S. R. Hutson (Eds.), *The social experience of childhood in the ancient Mesoamerica* (pp. 233–48). Boulder, CO: University of Colorado Press.

Besom, T. (2009). *Of summits and sacrifice: an ethnohistoric study of Inka religious practices.* Austin, TX: University of Texas Press.

Best, E. (1924). *The Maori,* vol. II. Wellington, NZ: H. H. Tombs.

Bhattacharyya, D. P. (1981). Bengali conceptions of mental illness. Unpublished Ph.D. dissertation. Indiana University, Bloomington, IN.

Bird-David, N. (2005). Studying children in "hunter-gatherer" societies: reflections from a Nayaka perspective. In B. S. Hewlett and M. E. Lamb (Eds.), *Hunter gatherer childhoods: evolutionary, developmental, and cultural perspectives* (pp. 92–101). New Brunswick, NJ: AldineTransaction.

Blanchy, S. (2007). Le *tambavy* des bébés à Madagascar: du soin au rituel d'ancestralité. In D. Bonnet and L. Pourchez (Eds.), *Du soin au rite dans l'enfance* (pp. 146–66). Paris: IRD.

Bonnet, D. (2007). La toilette des nourissons au Burkina Faso: une manipulation gestuelle et sociale du corps de l'enfant [Bathing Mossi babies: a social and cultural practice]. In D. Bonnet and L. Pourchez (Eds.), *Du soin au rite dans l'enfance* (pp. 113–28). Paris: IRD.

Boserup, E. (1970). *Women's role in economic development.* London: Allen and Unwin.

Bowlby, J. (1953). *Child care and the growth of love.* Hammondsworth: Penguin Books.

Broch, H. B. (1990). *Growing up agreeably: Bonerate childhood observed.* Honolulu, HI: University of Hawaii Press.

Buechler, H. C., and Buechler, J.-M. (1971). *The Bolivian Aymara.* New York: Holt, Rinehart and Winston.

Bugos, P. E., Jr., and McCarthy, L. M. (1984). Ayoreo infanticide: a case study. In G. Hausfater and S. B. Hrdy (Eds.), *Infanticide: comparative and evolutionary perspectives* (pp. 503–20). New York: Aldine.

Calvert, K. (2003). Patterns of childrearing in America. In W. Koops and M. Zucherman (Eds.), *Beyond the century of the child: cultural history and developmental psychology* (pp. 62–81). Philadelphia: University of Pennsylvania Press.

Campbell, J. K. (1964). *Honour, family, and patronage: a study of institutions and moral values in a Greek mountain community.* Oxford: Clarendon Press.

Casimir, M. J. (2010). *Growing up in a pastoral society: socialization among Pashtu nomads in Western Afghanistan.* Kölner Ethnologische Beiträge, 33. Köln: Institut für Ethnologie der Universität zu Köln.

Castle, S. E. (1994). The (re)negotiation of illness diagnoses and responsibility for child death in rural Mali. *Medical Anthropology Quarterly, 8*(3), 314–35.

Cerulli, E. (1959). *The consuetudinary law of northern Somalia,* vol. II. Rome, Italy: A Cura dell'Amministrazione Fiduciaria Italiana della Somalia.

Chagnon, N. A. (1968). *Yanomamo: the fierce people.* New York: Holt, Rinehart, and Winston.

Chapman, C. G. (1971). *Milocca: a Sicilian village.* Cambridge, MA: Schenkman.

Childs, G. M. (1949). *Umbundu kinship and character: being a description of social structure and individual development of the Ovimbundu of Angola.* London: Published for the International African Institute by Oxford University Press.

Clarke, A. M., and Clarke, A. D. B. (2000). *Early experience and the life path.* London: Jessica Kingsley.

Colón, A. R., with Colón, P. A. (2001). *A history of children: a socio-cultural survey across millennia.* Westport, CT: Greenwood Press.

Conklin, B. A., and Morgan, L. M. (1996). Babies, bodies, and the production of personhood in North America and a native Amazonian society. *Ethos, 24,* 657–94.

Covarrubias, M. (1937). *Island of Bali.* New York: Alfred E. Knopf.

Counts, D. A. (1985). Infant care and feeding in Kaliai, West New Britain, Papua New Guinea. In L. B. Marshall (Ed.), *Infant care and feeding in the South Pacific* (pp. 155–69). New York: Gordon and Beach Science.

Craig, S. R. (2009). Pregnancy and childbirth in Tibet: knowledge, perspective, and practices. In H. Selin and P. K. Stone (Eds.), *Childhood across cultures: ideas and practices of pregnancy, childbirth and the postpartum* (pp. 145–60). Amherst, MA: Springer.

Cunningham, H. (1995). *Children and childhood in Western Society since 1500.* New York: Longman.

Daly, M., and Wilson, M. (1984). A sociobiological analysis of human infanticide. In G. Hausfater and S. Blaffer Hrdy (Eds.), *Infanticide: comparative and evolutionary perspectives* (pp. 487–502). New York: Aldine.

D'Andrade, R., and Strauss, C. (1992). *Human motives and cultural models.* Cambridge University Press.

de Laguna, F. (1965). Childhood among the Yakutat Tlingit. In M. E. Spiro (Ed.), *Context and meaning in cultural anthropology* (pp. 3–23). New York: Free Press.

de León, L. (2013). "The j'Ik'al is coming!" Triadic directives and emotion in the socialization of Zinacantec Mayan children. In A. Breton and P. Nodédéo (Eds.), *Maya daily lives: Proceedings of the 13th European Maya Conference (Paris, 2008).* Markt Schwaben, Germany: Verlag Anton Saurwein.

De Lucia, K. (2010). A child's house: social memory, identity, and the construction of childhood in early postclassic Mexican households. *American Anthropologist, 112*(4), 607–24.

Denham, A. R., Adongo, P. B., Freydberg, N., and Hodgson, A. (2010). Chasing spirits: clarifying the spirit child phenomenon and infanticide in northern Ghana. *Social Science and Medicine, 71,* 608–15.

Dentan, R. K. (1978). Notes on childhood in a nonviolent context: the Semai case. In A. Montague (Ed.), *Learning non-aggression: the experience of nonliterate societies* (pp. 94–143). Oxford University Press.

de Suremain, C.-É. (2007). Au fil de la faja. Enrouler et dérouler la vie en Bolivie. In D. Bonnet and L. Pourchez (Eds.), *Du soin au rite dans l'enfance* (pp. 85–102). Paris: IRD.

Dettwyler, K. A. (1994). *Dancing skeletons: life and death in West Africa.* Prospect Heights, IL: Waveland Press.

Devereux, G. (1955). *A story of abortion in primitive societies.* New York: Julian Press.

Devleiger, P. (1995). Why disabled? The cultural understanding of physical disability in an African society. In B. Ingstad and S. Reynolds Whyte (Eds.), *Disability and culture* (pp. 94–133). Berkeley, CA: University of California Press.

DeVries, M. W. (1987). Cry babies, culture, and catastrophe: infant temperament among the Masai. In N. Scheper-Hughes (Ed.), *Child survival: anthropological perspectives on the treatment and maltreatment of children* (pp. 165–85). Dordrecht, NL: D. Reidel.

Dickeman, M. (1975). Demographic consequences of infanticide in man. *Annual Review of Ecology and Systematics, 6,* 107–37.

Duchesne, V. (2007). Le rituel de possession: un jeu d'enfants? Jeux enfantins et pratique religieuse. In D. Bonnet and L. Paurchez (Eds.), *Du soin au rite dans l'enfance* (pp. 231–40). Paris: IRD.

Dunn, P. (1974). "That enemy is the baby": childhood in imperial Russia. In L. deMause (Ed.), *The history of childhood* (pp. 383–405). New York: Harper and Row.

Dupuis, A. (2007). Rites requis par la naissance, la croissance et la mort des jumeaux. Leur aménagement dans le monde modern. Le cas de Nzebi du Gabon. In D. Bonnet and L. Pourchez (Eds.), *Du soin au rite dans l'enfance* (pp. 255–80). Paris: IRD.

Eickelkamp, U. (2011). Sand storytelling: its social meaning in Anangu children's lives. In U. Eickelkamp (Ed.), *Growing up in central Australia: new anthropological studies of Aboriginal childhood and adolescence* (pp. 103–30). Oxford: Berghahn Books.

Einarsdottir, J. (2004). *Tired of weeping: mother love, child death, and poverty in Guinea-Bissau.* Madison, WI: University of Wisconsin Press.

Erchak, G. M. (1976/77). Who is Zo? A study of Kpelle identical twins. *Liberian Studies Journal, 7*(1), 23–5.

(1992). *The anthropology of self and behavior.* New Brunswick, NJ: Rutgers University Press.

Evans-Pritchard, E. E. (1932). Heredity and gestation, as the Azande see them. *Sociologus, 8,* 400–14.

Fabian, S. M. (1992). *Space-time of the Bororo of Brazil*. Gainesville, FL: University Press of Florida.

Fajans, J. (1997). *They make themselves: work and play among the Baining of Papua New Guinea*. University of Chicago Press.

Faron, L. C. (1964). *Hawks of the sun: Mapuche morality and its ritual attributes*. University of Pittsburgh Press.

Faulkingham, R. H. (1970). Bases of legitimacy for social control in a Hausa village. Unpublished Ph.D. dissertation, Michigan State University, Lansing, MI.

Fermé, M. C. (2001). *The underneath of things: violence, history, and the everyday in Sierra Leone*. Berkeley, CA: University of California Press.

Ferraro, J. M. (2008). *Nefarious crimes, contested justice: illicit sex and infanticide in the Republic of Venice, 1557–1789*. Baltimore, MD: Johns Hopkins University Press.

Fisher, A. (1963). Reproduction in Truk. *Ethnology*, 2, 526–40.

Flinn, M. V., and England, B. G. (2002). Childhood stress: endocrine and immune responses to psychosocial events. In J. M. Wilce (Ed.), *Social and cultural lives of immune systems* (pp. 107–47). London: Routledge.

Fonseca, I. (1995). *Bury me standing: the Gypsies and their journey*. New York: Vintage Books.

Fortes, M. (1970). Social and psychological aspects of education in Taleland. In J. Middleton (Ed.), *From child to adult: studies in the anthropology of education* (pp. 14–74). Garden City, NY: Natural History Press.

Fouts, H. N. (2005). Families in Central Africa: a comparison of Bofi farmer and forager families. In J. L. Roopnarine (Ed.), *Families in global perspective* (pp. 347–63). Boston: Allyn & Bacon, Pearson.

Fricke, T. (1994). *Himalayan households: Tamang demography and domestic process*. New York: Columbia University Press.

Friedl, E. (1997). *Children of Deh Koh: young life in an Iranian village*. Syracuse, NY: Syracuse University Press.

Furth, C. (1987). Concepts of pregnancy, childbirth, and infancy in Ch'ing Dynasty China. *Journal of Asian Studies*, 46, 7–34.

Geertz, H. (1961). *The Javanese family: a study of kinship and socialization*. New York: Free Press.

Georgiadis, M. (2011). Child burials in Mesolithic and Neolithic southern Greece: a synthesis. *Childhood in the Past*, 4, 31–45.

Gillis, J. R. (2003). The birth of the virtual child: a Victorian progeny. In W. Koops and M. Zucherman (Eds.), *Beyond the century of the child: cultural history and developmental psychology* (pp. 82–95). Philadelphia: University of Pennsylvania Press.

Goldman, I. (1963). *The Cubeo: Indians of the northwest Amazon*. Urbana, IL: University of Illinois Press.

Goodich, M. E. (1989). *From birth to old age: the human life cycle in medieval thought, 1250–1350*. Lanham, MD: University Press of America.

Gorer, G. (1938). *Himalayan village: an account of the Lepchas of Sikkim*. London: Michael Joseph.

Gottlieb, A. (1995). Of cowries and crying: a Beng guide to managing colic. *Anthropology and Humanism*, 20, 20–8.

100 David F. Lancy

(2000). Luring your child into this life: a Beng path for infant care. In J. DeLoache and A. Gottlieb (Eds.), *A world of babies: imagined childcare guides for seven societies* (pp. 55–90). Cambridge University Press.

Graham, D. C. (1937). *The customs of the Ch'uan Miao.* Shanghai: Thomas Chu.

Green, E. C., Jurg, A., and Djedje, A. (1994). The snake in the stomach: child diarrhea in central Mozambique. *Medical Anthropology Quarterly, 8*(1), 4–24.

Gregor, T. (1970). Exposure and seclusion: a study of institutionalized isolation among the Mehinacu Indians of Brazil. *Ethnology, 9*(3), 234–50.

Grindal, B. T. (1972). *Growing up in two worlds: education and transition among the Sisala of northern Ghana.* New York: Holt, Rinehart, and Winston.

Guemple, D. L. (1979). Inuit socialization: a study of children as social actors in an Eskimo community. In K. Ishwaran (Ed.), *Childhood and adolescence in Canada* (pp. 39–71). Toronto: McGraw-Hill Ryerson.

Haffter, C. (1968). The changeling: history and psychodynamics of attitudes to handicapped children in European folklore. *Journal of the History of the Behavioral Sciences, 4,* 55–61.

Hampshire, K. (2001). The impact of male migration on fertility decisions and outcomes in northern Burkina Faso. In S. Tremayne (Ed.), *Managing reproductive life: cross-cultural themes in sexuality and fertility* (pp. 107–25). Oxford: Berghahn Books.

Hanawalt, B. A. (2003). The child in the Middle Ages and the Renaissance. In W. Koops and M. Zucherman (Eds.), *Beyond the century of the child: cultural history and developmental psychology* (pp. 21–42). Philadelphia: University of Pennsylvania Press.

Hardenberg, R. (2006). Hut of the young girls: transition from childhood to adolescence in a middle Indian tribal society. In D. K. Behera (Ed.), *Childhoods in South Asia* (pp. 65–81). Singapore: Pearson Education.

Harkness, S., and Super, C. (Eds.) (1995). *Parents' cultural belief systems: their origins, expressions, and consequences.* New York: Guilford Press.

Harkness, S., Super, C. M., and Keefer, C. H. (1992). Learning to be an American parent: how cultural models gain directive force. In R. D'Andrade and C. Strauss (Eds.), *Human motives and cultural models* (pp. 163–78). Cambridge University Press.

Harvey, T., and Buckley, L. (2009). Childbirth in China. In H. Selin and P. K. Stone (Eds.), *Childhood across cultures: ideas and practices of pregnancy, childbirth and the postpartum* (pp. 55–69). Amherst, MA: Springer.

Haxaire, C. (2007). Soins, toilette du nouveau-né et rite d'imposition du nom chez les Gouro de Côte d'Ivoire. In D. Bonnet and L. Pourchez (Eds.), *Du soin au rite dans l'enfance* (pp. 103–12). Paris: IRD.

Hearn, K. (2007). Ancient tomb found in Mexico reveals mass child sacrifice. *National Geographic News,* June 12 (news.nationalgeographic.com/news/2007/06/070612-tomb-child.html).

Heilbrunn Timeline of Art History (n.d.). Metropolitan Museum of Art (www.metmuseum.org/toah/hd/azss/ho_00.5.30.htm).

Helander, B. (1988). *The slaughtered camel: coping with fictitious descent among the Hubeer of southern Somalia.* University of Uppsala, Department of Anthropology.

Henderson, R. N. (1972). *The king in every man: evolutionary trends in Onitsha Ibo society and culture.* New Haven, CT: Yale University Press.

Henrich, J., Heine, S. J., and Norenzayan, A. (2010). The weirdest people in the world? *Behavioral and Brain Sciences, 33,* 61–81.

Hernandez, T. (1941). Children among the Drysdale River tribes. *Oceania, 12*(2), 122–33.

Heywood, C. (2001). *A history of childhood: children and childhood in the West from medieval to modern times.* Cambridge: Polity Press.

Hilger, M. I. (1951). *Chippewa child life and its cultural background.* Washington, DC: US Government Printing Office.

Hill, K., and Hurtado, A. M. (1996). *Ache life history: the ecology and demography of a foraging people.* Hawthorne, NY: Aldine de Gruyter.

Horn, C. B., and Martens, J. W. (2009). *"Let the little children come to me": childhood and children in early Christianity.* Washington, DC: Catholic University Press.

Hostetler, J. A., and Huntington, G. E. (1971/1992). *Amish children: education in the family, school, and the community* (2nd edn.). Orlando, FL: Harcourt Brace Jovanovich.

Houby-Nielsen, S. (2000). Child burials in ancient Athens. In J. S. Derevenski (Ed.), *Children and material culture* (pp. 151–66). London: Routledge.

Howard, A. (1973). Education in the 'Aina Pumehana': the Hawaiian-American student as hero. In S. T. Kimball and J. H. Burnett (Eds.), *Learning and culture* (pp. 115–29). Seattle, WA: University of Washington Press.

Howell, N. (1979). *Demography of the Dole !Kung.* New York: Academic Press.

Howell, S. (1988). From child to human: Chewong concepts of self. In G. Jahoda and J. M. Lewis (Eds.), *Acquiring culture: cross-cultural studies in child development* (pp. 147–68). London: Croom Helm.

Howrigan, G. A. (1988). Fertility, infant feeding and change in Yucatan. In R. A. LeVine, P. M. Miller, and M. M. West (Eds.), Parental behavior in diverse societies. *New Directions for Child Development, 40,* 37–50.

Hrdy, S. B. (1999). *Mother nature: maternal instincts and how they shape the human species.* New York: Ballantine.

(2006). Evolutionary context of human development: the cooperative breeding model. In C. S. Carter, L. Ahnert, K. E. Grossmann, S. B. Hrdy, M. E. Lamb, S. W. Porges, and N. Sachser (Eds.), *Attachment and bonding: a new synthesis* (pp. 9–32). Cambridge, MA: MIT Press.

Irons, W. (2000). Why do the Yomut raise more sons than daughters? In L. Cronk, N. Chagnon, and W. Irons (Eds.), *Adaptation and human behavior: an anthropological perspective* (pp. 223–36). New York: Aldine.

Isaac, B. L., and Feinberg, W. E. (1982). Marital form and infant survival among the Mende of rural Upper Bambara Chiefdom, Sierra Leone. *Human Biology, 54*(3), 627–34.

Jay, R. R. (1969). *Javanese villagers: social relations in rural Modjokuto.* Cambridge, MA: MIT Press.

Jenkins, C. L., Orr-Ewing, A. K., and Heywood, P. F. (1985). Cultural aspects of early childhood growth and nutrition among the Amele of Lowland Papua New Guinea. In L. B. Marshall (Ed.), *Infant care and feeding in the South Pacific* (pp. 29–50). New York: Gordon and Beach Science.

Jocano, F. L. (1969). *Growing up in a Philippine barrio*. New York: Holt, Rinehart, and Winston.

Johnson, M. C. (2000). The view from the Wuro: a guide to child rearing for Fulani parents. In J. DeLoache and A. Gottlieb (Eds.), *A world of babies: imagined childcare guides for seven societies* (pp. 171–98). Cambridge University Press.

Kağitcibaşi, C., and Ataca, B. (2005). Value of children and family change: a three-decade portrait from Turkey. *Applied Psychology: An International Review*, 54, 317–37.

Karen, R. (1998). *Becoming attached: first relationships and how they shape our capacity to love*. New York: Oxford University Press.

Karplus, Y., and Karplus, M. (1989). *Cultural variations in child caretaking practices among the Negev Bedouins: implications for the management of developmental disabilities*. Paper presented at the 4th World Congress, WAIPAD, Lugano, Switzerland.

Katz, E. (2007). Rites de vie, rites de mort (enfants Mixteèques du Mexique). In D. Bonnet and L. Pouchez (Eds.), *Du soin au rite dans l'enfance* (pp. 281–300). Paris: IRD.

Keller, H. (2007). *Cultures of infancy*. Mahwah, NJ: Erlbaum.

Kertzer, D. (1993). *Sacrificed for honor: Italian infant abandonment and the politics of reproductive control*. Boston, MA: Beacon Press.

Keshavjee, S. (2006). Bleeding babies in Badakhshan: symbolism, materialism, and the political economy of traditional medicine in post-Soviet Tajikistan. *Medical Anthropology Quarterly*, 20, 72–93.

Kim, U., and Choi, S.-H. (1994). Individualism, collectivism, and child development: a Korean perspective. In P. M. Greenfield and R. R. Cocking (Eds.), *Cross-cultural roots of minority child development* (pp. 227–59). Hillsdale, NJ: Erlbaum.

Kinaston, R. L., Buckley, H. R., Halcrow, S. E., Spriggs, M. J. T., Bedford, S., Neal, K., and Gray, A. (2009). Investigating foetal and perinatal mortality in prehistoric skeletal samples: a case study from a 3000-year-old Pacific island cemetery site. *Journal of Archaeological Science*, 36, 2780–7.

King, S. M. (2006). The making of age in ancient coastal Oaxaca. In T. Adren and S. R. Hutson (Eds.), *The social experience of childhood in ancient Mesoamerica* (pp. 169–200). Boulder, CO: University of Colorado Press.

Kinney, A. B. (1995). Dyed silk: Han notions of the moral development of children. In A. B. Kinney (Ed.), *Chinese views of childhood* (pp. 17–56). Honolulu, HI: University of Hawaii Press.

Klaus, H., Centurion, J., and Curo, M. (2010). Bioarchaeology of human sacrifice: violence, identity and the evolution of ritual killing at Cerro Cerrillos, Peru. *Antiquity*, 84, 1102–22.

Kleijueqgt, M. (2009). Ancient Mediterranean world, childhood and adolescence. In R. A. Shweder, T. R. Bidell, A. C. Dailey, S. D. Dixon, P. J. Miller, and J. Modell (Eds.), *The child: an encyclopedic companion* (pp. 54–6). University of Chicago Press.

Kojima, H. (2003). The history of children and youth in Japan. In W. Koops and M. Zucherman (Eds.), *Beyond the century of the child: cultural history and developmental psychology* (pp. 112–35). Philadelphia: University of Pennsylvania Press.

Kopp, C. B., Khoka, E. W., and Sigman, M. (1977). A comparison of sensorimotor development among infants in India and the United States. *Journal of Cross-Cultural Psychology, 8*(4), 435–51.

Kramer, K. L., and Greaves, R. D. (2007). Changing patterns of infant mortality and maternal fertility among Pumé foragers and horticulturalists. *American Anthropologist, 109*, 713–26.

Kulick, D. (1992). *Language shift and cultural reproduction: socialization, self, and syncretism in a Papua New Guinea village.* Cambridge University Press.

Kulick, D., and Stroud, C. (1993). Conceptions and uses of literacy in a Papua New Guinea village. In B. Street (Ed.), *Cross-cultural approaches to literacy* (pp. 30–61). Cambridge University Press.

Kuroda, H. (1998). A social historical view of the children of the Edo period. In Kumon Children's Research Institute (Ed.), *Children represented in Ukiyo-e* (pp. 10–12). Osaka, Japan: Kumon Institute of Education.

Lancy, D. F. (2007). Accounting for variability in mother–child play. *American Anthropologist, 109*(2), 273–84.

(2008). *The anthropology of childhood: cherubs, chattel, changelings.* Cambridge University Press.

(2010). When nurture becomes nature: ethnocentrism in studies of human development. *Behavioral and Brain Sciences, 33*, 39–40.

Lancy, D. F., and Grove, M. A. (2010). The role of adults in children's learning. In D. F. Lancy, S. Gaskins and J. Bock (Eds.), *The anthropology of learning in childhood* (pp. 145–80). Lanham, MD: Alta-Mira Press.

(2011a). "Getting noticed": middle childhood in cross-cultural perspective. *Human Nature, 22*, 281–302.

(2011b). Marbles and Machiavelli: the role of game play in children's social development. *American Journal of Play, 3*, 489–99.

Langness, L. L. (1981). Child abuse and cultural values: the case of New Guinea. In J. Korbin (Ed.), *Child abuse and neglect* (pp. 13–34). Berkeley, CA: University of California Press.

Leavitt, S. C. (1989). Cargo, Christ, and nostalgia for the dead: themes of intimacy and abandonment in Bumbita Arapesh social experience. Unpublished Ph.D. dissertation, University of California, San Diego.

Lebegyiv, J. (2009). Phases of childhood in early Mycenaean Greece. *Childhood in the Past, 2*, 15–32.

Lebra, T. S. (1994). Mother and child in Japanese socialization: a Japan–U.S. comparison. In P. M. Greenfield and R. R. Cocking (Eds.), *Cross-cultural roots of minority child development* (pp. 259–74). Hillsdale, NJ: Erlbaum.

Lee, K. A. (1994). Attitudes and prejudices towards infanticide: Carthage, Rome and today. *Archaeological Review from Cambridge, 13*, 65–79.

Leighton, D., and Kluckhohn, C. C. (1948). *Children of the people.* Cambridge, MA: Harvard University Press.

Leis, N. B. (1982). The not-so-supernatural power of Ijaw children. In S. Ottenberg (Ed.), *African religious groups and beliefs* (pp. 150–69). Meerut, India: Archana.

104   *David F. Lancy*

Le Mort, F. (2008). Infant burials in pre-pottery neolithic Cyprus: evidence from Khiroitia. In K. Bacvarov (Ed.), *Babies reborn: infant/child burials in pre- and protohistory* (pp. 23–32). BAR International Series 1832. Oxford: Archaeopress.

Lepowsky, M. A. (1987). Food taboos and child survival: a case study from the Coral Sea. In N. Scheper-Hughes (Ed.), *Child survival: anthropological perspectives on the treatment and maltreatment of children* (pp. 71–92). Dordrecht, NL: D. Reidel.

Lessa, W. A. (1966). *Ulithi: a Micronesian design for living.* San Francisco, CA: Holt, Rinehart, and Winston.

LeVine, R. A. (2004). Challenging expert knowledge: findings from an African study of infant care and development. In U. P. Gielen and J. Roopnarine (Eds.), *Childhood and adolescence: cross-cultural perspectives and applications* (pp. 149–65). Westport, CT: Praeger.

    (2007). Ethnographic studies of childhood: a historical overview. *American Anthropologist, 109*, 247–60.

LeVine, R. A., and Norman, K. (2001). The infant's acquisition of culture: early attachment reexamined in anthropological perspective. In C. C. Moore and H. F. Matthews (Eds.), *The psychology of cultural experience* (pp. 83–104). Cambridge University Press.

LeVine, S., and LeVine, R. A. (1981). Child abuse and neglect in sub-Saharan Africa. In J. Korbin (Ed.), *Child abuse and neglect: cross-cultural perspectives* (pp. 35–55). Berkeley, CA: University of California Press.

Lewis, M. E. (2007). *The bioarchaeology of children: perspectives from biological and forensic anthropology.* Cambridge University Press.

Liamputtong, P. (2009). Nyob Nruab Hlis: thirty days confinement in Hmong culture. In H. Selin and P. K. Stone (Eds.), *Childhood across cultures: ideas and practices of pregnancy, childbirth and the postpartum* (pp. 161–73). Amherst, MA: Springer.

Little, C. A. J. L. (2008). Becoming an Asabano: the socialization of Asabano children, Durinmin, West Sepik Province, Papua New Guinea. Unpublished master's thesis, Trent University, Peterborough, ON, Canada.

Loeb, E. M. (1962). Shaman and seer. *American Anthropologist, 31*, 60–84.

Mabilia, M. (2000). The cultural context of childhood diarrhea among Gogo infants. *Anthropology and Medicine, 7*, 191–208.

MacGinnis, J. (2011). *Aspects of child labour and the status of children in Mesopotamia in the first millennium BC.* Paper given at Fourth Annual Society for the Study of Childhood in the Past Conference, Cambridge, October 1.

Maclean, U. (1994). Folk medicine and fertility: aspects of Yoruba medical practice affecting women. In C. P. MacCormack (Ed.), *Ethnography of fertility and birth* (pp. 151–69). Prospect Heights, IL: Waveland Press.

Maiden, A. H., and Farwell, E. (1997). *The Tibetan art of parenting.* Boston, MA: Wisdom.

Mangin, E. B. (1921). *Essay on the manners and customs of the Mossi people in the Western Sudan.* Paris: Augustin Challamel.

Martin, D. (2001). The meaning of children in Hong Kong. In S. Tremayne (Ed.), *Managing reproductive life: cross-cultural themes in sexuality and fertility* (pp. 157–71). Oxford: Berghahn Books.

McGilvray, D. B. (1994). Sexual power and fertility in Sri Lanka: Batticaloa Tamils and Moors. In C. P. MacCormack (Ed.), *Ethnography of fertility and birth* (pp. 15–63). Prospect Heights, IL: Waveland Press.

Meehan, C. L. (2009). Maternal time allocation in two cooperative childrearing societies. *Human Nature, 20,* 375–93.

Meskell, L. (1994). Dying young: the experience of death at Deir el Medina. *Archaeological Review from Cambridge, 13,* 35–45.

Middleton, J. (1965). *The Lugbara of Uganda.* New York: Holt, Rinehart, and Winston.

Miller, B. (1987). Female infanticide and child neglect in rural north India. In N. Scheper-Hughes (Ed.), *Child survival: anthropological perspectives on the treatment and maltreatment of children* (pp. 95–112). Dordrecht, NL: D. Reidel.

Mintz, S. (2004). *Huck's raft: a history of American childhood.* Cambridge, MA: Belknap Press.

Montague, S. P. (1985). Infant feeding and health care in Kaduwaga Village, the Trobriand Islands. In L. B. Marshall (Ed.), *Infant care and feeding in the South Pacific* (pp. 83–96). New York: Gordon and Beach Science.

Morel, M.-F. (2007). Histoire du maillot en Europe occidental. In D. Bonnet and L. Pourchez (Eds.), *Du soin au rite dans l'enfance* (pp. 62–84). Paris: IRD.

Morgan, L. M. (1998). Ambiguities lost: fashioning the fetus into a child in Ecuador and the United States. In N. Scheper-Hughes and C. Sargent (Eds.), *Small wars: the cultural politics of childhood* (pp. 58–74). Berkeley, CA: University of California Press.

Morton, H. (1996). *Becoming Tongan: an ethnography of childhood.* Honolulu, HI: University of Hawaii Press.

Moses, S. (2008). Çatalhöyük's foundation burials: ritual sacrifice or convenient deaths? In K. Bacvarov (Ed.), *Babies reborn: infant/child burials in pre- and protohistory* (pp. 45–52). BAR International Series 1832. Oxford: Archaeopress.

Mull, D. S., and Mull, J. D. (1987). Infanticide among the Tarahumara of the Mexican Sierra Madre. In N. Scheper-Hughes (Ed.), *Child survival: anthropological perspectives on the treatment and maltreatment of children* (pp. 113–32). Dordrecht, NL: D. Reidel.

Murphy, Y., and Murphy, R. F. (1985). *Women of the forest.* New York: Columbia University Press.

Musharbash, Y. (2011). Warungka: becoming and unbecoming a Warlpiri person. In U. Eickelkamp (Ed.), *Growing up in central Australia: new anthropological studies of aboriginal childhood and adolescence* (pp. 63–81). Oxford: Berghahn Books.

Nath, Y. V. S. (1960). *Bhils of Ratanmal: an analysis of the social structure of a western Indian community.* The M.S. University Sociological Monograph Series I. Baroda, India: Maharaja Sayajirao University of Baroda.

Ndege, G. O. (2007). *Culture and customs of Mozambique.* Westport, CT: Greenwood Press.

106   *David F. Lancy*

Newton, R., and Schore, A. (2008). *The attachment connection: parenting a secure and confident child using the science of attachment theory.* Oakland, CA: New Harbinger.

Nichter, M., and Nichter, M. (1987). A tale of Simeon: reflections on raising a child while constructing fieldwork in rural south India. In J. Cassell (Ed.), *Children in the field: anthropological experiences* (pp. 65–89). Philadelphia: Temple University Press.

Nicolaisen, I. (1988). Concepts and learning among the Punan Bah of Sarawak. In G. Jahoda and I. M. Lewis (Eds.), *Acquiring culture: cross-cultural studies in child development* (pp. 193–221). London: Croom Helm.

Nimmo, H. A. (1970). Bajau sex and reproduction. *Ethnology, 9,* 251–62.

Ochs, E., and Schieffelin, B. B. (1984). Language acquisition and socialization: three developmental stories and their implications. In R. Shweder and R. L. LeVine (Eds.), *Culture theory: essays on mind, self, and society* (pp. 276–320). Cambridge University Press.

Orme, N. (2003). *Medieval children.* New Haven, CT: Yale University Press.

Paradise, R. (1996). Passivity or tacit collaboration: Mazahua interaction in cultural context. *Learning and Instruction, 6,* 379–89.

Pearsall, M. (1950). *Klamath childhood and education.* Berkeley, CA: University of California Press.

Picchi, D. (2000). *The Bakairí Indians of Brazil: politics, ecology, and change.* Prospect Heights, IL: Waveland Press.

Platt, K. (1988). Cognitive development and sex roles of the Kerkennah Islands of Tunisia. In G. Jahoda and I. M. Lewis (Eds.), *Acquiring culture: cross-cultural studies in child development* (pp. 271–87). London: Croom Helm.

Pomponio, A. (1992). *Seagulls don't fly into the bush.* Belmont, CA: Wadsworth.

Pourchez, L. (2007). Les transformations du corps de l'enfant: façonnage du visage et bandage du tronc de l'enfant à l'île de la Réunion. In D. Bonnet and L. Pourchez (Eds.), *Du soin du rite dans l'enfance* (pp. 43–59). Paris: IRD.

Rao, A. (1998). *Autonomy: life cycle, gender, and status among Himalayan pastoralists.* Oxford: Berghahn Books.

Rattray, R. S. (1927). *Religion and art in Ashanti.* Oxford: Clarendon Press.

Rawson, B. (2003). *Children and childhood in Roman Italy.* Oxford University Press.

Razy, É. (2007). *Naître et devenir: anthropologie de la petite enfance en pays Soninké, Mali* [Birth and becoming: the anthropology of infancy in Soninké, Mali]. Nanterre, France: Société D'ethnologie.

Read, M. (1960). *Children and their fathers.* New Haven, CT: Yale University Press.

Rega, E. (1997). Age, gender and biological reality in the Early Bronze Age cemetery at Morkrin. In J. Moore and E. Scott (Eds.), *Invisible people and processes* (pp. 229–47). London: Leicester University Press.

Reichel-Dolmatoff, G. (1976). Training for the priesthood among the Kogi of Columbia. In J. Wilbert (Ed.), *Enculturation in Latin America* (pp. 265–88). Los Angeles, CA: UCLA Latin American Center Publications.

Remorini, C. (2011). Becoming a person from the Mbya Guarani perspective: a brief comment. Paper presented at the symposium, "The Cultural Construction of Identity: How Children Become Persons," Third Annual Conference AAA Childhood/Youth Interest Group, Las Vegas, NV, February 23.

Reynolds, P. (1991). *Dance civet cat: child labour in the Zambezi Valley.* Athens, OH: Ohio University Press.

Riches, D. (1974). The Netsilik Eskimo: a special case of selective female infanticide. *Ethnology, 13,* 351–61.

Riesman, P. (1992). *First find yourself a good mother.* New Brunswick, NJ: Rutgers University Press.

Rival, L. (1998). Androgynous parents and guest children: the Huaorani couvade. *Journal of Royal Anthropological Institute, 4,* 619–42.

Roach, J. (2010). "Chilling" child sacrifices found at prehistoric site. *National Geographic News,* December 23 (http://news.nationalgeographic.com/news/2010/12/101223-child-sacrifices-bloodletting-archaeology-science/).

Roach, P. (2009). *Others in mind: social origins of self-consciousness.* Cambridge University Press.

Roscoe, J. (1924). *The Bagesu and other tribes of the Uganda protectorate.* Cambridge University Press.

Sachs, D., and Vu, L. Q. (2005). Vietnam unearths its royal past. *National Georgraphic Magazine,* Interactive Edition, June (http://ngm.nationalgeographic.com/ngm/0506/resources_geo.html?fs=seabed.nationalgeographic.com#bibliography).

Sargent, C. F. (1988). Witchcraft and infanticide in Bariba culture. *Ethnology, 27*(1), 79–95.

Scheer, J., and Groce, N. (1988). Impairment as a human constant: cross-cultural and historical perspectives on variation. *Journal of Social Issues, 44,* 23–37.

Scheper-Hughes, N. (1987). "Basic strangeness": maternal estrangement and infant death: a critique of bonding theory. In C. Super (Ed.), *The role of culture in developmental disorder* (pp. 131–51). New York: Academic Press.

Schiefenhovel, W. (1989). Reproduction and sex-ratio manipulation through preferential female infanticide among the Eipo, in the highlands of Western New Guinea. In A. E. Rasa, C. Vogel, and E. Voland (Eds.), *The sociobiology of sexual and reproductive strategies* (pp. 170–93). New York: Chapman and Hall.

Scott, E. (1999). *The archaeology of infancy and infant death.* Oxford: Archaeopress.

Sear, R., and Mace, R. (2008). Who keeps children alive? A review of the effects of kin on child survival. *Evolution and Human Behavior, 29,* 1–18.

Sellen, D. W. (1998). Infant and young child feeding practices among African pastoralists: the Datoga of Tanzania. *Journal of Biosocial Science, 3,* 481–99.

Senior, L. M. (1994). Babes in the "hood": concepts of personhood and the spatial segregation of infants from adults in archaeological burial practices. Paper presented at the 59th annual meeting of the Society for American Archaeology, Anaheim, CA, April 22.

Sharer, R. J. (1994). *The ancient Maya* (5th edn.). Stanford University Press.

Shein, M. (1992). *The Precolumbian child.* Culver City, CA: Labyrinthos.

Shostak, M. (1982). *Nisa: the life and words of a !Kung woman.* Cambridge, MA: Harvard University Press.

Sillar, B. (1994). Playing with god: cultural perceptions of children, play, and miniatures in the Andes. *Archaeological Review from Cambridge, 13,* 47–63.

Smith, P., and Kahila, G. (1992). Identification of infanticide in archeological sites: a case study from the Late Roman-Early Byzantine periods at Ashkelon, Israel. *Journal of Archeological Science, 19,* 667–75.

Spielmann, K. A. (1989). Dietary restrictions on hunter-gatherer women and the implications for fertility and infant mortality. *Human Ecology, 17,* 321–45.

Spitz, R. A. (1945). Hospitalism – an inquiry into the genesis of psychiatric conditions in early childhood. *Psychoanalytic Study of the Child, 1,* 53–74.

Sprott, J. W. (2002). *Raising young children in an Alaskan Iñupiaq village: the family, cultural and village environment of rearing.* Westport, CT: Bergin and Garvey.

Stager, L. E., and Greene, J. A. (2000). Were living children sacrificed to the gods? *Archeology Odyssey, 3*(6), 29–31.

Stasch, R. (2009). *Society of others: kinship and mourning in a West Papuan Place.* Berkeley, CA: University of California Press.

Stearman, A. M. (1989). *Yuqui: forest nomads in a changing world.* New York: Holt, Rinehart, and Winston.

Stearns, P. N. (2010). Defining happy childhoods: assessing a recent change. *Journal of the History of Childhood and Youth, 3,* 165–86.

Steiner, L. M. (2007). *Mommy wars: stay-at-home and career moms face off on the choices, their lives, their families.* New York: Random House.

Stoller, P. (1989). *Fusion of the worlds: an ethnography of possessions among the Songhay of Niger.* University of Chicago Press.

Strassmann, B. I. (1997). Polygyny as a risk factor for child mortality among the Dogon. *Current Anthropology, 38,* 688–95.

Sussman, G. (1982). *Selling mother's milk: the wet-nursing business in France, 1715–1914.* Urbana, IL: University of Illinois Press.

Teixeira, M. (2007). Parachever l'humanité toilette, massage et soins des enfants Manjak (Guinée-Bissau, Sénégal). In D. Bonnet and L. Pourchez (Eds.), *Du soin au rite dans l'enfance* (pp. 129–45). Paris: IRD.

Telban, B. (1997). Being and "non-being" in Ambonwari (Papua New Guinea) ritual. *Oceania, 67,* 308–25.

Tiesler, V. (2011). Becoming Maya: infancy and upbringing through the lens of pre-Hispanic head shaping. *Childhood in the Past, 4,* 117–32.

Tizard, J., and Tizard, B. (1974). The institution as an environment for development. In M. P. M. Richards (Ed.), *The integration of a child into a social world* (pp. 137–52). Cambridge University Press.

Tjitayi, K., and Lewis, S. (2011). Envisioning lives at Ernabella. In U. Eickelkamp (Ed.), *Growing up in central Australia: new anthropological studies of Aboriginal childhood and adolescence* (pp. 49–62). Oxford: Berghahn Books.

Tomlinson, M., Murray, L., and Cooper, P. (2010). Attachment theory, culture, and Africa: past, present, and future. In P. Erdmand and K.-m. Ng (Eds.), *Attachment: expanding the cultural connections* (pp. 181–209). New York: Routledge.

Trivers, R. L. (1972). Parental investment and sexual selection. In B. Campbell (Ed.), *Sexual selection and the descent of man* (pp. 136–79). Chicago: Aldine.
Tronick, E. Z., Thomas, R. B., and Daltabuit, M. (1994). The Quechua manta pouch: a caretaking practice for buffering the Peruvian infant against the multiple stressors of high altitude. *Child Development, 65,* 1005–13.
True, M. M., Pisani, L., and Oumar, F. (2001). Infant–mother attachment among the Dogon of Mali. *Child Development, 72,* 1451–66.
Tulloch, M. I. (2004). Parental fear of crime: a discursive analysis. *Journal of Sociology, 40,* 362–77.
van IJzendoorn, M. H., and Sagi-Schwartz, A. (2008). Cross-cultural patterns of attachment: universal and contextual dimensions. In J. Cassidy and P. R. Shaver (Eds.), *Handbook of attachment: theory, research and clinical applications* (pp. 713–34). New York: Guilford Press.
Viccars, J. D. (1949). Witchcraft in Bolobo, Belgian Congo. *Africa, 19*(3), 220–9.
Wagley, C. (1977). *Welcome of tears: the Tapirapé Indians of central Brazil.* New York: Oxford University Press.
Wee, V. (1992). Children, population policy, and the state in Singapore. In S. Stephens (Ed.), *Children and the politics of culture* (pp. 184–217). Princeton University Press.
Weisner, T. S., and Gallimore, R. (1977). My brother's keeper: child and sibling caretaking. *Current Anthropology, 18,* 169–90.
Whittemore, R. D. (1989). Child caregiving and socialization to the Mandinka way: toward an ethnography of childhood. Unpublished PhD dissertation, University of California, Los Angeles.
Wiedemann, T. (1989). *Adults and children in the Roman Empire.* New Haven, CT: Yale University Press.
Wileman, J. (2005). *Hide and seek: the archaeology of childhood.* Stroud: Tempus.
Wiley, A. S. (2004). *An ecology of high-altitude infancy.* Cambridge University Press.
Wolf, M. (1972). *Women and the family in rural Taiwan.* Stanford University Press.
Woolf, A. (1997). At home in the long Iron Age: a dialogue between households and individuals in cultural reproduction. In J. Moore and E. Scott (Eds.), *Invisible people and processes* (pp. 68–78). London: Leicester University Press.
Yanagisawa, S. (2009). Childbirth in Japan. In H. Selin and P. K. Stone (Eds.), *Childhood across cultures: ideas and practices of pregnancy, childbirth and the postpartum* (pp. 85–94). Amherst, MA: Springer.
Zeitlin, M. (1996). My child is my crown: Yoruba parental theories and practices in early childhood. In S. Harkness and C. M. Super (Eds.), *Parent's cultural belief systems: their origins, expressions, and consequences* (pp. 407–27). New York: Guilford Press.
Zelizer, V. A. (1985). *Pricing the priceless child: the changing social value of children.* New York: Basic Books.

Part II

Multiple attachments: allomothering,
stranger anxiety, and intimacy

4   Maternal and allomaternal responsiveness: the significance of cooperative caregiving in attachment theory

Courtney L. Meehan and Sean Hawks

Introduction

Bowlby (1969) and Ainsworth (1967), as well as many who have followed (e.g., Howes and Spieker, 2008; Kermoian and Leiderman, 1986; Lamb and Lewis, 2010; Marvin, van Devender, Iwanaga *et al.*, 1977; Sagi, van IJzendoorn, Aviezer *et al.*, 1995; Seymour, 2004; Tronick, Morelli, and Ivey, 1992; True, 1994; van IJzendoorn, Sagi, and Lambermon, 1992; van IJzendoorn and Sagi-Schwartz, 2008), clearly recognized that children have multiple attachment figures. Nevertheless, the vast majority of research remains heavily biased towards the mother–child relationship. In addition, while not exclusive, research continues to emphasize Western contexts. Western children often have less access to and less stable allomaternal attachment figures than what is commonly experienced by children cross-culturally. The result is a dearth of studies that explore the role and significance of nonmaternal attachments to the formation of children's internal working models and developmental outcomes (Howes and Spieker, 2008; Vermeer and Bakermans-Kranenburg, 2008).

The emphasis on the mother–child dyad has been argued to be a product of our recent history and Western culture (Hrdy, 2009). Bowlby formulated his ideas on attachment at a time when human caregiving was

This research was supported by a US National Science Foundation CAREER Award (BCS-#9055213) and a grant from the Leakey Foundation. We would like to thank the Aka families who have so generously shared their lives with us; Courtney Helfrecht, Mark Caudell, Jennifer Wilcox Roulette, Michelle Dillon, Angela Sulfaro, Emily Wolfe, Shantel Eggar, Rebecca Prescott, and Courtney Malcom for assistance with data collection; our local field assistants, Mboula, Eduard, Moboulou, Francis Aubin, Kolet, Guy Alain, Banzengola, Matthieu, Dopeningue, Herve, Dopeningue, and Mesmin; and Robert Quinlan, for statistical advice during the development of this chapter. For logistical support, we offer our sincere thanks to Timothee Tikouzou. We would also like to thank the Ministere de l'Education Nationale de la Recherché Scientifique et de la Technologie in the Central African Republic.

assumed to be consistent with the continuous care and contact model (CCCM). The CCCM is defined by intense maternal investment – mothers remain in tactile contact and offer all care to their infants. Hrdy (1999) argues that CCCM fits well with perceptions of how Western mothers should care for their children. As a result, the mother–child dyad began to be studied as the unit of investigation. Yet, human child rearing does not conform to the CCCM. Mothers freely share their offspring and rely on the assistance of allomothers (nonmaternal caregivers) while their children are immature (Hrdy, 2007, 2009). As such, like other species who rely on investment by others, humans are now considered to be cooperative breeders (Crittenden and Marlowe, 2008; Hewlett and Lamb, 2005; Hrdy, 2009; Kramer, 2005, 2010; Kramer and Ellison, 2010; Meehan, 2005a, 2008). The inclusion of allomothers does not suggest that mothers are not primary caregivers or a child's primary attachment figure. However, research into human cooperative breeding is transforming our notion of who may be necessary for successful physical, social, and emotional development.

Throughout evolutionary history and in most of the world today, the mother–child dyad was and is immersed in dense social and caregiving networks. These support networks form an integral part of human sociality. Our prosocial behavior, unparalleled in other primates, results in widespread and daily cooperation with kin and nonkin in food procurement, the sharing of public goods, and childcare to children who are not our own (Burkart, Hrdy, and van Schaik , 2009; Gurven, 2004; Hill, 2002; Hill, Walker, Bozicevic *et al.*, 2011; Silk, 2006). These cooperative social networks form an essential component of successful human reproduction and child rearing (Hrdy, 2009). Thus, while the mother–child dyad has been emphasized in child development research and in attachment theory, the dyad does not exist in isolation – it is embedded in and influenced by the greater social network in which it resides.

Here our focus is to shed light on the role of allomothers in the development of children's attachment relationships. We review current evidence on human cooperative breeding and consider its implications for attachment theory. Then, utilizing data collected among the Aka tropical forest foragers, a small-scale foraging population, we show the breadth and effects of multiple attachment relationships and suggest how multiple attachments may affect the formation of children's internal working models.

Human cooperative breeding

Human mothers are unique among extant apes in that their level of commitment and willingness to invest in their offspring is contingent upon their perception of nonmaternal care (Hrdy, 2005a). It is not remarkable that mothers evaluate their social environments considering the complexity of human life-history traits and the unusual and lengthy dependency that human children display. Human children are highly altricial at birth, requiring tremendous nutritional investment through breast-feeding and continuous caregiving (Chisholm, 1999; Hewlett and Lamb, 2002; Hrdy, 2005b, 2009). Among contemporary foragers and many other small-scale societies, infant care requires almost constant physical contact (Blurton Jones, Hawkes, and O'Connell, 2005; Hewlett, 1991; Hewlett, Lamb, Leyendecker et al., 2000). The life-history traits of lengthy childhood, high fertility, and simultaneous, multiple, dependent offspring (Blurton Jones et al., 2005; Hawkes, O'Connell, and Blurton Jones, 1997, 1998; Kramer, 2010), have lead anthropologists to investigate the effects of others on human reproduction and child development. Findings have illustrated that human mothers could not successfully rear children to independence alone (Kaplan, 1994) and that allomaternal investment is extensive cross-culturally (e.g., Crittenden and Marlowe, 2008; Fouts, 2011; Gottlieb, 2004; Hewlett and Lamb, 2005; Ivey Henry, Morelli, and Tronick, 2005; Lancy, 2008; Marlowe, 2005; Meehan, 2005a, 2008). Cooperative breeding, care and provisioning by non-parental caregivers, enables a mother to produce and raise costly and slowly maturing offspring, something that she would not be able to on her own, or with only support from the father (Hrdy, 2005a; Kramer, 2010).

Although not limited to small-scale forager populations, the ubiquitous nature of nonmaternal care is unambiguous in these groups. Aka allomothers in the Central African Republic contribute approximately one-quarter of all caregiving in late infancy (Meehan, 2005b). Childcare is undertaken by multiple individuals who span age, sex, and kin and nonkin categories (i.e., juvenile females/males, adult females/males, and elderly males/females) (Meehan, 2005a). In late infancy, children interact with just over twenty caregivers each day, and half of these caregivers invest in intensive forms of caregiving (e.g., holding, soothing, feeding, showing affection, etc.) (Meehan, 2009). Among the Efe foragers in the Ituri Forest, newborn infants are in physical contact with allomothers 39% of the time, and they are transferred to different caregivers 3.7 times per hour. At 18 weeks, infants are in physical contact with allomothers 60% of the time, and children are transferred to different caregivers 8.3 times per hour (Tronick, Morelli, and Winn, 1987). Allomothers among the Hadza, a mobile hunter-gatherer group in northern Tanzania, also demonstrate extensive allomaternal care. Thirty-one percent of all child holding is by allomothers (Crittenden and Marlowe, 2008). Even among the !Kung, who greatly influenced the

CCCM, allomothers are an integral part of infant and young children's lives (Konner, 2005). For instance, !Kung mothers attend to the majority of infant crying bouts, but allomothers respond to infant distress a remarkable 42% of the time. Fourteen percent of the responses are joint responses by a mother and allomother(s). Thus, !Kung mothers often have assistance in responding to their infants' cries (Kruger and Konner, 2010).

Furthermore, allomothers offer nutritional benefits to children (Hawkes et al., 1997; Sear, Mace, and McGregor, 2000; Sear, Steele, McGregor et al., 2002). Their presence is often associated with improved child survivorship (see Beise, 2005; Euler and Weitzel, 1996; Hawkes et al., 1997; Jamison, Cornell, Jamison et al., 2002; Pashos, 2000; Sear et al., 2000; Sear et al., 2002; Sear and Mace, 2009; Voland and Beise, 2005), and they have been repeatedly noted to increase maternal fertility (Flinn, 1989; Kramer, 2005; Leonetti et al., 2005; Turke, 1988). There is also evidence that the presence of allomothers reduces child stress responses (Flinn and Leone, 2009) and increases maternal responsiveness to children (Hrdy, 2007; Olds, Henderson, Chamberlin et al., 1986, 2002), and this, in turn, improves mother–child interactions.

Multiple attachments and internal working models

While the frequency of nonmaternal care has been well documented in many small-scale societies, far less is known about whether children form attachment relationships with these caregivers and their role in the development of children's internal working models. Under most circumstances, attachments to allomothers are assumed to be secondary in order of importance and in the temporal scale of formation (Howes and Spieker, 2008). The first assumption is supported by cross-cultural evidence, and we do not question the primary attachment role of mothers. As Hrdy (2009, p. 68) notes, "Of all the attachments mammalian babies form, none is more powerful than that between baby primates and their mothers." Even in cultures with extensive allomaternal investment, mothers are primary caregivers (Hrdy, 2009; Meehan, 2005b, 2013; Meehan, Quinlan, and Malcolm, 2013) and essential to child survivorship (Sear and Mace, 2009). However, acknowledging the mother as the primary attachment figure should not negate the role that others play in children's attachment systems or in the formation of the mother–child relationship. The latter assumption, regarding subsequent attachment formation with nonmaternal caregivers, is probably based on Western socioecology. In the West, mothers (and fathers) represent children's first attachment figure(s), and only subsequently, when children enter childcare, do they develop additional attachment relationships (Howes and Spieker, 2008). Yet, in cultures where cooperative caregiving from birth is the norm (see Gottlieb, this volume), children's social relationships are not restricted to the mother–infant dyad, and we should expect children to simultaneously form attachment relationships with individuals other than their mother. Our ability to investigate the multiple influences that shape children's attachment security is dependent upon investigating attachment relationships beyond the mother–child dyad (Thompson, 2000; Vermeer and Bakermans-Kranenburg, 2008).

For example, hunter-gatherer children enter into the social milieu from the moment of birth. While not universal, multiple hunter-gatherer populations practice nonmaternal breast-feeding. Ongee, Efe, Aka, and Agta allomothers frequently breast-feed children who are not their own (Hewlett and Lamb, 2002, 2005). Efe allomothers, who represent the best-known example of this practice, are the first to breast-feed a child. Maternal breast-feeding does not commence until several days after birth when the mother's milk comes in (Tronick et al., 1987). Furthermore, Efe allomothers are the first to hold newborn infants and maternal contact, only occurs several hours later. From there, infants spend more than one-third to over 50% of their time in the care of others (Tronick et al., 1987, 1992). While the Efe may seem to represent a unique example (Ivey, 2000), a multitude of recent studies suggest that the focus on mothers and children isolated from their larger social network is inconsistent with the ways in which children are frequently reared throughout the world (Gottlieb, 2004; Howes and Spieker, 2008; Kramer, 2010; Lamb, 1999; Lancy, 2008; van IJzendoorn and Sagi-Schwartz, 2008).

A better understanding of the formation of multiple, simultaneous attachment relationships has clear theoretical implications for attachment theory, particularly in regard to children's socioemotional development and the organization of children's internal working models (Howes and Spieker, 2008; Tronick et al., 1992; van IJzendoorn et al., 1992). Internal working models are cognitive schemata reflecting feelings towards the self and others (Bowlby, 1973). Such a schema is formed early in life from a child's repeated interactions with his or her caregivers. It is during these interactions that children learn about their social and caregiving environment and develop models of others and self (Ahnert, 2005; Bowlby, 1973). When caregivers respond appropriately, promptly, and with warmth, children develop "secure" trusting internal working models (Ahnert, 2005; Bowlby, 1973; Hewlett et al., 2000; Lamb et al., 1984). These models guide an individual's behavior and interactions with others, often unconsciously (Verschueren, Marcoen, and Schoefs, 1996). That it operates partly unconsciously makes it self-fulfilling (for example, those with trusting internal working models are more likely to cultivate trusting relationships and believe that others are generally trustworthy) (Dykas and Cassidy, 2011).

Van IJzendoorn *et al.* (1992) summarized four models which explain how children organize their relationships with multiple caregivers. First, monotropy suggests that the mother–child relationship is *the* primary relationship. Others are considered "ineffective in determining child development." Second, hierarchy suggests that the mother–child relationship is primary and the most predictive of later functioning, although it is not the only influence. Third, the independence model suggests that caregivers fulfill a variety of roles in children's lives, and multiple caregivers influence later functioning in children, suggesting distinct, but equal, importance between relationships. Fourth, the integrated model, proposes that attachment relationships are integrated. Later socioemotional functioning is the result of the quality of a child's entire attachment network. Relationships with nonmaternal caregivers are integrated into a child's internal working model.

Excluding research on fathers and day-care providers (cross-culturally an unusual category of nonmaternal caregivers), minimal research documents children's interactions and attachments with nonmaternal attachment figures, limiting our ability to explore how others might affect the organization of internal working models. Here, we take steps towards incorporating the social world of infants and young children by highlighting the breadth of children's attachment networks and exploring how others may influence children's felt security and, in turn, the formation of their internal working models. To do so, we focus on data collected on the Aka tropical forest foragers. While the Aka are certainly not representative of all forager populations or all societies that practice cooperative child rearing, their system of shared caregiving offers a window into the experiences of children around the world who are reared in extended social units.

Multiple attachments: a case study among Aka foragers

The Aka are tropical foragers who reside in the Congo basin rain forest. The focal Aka population is associated with two horticultural villages in the Central African Republic. Like most hunter-gatherers, the Aka are strongly egalitarian – individuals do not attempt to draw attention to themselves or find fault with others, and they have a strong respect for the autonomy of others (Hewlett, Fouts, Boyette *et al.*, 2011). Extensive cooperation and sharing characterize Aka social relationships (Hewlett *et al.*, 2000). Food resources are shared widely with related and unrelated individuals (Bahuchet, 1990).

Infancy and early childhood among hunter-gatherers is indulgent (Hewlett, 1991). Like the !Kung and other hunter-gatherer groups, infants and young children are usually held in a sling on the mother or other caregiver's side, where a child can easily see the faces of his or her caregivers. This position also allows for on-demand breast-feeding (Hewlett, 1991; Konner, 2005). Aka children cry infrequently in comparison with horticultural or Western children (Hewlett et al., 2000). When children do cry, others respond to infants' cries promptly: there is no difference between mothers and allomothers in how quickly they respond to or effectively soothe a child's fussing or crying (Meehan and Hawks, 2011, 2013). As infants become mobile, maternal physical access (holding, touching, and proximity) decreases, while nonmaternal touching and proximity increase (Meehan and Hawks, 2011). As a whole, allomothers also reduce maternal energy expenditure and frequently offer care when mothers are engaged in work activities, decreasing the costs associated with childcare/labor trade-offs (Meehan, 2009; Meehan et al., 2013).

Aka camps consist of approximately twenty to thirty-five individuals (Hewlett et al., 2000). Houses are small, dome-shaped leaf and stick structures with only enough room to fit a bed and a few household items. The Aka practice a flexible post-marital residence pattern. Couples generally reside matrilocally during early marriage, although there is tremendous flexibility, and couples frequently move back and forth between the wife's or husband's camp for years (Bahuchet, 1991; Meehan, 2005a). Camp life is open and public, with the houses arranged in a circle. This intimate living situation places children into the fabric of social life.

Below, we provide evidence that Aka children form attachment relationships with many individuals. While attachment researchers have long recognized attachment to nonmaternal caregivers, methodologies for assessing attachment security do not take cultural variation into consideration, nor do they allow researchers to fully explore the extent of children's attachment networks. Current methods examine attachment relationships in a dyadic fashion, are conducted in a controlled environment (i.e., the strange-situation procedure), and emphasize particular caregivers when examining children's attachment relationships. These emphases are based on Western socioecology. For instance, fathers and day-care providers are often highlighted as nonmaternal attachment figures, but there are no studies that explore children's attachment to grandparents (Howes and Spieker, 2008), probably a common attachment figure around the world and an essential caregiver throughout our evolutionary history (Hawkes et al., 1997, 1998). Perhaps these emphases are not surprising – LeVine (this volume) notes that Ainsworth developed the strange situation to replicate the experiences of Western infants at that time.

Next, our data suggest that while hunter-gatherer childcare patterns have been well described (Crittenden and Marlowe, 2008; Fouts, Hewlett, and Lamb, 2001; Hewlett, 1991; Hewlett, Lamb, Shannon *et al.*, 1998; Ivey Henry *et al.*, 2005; Meehan, 2005a; Tronick *et al.*, 1992), we still know very little about the intracultural variation in maternal and allomaternal caregiving styles among these populations. Understanding children's experiences across their attachment network is essential, as much has been attributed to hunter-gatherer caregiving patterns. For instance, early childhood among foragers is characterized by intense, intimate, and sensitive care (Hewlett, 1991), and this responsive and caring environment is associated with the development of positive internal working models (IWM) (Hewlett *et al.*, 2000). Despite the risky environments in which these foragers often live, individuals view their world and others as giving and trustworthy (Bird-David, 1990; Hewlett *et al.*, 2000). Children believe that their needs will be attended to and develop a general trusting view of other people as they grow up (Hewlett *et al.*, 2000). Yet, our data show that children do not always receive concordant care from their mothers and allomothers. Despite frequent observation of others' caregiving styles, there is only minimal evidence that caregivers mirror each other's interaction styles.

Finally, we illustrate the effects of allomaternal attachment figures on child behavior, the mother–child attachment relationship, and on early child developmental outcomes (weight and height for age). Studies have consistently shown that others affect maternal behavior and responsiveness. Access to social support reduces the occurrence of child abuse (Olds *et al.*, 1986, 2002) and improves maternal–child interactions and secure attachments (Jacobson and Frye, 1991; Spieker and Bensley, 1994). A lack of social support in the early postnatal period is associated with postpartum depression (Hagen, 1999), which in turn has been linked to low maternal sensitivity, responsiveness, and attunement with children, all of which are tied to the development of insecure attachments (Beck, 1995; Crnic, Greenburg, Ragozin *et al.*, 1983; Hagen, 1999; Lyons-Ruth, Connell, Grunebaum *et al.*, 1990; Slykerman, Thompson, Pryor *et al.*, 2005). Findings such as these suggest that allomaternal care is not supplementary but a critical component in maternal sensitive and responsive care. Still, little is known about how others might affect children's behavior to their mothers and how that may affect the mother–child attachment relationship. Below, we illustrate the importance of examining the whole of a child's attachment network and show that allomaternal responsiveness impacts children's felt security, child–mother interactions, and early developmental outcomes.

We conclude with a discussion on the implications of allomaternal attachment relationships on the organization of children's internal working models. Multiple attachments raise several questions for attachment theory (Howes and Spieker, 2008; van IJzendoorn et al., 1992). Is a child's attachment to his or her mother the principal relationship? Are attachment relationships domain-specific? Are children's attachment relationships to others integrated in the development of their internal working models? Research in small-scale societies, where cooperative care is ubiquitous and children have the opportunity to form multiple and simultaneous attachment relationships, offers a unique opportunity to begin to explore these questions.

Aka maternal and allomaternal attachment figures

As mentioned above, the social, caregiving, and attachment networks of Aka children are dense. Here children's social networks (the number of people in camp) averaged twenty-eight people. Their extended caregiving network (those who engage with or come within a forearm's distance of the child), averaged just over twenty-one individuals. Mothers are clearly the primary attachment figures, and mothers receive approximately three-quarters of all attachment displays (Meehan and Hawks, 2013). However, mothers are not the only individuals with whom children form attachment relationships. Children display attachment behaviors to an average of just over five caregivers. This is slightly lower than a previously reported average of six attachment figures on a smaller sample (Meehan and Hawks, 2011, 2013). Nevertheless, the number of attachment figures is quite large. Additionally, while children have multiple attachment figures, they clearly do not display attachment behaviors to the whole of their social or caregiving network (Table 4.1).

Attachment behaviors (Table 4.2) recorded during observations[1] are characterized by actions in which the child sought to maintain or establish

---

[1] Quantitative data were collected through a focal sampling technique (Altmann, 1974), successfully in multiple child-focused studies (e.g., Fouts, 2011; Hewlett et al., 2000; Meehan, 2005a, 2008, 2009). The researcher observes and follows a focal individual over several days covering all daylight hours (6 am–6 pm). Observations occur in 4-hour intervals from 6 am to 10 am, 10 am to 2 pm, and 2 pm to 6 pm. The 4-hour observations are spread over multiple days to capture the variation in children's daily activities. Observations start at the top of each hour and last for 45 minutes, allowing the observer a 15-minute break at the end of each 45-minute segment (e.g., observe and record from 6:00:00 am to 6:44:59 am and break from 6:45:00 am to 6:59:59 am). Due to the 15-minute break following every 45 minutes of observations, infants are actually observed for 9 of the 12 daylight hours. Observers carry tape recorders with earphones that direct the observer to start observing at the top of the minute, record during 0:00:20–29 seconds, resume observing at 0:00:30 seconds, record at 0:00:50–59 seconds, etc. Thus, observations are divided into 30-second intervals. The 30-second

Table 4.1 *Summary statistics for focal mothers and children*

Variable	Mean	Std. deviation	Min.	Max.
Infant age (months)[a]	18.403	8.161	6.5	32.75
Mother age (years)	27.871	5.488	20	42
Social network[b]	29.129	9.348	8	46
Extended caregiver network[c]	21.903	8.105	8	41
Caregiver network[d]	10.129	3.956	5	20
Attachment figure network	5.065	2.568	1	11
Number of attachment bouts	40.323	25.793	3	102

$n = 31$.

[a] Previous analysis showed a clear emergence in attachment-related behaviors in children just after 6 months of age; therefore, children less than 6 months of age were eliminated from the sample (Meehan and Hawks, 2013).

[b] Camp size.

[c] Number of caregivers who came within a forearm's distance.

[d] Number of high-investing caregivers.

Table 4.2 *Infant attachment behaviors and descriptions*

Attachment behavior	Description
Approach	Approaches caregiver with intent to gain proximity
Seek	Attempts to be held through gestures or vocalizations
Reach	Reaches for caregiver
Touch	Touches caregiver to maintain physical contact
Proffer	Proffers an object or food item to caregiver
Crawl in lap	Crawls into lap of caregiver
Kiss/hug/nuzzle	Kisses, hugs, or nuzzles a caregiver
Bury face	Buries face in caregiver's breast
Follow	Follows caregiver as he/she moves away to maintain proximity
Cling	Clings to the body or clothing of caregiver

contact or proximity. These behaviors are not passive interactions, such as being held, general physical contact, and visual or verbal contact, and we argue that they do not illustrate common caregiver–child interactions. These displays demonstrate a more significant relationship than what is typically observed between a child and his or her larger caregiving network (Meehan and Hawks, 2013).

Aka children have multiple attachment figures, and these individuals comprise different age, sex, and relationship categories. All infants

observations yield 1,080 observations per child or 33,480 observations for the 31 children included in this sample.

display attachment behaviors to their mothers. However, beyond mothers, who children form attachment relationships with is fluid (Table 4.3). Access to particular caregivers or categories of caregivers does not guarantee that children display attachment behaviors towards these individuals. Nineteen children had access to their father, but only twelve displayed attachment behaviors towards him. Twenty-five children had a living grandmother in camp, but only nine children displayed attachment behaviors to her. Approximately 30% of latter-born children did not display attachment behaviors to their siblings. Thus, the presence of a close kin member does not necessarily result in a child displaying attachment behaviors towards that individual. The largest category of attachment figures was individuals other than those listed above. Close to 50% of children's attachment figures are *others*, camp members who occupy different relational, sex, and age categories. Attachments to other camp members were the norm. Seventy-seven percent displayed attachment behaviors towards others, but these relationships were not universal. Due to the high density of allomaternal care, children have the opportunity to develop strong relationships with others, yet children do not form attachment relationships with all of their caregivers.

Aka maternal and allomaternal responsiveness and concordance

To understand how caregiver responsiveness might affect child behavior, the mother–child relationship, or the development of children's internal working models, we examined caregivers' responsiveness to children's attachment bouts. Whether or not children receive concordant responses from mothers and allomothers will affect children's overall sense of security. We assumed Aka caregivers would show significant concordance in caregiving styles – children whose mothers were highly responsive to attachment bouts would have highly responsive allomothers. The frequency of interaction between individuals in Aka camps allows caregivers to observe and model caregiving behaviors after one another. Concordant care between mothers and others in the child's network of attachment figures would indicate that caregivers match their level of responsiveness and conform to a widely shared model of caregiving. Lack of concordant caregiving would suggest that children may experience different levels of felt security across their attachment network.

We conducted principal-components analysis (PCA) on attachment figures' responses to children's attachment bouts.[2] PCA reveals three

---

[2] PCA is a data-reduction method that reduces a large number of variables into a few compact "latent" variables, called components. Components reveal an underlying structure

Table 4.3 *Categories of attachment figures^a to whom infants displayed attachment behaviors*

Infant name^b	Infant sex	Mother	Father	Grandmother	Siblings	Others^c	Total
Dumasi	M	1	–	1	–	6	8
Samedi	M	1	1	0	1	1	4
Mony	M	1	–	1	0	4	6
Ameny	F	1	1	1	1	7	11
Likanda	M	1	–	–	–	5	6
Dikamo	M	1	0	0	0	1	2
Mbondo	M	1	1	0	1	1	4
Nzambe	M	1	–	0	2	1	4
Mbeki	F	1	0	0	1	1	3
Caffe	F	1	1	1	2	2	7
Mobemba	M	1	0	0	0	3	4
Mabela	M	1	1	1	0	2	5
Tengbe	M	1	1	1	1	4	8
Nzanga	M	1	1	–	3	0	5
Yembu	M	1	1	1	2	3	8
Imo	M	1	–	–	0	0	1
Possa	M	1	–	1	–	4	6
Lundi	M	1	0	0	1	3	5
Botemo	M	1	–	0	0	1	2
Guyndako	M	1	–	0	1	1	3
Wele	M	1	–	0	0	8	9
Kobele	F	1	–	0	5	5	11
Mbenza	M	1	0	1	1	0	3
Ebake	F	1	1	0	1	0	3
Ejeni	M	1	0	1	–	1	3
Munga	F	1	1	0	0	3	5
Bozjambo	M	1	1	0	2	0	4
Baboko	M	1	0	–	2	4	7
Madiki	M	1	1	0	1	0	3
Njubi	M	1	–	0	1	0	2
Gba Gba	F	1	–	–	2	2	5

^{a} To capture the range of caregivers, all individuals interacting or in proximity to a focal child are given a unique identifier. Mothers and fathers discussed in the analysis are the biological parents of the focal children. Siblings were full brothers and sisters. Children under 4 are not considered allomothers and are eliminated from the analysis. Their elimination is due to the difficulty in determining motivation in a 3-year-old allomother and because the care offered by these children is usually of poorer quality.

^{b} All names are pseudonyms.

^{c} *Others* are all other attachment figures who are not mother, father, grandmothers, or siblings.

Table 4.4 *Principal-components analysis (PCA) loadings[a]
for caregiver responses[b] to attachment behaviors (high
loadings in boldface)*

Variable	Component 1 Sensitive care 44.8% of variance	Component 2 Positive affect 17.3% of variance	Component 3 Negative affect 15.2% of variance
Nurse	**.4596**	−.0776	−.0019
Feed	**.4579**	−.0346	−**.3179**
Watch/check	**.4116**	.0834	−.0047
Vocalize	**.3875**	−.0153	.1150
Physical contact	**.3595**	.0392	.2336
General care	**.3481**	.1087	.1011
Affection	.0080	**.6491**	−.0796
Soothe	.0008	**.6459**	.0033
Reject	.0476	−.2172	**.6914**
Ignore	−.0821	.2941	**.5800**

$n = 157$.
[a] PCA components obtained after varimax rotation.
[b] Caregiver behavior was coded in response to a child's attachment
bout. A bout is a continuous display of attachment behaviors, not
separated by more than 30 seconds. Individual responses were caregiving behaviors that occurred during an attachment display or within
30 seconds following an attachment bout.

underlying variables, or components, for caregiver responses to infants'
attachment behaviors (Table 4.4). Component 1 contains nurse, feed,
watch/check, vocalize, physical contact, and general care; component
2 contains affection and soothe; and component 3 contains positive loads
for reject and ignore, and loads negatively for feed. This component is
most highly characterized by rejecting and ignoring behaviors. The loadings on component 1 indicate sensitive and attentive care, so we have
labeled it sensitive care. Component 2 contains variables related to positive affect, and component 3 is most highly characterized by behaviors
associated with negative affect.

in the data. These components contain all of the information from the original variables, but they are more easily employed in more common statistical techniques, such as
t-tests or linear regression. The technique constructs these latent variables by determining
which of the original variables are correlated to one another. These variables have certain
correlations with the new latent variables, called loadings. A variable is said to "load
highly" on a component if its loading is ±.3. Variables that load highly on a component
define the component and the component can then be named (Kline, 1994).

Using caregiver scores for sensitivity, positive affect, and negative affect, we investigated the caregiving styles of mothers, fathers, grandmothers, siblings, and other nonparental caregivers. As all scores are based on caregivers' responses to attachment bouts that were specifically directed to them, we were able to compare responses by varied attachment figures to equivalent stimuli. A positive association between mothers and others would indicate that children receive consistent responses across their attachment figures, either positive or negative. A negative association would indicate that a child with a mother who scored low on sensitivity had allomothers who were highly sensitive or the reverse. No association indicates that there was no relationship (i.e., no concordance) between maternal and allomaternal response styles.

With a few exceptions, our results indicate minimal concordance between maternal and allomaternal response styles. Siblings represent the clear exception. Siblings demonstrate significant concordance with mothers in regard to sensitive care and trend towards concordance in negative affect. Sibling and maternal positive affect care were not associated. The lack of concordance in positive affective response behavior was not unexpected. We previously found that juveniles are equally as sensitive and just as unlikely to be rejecting as adults. However, juveniles do not score as high on positive affective behaviors as do adults (Meehan and Hawks, 2011, 2013), suggesting that while children are attentive, responsive caregivers, they are not as emotionally aware as adults are (Meehan and Hawks, 2013).

As Aka married couples spend a considerable amount of time together and are able to observe each other's interaction styles throughout the day (Hewlett, 1992), we predicted that paternal and maternal response style would be significantly associated. However, our sample size for investigating concordance in responses to attachment displays between mothers and fathers was limited. Seventy-seven percent of the focal children's parents were married; however, only 61% ($n = 19$) of these children's fathers were present during the observations. If a father was not present at the time of the observation, it clearly eliminated a child's opportunity to display attachment behaviors to them. Furthermore, only twelve out of the nineteen children who had the opportunity to display attachment behaviors to their fathers did so. Nonetheless, there is no indication of concordance in response behavior to children's attachment bouts between mothers and fathers. Maternal and paternal response styles to attachment bouts showed no similarity.

Aka grandmothers represent an important allomaternal category, providing high frequencies of allomaternal care (Meehan, 2008; Meehan et al., 2013). We predicted concordance between maternal and grandmaternal response style; however, several important caveats are noted below. Sample size was again a concern. Twenty-five out of thirty-one children had access to a grandmother; however, only nine of these children displayed attachment behaviors to their grandmother. Thus, we cautiously present results. Results indicate no significant association between maternal and grandmaternal response style to attachment bouts. However, we were not able to conduct separate analyses on maternal and paternal grandmothers. Out of the nine grandmothers who were attachment figures, six were maternal grandmothers and three were paternal grandmothers. We broadly predicted that mothers would mirror the caregiving styles of more experienced and knowledgeable grandmothers, but also assumed that maternal grandmothers and their daughters would have far greater concordance in caregiving styles than would paternal grandmothers and their daughter-in-laws. Unfortunately, sample size precluded us from exploring this question.

We also investigated concordance with other attachment figures. The category of *others* represents the largest percentage of infants' attachment figures (see Table 4.2). These individuals encompass a variety of kin and nonkin categories, men and women, and younger and older individuals. Mean sensitivity, positive affect, and negative affect scores from the PCA analysis were calculated for each focal child's caregivers and compared to the child's mother's response style (Table 4.5). *Others* do not show concordant behavior with mothers in terms of sensitivity or negative affect, although the former show significant concordance in positive affect response behavior.

Effects of mothers and allomothers' responsiveness on child behavior

Previous research noted that allomaternal sensitivity affects children's distress levels during mother–child separations (Meehan and Hawks, 2011, 2013). That finding in combination with our current results, a general lack of concordance in caregiving styles, suggests that children experience variation in felt security across their attachment network. Thus, we examined whether maternal and allomaternal responsiveness, sensitivity, and positive affect or negative affect, influenced child behavior following naturalistic mother–child separations.[3] We focused on child

---

[3] We coded whether the children responded to their mothers at reunion by displaying attachment behaviors or other visual, verbal, or physical means to garner or engage the mother's attention. Behaviors included all attachment behaviors listed in Table 4.1 as well as, *looking, fussing/crying, nondistress vocalizing, shared visual orientation, smiling,* and *physical contact* with mother. Fussing was coded if the child was awake and showed signs of agitation – emitting whining sounds or moans, but was not crying. Crying was recorded if a child was visibly agitated and had tears.

Table 4.5 *Correlation between others' and mothers' responses to attachment behaviors (statistically significant values in boldface)*

	n^a	Maternal sensitivity		Maternal positive affect		Maternal negative affect	
		Pearson's r	p	Pearson's r	p	Pearson's r	p
Sibling sensitivity	19	**.7128**	**<.01**	−.0962	.70	.3570	.13
Sibling positive affect	19	−.1468	.55	.2715	.26	−.3749	.11
Sibling negative affect	19	.1197	.63	−.1628	.51	**.4345**	**.06**
Paternal sensitivity	12	.0396	.90	.0349	.91	−.1779	.58
Paternal positive affect	12	−.1890	.56	−.1617	.62	−.3473	.27
Paternal negative affect	12	−.0747	.82	−.0390	.90	−.3760	.23
Grandmaternal sensitivity	10	−.3480	.32	−.4167	0.23	−.1887	.60
Grandmaternal positive affect	10	−.0051	.99	−.0837	.64	.2937	.41
Grandmaternal negative affect	10	−.2305	.52	.2737	.44	.3618	.30
Other sensitivity[b]	24	.2057	.34	.4226	.04	−.2101	.32
Other positive affect[b]	24	.0866	.69	**.4388**	**.03**	.1274	.55
Other negative affect[b]	24	−.0081	.97	−.0072	.97	.1992	.35

[a] Number of focal infants.
[b] "Other" refers to all other attachment figures (e.g., aunts, uncles, cousins, etc.).

behavior during reunion episodes because mother–child separations are infrequent events and therefore have the potential to cause stress. Aka children were separated from their mothers only approximately 2.9 times across the 9-hour observation period (Meehan and Hawks, 2013), a rate lower than that Ainsworth reported for both the Ganda and Baltimore samples (Ainsworth, 1977). When Aka children are left in the care of others during mother–child separations, some children show clear signs of distress, measured through crying frequency (Meehan and Hawks, 2013). Distress during separations was also noted by Ainsworth (1977) in the Ganda sample. Ganda children loudly protested maternal separations, despite the fact that those who were caring for them were familiar. Ganda allomothers did not mitigate all child stress during separations.

Additionally, while the majority of children quickly seek out or engage their mother upon her return, one-quarter of Aka children were previously found to show no response or ignore their mothers at reunion (Meehan and Hawks, 2013). While we are not able to classify attachment security (i.e., secure, insecure/disorganized, ambivalent/avoidant), the infrequency of separations, child distress during separations, and variation in child responses to their mothers at reunion suggests that observational data during reunion episodes are useful for assessing children's felt security and the mother–child relationship.

We examined the behaviors of children towards their mother during the first 3 minutes of a reunion. Episodes started as a mother re-entered camp following a separation. Naturalistic separations between mothers and children often occur when the mother needs to accomplish a task quickly or when it is more difficult to accomplish while holding a child (e.g., chopping/carrying firewood). We documented whether children engaged their mother through attachment behaviors and other forms of visual, physical, and verbal contact, or whether they did not engage her upon her return.[4]

Maternal responsiveness (sensitivity, positive affect, and negative affect) does not predict child behavior during reunion episodes. There is also no association between sibling, paternal, or grandmaternal responsiveness and children's engagement with their mother at reunion. As mentioned above, the sample size for the individual categories of siblings, fathers, and grandmothers was limited; therefore, we hope to investigate more fully their influence on child behavior at a later date. However, *others*, the largest category of nonmaternal attachment figures, predicted child responsiveness (Table 4.6). *Others'* positive affect scores were marginal, but positively associated with children directing attachment behaviors and physically, verbally, or visually trying to engage their mothers' attention or care. *Others'* negative affect scores were significantly negatively associated with child response at the mother's return. Children with caregivers who score high on positive affect are more likely to engage their mothers upon her return. When children have allomothers who display negative, rejecting behaviors, they are less likely to engage their mothers during reunion episodes. Twenty-nine percent of the variance in infant responsiveness to their mothers at reunion was predicted by children's experience with these nonmaternal attachment figures.

---

[4] There was variation in the frequency of mother–child separations across the focal families. Therefore, we calculated the percentage of times that children engaged and/or ignored their mothers during reunion episodes.

Table 4.6 *Multiple linear regression models showing relationship between allomaternal caregiving style and child behavior following mother–child separations*

	Coefficient (b)	Std. error	p value	Model statistics
Model #1: Percent infant responded to maternal reunion				
Allomaternal positive affect	.4569	0.2631	.099	$n = 22$
Allomaternal negative affect	−.4346	0.1714	.020	$R^2 = .3556$
Constant	.8240	0.1301	<.000	adj. $R^2 = .2878$
				$p = .0154$

Table 4.7 *Multiple linear regression models showing relationship between allomaternal caregiving style and child developmental outcomes*

	Coefficient (b)	Std. error	p value	Model statistics
Model #1: weight for age (residuals)				
Allomaternal negative affect	−1.4945	0.8552	.094	$n = 24$
Constant	−.4440	0.3592	.230	$R^2 = .1219$
				adj. $R^2 = .0820$
				$p = .0945$
Model #2: height for age (residuals)				
Allomaternal negative affect	−6.1803	2.6559	.030	$n = 24$
Constant	−2.1721	1.1156	.064	$R^2 = .1975$
				adj. $R^2 = .1610$
				$p = .0296$

Effects of mothers and others on early childhood developmental outcomes

Lastly, we explored whether variation in attachment figures' responsiveness affected early childhood developmental outcomes (Table 4.7). Previous research among urban Chilean infants showed higher incidence of disorganized attachment among infants who chronically failed to attain appropriate weight for age (Valenzuela, 1990). Aka focal children's expected height- and weight-for-age residuals were calculated. We again used caregivers' PCA scores for sensitivity and positive affect, and negative affect as measures for children's experience with attachment figures.

Overall caregiver responsiveness (mothers and all allomothers), maternal responsiveness, and overall allomaternal responsiveness were not predictive of children's height and weight for age. However, on closer examination, the category of *others* again demonstrated a small, but significant effect on children's early growth. Others' negative affect, which as we mentioned above was predictive of child nonresponsiveness during mother–child reunion episodes, was negatively associated with expected height and weight for age in children. The fact that the adjusted R^2 values are quite low is not unexpected. Childhood growth and overall health are informed by a multitude of genetic and environmental factors. However, our results offer some evidence that allomothers' caregiving style influences not only child behaviors but also early childhood developmental outcomes.

Discussion

Our focus for this chapter was to highlight the extent of nonmaternal attachment figures and explore the impact of these individuals on children. We chose to present data among a small-scale foraging population, as there is a dearth of data on the role and effect of nonmaternal caregivers in attachment theory, and forager populations offer an opportunity to examine these issues. Aka children form attachment relationships with a subset of their larger caregiving network (see also Meehan and Hawks, 2013). Attachment networks are large and attachment figures represent a variety of kin, nonkin, sex, and age categories. Furthermore, attachment figures are frequently individuals outside children's closest familial relationships (i.e., *not* fathers, grandmothers, or siblings). The variety of individuals with whom children form attachment relationships also suggests that research that emphasizes caregivers who are prominent in Western societies may underestimate children's attachment networks.

Previous research by us and others (Hewlett, 1991; Hewlett *et al.*, 2000; Meehan, 2005a, 2009; Meehan and Hawks, 2013) show that Aka mothers, fathers, and alloparents are highly responsive caregivers. The positive and trusting view of their environment and others has been argued, in part, to be the consequence of such warm, sensitive, and responsive caregiving received in infancy and early childhood (Hewlett *et al.*, 2000). Yet, until now, we knew little about intracultural variation in caregiving styles. Our results indicate that children do not always receive concordant responses to attachment bouts from mothers and allomothers. Maternal and sibling sensitive and negative affect behaviors were concordant, but we found no concordance between mothers and fathers, or mothers and grandmothers. With the exception of positive affect, there was no association between mothers and *others*. These results suggest that siblings model their interactions with latter-born siblings after their own experiences with their mother and observation of their mother's behavior to the focal child. The lack of concordance in most other categories estab-lishes clear intracultural variation in Aka caregiver interaction styles and suggests that children's felt security across caregivers is not consistent. Additionally, the lack of concordance between caregiver's response styles provides an important case study to examine questions surrounding the organization of internal working models. If children experience variation in responsiveness across their attachment network, how do these poten-tially discordant relationships affect children's felt security, their primary attachment relationship, and the organization of their internal working model?

It was not possible for us to examine later socioemotional functioning, a key analytic measurement in previous research examining the organi-zation of internal working models (van IJzendoorn and Sagi-Schwartz, 2008; van IJzendoorn *et al.*, 1992). However, we used children's behav-ior during reunion episodes as a measurement of child-felt security and early growth indicators as a measurement of the effects of the attach-ment network on child outcomes. Focusing on caregiver responsiveness and indicators of children's felt security enabled us to explore whether children's relationships with their mother and others was domain specific or whether there was evidence that children integrate their attachment relationships.

The cross-cultural evidence regarding multiple attachments and the role that others play is unmistakably at odds with monotropy (van IJzen-doorn *et al.*, 1992). Even the hierarchy model neglects to include the contributions of allomothers who are clearly affecting children's secu-rity and development (van IJzendoorn *et al.*, 1992). Aka children are reared in a culture where they are surrounded by familiar individuals. Caregiving and attachment networks are stable, and these relationships begin at birth and form simultaneously with the mother–child attachment relationship; thus, to suggest that they are an ineffective determinate of children's development conflicts with our results. Allomaternal respon-siveness affects children's behavior during naturalistic mother–child sep-arations (Meehan and Hawks, 2013), and, as we show here, it affects how children interact with their mothers following separation. Children with allomothers who scored low on positive affect and high on negative affect were significantly less likely to respond to their mother at reunion. Additionally, others' negative affect scores were positively associated with lower than expected height and weight for age, suggesting that there are not only emotional but also physical consequences to children's nonma-ternal attachment relationships.

These results provide some evidence that in a multiple caregiving soci-ety, such as that of the Aka, children's overall sense of felt security results from the integration of multiple attachment relationships. We do not see any kind of "specialization" by other caregivers (van IJzendoorn *et al.*, 1992). That is, Aka life does not consist of separate settings where children only interact with particular attachment figures in specific contexts. Daily life is open and public, with no distinct times when one should work, play, etc.

Clearly, one of the most interesting patterns that emerged was that allomaternal, not maternal, responsiveness (sensitivity, positive affect, and negative affect) was predictive of both child behavior during reunion episodes and to a small extent, early growth indicators. The lack of association between maternal responsiveness and child behavior or outcomes in these analyses might suggest that measuring responsiveness to attachment bouts may not be key to determining the ways in which children form and assess their attachment relationships with their mother. That maternal responsiveness to attachment bouts was not predictive of child behavior or outcomes certainly does not indicate that mothers' caregiving style is unimportant to the child's felt security or socioemotional functioning. Rather, the results indicate that the mother–child attachment relationship is formed and assessed in a different manner. Mothers are the child's most intimate caregiver, providing the majority of care, breast-feeding, and holding early in life (Meehan *et al.*, 2013). *Others*, while frequent participants, by any cross-cultural standard, do not spend as much individual time with the child as mothers and immediate family members. Therefore, evaluation of children's attachment relationships with others is based on fewer interactions. Due to the frequency of mother–child interaction, one instance of maternal rejection may not be as significant as a rejection by another.

It is also important to note that Aka children share a family bed, only 50–70 cm wide, with their mothers, fathers, and siblings (Hewlett, 1992, 2007). The close quarters result in skin-to-skin contact, enabling children many opportunities to monitor and assess their relationships with these individuals. Communal sleeping arrangements are argued to be particularly important to the development of a primary attachment relationship in multiple caregiving environments (Sagi, van IJzendoorn, Aviezer *et al.*, 1994; van IJzendoorn *et al.*, 1992) and may offer additional insight into why others' responsiveness to attachment behaviors was more predictive of children's behavior during reunion than that of mothers, fathers, and siblings. Children's assessment of felt security with their immediate family may be in response to their overall level of interaction throughout the day and night and not simply when they express attachment behaviors. This does not explain why Aka grandmothers' responsiveness was not predictive, although the grandmother–child relationship is also quite intimate. Grandmothers are one of the highest investing allomothers, meaning they spend a considerable amount of time in direct contact with their grandchildren (Meehan, 2008; Meehan *et al.*, 2013). Additionally, co-sleeping with grandmothers occurs, although usually at older ages (Hewlett, 2007).

We recognize several limitations to this study. First, we have a relatively small sample size, an inherent consequence of the time necessary to collect detailed behavioral and network data on children. Second, we realize that we focus on measurements of caregiver responsiveness and indicators of child's felt security, not measurements of attachment security (i.e., the strange-situation procedure). However, one of the primary goals of this chapter was to document the density, breadth, and characteristics of attachment relationships in a small-scale, cooperative, child-rearing society, a goal that cannot be achieved through the use of traditional attachment security measurements. As mentioned earlier, selecting particular categories of caregivers would have resulted in an ethnocentric bias based on Western socioecology. We chose naturalistic observations of these attachment relationships to gain an accurate representation of a child's attachment network.

Early in this chapter, we emphasized that the mother–child dyad does not exist in isolation. Cross-culturally, allomothers play an essential role in childcare; provisioning; maternal behavior; and the child's physical, social, and emotional development (see references herein). Despite these findings, nonmaternal caregivers have yet to be fully integrated into the mainstream of attachment studies. We, as others have before us, argue that specifically focusing on the mother–child relationship may limit our understanding of who and what contributes to maternal responsiveness, the mother–child attachment relationship, and the organization of children's internal working models (Howes and Spieker, 2008; Thompson, 2000; van IJzendoorn *et al.*, 1992). The majority of children in the world are born into a dense social world, childcare is a joint venture, and child development occurs within this social framework. That framework is essential to understanding attachment.

References

Ahnert, L. (2005). Parenting and alloparenting: the impact on attachment in humans. In C. S. Carter, L. Ahnert, K. E. Grossmann, S. B. Hrdy, M. E. Lamb, S. W. Porges, and N. Sachser (Eds.), *Attachment and bonding: a new synthesis* (pp. 229–44). Cambridge, MA: MIT Press.

Ainsworth, M. D. S. (1967). *Infancy in Uganda: infant care and the growth of love.* Baltimore, MD: Johns Hopkins University Press.

(1977). Infant development and the mother–infant interaction among Ganda and American families. In P. H. Leiderman, S. R. Tulkin, and A. Rosenfeld

(Eds.), *Culture and infancy: variations in the human experience* (pp. 119–49). New York: Academic Press.

Altmann, J. (1974). Observational study of behavior: sampling methods. *Behaviour, 49,* 227–67.

Bahuchet, S. (1990). Food sharing among the pygmies of Central Africa. *African Study Monographs, 11,* 27–53.

(1991). Spatial mobility and access to resources among the African Pygmies. In M. S. Casimir and A. Rao (Eds.), *Mobility and territoriality* (pp. 205–57). New York: Berg.

Beck, C. T. (1995). The effects of postpartum depression on maternal–infant interaction: a meta-analysis. *Nursing Research, 44*(5), 298–304.

Beise, J. (2005). The helping and the helpful grandmother: the role of maternal and paternal grandmothers in child morality in the seventeenth- and eighteen-century population of French settlers in Quebec, Canada. In E. Voland, A. Chasiotis, and W. Schiefendhovel (Eds.), *Grandmotherhood: the evolutionary significance of the second half of female life* (pp. 215–38). New Brunswick, NJ: Rutgers University Press.

Bird-David, N. (1990). The giving environment: another perspective on the economic system of gatherer-hunters. *Current Anthropology, 31*(2), 189–96.

Blurton Jones, N. G., Hawkes, K., and O'Connell, J. F. (2005). Older Hadza men and women as helpers: residence data. In Hewlett and Lamb, *Hunter-gatherer childhoods,* pp. 214–36.

Bowlby, J. (1969). *Attachment and loss,* vol. I: *Attachment.* New York: Perseus Books.

(1973). *Attachment and loss,* vol. II: *Separation: anxiety and anger.* New York: Basic Books.

Burkart, J. M., Hrdy, S. B., and van Schaik, C. P. (2009). Cooperative breeding and human cognitive evolution. *Evolutionary Anthropology: Issues, News, and Reviews, 18,* 175–86.

Chisholm, J. (1999). *Death, hope, and sex: steps to an evolutionary ecology of mind and morality.* Cambridge University Press.

Crittenden, A. N., and Marlowe, F. W. (2008). Allomaternal care among the Hadza of Tanzania. *Human Nature, 19,* 249–62.

Crnic, K. A., Greenburg, M. T., Ragozin, A. S., Robinson, N. M., and Basham, R. B. (1983). Effects of stress and social support on mother and premature and full-term infants. *Child Development, 54*(1), 209–17.

Dykas, M. J., and Cassidy, J. (2011). Attachment and the processing of social information across the life span: theory and evidence. *Psychological Bulletin, 137*(1), 19–46.

Euler, H., and Weitzel, B. (1996). Discriminative grandparental solicitude as reproductive strategy. *Human Nature, 7,* 39–59.

Flinn, M. V. (1989). Household composition and female reproductive strategies. In A. Rasa, C. Vogel, and E. Voland (Eds.), *Sexual and reproductive strategies* (pp. 206–33). London: Chapman and Hall.

Flinn, M. V., and Leone, D. (2009). Alloparental care and the ontogeny of glucocorticoid stress response among stepchildren. In G. R. Bentley and R. Mace (Eds.), *Substitute parents: biological and social perspectives on alloparenting in human societies* (pp. 212–31). Oxford: Berghahn Books.

Fouts, H. N. (2011). Multiple caregivers' touch interactions with young children among the Bofi foragers in central Africa. *International Journal of Psychology*, 46(1), 24–32.

Fouts, H. N., Hewlett, B. S., and Lamb, M. E. (2001). Weaning and the nature of early childhood interactions among Bofi foragers in central Africa. *Human Nature*, 12(1), 27–46.

Gottlieb, A. (2004). *The afterlife is where we come from: the culture of infancy in West Africa*. University of Chicago Press.

Gurven, M. (2004). To give and to give not: the behavioral ecology of human food transfers. *Behavioral and Brain Sciences*, 27, 543–83.

Hagen, E. (1999). The functions of postpartum depression. *Evolution and Human Behavior*, 20, 325–59.

Hawkes, K., O'Connell, J. F., and Blurton Jones, N. G. (1997). Hazda women's time allocation, offspring provisioning, and the evolution of long post-menopausal life spans. *Current Anthropology*, 38, 551–77.

Hawkes, K., O'Connell, J. F., Blurton Jones, N. G., Charnov, E. L., and Alvarez, H. P. (1998). Grandmothering, menopause, and the evolution of human life histories. *Proceedings of the National Academy of Sciences of the United States of America*, 95, 1336–9.

Hewlett, B. S. (1991). *Intimate fathers: the nature and context of Aka Pygmy paternal infant care*. Ann Arbor, MI: University of Michigan Press.

(1992). Husband–wife reciprocity and the father–infant relationship among Aka pygmies. In B. S. Hewlett (Ed.), *Father–child relations: cultural and biosocial contexts* (pp. 153–76). New York: Aldine de Gruyter.

(2007). Why sleep alone? An integrated evolutionary approach to intra-cultural and intercultural variability in Aka, Ngandu, and Euro-American co-sleeping. Paper presented at the annual meeting of the Society for Cross-Cultural Research, San Antonio, TX.

Hewlett, B. S., Fouts, H. N., Boyette, A. H., and Hewlett, B. L. (2011). Social learning among Congo basin hunter-gatherers. *Philosophical Transactions of the Royal Society of London. Series B, Biological Sciences*, 366, 1168–78.

Hewlett, B. S., and Lamb, M. E. (2002). Integrating evolution, culture, and developmental psychology: explaining caregiver–infant proximity and responsiveness in central Africa and the USA. In H. Keller, Y. H. Poortinga, and A. Scholmerich (Eds.), *Between culture and biology: perspectives on ontogenetic development* (pp. 241–69). Cambridge University Press.

(Eds.) (2005). *Hunter-gatherer childhoods: evolutionary, developmental, and cultural perspectives*. New Brunswick, NJ: Aldine Transaction.

Hewlett, B. S., Lamb, M. E., Leyendecker, B., and Scholmerich, A. (2000). Internal working models, trust, and sharing among foragers. *Current Anthropology*, 41, 287–97.

Hewlett, B. S, Lamb, M. E., Shannon, D., Leyendecker, B., and Scholmerich, A. (1998). Culture and early infancy among central African foragers and farmers. *Developmental Psychology*, 34, 653–1.

Hill, K. (2002). Altruistic cooperation during foraging by the Ache, and the evolved human predisposition to cooperate. *Human Nature*, 13(1), 105–28.

Hill, K., Walker, R. S., Bozicevic, M., Eder, J., Headland, T., Hewlett, B., Hurtado, A. M., *et al.* (2011). Co-residence patterns in hunter-gatherer societies show unique human social structure. *Science, 331,* 1286–9.

Howes, C., and Spieker, S. (2008). Attachment relationships in the context of multiple caregivers. In J. Cassidy and P. Shaver (Eds.), *The handbook of attachment: theory, research, and clinical applications* (2nd edn., pp. 317–32). New York: Guilford Press.

Hrdy, S. B. (1999). *Mother nature: a history of mothers, infants, and natural selection.* New York: Pantheon Books.

(2005a). Comes the child before man: how cooperative breeding and prolonged post-weaning dependence shaped human potential. In Hewlett and Lamb, *Hunter-gatherer childhoods,* pp. 65–91.

(2005b). Evolutionary context of human development: the cooperative breeding model. In C. S. Carter and L. Ahnert (Eds.), *Attachment and bonding: a new synthesis* (pp. 9–32). Cambridge, MA: MIT Press.

(2007). Evolutionary context of human development: the cooperative breeding model. In C. A. Salmon and T. K. Shackelford (Eds.), *Family relationships: an evolutionary perspective* (pp. 39–68). New York: Oxford University Press.

(2009). *Mothers and others: the evolutionary origins of mutual understanding.* Cambridge, MA: Belknap Press of Harvard University.

Ivey, P. K. (2000). Cooperative reproduction in Ituri Forest hunter-gatherers: who cares for Efe infants? *Current Anthropology, 41*(5), 856–66.

Ivey Henry, P., Morelli, G. A., and Tronick, E. Z. (2005). Child caretakers among the Efe foragers of the Ituri Forest. In Hewlett and Lamb, *Hunter-gatherer childhoods,* pp. 347–88.

Jacobson, S. W., and Frye, K. F. (1991). Effect of maternal social support on attachment: experimental evidence. *Child Development, 62*(3), 572–82.

Jamison, C. S., Cornell, L. L., Jamison, P. L., and Nakazato, H. (2002). Are all grandmothers equal? A review and a preliminary test of the 'grandmother hypothesis' in Tokugawa, Japan. *American Journal of Physical Anthropology, 119,* 67–76.

Kaplan, H. (1994). Evolutionary and wealth flows theories of fertility: empirical tests and new models. *Population and Development Review, 20,* 753–91.

Kermoian, R., and Leiderman, P. H. (1986). Infant attachment to mother and child caretaker in an East African community. *International Journal of Behavioral Development, 9,* 455–69.

Kline, P. (1994). *An easy guide to factor analysis.* New York: Routledge.

Konner, M. J. (2005). Hunter-gatherer infancy and childhood: the !Kung and others. In Hewlett and Lamb, *Hunter-gatherer childhoods,* pp. 19–64.

Kramer, K. L. (2005). Children's help and the pace of reproduction: cooperative breeding in humans. *Evolutionary Anthropology, 14,* 224–37.

(2010). Cooperative breeding and its significance to the demographic success of humans. *Annual Review of Anthropology, 39,* 417–36.

Kramer, K. L., and Ellison, P. T. (2010). Pooled energy budgets: resituating human energy-allocation trade-offs. *Evolutionary Anthropology, 19,* 136–47.

Kruger, A., and Konner, M. (2010). Who responds to crying? *Human Nature, 21,* 309–29.

Lamb, M. E. (Ed.) (1999). *Parenting and child development in "nontraditional" families.* Mahwah, NJ: Erlbaum.

Lamb, M. E., and Lewis, C. (2010). The development and significance of father–child relationships in two-parent families. In M. E. Lamb (Ed.), *The role of the father in child development* (5th edn., pp. 94–153). Hoboken, NJ: Wiley.

Lamb, M. E., Thompson, R., Gardner, W. P., Charnov, E., and Estes, D. (1984). Security of infantile attachment as assessed in the strange situation: its study and biological interpretation. *Behavioral and Brain Sciences, 7,* 127–47.

Lancy, D. F. (2008). *The anthropology of childhood: cherubs, chattel, changelings.* Cambridge University Press.

Leonetti, D. L., Nath, D. C., Heman, N. S., and Neill, D. B. (2005). Kinship organization and the impact of grandmothers on reproductive success among the matrilineal Khasis and patrilineal Bengali of northeast India. In E. Voland, A. Chasiotis, and W. Schiefenhovel (Eds.), *Grandmotherhood: the evolutionary significance of the second half of the female life* (pp. 195–214). New Brunswick, NJ: Rutgers University Press.

Lyons-Ruth, K., Connell, D. B., Grunebaum, H. U., and Botein, S. (1990). Infants at social risk: maternal depression and family support services as mediators of infant development and security of attachment. *Child Development, 61*(1), 85–98.

Marlowe, F. (2005). Who tends Hadza children? In Hewlett and Lamb, *Hunter-gatherer childhoods,* pp. 177–190.

Marvin, R. S., van Devender, T. L., Iwanaga, M. I., LeVine, S., and LeVine, R. A. (1977). Infant–caregiver attachment among the Hausa of Nigeria. In H. McGurk (Ed.), *Ecological factors in human development* (pp. 247–60). New York: North-Holland.

Meehan, C. L. (2005a). The effects of residential locality on parental and alloparental investment among the Aka of the Central African Republic. *Human Nature, 16,* 58–80.

(2005b). Multiple caregiving and its effect on maternal behavior among the Aka foragers and the Ngandu farmers of central Africa. Unpublished Ph.D. dissertation, Department of Anthropology, Washington State University.

(2008). Cooperative breeding in humans: an examination of childcare networks among foragers and farmers. Paper presented at the American Anthropological Association Meeting, Philadelphia, PA.

(2009). Maternal time allocation in cooperative childrearing societies. *Human Nature, 20,* 375–93.

(2013). Allomothers and child well-being. In A. Ben-Arieh, F. Casas, I. Frones, and J. E. Korbin (Eds.), *Handbook of child well-being: theories, methods and policies in global perspective (pp. 1787–1816).* Dordrecht: Springer.

Meehan, C. L., and Hawks, S. (2011). Cooperative breeding and attachment in early childhood: a case study among the Aka. Paper presented at the Lemelson/Society for Psychological Anthropology Conference: Rethinking Attachment and Separation in Cross-Cultural Perspective, Spokane, WA.

(2013). Cooperative breeding and attachment among the Aka foragers. In N. Quinn and J. Mageo (Eds.), *Attachment reconsidered: cultural perspectives on a Western theory* (pp. 85–113). New York: Palgrave Macmillan.

Meehan, C. L., Quinlan, R., and Malcolm, C. D. (2013). Cooperative breeding and maternal energy expenditure among Aka foragers. *American Journal of Human Biology*, 25(1), 42–57.

Olds, D., Henderson, C., Jr., Chamberlin, R., and Tatelbaum, R. (1986). Preventing child abuse and neglect: a randomized trial of nurse home visitation. *Pediatrics*, *78*, 65–78.

(2002). Preventing child abuse and neglect: a randomized controlled trial. *Pediatrics*, *110*, 486–496.

Pashos, A. (2000). Does paternal uncertainty explain grandparental solicitude? A cross-cultural study in Greece and Germany. *Evolution and Human Behavior*, *21*, 97–109.

Sagi, A., van IJzendoorn, M. H., Aviezer, O., Donnell, F., Koren-Karie, N., Joels, T., and Harel, Y. (1995). Attachments in a multiple-caregiver and multiple-infant environment: the case of the Israeli kibbutzim. *Monographs of the Society for Research in Child Development*, *60*, 71–91.

Sagi, A., van IJzendoorn, M. H., Aviezer, O., Donnell, F., and Mayseless, O. (1994). Sleeping out of home in a kibbutz communal arrangement: it makes a difference for infant–mother attachment. *Child Development*, *64*, 992–1004.

Sear, R., and Mace, R. (2009). Family matters: kin, demography, and child health in a rural Gambian population. In G. Bently and R. Mace (Eds.), *Substitute parents: biological and social perspective on alloparenting in human societies* (pp. 50–76). Oxford: Berghahn Books.

Sear, R., Mace, R., and McGregor, I. A. (2000). Maternal grandmothers improve nutritional status and survival of children in rural Gambia. *Proceedings of the Royal Society of London. Series B, Biological Sciences*, *267*, 1641–7.

Sear, R., Steele, F., McGregor, I. A., and Mace, R. (2002). The effects of kin on child mortality in rural Gambia. *Demography*, *39*, 43–63.

Seymour, S. (2004). Multiple caretaking of infants and young children: an area in critical need of a feminist psychological anthropology. *Ethos*, *32*, 538–56.

Silk, J. B. (2006). Who are more helpful, humans or chimpanzees? *Science*, *311*, 1248–9.

Slykerman, R. F., Thompson, J. M. D., Pryor, J. E., Becroft, D. M. O., Robinson, E., Clark, P. M., Wild, C. J., *et al.* (2005). Maternal stress, social support and preschool children's intelligence. *Early Human Development*, *81*(10), 815–21.

Spieker, S. J., and Bensley, L. (1994). Roles of living arrangements and grandmother social support in adolescent mothering and infant attachment. *Developmental Psychology*, *30*(1), 102–11.

Thompson, R. A. (2000). The legacy of early attachments. *Child Development*, *71*, 145–52.

Tronick, E. Z., Morelli, G. A., and Ivey, P. K. (1992). The Efe forager infant and toddler's pattern of social relationships: multiple and simultaneous. *Developmental Psychology*, *28*, 568–77.

Tronick, E. Z., Morelli, G. A., and Winn, S. (1987). Multiple caretaking of Efe (pygmy) infants. *American Anthropologist*, *89*, 96–106.

True, M. M. (1994). Mother–infant attachment and communication among the Dogon of Mali. Unpublished Ph.D. dissertation, Department of Psychology, University of California, Berkley.

Turke, P. (1988). Helpers at the nest: child care networks on Ifaluk. In L. Betzig, M. Borgerhoff-Mulder, and P. Turke (Eds.), *Human reproductive behavior* (pp. 173–88). Cambridge University Press.

Valenzuela, M. (1990). Attachment in chronically underweight young children. *Child Development, 61,* 1984–96.

van IJzendoorn, M. H., Sagi, A., and Lambermon, M. W. E. (1992). The multiple caretaker paradox: data from Holland and Israel. *New Directions for Child and Adolescent Development, 57,* 5–24.

van IJzendoorn, M. H., and Sagi-Schwartz, A. (2008). Cross-cultural patterns of attachment: universal and contextual dimensions. In J. Cassidy and P. R. Shaver (Eds.), *Handbook of attachment: theory, research, and clinical applications* (pp. 880–905). New York: Guilford Press.

Vermeer, H. J., and Bakermans-Kranenburg, M. J. (2008). Attachment to mother and nonmaternal care: bridging the gap. *Attachment and Human Development, 10,* 263–73.

Verschueren, K., Marcoen, A., and Schoefs, V. (1996). The internal working model of self, attachment, and competence in five-year-olds. *Child Development, 67,* 2495–2503.

Voland, E., and Beise, J. (2005). The husband's mother is the devil in house: data on the impact of the mother-in-law on stillbirth mortality in historical Krummhörn (1750–1874) and some thoughts on the evolution of the post-reproductive female life. In E. Voland, A. Chasiotis, and W. Schiefendhovel (Eds.), *Grandmotherhood: the evolutionary significance of the second half of female life* (pp. 239–276). New Brunswick, NJ: Rutgers University Press.

5 Bonding and belonging beyond WEIRD worlds: rethinking attachment theory on the basis of cross-cultural anthropological data

Birgitt Röttger-Rössler

Introduction

Henrich, Heine, and Norenzayen (2010) have complained that the majority of psychological statements claiming universal validity are actually based on empirical studies of samples consisting exclusively of WEIRD (*W*estern, *E*ducated, *I*ndustrialized, *R*ich, and *D*emocratic) people – that is, people who form a very particular and small part of the world population.[1] This criticism also applies to the attachment theory formulated by the psychoanalyst and pediatrician John Bowlby (1969), and further developed by his student Mary Ainsworth (Ainsworth, 1967; Ainsworth, Bell, and Stayton, 1974; Ainsworth, Blehar, Waters *et al.*, 1978), that continues to hold – despite increasing criticism – a central position in developmental psychology. One major criticism addresses the "cultural blindness" of attachment theory (LeVine and Norman, 2001; Otto, 2011; Rothbaum, Weisz, Pott *et al.*, 2000). Although Bowlby (1982, p. 50) certainly considered the cultural context to be important in his conceptions and Mary Ainsworth laid the foundations of her work in a study carried out in Uganda, neither John Bowlby nor Mary Ainsworth nor subsequent attachment theorists have paid any systematic attention to culture and integrated this into the theory as a decisive element (Otto, 2011).

---

[1] Henrich *et al.* (2010) have shown that the bulk of the database in the experimental branches of psychology, cognitive science, and economics is about Western, and more specifically American, undergraduates. He and his coauthors analyzed the leading journals in six subdisciplines of psychology between 2003 and 2007 and found that 68% of subjects came from the USA and 96% from Western, industrialized countries. The majority of samples (80%) were composed solely of undergraduates in psychology and the make-up of these samples appeared to reflect the country of residence of the authors: 73% of first authors were at American universities and 99% were at universities in Western countries. "This means that 96 per cent of psychological samples come from countries with only 12 per cent of the world's population" (Henrich *et al.*, 2010, p. 63).

In this chapter, I shall critically examine some central hypotheses of attachment theory and draw on empirical data from an Indonesian society to show how these assumptions are based on Eurocentric axioms that transfer in only a very limited way to other cultural contexts.

Attachment theory

Attachment theory focuses on the prolonged period of helplessness in human infants – that is, on infants' biologically given need to elicit their mothers' or caregivers' protection and care. According to Bowlby (1969, 1982), attachment behaviors such as smiling, crying, clinging to, or approaching the mother are rooted in evolution, providing a survival advantage by increasing mother–child proximity and thus maximizing the beneficial outcomes a mother can provide. Bowlby assumes that the attachment behavioral system is activated primarily by stress either arising within the child (e.g., pain, hunger) or induced by external cues (e.g., an unfamiliar person, a loud noise, etc.). Caregivers normally respond intuitively to infant stress signals and help their infants to regain their physical and mental equilibrium through appropriate caring behaviors. According to Bowlby, a child's attachment builds up over several phases during the first year of life. Whereas, initially, in the "preattachment" phase (first–sixth week of life), infants can switch caregivers with hardly any problems arising, the following 6 months reveals an increasingly close attachment to one or more caregivers ("attachment in the making") that then consolidates as the infant becomes increasingly mobile after the seventh or eighth month of life and reveals clear contours by the age of 1 year ("clear-cut attachment").

Bowlby postulates that the kinds of attachment experienced in early infancy are represented mentally in an "internal working model" that decisively influences the child's further socioemotional development and her own ability to form attachments.

Mary Ainsworth, a student and colleague of John Bowlby, extended this theoretical model and made it accessible to empirical analysis. While engaged in field research in Uganda, she observed everyday mother–child interactions and, above all, how children react when the mother suddenly disappears from their reach and sight. Ainsworth established that the children's reactions could be classified into three groups: most children reacted to the mother's disappearance with pain of separation (crying) and to her reappearance with signals of joy (laughter, crawling towards the mother), before soon going back to exploring their environment from the secure base of their mother's presence. Ainsworth described these children as being securely attached. Some children displayed no emotions at all either when their mother disappeared or reappeared; they seemed to be unimpressed by their mothers' presence or absence, and simply carried on doing whatever they were doing. Ainsworth called this group the "insecure-avoidant" (anxious-avoidant) children. A further proportion of the children reacted excessively and contradictorily (simultaneously sad and angry) to their mother's disappearance and exhibited very ambivalent behavior when she returned – that is, equally consoled and angry, both clinging to the mother and spurning her. Ainsworth classified these children as having an "insecure-ambivalent" (anxious-resistant) attachment. Later, Ainsworth tried to replicate these findings in the USA, but found that 1-year-old American children who were at home – that is, in a familiar environment – were not upset when their mothers left them. Therefore, she developed an experimental design, the so-called strange situation, which is a kind of minidrama with fixed sequences: children and their mothers are invited to an unfamiliar laboratory where the children are first confronted with a stranger in the presence of their mothers. In a later sequence, the mothers leave the child alone with this stranger.[2] According to attachment theory, the child's reactions to the departure and the return of the mother provide indications regarding the child's attachment security, the type of attachment. The strange situation became the central methodological paradigm in psychological attachment research. However, as Otto (2011, p. 410) emphasizes, this represents a paradox, because during the course of the attachment research hype of subsequent years, the method originally developed as an adaptation to the US context was transferred to the greatest range of different cultures:

> Since then, hundreds of babies with the most different socio-cultural background have had and continue to have their attachment behavior classified according to the Strange Situation although the appropriateness of the procedure for the specific context mostly remained untested. (Otto, 2011, p. 410, translated)[3]

Using the strange situation in their American study in Baltimore, Ainsworth *et al.* (1978) found a correlation between children's attachment security and maternal interaction style: children who were handled sensitively by their mothers displayed a high attachment security in the strange situation, whereas those with less sensitive mothers more

---

[2] The strange situation is always videographed, thus making it easy to reproduce and assess.
[3] LeVine and Norman (2001, p. 129) suspect that the attractiveness of this method "is due to its evolutionary rationale, its convenient and reliable assessment procedure (the videotaped Strange Situation), and its clinically interpretable categories (secure–insecure, optimal–suboptimal, sensitive–insensitive) – all features that are problematic from an anthropological point of view."

frequently displayed insecure attachment behavior. This "maternal sensitivity" forms a key concept in the attachment-theory approach and is defined according to Ainsworth through (1) the reliable perception and (2) correct interpretation of the child's signals, as well as (3) appropriate and (4) prompt reactions by the mothers.

The central theses of the attachment theory formulated by Bowlby and Ainsworth can be summarized into four key assumptions (Rothbaum *et al.*, 2000; Otto, 2011, p. 399):

(1) *Universality:* all neonates (except those with major neurophysiological damage) develop an attachment to their attachment figure or figures during the first year of life.

(2) *Sensitivity:* the most important precondition for infant attachment security is sensitive parental behavior.

(3) *Normativity:* the majority of children in all societies develop a secure attachment; uncertain attachments are found in only up to 40% of cases.[4]

(4) *Competence:* attachment security leads to a more competent coping with further socioemotional and cognitive developmental tasks, whereas the other two insecure-avoidant forms of attachment are taken to be suboptimal preconditions for further child development.

The pattern of attachment consistent with healthy development is that of secure attachment, in which the individual is confident that his parent (or parent figure) will be available, responsive, and helpful should he encounter adverse or frightening situations. With this assurance he feels bold in his explorations of the world and also competent in dealing with it. This pattern is found to be promoted by a parent in the early years especially by a mother being readily available, sensitive to her child's signals, and lovingly responsive when he seeks protection and/or comfort and/or assistance. (Bowlby, 1988, p. 166)

In the following, I shall use ethnographic data from an Indonesian society to critically discuss the central assumptions of attachment theory sketched above. I shall start descriptively, by giving an insight into the most important aspects of the socialization practices and parenting models among the Makassar in Indonesia along with the attachment models to be found in this society. Based on this material, I shall consider the implications of the sensitivity and competence hypotheses and discuss how far the strange situation is an appropriate method for studying attachment

---

[4] In their definitive American study, Mary Ainsworth and her colleagues used the strange situation to gather data from 106 one-year-old children from Baltimore. They found the following distribution of attachment styles: 66% securely attached children, 12% anxious-resistant children, and 22% anxious-avoidant children (Ainsworth *et al.*, 1978). This distribution was confirmed in later cross-cultural studies (e.g., van IJzendoorn and Kroonenberg, 1988) and is now taken to be the standard normal distribution.

behavior in societies whose social, economic, and familial structures are organized in completely different ways from those of WEIRD people and whose children thereby grow up under completely different socialization conditions and demands. I shall supplement this discussion with some ideas on the role of childhood agency. This has received hardly any attention in attachment research, although I believe it represents a significant analytical dimension with which to distinguish societal attachment ideologies from actual practices.

Beyond mothers: an ethnographic example

Recent developmental and attachment research, above all, in cultural psychology, has already stressed repeatedly that mothers cannot always be viewed as the child's central reference person and therefore *attachment figure* in all societies. In many cases, a larger social grouping – mostly in the form of multigenerational families – in which not only aunts, uncles, and grandparents but also, particularly, older siblings play a decisive role, is responsible for rearing children ("alloparenting" or "multiple caregiving").[5] Gottlieb (this volume) gives a fascinating picture of how Beng children from the Ivory Coast grow up in extended family groupings.

The relations described by Gottlieb strongly match socialization conditions among the Makassar, a hierarchically organized Islamic society indigenous to the Indonesian island of Sulawesi. There are about 2 million Makassar, who subsist on rice cultivation in the interior and fishing and sea trade on the coast. The following description is based on several field studies that I carried out between 1984 and 2007 in a prototypical highland village in the Gowa district of south Sulawesi. The main source of income in this village is rice cultivation.[6]

Following birth, mother and infant spend their first 4–6 weeks together in the closest possible contact. During this postnatal period, neither may leave the house; they remain completely indoors where they are cared for and receive visitors. They are allowed to leave the house only after going through a purification ritual, the *atturungeng* (BM).[7] This is

[5] See, for example, Hrdy (2005).
[6] Most of the data presented here were gathered during two 1-year periods of field research (1984–5; 1990–1). During later field visits, I noticed no changes from the conditions described here in rural contexts, although I did not use these visits to systematically study changes in the forms of socialization.
[7] Terms in the local language, Bicara Mangkasara, are marked by the abbreviation *BM*, while idioms in the national language of Indonesia, Bahasa Indonesia, are marked by the abbreviation *BI*.

generally carried out 40 days after the birth (and hence also after the end of post-birth vaginal discharge) and markedly extends the radius of activity for both mother and infant.[8] After this transitional ritual, the mother returns more and more to her usual activities, particularly in the agricultural context, and the circle of reference persons for the infant greatly increases. If a household has enough young and strong female workers at its disposal, a mother may spend a comparatively long period of time with her baby; otherwise, grandmothers, older aunts, sisters, or young girls in the extended family take over the care. Depending on the size of the household and the mother's productive tasks, she will often spend only the breast-feeding times with her infant. However, here as well, it is not unusual for other women who are also currently breast-feeding to take over when the mother cannot be present. It is also common practice for grandmothers or older aunts to give infants their breasts to suckle in order to help them sleep, to calm them when distressed, or also simply as gestures of tenderness and intimacy.[9] Hence, right from the start, infants have close bodily contact with several reference persons. Basically, babies and infants are cared for proactively; that is, caregivers respond immediately to the smallest signals from the infant so that it is never exposed to long-lasting stress or has any need to communicate its discomfort with any vehemence. Screaming and crying babies are correspondingly a rarity, and generally encountered only in cases of illness. Until they themselves become mobile, babies and infants are mostly in bodily contact with their caregivers; they are carried around or transported in a baby sling on the hip or back. They are laid down in small hammocks or on cushions only to sleep, but, even then, they are always within direct reach of their caregivers. At night, children always sleep alongside their reference persons, infants preferably with their mothers, but, after they have been weaned, with various other reference persons. Basically, even adult Makassars never sleep alone. This all indicates that the local conception of a sensitive approach to infants is founded essentially on bodily

---

[8] *Atturungeng* means, literally, "to climb down." This refers to the fact that mother and infant first climb down from the traditional stilt house during the rite. The ritual involves various purificatory washings to cleanse the mother of impurity and drive away malicious powers. It reintegrates the woman, who has recently given birth and was in a liminal phase, into society; names the neonate; and welcomes her or him to society (see also Rössler, 1987, pp. 34–5).

[9] In Makassar society, infants are generally breast-fed for at least 2 years *ad libitum* and receive additional food from 6 months onwards. Weaning is generally very "gradual" with mothers increasingly denying the breast to the infant and declaring it to be "dry." However, the child generally retains the other "breast partners" for a long time. One can frequently observe 5–6-year-old children being given their grandmother's or aunt's breast to suckle when they seek intimacy or consolation.

based interaction and communication processes between reference person and child. The focus is literally on directly "feeling" children's needs from their slightest expressive signals, so that caregivers can respond before a child becomes clearly distressed. Put briefly, the Makassar do their best to anticipate and avoid negative stress, so that infants have few chances of developing and expressing the emotions of discomfort, anxiety, and fear – which Bowlby views as primary emotions of the attachment system.[10]

Infant care in Makassar society is organized to enable women to combine both productive and reproductive tasks. In a subsistence economy in which female work is a crucial economic factor, cultural childcare models in which mothers are the primary/sole attachment figure would be absolutely counterproductive. Meaningful systems here are so-called alloparenting or multiple caregiving models in which rearing children is a communal task. Although these have been described repeatedly, particularly in comparative cultural psychology, their consequences for attachment theory, in my opinion, have not been analyzed systematically (see also Keller, this volume; Meehan and Hawks, this volume; Otto, this volume). My premise is that multiple caregiving systems lead to forms of attachment that Bowlby and Ainsworth's theory is unable to handle and that cannot be assessed and portrayed with the inflexible strange-situation method. An important step would be to start by determining the decisive patterns and ideologies of attachment in the different multiple-caregiving systems. In Makassar society, for example, grandmothers/grandparents are very decisive attachment figures for infants. According to local conceptions, young children and old people belong close together. "Only the aged have the necessary patience for young children" is the corresponding local maxim, and grandparent–infant dyads are an everyday picture in Makassar villages (Figure 5.1).

Samplings of time allocation have shown that in purely rice-farming households, infants who need intensive supervision (from the age of 2–3 months to 2–3 years) spend far more time (two-thirds) with grandparents or great-aunts and great-uncles than with their own parents, who are occupied mostly in work in the fields. This togetherness frequently develops into very close and long-term emotional attachments.[11] According

---

[10] For a criticism of the bias in Bowlby's focus on negative emotions in his attachment theory with the consequence that the assessment of maternal sensitivity is based primarily on the response to negative signals from the child, see Otto (2011, p. 416); see also Keller, Völker, and Yovsi (2005).

[11] The close relationships between the oldest and the youngest are also reflected in many childhood memories of adults. It is nearly always the grandparents, great-aunts, or great-uncles who play the primary roles in these narratives.

148   *Birgitt Röttger-Rössler*

Figure 5.1 Grandparent–infant dyad during everyday life in Makassar villages (© Birgitt Röttger-Rössler, photographer Martin Rössler).

to the local ideas, infants require, above all, patient, constant, attentive, loving, and indulgent care. The older generation is considered to be predestined for this form of emotional attention, which is called in the Makassar language *a'laju-la'ju*. Parents, it is said, are generally too active and too involved with their own concerns for this.[12] A frequently observed scenario in daily life is that infants who are upset, have fallen over, or simply seek closeness will prefer their grandmothers or great-aunts to their mothers when both are present. However, they may also turn to older siblings, other relatives living in the household, or even nonrelatives who have become significant reference persons for the child. In my opinion, the active role of the child, the child's agency, plays a central, though

[12] In the Makassar conception of emotions and emotion terminology, *a'laju-la'ju*, the patient, considerate, caring, and indulgent love of young children attributed primarily to grandparents, is distinguished from *rimang*, a more child-rearing and caring form of affection/love of adults for young children. This – generally less patient – attachment emotion is considered to be characteristic for the affective attitude of parents or older siblings towards children (see, for more detail, Röttger-Rössler, 2004, pp. 170–1).

scarcely acknowledged, role in the formation of emotional attachments. From the multitude of reference persons available to Makassar children in their large, multigeneration families, they take a thoroughly active role in choosing their main reference person by preferring to affiliate with specific persons. According to local conceptions, it is completely "natural" for children to attach themselves to those who match them best in terms of temperament and character. The biological parents are in no way considered to be predestined for this; there is no "mother love" ideology. In other words, according to Makassar beliefs, children in no way have a primary need for their mothers or biological parents in order to grow up well. In contrast, the many conversations and interviews in which I discussed child-rearing ideas were dominated by the idea that being attached closely to a mother whom the child does not match in terms of temperament and character can impair development because of the inevitable tensions and conflicts. A child should be reared primarily by those who best fit her "essential nature" (BI: *sifat*). Local conceptions permit irreconcilable essential natures in parents and children and do not conceptualize close emotional parent–child attachments as being a quasi-naturally given "automatism." Likewise, differences in the intensity of parental affection to individual children are taken for granted as logical and unavoidable consequences of the incompatibility of essential natures.

These ideas are accompanied by a care system that is not only personally but also spatially highly flexible. For example, many young children also change home with their chosen main reference partner – that is, they leave the household of their biological parents. If an older sister or cousin to whom a child has attached herself closely gets married, the child will often move to the bride's new home as well. Frequently, a child's grandparents will move from one child's household to another and then take the grandchild to whom they have a special closeness with them.[13] The

---

[13] We can back this up with some data. According to the household survey carried out by my husband and colleague Martin Rössler in a sample of 50 households (from the total of 180 households in the village studied) for the years 1990/1 and 2005, 11% (1990/1) or 10.5% (2005) of the households contained children who were living not with their parents but with their grandparents or other close relatives. A total of 41% of the households in the sample consisted of multigenerational families. This percentage remained more or less constant over the years, even when the multigenerational households naturally changed their constitution constantly through births and deaths. However, the remaining 59% of households in no way consisted of nuclear families; they simply did not contain at least three generations. It is important to note here that the borders of a house or household are permeable; they do not coincide with family borders. As a rule, close relatives, parents and children, or siblings live in the immediate vicinity of each other. In other words, a child's everyday interaction partners are spread across several houses.

freedom of choice available to even very young children is enormous. I was able to document several cases in which children as young as 2 years – such as little Pia – decided with whom they wanted to live: Pia had spent the first 2 years of her life with her parents in the house of her mother's family. When her parents moved to a small town and took her with them, Pia suffered greatly due to the separation from her grandmother and insisted on returning to her. After only a few weeks, the parents gave in to the child's demands and brought Pia back to her grandparents, with whom she then grew up, seeing her parents only occasionally. Cases such as that of 3-year-old Baso are also typical. He frequently visited his grandparents in the neighboring village together with his mother and his older siblings. Although he had never stayed there for any length of time before, when visiting the grandparents one day at the age of 3 years, Baso simply announced that he did not want to go back home with his parents but to spend a few days with his grandparents. These few days turned into several years.[14]

This changing of household communities on the basis of close emotional ties between children and specific adults has to be distinguished from what are likewise highly flexible patterns of fosterage and adoption. Frequently, children from poor households grow up with more affluent family members (generally siblings or first-degree cousins of one of the parents) in other villages who then take on full financial responsibility for these children. They not only feed and clothe them but also organize their education and, later, their marriages. The children contribute their labor by helping exclusively in the fields or in the household of their foster family, and not their biological family. These types of fosterage motivated primarily by economic privation are informal. That is, they are not accompanied by legal duties and rights (such as rights of ownership and inheritance, etc.). In the Makassar context, the latter – that is, legalized and officially registered adoptions – are generally carried out only by affluent, childless couples, who thereby gain children as heirs and prevent any conflicts over inheritance. Here as well, it is always the children of relatives who are adopted; however, they do not have to live with the adoptive parents when they prove to have "irreconcilable essential natures." Thus, children can exert a decisive influence on where they primarily live and with whom they want to have their closest ties. In short, the Makassar use what Bowie (2004b, p. 9) calls an "additive model of parenthood" – that is, they do not polarize biological and social parenthood. Adoptive parenthood coexists with biological parenthood; it does not aim to replace or deny biological parenthood, and is therefore

---

[14] See Bodenhorn (2000), who reports similar findings among the Iñupiat in north Alaska.

not threatened by it. Practices of fosterage and adoption similar to the system described here are widespread and well confirmed in anthropological literature (Bodenhorn, 2000; Bowie, 2004a; Brady, 1976; Caroll, 1970; Terrel and Modell, 1994; Young, 2000).

All this reveals that children are perceived not as the personal "property" of their biological or socially legal parents in Makassar society, but as part of a large, transgenerational group of relatives (this is also the case with the Cameroonian Nso – see Otto, this volume), within which – and this is the decisive aspect – children can negotiate the choice of the persons to become their central attachment figures, and this is already decisively negotiable for young children as well.

From an anthropological perspective, such flexible multiple caregiving and fosterage systems are interpreted as meaningful social and environmental adaptations (Bowie, 2004b; Young, 2000). Sharing children among kin is a major risk-minimization strategy – in both economic and social-psychological terms. First, multiply and transgenerationally shared caregiving allows women to invest their labor and productivity in economic tasks (in this case, working in the fields), and, particularly in subsistence economies, this is absolutely essential to the survival of the community.[15] Second, fosterage arrangements lower the economic burden on families with many children or few resources, and the various attachments/close emotional ties to several reference persons ensure the emotional security of children if they lose important attachment figures through, for example, death – which is in no way a secondary concern in societies with high mortality rates.

A further significant aspect is that children are encouraged actively to enter into a multitude of relationships and build up their own alliances from an early age. The personal networks of relationships that individuals build up over the course of their lives are decisively important for their economic and social security. Relatives are viewed basically as the most preferable and most reliable relationship partners. The bilateral kinship system of the Makassar grants every individual what is finally an almost incomprehensible number of persons with whom they are related on either the paternal or maternal side. The formation of personal alliance systems within this major social resource is therefore of great importance. The more active relationships with relatives an individual has at her disposal, the more networks of reciprocity in which she is embedded, the more secure, and finally the more successful she will be. Hence, what counts are the enacted kin relations. Kinship is just a potential, a social

[15] On the economy of the Makassar, which was still very much subsistence-oriented in the 1980s and 1990s, see Rössler (1997).

resource. Relatedness among kin is always the outcome of everyday practices, of "small, seemingly trivial, or taken for granted acts like sharing a meal, giving a dish of cooked food . . . dropping into a nearby house for a quiet chat, a coffee or a betel quid" (Carsten, 2000, p. 18).

A willingness to communicate and the ability to reach out actively to others and form a multitude of personal relationships are viewed as decisive social competencies in this society. Those who are less sociable (BI: *yang tidak suka bergaul*) are thought to be disturbed and are pitied. In line with such values, children are trained to develop their communication skills and encouraged to reach out to different individual relatives, to attach themselves to them, and to sleep in their homes. Sleeping over in others' houses has a generally high status in Makassar society: spending the night together symbolizes closeness and togetherness; correspondingly, adults who wish to consolidate their relationships also encourage the other party to stay for the night (BI: *bermalam*) in their houses.[16] Children who affiliate narrowly with only one or two reference persons, who react defensively or anxiously to others, and who never want to sleep in other houses are viewed accordingly in the local conceptions as being socially incompetent and abnormal (BI: *bukan biasa*).

However, after roughly the third year of life, clear borders are imposed on the strongly encouraged sociability in the child. The main developmental task for children at this age is to learn social differentiations. Children now have to learn that they can no longer approach all people frankly and freely, but should be reserved and shy (BI: *malu*) towards people they do not know and generally respectful to all older persons. From now on, they successively have to learn the complex social etiquette required by the hierarchic structure of their society. The first step is to recognize the seniority principle: the child must address all people who are older in years – including older siblings – with specific, graded forms of respect.[17] When it comes to complete strangers, the child has to behave in an extremely reserved way.

At the same time, that is, at the age of 3 years, Makassar children begin increasingly to spend their time in same-aged peer groups and move

---

[16] Refusing an invitation to spend the night is generally conceived as an affront and a rejection of the offer of friendship. During our field research in Sulawesi, this was often a major problem for me and my husband: we did not want to reject anybody, but we also did not want to have to spend every single night in other people's houses.

[17] On the level of language, this goes hand in hand with the acquisition of lexical etiquette. The Makassar language – like all Indonesian languages – possesses a comprehensive "honorific subsystem" with different forms of address and reference, personal pronouns, and so forth for different social rank dyads. See Rössler and Röttger-Rössler, 1988; Yatim, 1983; see also Errington, 1988.

outside the direct reach of adults. Until they enter school (in the sixth to seventh year of life), they spend their days in a way that is scarcely regulated by adults and only supervised loosely. Younger children (aged 3–5 years) are told not to stray too far away from the village or the parental houses, or to do so only in the company of older siblings. Otherwise, children are left to themselves; they are first introduced to domestic chores playfully; and then, from the sixth year of life onwards, increasingly systematically (once school is over). These considerable free spaces for children provide a kind of protective zone within an increasingly complex social world in which children from the age of 3 years onwards have to learn to rank themselves and behave adequately. The markedly hierarchic social structure and the seniority principle that places everybody on a higher level than the children except for their peers and younger children requires them to engage in complex social classifications and to acknowledge and take into account a multitude of social differences and distances of rank in their interaction with adults. Cultural psychology uses terms such as "power distance" (Hofstede, 2001; Hofstede and Bond, 1988) or "interpersonal distance" (Matsumoto, 1996; Triandis and Gelfand, 1998) when referring to such vertically arranged structures of social inequality that stress values such as obedience, respect, and deference and expect all children after a certain age to display these. Children aged 3 and older can interact as equals – that is, in a spontaneous, lively way disregarding social etiquette – only with their peers.[18] For adults as well, relations to peers and persons of the same sex remain the only hierarchy-free spaces throughout life, and this is why they attach great importance to peer relationships.

Significance for attachment theory

In the following, I shall draw on the ethnographic description above and start by criticizing the strange situation as the main instrument for assessing attachment qualities before going on to discuss the problematic sensitivity and competence assumptions in attachment theory. In the second part of the discussion, I shall address childhood agency – a much neglected aspect in attachment research that, in my opinion, needs to be introduced as a major analytical dimension in attachment research.

---

[18] However, the close ties that young children have built up with various adult relatives do, to some extent, remain unaffected by this. In other words, children can continue to act relatively freely with these persons, although they still have to show them the necessary forms of respect.

154   *Birgitt Röttger-Rössler*

Strange situation – a strange method

There are several reasons why using the strange situation as the main method for assessing attachment qualities seems to be questionable if not completely inappropriate when it comes to adequately assessing forms of attachment that – as shown in the ethnographic example sketched above – deviate strongly from the parameters of the Western European and US middle-class structures for which the method was developed.

One central deficit is the marked mother bias of the strange-situation design. To take appropriate account of conditions in Makassar society, it would actually be necessary to start off by collecting a sociogram of reference persons for each child being tested. For children whose primary attachment figures in daily life are not their mothers, it seems rather meaningless to test them only together with their mothers as in the majority of strange-situation studies – including those carried out in Indonesia by Zevalkink, Riksen-Malraven, and van Lieshout (1999, 2001), which I shall take a closer look at in the following.

Zevalkink *et al.* studied attachment patterns in the Sundanese of west Java, who belong to one of the largest ethnic groups in the Indonesian archipelago. They studied forty-six mother–child dyads with the strange situation. The sample was composed of nineteen dyads from lower-middle-class families and twenty-seven dyads from families with low socioeconomic status (SES) who had migrated only recently from rural areas to the city of Bandung.[19] Zevalkink *et al.*'s (1999, pp. 28–9) analysis produced the following results on the four types of attachment (ABCD) differentiated in attachment theory: the majority of children (52.2%) were classified as securely attached (type B) in line with the global distribution reported in the meta-analyses by van IJzendoorn and Kroonenberg (1988); 19.9%, as insecure-resistant (type C); a further 19.9%, as insecure-disorganized (type D); and 6.5%, as insecure-avoidant (type A), which deviates strongly from the global distribution of 21.0% (Zevalkink *et al.*, 1999, p. 30). These findings were then related to the social context of the families of origin, revealing that all the insecure-resistant children came from low-SES families and the majority of disorganized children came from extended families (Zevalkink *et al.*, 1999, pp. 33, 35). Regarding the mother–child relations in the low-SES families, Zevalkink *et al.* (1999) found some contradictions. The study's initial

[19] Socioeconomic status (SES) was defined by the family income, parental occupational status, and educational level of both parents. This means that in low-SES families, parents were employed as unskilled or semiskilled laborers and had a basic level of education. In lower-middle-SES families, parents had skilled-labor or white-collar jobs and had completed secondary education (Zevalkink *et al.*, 1999, p. 25).

participating observations (before the experimental part) carried out in the individual family homes – that is, in the children's familiar everyday environment– had given an impression of sensitively responsive mothers. However, this could not be reproduced in the test. In the experiment itself, in which every mother–child dyad was initially given five tasks, such as a jigsaw puzzle or building a tower with cubes in structured play episodes, the same mothers were less sensitive towards and supportive of their children. "We found that the quality of maternal support for insecure-resistant children was relatively high at home, showing a picture of an involved mother, who, however, behaved more irritated and hostile towards the child in the structured play session than other mothers" (Zevalkink *et al.*, 1999, p. 36).[20]

Nonetheless, this discrepancy did not lead the authors to question the suitability of an experimental design that had transformed sensitively acting mothers in the home environment into "hostile mothers" in the "strange situation" of the experiment. Instead, they evaluated the maternal sensitivity at home as a pragmatic behavior in response to the impoverished living conditions of the low-SES families, and the initial maternal sensitivity was deconstructed as being only apparent:

Mothers of resistant children lived in significantly poorer physical conditions than the other mothers. Under these conditions it is more dangerous for the child's well-being to put the child on the ground to play (e.g., mud floor, open kitchen fire). Therefore, even inside the home these mothers needed to carry their children more often than other mothers. This physical closeness may have made the resistant children relatively at ease at home, which may have made their mothers look more competent in responding to the child's signals. But our finding . . . shows that, in other respects, they lacked fundamental competence in caring for their children's well-being. (Zevalkink *et al.*, 1999, p. 36)

In my opinion, this interpretation reveals an unreflected transfer of Western European middle-class ideals of maternal behavior. The quality of maternal sensitivity is evaluated here mostly in terms of the supportive maternal behavior in the experiment, with a calm, confident attitude that encourages and helps children to solve the task for themselves being viewed as a clear indicator of "maternal competence." The authors completely ignored the fact that the mothers in the low-SES families (from which all the children categorized as insecure-resistant came) had recently migrated to the city of Bandung from rural regions, and therefore came from contexts in which mother–child interactions and hence

---

[20] See also Zevalkink and Riksen-Walraven (2001). This cross-cultural study of maternal behavior in structured play sessions gives a further, more detailed description of the Sundanese experiments.

the corresponding competence models are determined by completely different socioeconomic demands and structures. Mothers from the low-SES families, who carry their infants continually close to their bodies in order to perform various productive tasks and duties while simultaneously always being able to react promptly or proactively to their child's signals, display a behavior adapted to their socioeconomic conditions that is correspondingly extremely competent and sensitive. Among the rural Sundanese, as among the Makassar, parental sensitivity may well be conceived as a direct, body-based "feeling." Intensive maternal play with young children (assisted by toys) is not an element of this milieu-specific parenting model, and it is correspondingly not very surprising that mother and child did not know how to deal confidently with this strange task in the test. The unfamiliar artifacts used in the test will also have played a major role. Manufactured toys are completely unusual in a rural context. For example, a simple jigsaw puzzle, which I had brought with me for my own children, was a source of general amazement. The Indonesian children did not know what to do with it, and even adults with secondary education were either incapable of, or had great difficulty in, putting together a simple, 60-piece puzzle. It is very likely that such context-insensitive objects markedly increased the uncertainty and stress of the mothers (and thus of their children as well). Another major factor is that the low-SES mothers – due to the hierarchical orientation of Sundanese society – certainly felt insecure and inferior to the European researcher, and this may well have further disturbed their behavior. In my opinion, such context factors distort the power of the results and thereby the utility of this method. The quality of maternal sensitivity during the videotaped structured play sessions was assessed with five 7-point rating scales developed by Erickson, Sroufe, and Egeland (1985). These assessed

supportive presence (i.e., expression of positive regard and emotional support for the child), respect for autonomy (i.e., recognition of child's individuality and motives), hostility (i.e., expression of anger, discounting or rejection of child), structure and limit setting (i.e., adequacy of mother's attempts to communicate her expectations with regard to child's behavior and enforce her agenda adequately), and quality of instruction (i.e., the degree to which instructions are timed to the child's focus, stated clearly, paced at a rate that allows comprehension, and graded in logical steps understandable to the child). (Zevalkink *et al.*, 1999, p. 27)

These formulations show that pedagogic ideals from the Western European middle classes are being generalized and set up as a standard of sensitive parental behavior. Just as in the rural Makassar, the essential encouragement of the child's striving for autonomy through deliberate and thoughtfully administered instructions was probably far from the ethnotheories on ideal parental behavior among the low-SES families. Young children need to be protected, cared for, fed, and monitored so that nothing untoward happens to them and so that they lack nothing. To promote their development through targeted pedagogic measures is not an element in this model that views learning or the acquisition of competencies primarily as a "natural" maturation process and less as a product of parental instruction. Further on, I shall show how significant the culture-specific conceptions of the way in which children learn are when appraising parental behavior.

It is not surprising that the categorizations based on these criteria resulted in a more positive picture of the children from lower-middle-class families in Zevalkink et al.'s sample. They were mostly classified as securely attached. These comparatively affluent families, in which the parents held skilled-labor or white-collar jobs and a higher level of education, were characterized, according to Zevalkink et al. (1999, p. 25), by a marked " 'Western lifestyle', 'Western' values and high educational aspirations for their children." Toys along with the tasks and implicit expectations linked to the test scenario will have been far less of a "strange situation" for these mothers.

It is also worth looking at Zevalkink et al.'s (1999, p. 36) finding that the majority of children classified in the insecure-disorganized type of attachment (D) came from extended families. The authors suspected that the reason for this "overrepresentation of disorganized children in extended families" was that the presence of further members of the family could have hindered the formation of a secure attachment to the mother. This may well have been the case. As shown for the Makassar, children in multiple caregiving contexts have far more potential attachment partners than those in nuclear family systems, in which the focus is generally on the mothers. However, one has to ask whether this has negative consequences for the children, or whether it is correct to classify children as insecure-disorganized when they display behavior suggesting such a classification in artificial interactions with their mother – who may well not be their main reference person. The unreflected transfer of the ideal of the mother as the most important, best, and "most natural" reference person for her children is particularly striking here. However, in their attempt to interpret this finding, Zevalkink et al. even go one step further and suspect that mothers in extended families are exposed to a greater risk of mental illness, and that this, in turn, prevents them from being sensitive mothers:

For instance, Pakistani mothers in extended families have been found to be at a greater risk for both depression and anxiety (Shah and Sonuga-Barke 1995). Like Pakistani mothers, Sundanese–Indonesian mothers are perhaps also at a greater risk for developing depression and anxiety when living in an extended family. This may be reflected by their low quality of support towards their children compared to mothers of other children. (Zevalkink *et al.*, 1999, p. 36)

Without wanting to discuss the Pakistani study cited here in any detail, we should consider that what is possibly a higher prevalence of depression among women in Pakistan certainly correlates not just with living in extended families but also with such diverse factors as gender roles, the status of daughters-in-law in virilocal residence, and so forth. This cannot simply be transferred from one "non-Western" society to another. However, apart from this, I find the latent depreciation of conditions that do not comply with the WEIRD standard (nuclear family, mother ideology, education focus, emphasis on child autonomy) in this reasoning to be highly problematic.

It seems to be generally questionable how far one can assess attachment securities with the strange situation in societies in which secure attachments do not consist primarily in close ties to the mother but in a *multitude of attachments*. A major task for a context-sensitive, cross-cultural attachment research would be to develop a set of methods that permits an adequate assessment of the concepts and forms of attachment in societies with multiple caregiving systems.

Children's agency – a neglected dimension

Children who grow up in societies such as that of the Makassar with multiple caregiving systems frequently have far greater opportunities to contribute personally to shaping their relationships than children growing up in the narrow nuclear families that are so typical of the Western European or American middle and upper classes. The latter possess far fewer interaction partners and, as a result, fewer attachment opportunities – without even considering that they do not possess a comparable autonomy for shaping their relationships due to their completely different kinship and parenting models. According to the dominant Western conceptions, children "belong" to their biological parents, who have a legally protected right to custody over them – something that they may lose only after confirmation that they are no longer able to ensure their child's well-being. A close emotional bond between parents and child, particularly between mother and child, is taken to be biologically determined, and this is why the biological parents – as long as they are physically and mentally fit – are considered to be the best caregivers for their children.

Psychological research has given hardly any consideration to the different consequences that these different cultural models have for children's agency. This casts doubt on a central paradigm of research in cultural psychology that distinguishes between "socio-centrically" oriented societies and those with an "individual-centered" orientation. Markus and Kitayama (1991), who introduced these concepts to psychology, postulated that these different societal orientations each correlate with a specific self-concept: the "interdependent" and the "independent self." They proposed that interdependence involves "seeing oneself as part of an encompassing social relationship and recognizing that one's behavior is... to a large extent organized by what the actor perceives to be the thoughts, feelings, and actions of others in the relationship" (Markus and Kitayama, 1991, p. 27). The antithesis to this is the independent self of so-called individualistically oriented cultures, which are essentially the Western European and Euro-American societies. To clarify the "independent self," cultural psychology frequently cites the social anthropologist Clifford Geertz – as do Markus and Kitayama – who characterizes this self as "a bounded, unique... center of awareness, emotion, judgment, and action organized into a distinctive whole and set contrastively both against other such wholes and against a social and natural background" (Geertz, 1975, p. 48). In the field of developmental psychology, it has been particularly Heidi Keller who, in an impressive series of empirical studies, has shown that these different orientations and self-concepts in a society are accompanied by different parenting goals, strategies, and styles:

The model of independence incorporates a roughly equal interactional exchange between parent and infant, assigning the infant wishes, desires, and wants that need to be taken seriously. The concept is child centered and nurtures the infant's individuality. The model of interdependence incorporates a hierarchical, role-defined social model with the parental responsibility to monitor health, teach life skills, and stimulate growth and development. As such, the model is adult centered and assigns the infant the proper place in community. The model of interdependence is closed and community controlled with the consequence that intracultural variability is low. The independent model, on the other hand, embodied more personal variability with individual nuances to the general pictures. This attitude reflects the importance of individual choices. However, mothers with an independent cultural model also share the universe of meaning and feel that their worldview is part of an established knowledge system. (Keller, 2007, p. 138)

These classifications, which have been replicated consistently in a host of cultural psychological studies (Hofstede, 1980, 2001; Triandis, Bontempo, Villareal *et al.*, 1988), are based on ideal orientations; that is, they relate predominantly to the normative blueprints that various societies possess on the relation between the individual and the community. Nonetheless, there is generally a strong discrepancy between a society's norms and values and the everyday social reality, and this discrepancy is finally the motor that drives social change. Although conceptual models, norms, and values shape social institutions and real social behavior in many ways, they never do this completely. From the perspective of children's scope for autonomy and agency, there is a clear need to qualify the concepts of the "independent" and "interdependent self" or the "power distance" with which cultural psychology tries to portray differences in the ideal basic orientations of various societies. If we look at the daily lives of children in an average Western European family, we can see that they have far less real scope for autonomy, even though children's individuality and autonomy are a central value in Western European child-rearing concepts. As pointed out above, this is due in part to the different family structures. The typical nuclear family in Western Europe with only a few members generally does not even give young children the opportunity to choose attachment figures other than their parents. In addition, the dominant discourse in society and the institutions entangled with it assigns parents the role of the "natural" and therefore automatically best caregivers for children and correspondingly grants them a legally codified right of custody.[21]

However, the markedly lower action scope of children in Western European societies compared to the Makassar is qualified quite fundamentally by two further factors. First, whereas, as we have seen, Makassar children can move around the village and the surrounding fields with their peers with hardly any adult "interference" as soon as they are sufficiently mobile and have an adequate grasp of language (by about the age of 3 years), Western European children are, almost without exception, supervised, guided, and led by adults – be it in the parental home, in day care, or in preschools. This is particularly the case in the urban context, whereas children in rural environments often have a somewhat larger freedom of movement because of the sufficient amount of free space available to them.[22] In my opinion, the different degrees of social institutionalization and the accompanying centralization of child supervision have yet to receive enough attention in cultural psychological research. Viewed from the perspective of children's agency, children in Makassar society have much more free space that is controlled only peripherally by adults

---

[21] In this context, one should recall the length of the processes needed to take custody away from parents or one parent if they are unable to care appropriately for, or even deliberately injure, their child.

[22] See Keller, Lohaus, Kuensemueller *et al.* (2004), who also stress that the differences between rural and big-city life-worlds seem to have a more fundamental impact on socialization practices and parenting styles than differences between cultures.

than children in Western Europe. Hence, on the level of concrete, every-day behavior, children in the hierarchically structured Makassar society – which is clearly one of the "power distant/vertical societies" that demands that children show adaptation, respect, obedience, and a subjugation of their own interests in the presence of adults – clearly have more action scope. From the age at which Makassar children are increasingly required to show respect and obedience, they spend increasingly less time in the direct presence of adults – thereby greatly defusing this imperative. In the Western European majority societies, the autonomy of the child, the fundamental equality of children and adults, and democratic child-rearing principles are emphasized in theory, but, in practice, children are supervised almost 24 hours a day, and adults guide and constrain their activities. Despite the egalitarian pedagogic ethos, adults are *de facto* those in power who impose clear limits on children's strivings for autonomy. In summary, children's autonomy and equality are a social ideal that either does not correspond to social reality or is something that would be hard to achieve in the increasingly complex environments of highly technological societies with the growing risks these impose on their children.

The second factor that impinges directly on children's action scope results from which ideas about childhood learning are generated within a particular culture; that is, the ideas about when, what, how, and through whom children should learn. Cultural beliefs regarding timetables for developing competencies vary widely between societies along with the ideas about what lessons children should learn and who is "in charge" of teaching them (Halberstadt and Lozada, 2011). With regard to chil-dren's agency, it is the dominant ideas within a culture or social group on how children learn that are particularly crucial. Halberstadt and Lozada (2011, p. 162) distinguish between two prototypes here: (1) cultural belief systems in which it is assumed that children learn primarily "via matura-tion" – that is, quasi-automatically – and (2) belief systems that conceive learning as a process requiring systematic instruction and teaching. For example, Tamang mothers in Nepal (Cole and Tamang, 1998), Chi-nese mothers in Taiwan (Chen and Luster, 2002), and Mayan mothers in Yucatan, Mexico (Gaskins, 1996) believe that development is largely maturational and that children mainly grow up "naturally." In contrast, the Chetri in Nepal (Cole and Tamang, 1998), the Nso in Cameroon (Keller, 2003), and the Javanese in Indonesia (Geertz, 1959), for exam-ple, believe that learning is a process that requires teaching (see also Halberstadt and Lozada, 2011, p.162). Societies in which it is assumed that learning does not function without instruction can be further dif-ferentiated according to who is primarily responsible for this instruction. For example, the Javanese consider that the main responsibility lies with the parents, whereas the Kipsigis in Kenya (Super and Harkness, 1982, 1986) assume that children learn by observing and imitating others, particularly their peers (Halberstadt and Lozada, 2011, p. 162). Such factors influence the given ideas on parental tasks. However, cultures cannot be classified completely in either one or the other prototype. Instead, it has to be assumed that whether children acquire knowledge by themselves or through purposeful instruction depends on its content – that is, on which abilities and competencies the children should learn in the specific society. For example, among the Makassar, the social hierarchy and etiquette are learned primarily through purposeful child-rearing strategies, whereas children learn practical abilities along with the necessary knowledge of agriculture successively through learning by doing – that is, by helping in the fields and in the household. The contents of the complex oral literature, as well as local history and genealogical knowledge, are acquired by listening to adults, whereby the children themselves determine the tempo and extent of this learning. The same applies to the acquisition of the ritual knowledge that is related primarily to the traditional belief system.[23] Basic knowledge of Islam in the form of the ability to recite the Koran, in contrast, is learned in the form of explicit instruction from local imams.[24] At the age of 7 years, this learning is then extended by the school as a major educational institution teaching fixed and centralized contents that go beyond local horizons.[25] When they are not at school, which they have to attend in the morning during the primary school years, Makassar children can themselves determine to a large extent the content, extent, and tempo of what they want to learn in most domains. Hence, here as well, they have a major scope for autonomy and thus have much opportunity to develop individually (Figure 5.2).

In contrast, children in contemporary Western European societies are fixed into a tight time schedule of pedagogic leisure time and learning programs, and competence expectations. This begins in day-care centers and nurseries, which children often attend after their first birthday, and continues in an increasingly regulated form in preschools. Despite the high value assigned to children's autonomy in child-rearing concepts and

[23] The Makassar in the highlands of south Sulawesi practice a syncretistic Islam. In other words, elements of the earlier, pre-Islamic belief system continue to be significant and particularly shape agricultural rituals as well as rites of passage.

[24] From about the age of 8 years, boys and girls go separately to the imam twice a week for instruction in reciting the Koran. As a rule, this instruction continues for 2 years or until the children can recite the entire Koran, this occasion being marked by a religious ritual.

[25] In Indonesia, school is compulsory for a minimum of 6 years. Six-year primary schools have been set up in all larger villages.

Figure 5.2 Makassar children playing with bamboo sticks with two wooden wheels (© Birgitt Röttger-Rössler, photographer Martin Rössler).

parenting goals, children's scope is extremely restricted on the action level. Educators, pediatricians, developmental psychologists, and other specialists use their research and their expert knowledge to define which motor, cognitive, social, and emotional competencies a "normal" child should have at which age and how parents and educators should best promote this. Parents – and, above all, the mothers – are viewed by the binding Western European ethnotheories as those most responsible for the healthy bodily, mental, and emotional development of their children. This is something they should promote purposefully, and they can refer to a vast amount of self-help literature that will help them to fulfill this task.

Without going into more detail, this rather simplistic comparison should suffice to show that the central concepts of "interdependent versus independent selves and societies" in cultural psychology refer primarily to cultural ideologies and can take completely different – and even contradictory – accents in social practice. In my opinion, it is important to extend these models by systematically taking the children's action scope into account. Important dimensions for this are (1) how far children have a choice regarding their main reference person and can shape their attachments themselves; (2) how far they have the opportunity to shape some of their time autonomously and outside the direct control of adults; and (3) how far they are also able to codetermine their learning tempo – that is, to influence when and to what extent they acquire which socially and culturally anticipated competencies. In a recent paper, Heidi Keller (2012) has also pointed to the wide-ranging *action autonomy* of children in various non-Western cultures with a strong interdependent or "communal" orientation (p. 13). She defines *action autonomy* as "an individual's capacity to act in a responsible and self-controlled way with respect to fulfilling responsibilities and obligations" and distinguishes it from *psychological autonomy*. The first, she argues, mainly extends to activities that are socially expected and thus "may be performed without negotiations of one's own and others' intentions and wishes," while the second refers to the "inner world" – that is, to the individual's own aspirations, wishes, and intentions (p. 14). However, my above reported findings lead me to question this dichotomy. Does not the remarkable influence Macassarese children may exercise on the choice of who will become their closest attachment figure, how they spend their days together with their peers, and to what extent they engage in learning demonstrate that their own aspirations and wishes – their "inner world" – is ascribed an important role by the local society? On the other hand, do not the multiple social regulations, obligations, and expectations which children in educated Western, middle-class contexts have to meet constitute a kind of heteronomy, a clear limitation on their own intentions and thus on their psychological autonomy?

Conclusion

The primary goal of my chapter has been to use ethnographic material from Indonesia to point to some "cultural blind spots" in attachment research. From my perspective, these are as follows:

(1) *The persistence of a strong "mother bias" in attachment research – that is, a failure to pay attention to local attachment models.* Attachment research with its rigid adherence to the strange situation, which primarily tests the interaction between mothers and children, is inappropriate for societies such as the Makassar that are characterized by alloparenting or multiple transgenerational caregiving as well as strong fosterage systems and corresponding "models of additive parenthood."

(2) *The failure to take account of local ideas on what is a sensitive and appropriate way of handling babies and young children.* This also includes the neglect of culture-specific ideas on childhood learning, on adequate forms of instruction, and on who is responsible for these. I have

given a brief sketch of how the responsibilities for child rearing and instruction are distributed among the Makassar and numerous other societies, and have shown how they are in no way predominantly the responsibility of parents or mothers – without even considering how these responsibilities change depending on a child's age. However, when the tasks of the parents or mothers in one cultural group are considered to lie primarily in body-centered care, feeding, and protection from danger, and not so much in a purposeful pedagogy, it is misleading to confront mother–child dyads with pedagogic play tasks in the strange situation – as I have shown in my criticism of the studies by Zevalkink *et al.* Experimental tasks dedicated to a Western European and middle-class-specific education ideal are completely inappropriate for reflecting the local conceptions of parental sensitivity and competence.

(3) *The almost complete neglect of children's agency.* My concern has been to show that the systematic consideration of children's scope for autonomy offers an important analytical tool for assessing the discrepancy between societal ideology and social reality. In this context, I have argued that the central culture psychological concepts of "independent" or "individual-centered" versus "interdependent" or "socio-centered" societies become unconvincing from an agent- and action-centered perspective.

The importance of the different ethnotheories on children's competencies and their adequate development is something that I have only touched on implicitly. An appropriate judgment of parental sensitivities can be made only in relation to local ideas on what children should be able to do when; that is, only against the background of the specific cultural and social competence concepts.

Judging the attachment, care, child rearing, and competence models of the "non-White Majority World" (Gielen and Chumachenko, 2004) on the basis of WEIRD standards and norms is – as the Cameroonian psychologist Bame Nsamenang (2011, p. 235) so rightly points out – a drastic form of "cultural imperialism." It is time for psychological attachment research to face up to such criticism and develop culture-sensitive models and procedures. Books such as the present volume are an important and encouraging step in this direction.

References

Ainsworth, M. D. S. (1967). *Infancy in Uganda: infant care and the growth of love.* Oxford: Johns Hopkins University Press.

166   *Birgitt Röttger-Rössler*

Ainsworth, M. D. S., Bell, S. M., and Stayton, D. (1974). Infant–mother attachment and social development. In M. P. Richards (Ed.), *The introduction of the child into a social world* (pp. 17–57). London: Academic Press.

Ainsworth, M. D. S., Blehar, M. C., Waters, E., and Wall, S. (1978). *Patterns of attachment: a psychological study of the strange situation*. Hillsdale, NJ: Erlbaum.

Bodenhorn, B. (2000). 'He used to be my relative': exploring the bases of relatedness among the Inupiat of northern Alaska. In Carsten, *Cultures of relatedness*, pp. 128–48).

Bowie, F. (Ed.) (2004a). *Cross-cultural approaches to adoption*. New York: Routledge.

(2004b). Adoption and the circulation of children: a comparative perspective. In Bowie, *Cross-cultural approaches to adoption* (pp. 3–20).

Bowlby, J. (1969). *Attachment and loss*, vol. I: *Attachment*. New York: Basic Books.

(1982). *Attachment* (2nd edn.). New York: Basic Books.

(1988). *A secure base: parent–child attachment and healthy human development*. New York: Basic Books.

Brady, I. (1976). *Transactions in kinship: adoption and fosterage in Oceania*. Honolulu, HI: University of Hawaii Press.

Caroll, V. (Ed.) (1970). *Adoption in eastern Oceania*. Honolulu, HI: University of Hawaii Press.

Carsten, J. (Ed.) (2000). *Cultures of relatedness: new approaches to the study of kinship*. Cambridge University Press.

Chen, F., and Luster, T. (2002). Factors related to parenting practices in Taiwan. *Early Child Development and Care, 172*, 413–30.

Cole, P. M., and Tamang, B. L. (1998). Nepali children's ideas about emotional displays in hypothetical challenges. *Developmental Psychology, 34*, 640–6.

Erickson, M. F., Sroufe, A. L., and Egeland, B. (1985). The relationship between quality of attachment and behavior problems in preschool in a high-risk sample. *Monographs of the Society for Research in Child Development, 50*(1/2), 147–66.

Errington, J. J. (1988). *Structure and style in Javanese: a semiotic view of linguistic etiquette*. Philadelphia: University of Pennsylvania Press.

Gaskins, S. (1996). How Mayan parental theories come into play. In S. Harkness and C. M. Super (Eds.), *Parents' cultural belief systems: their origins, expressions, and consequences* (pp. 345–63). New York: Guilford Press.

Geertz, C. (1975). On the nature of anthropological understanding. *American Scientist, 63*, 47–53.

Geertz, H. (1959). The vocabulary of emotion: a study of Javanese socialization processes. *Psychiatry: Journal for the Study of Interpersonal Processes, 22*, 225–37.

Gielen, U. P., and Chumachenko, O. (2004). All the worlds' children: the impact of global demographic trends and economic disparities. In U. P. Gielen and J. Roopnarine (Eds.), *Childhood and adolescence: cross-cultural perspective and applications* (pp. 81–109). Oxford University Press.

Halberstadt, A. G., and Lozada, F. T. (2011). Emotion development in infancy through the lens of culture. *Emotion Review*, *3*(2), 158–68.

Henrich, J., Heine S. J., and Norenzayan, A. (2010). The weirdest people in the world? *Behavioral and Brain Sciences*, *33*, 61–135.

Hofstede, G. (1980). *Culture's consequences: international differences in work-related values*. Thousand Oaks, CA: Sage.

(2001). *Culture's consequences: comparing values, behaviors, institutions, and organizations across nations*. Thousand Oaks, CA: Sage.

Hofstede, G., and Bond, M. H. (1988). The Confucius connection: from cultural roots to economic growth. *Organizational Dynamics*, *16*(4), 5–21.

Hrdy, S. B. (2005). Evolutionary context of human development: the cooperative breeding model. In C. S. Carter, L. Ahnert, K. E. Grossmann, S. B. Hrdy, M. E. Lamb, S. W. Porges *et al.* (Eds.), *Attachment and bonding: a new synthesis* (Dahlem Workshop Reports) (pp. 9–32). Cambridge, MA: MIT Press.

Keller, H. (2003). Socialization for competence: cultural models of infancy. *Human Development*, *46*, 288–311.

(2007). *Cultures of infancy*. New York: Taylor and Francis.

(2012). Autonomy and relatedness revisited: cultural manifestations of universal human needs. *Child Development Perspectives*, *6*(1), 12–18.

Keller, H., Lohaus, A., Kuensemueller, P., Abels, M., Yovsi, R., Voelker, S., Jensen, H., *et al.* (2004). The bio-culture of parenting: evidence from five cultural communities. *Parenting: Science and Practice*, *4*(1), 25–50.

Keller, H., Voelker, S., and Yovsi, R. D. (2005). Conceptions of parenting in different cultural communities: the case of west African Nso and northern German women. *Social Development*, *14*(1), 158–80.

LeVine, R.A., and Norman, K. (2001). Attachment in anthropological perspective. In R. A. LeVine and R. S. New (Eds.), *Anthropology and child development: a cross-cultural reader* (pp. 127–42). Malden, MA: Blackwell.

Markus, H. R., and Kitayama, S. (1991). Culture and self: implications for cognition, emotion, and motivation. *Psychological Review*, *98*(2), 224–53.

Matsumoto, D. (1996). *Culture and psychology*. Pacific Grove, CA: Brooks Cole.

Nsamenang, A. B. (2011). The culturalization of developmental trajectories: a perspective on African childhoods and adolescences. In L. A. Jensen (Ed.), *Bridging cultural and developmental approaches to psychology: new syntheses in theory, research, and policy* (pp. 235–54). Oxford University Press.

Otto, H. (2011). Bindung – Theorie, Forschung und Reform [Attachment – theory, research, and reform]. In H. Keller (Ed.), *Handbuch der Kleinkindforschung* (pp. 390–428). Bern: Hans Huber Verlag.

Rössler, M. (1987). *Die soziale Realität des Rituals. Kontinuität und Wandel bei den Makassar von Gowa (Süd-Sulawesi/Indonesien)*. Berlin: Dietrich Reimer Verlag.

(1997). *Der Lohn der Mühe. Kulturelle Dimensionen von "Wert" und "Arbeit" im Kontext ökonomischer Transformationen in Süd-Sulawesi, Indonesien*. Münster: Lit Verlag.

168   *Birgitt Röttger-Rössler*

Rössler, M., and Röttger-Rössler, B. (1988). Sprache und soziale Wertschätzung: Soziolinguistische Aspekte des Makassarischen. In K.-H. Pampus and B. Nothofer (Eds.), *Die deutsche Malaiologie* (pp. 169–96). Heidelberg: Groos.

Rothbaum, F., Weisz, J., Pott, M., Miyake, K., and Morelli, G. (2000). Attachment and culture: security in the United States and Japan. *American Psychologist*, 55(10), 1093–1104.

Röttger-Rössler, B. (2004). *Die kulturelle Modellierung des Gefühls. Ein Beitrag zur Theorie und Methodik ethnologischer Emotionsforschung anhand indonesischer Fallstudien.* Münster: Lit Verlag.

Super, C. M., and Harkness, S. (1982). The infant's niche in rural Kenya and metropolitan America. In L. L. Adler (Ed.), *Cross-cultural research at issue* (pp. 47–55). New York: Academic Press.

—— (1986). The developmental niche: a conceptualization at the interface of child and culture. *International Journal of Behavioral Development*, 9, 545–69.

Terrel, J., and Modell, J. (1994). Anthropology and adoption. *American Anthropologist*, 96, 155–61.

Triandis, H. C., Bontempo, R., Villareal, M. J., Asai, M., and Lucca, N. (1988). Individualism and collectivism: cross-cultural perspectives on self-ingroup relationships. *Journal of Personality and Social Psychology*, 54(2), 323–38.

Triandis, H. C., and Gelfand, M. J. (1998). Converging measurements of horizontal and vertical individualism and collectivism. *Journal of Personality and Social Psychology*, 74, 118–28.

van IJzendoorn, M. H., and Kroonenberg, P. (1988). Cross-cultural patterns of attachment: a meta-analysis of the strange situation. *Child Development*, 59(1), 147–56.

Yatim, N. (1983). *Subsistem Honorifik Bahasa Makasar. Sebuah Analisis Sosiolinguistik.* Disertasi Universitas Hasanuddin.

Young-Leslie, H. (2000). Fostering: case study – Oceania. In C. Kramarae and D. Spender (Eds.), *Routledge international encyclopedia of women: global women's issues and knowledge* (pp. 853–55). New York: Routledge.

Zevalkink, J., and Riksen-Walraven, M. (2001). Parenting in Indonesia: inter- and intracultural differences in mothers' interactions with their young children. *International Journal of Behavioral Development*, 25(2), 167–75.

Zevalkink, J., Riksen-Walraven, M., and van Lieshout, C. F. M. (1999). Attachment in the Indonesian caregiving context. *Social Development*, 8(1), 21–40.

6 Concentric circles of attachment among the Pirahã: a brief survey

Daniel L. Everett

Introduction

This is a descriptive chapter sketching some ways in which Pirahã children develop attachments to their mothers and other Pirahãs from birth to early childhood. I am not a specialist in this area and focus on those things that I consider to be among the most salient exemplars of cultural and personal attachment and identification, from mothers to family to village to full social group.

This study in part responds to the call of R. A. Levine (this volume) for more cross-cultural studies of attachment. The importance of such studies is twofold. First, they add to our understanding of the range of attachment possibilities selected by our species. Second, they help us at least to begin to tease apart the relative contributions of nature and nurture in the shaping of human development.

The place to begin is with fundamental questions that bring our foundational assumptions to light. For example, what makes humans different from other species? Of the many answers one might suggest to this question, perhaps the majority fail to capture our core differences by focusing on superficial qualities. For example, humans are largely hairless among the primates. But shave a gorilla and you do not thereby derive a human. Hairlessness is superficial. Another answer might be that humans are cooperative. This is certainly true. Yet that statement alone does not single humans out from the line-up of the animal kingdom. Canines (imagine wolves hunting as a pack), Papios (e.g., baboons defending their troop from lions), and Felidae (think of a pride of lions attacking a band of baboons) all cooperate. So humans are not (merely) the "cooperative species".

One thing that does set humans apart from other species is their ability to accumulate knowledge by means of language. If a chimp, for example, learns that a particular plant is poisonous, its offspring might learn that valuable lesson if they observe their parent avoid the plant (or get sick and die from it). But European chimps (in zoos) do not know about

169

poisonous plants in "the old country" (Africa) because of lore passed down through their grandparents. Chimps do not build tools whose basic design is elaborated with additions and improvements in each succeeding generation. Culture entails the transgenerational transmission and elaboration of knowledge.

Through language, each generation learns not only from the generation before them but also potentially from all the generations that have ever lived. Language is not the only tool by which we construct knowledge, values, ways of behaving, and so on. But it is the most important, even as it itself is shaped by culture (Everett, 2012a).

One way is through language, of course. Another is imitation. Imitation is a major part of the transmission of culture, even across generations. And as actions that we imitate change across time, imitation alone can carry some cumulative cultural knowledge (e.g., the transmission of a bow and arrow's design changes down through the history of a specific culture by mere imitation of the latest and best design). But imitation alone is not enough. Your local library proves it. Google proves it. I cannot learn the theory of relativity by merely imitating your actions or your words. Language becomes crucial for the construction and transmission of culture.

The principal thesis of this chapter is that language and culture are the essential mechanisms of attachment, beyond whatever, if any, innate program for attachment there might be. Language and culture develop symbiotically – neither is possible without the other. Through the development of language and culture, cognitive patterns are formed which recursively cycle back on one another and the larger symbiosis of identity formation and attachment to a particular place, family, people, and so on.

The plan of presentation I adopt here is organized around the acquisition of what we might refer to as "concentric circles of attachment." At each stage of development, the child is attaching to various sets of individuals, each more inclusive than the other – mother, parents, family, village, larger Pirahã population.[1] But activities and lessons differ by age. I will discuss many of the cultural and linguistic lessons that reinforce attachment and identification among the Pirahãs.

Definitions of culture and language

Before we can begin this descriptive discussion, however, I need to make clear what I mean by "language" and "culture" since they are both abstract terms.

---

[1] I use "attachment" here in a potentially nonstandard meaning that includes "identification with."

Let's begin with "culture." Culture derives from the Latin word for cultivation. As we cultivate our minds, we simultaneously develop identity and connections between ourselves and others of our community. As others cultivate their own minds in a similar manner, we can in some sense be said to share a form and output of cultivation, a culture. But this is simply to elaborate the metaphor.

There have been many attempts to define culture as a scientific concept over the years, with so little consensus that many anthropologists have just (mistakenly) thrown out "culture" as an outdated and useless concept.

One of the most famous attempts to grapple with culture as a scientific way of talking is found in the book published in 1952, *Culture: A Critical Review of Concepts and Definitions*, by the American anthropologists Clyde Kluckhohn and Alfred Kroeber. Though the authors suggested their own definition of culture, their work did not resolve the problem:

Culture consists of patterns, explicit and implicit, of and for behavior acquired and transmitted by symbols, constituting the distinctive achievements of human groups, including their embodiments in artifacts; the essential core of culture consists of traditional (i.e. historically derived and selected) ideas and especially their attached values; culture systems may, on the one hand, be considered as products of action, and on the other as conditioning elements of further action. (Kroeber and Kluckhohn, 1952, p. 357)

We still are left with the question of how to use the word "culture," the essential issue. Is religion culture? Is art? Are language, artifacts, and ritual culture? Is the way of life in Alabama culture?

In my own thinking (Everett, 2012a), culture is a body of transmitted tacit and overt knowledge, values, and hermeneutics of previous generations, and the aspirations of the current generation. The forms of knowledge, values, and hermeneutics are prioritized in some way by the group, with individual variation expected. Values are always ranked by the group, with some individual variation inevitable – a form of cultural mutation. Ranked values are the primary determinants of overt behavior, being linked to social constraints to ensure that they are followed as ranked. For example, if "being in shape" and "eating gourmet food" are values of a particular culture and the former outranks the latter, then those who are overweight will have violated the value ranking and will suffer some sort of social sanction, whether ridicule or relative difficulty in mating, etc. Rank them the other way and fat people will be welcome.

Cultural transmission, like genetic transmission, is always corrupted in some way, leading to "mutations" (see Newson, Richerson, and Boyd, 2007). For example, among the Sateré people of the Amazon, there is a famous wooden club, the "Poranting," that has writing/marking on both sides. The people say that one side tells them the good they should do and the other has the bad things they are to avoid. The problem is that they have forgotten which side is which. Assuming that it was ever clear what the two sides said, this is a case of transmission breakdown. But cases of smaller magnitude abound. Consider something as concrete as the making of a blowgun. I have witnessed the transmission of this skill in Arawan societies of the Amazon from father to son. Sons observe, imitate, and work alongside their fathers. Surprisingly little linguistic instruction takes place in this skill transmission (at least relative to anything my dad ever taught me how to do). The wood for the blowgun comes from a narrow range of wood species. The vine used to tie the blowgun and render it airtight is limited to a couple of types. The needle used for the darts likewise requires highly specific knowledge of local flora. The kind of large jungle vine used to extract the poison (strychnine) and the other ingredients of the poison that help it enter the bloodstream more effectively: all of these steps and bits of knowledge, even without language, can be transmitted faithfully or inaccurately. For example, someone might accidentally use a different type of wood, or a different way of tying the blowgun, or a different binding agent for the poison. Error or innovation may occur at any step of the transmission process in one father–son pair, leading to a divergence from the cultural norm. From the perspective of the culture it does not matter whether the deviation was intentional or not. There is a deviation, a potential for mutation – a different type of blowgun or an inferior or superior weapon. Clearly, such deviations have occurred because in closely related Arawan cultures, blowguns differ (as do the cultures themselves!) in nontrivial ways. The technology varied and the language varied due to imperfect imitation and innovation. Such examples show that not all (however important) cultural knowledge is propositional.

And propositional information is the domain of language. What is language? Well, just as some anthropologists are skeptical of something as abstract as "culture" (Kuper, 1999), some linguists consider language to be an abstraction. We talk, for example, about the "German language" or the "English language," but what do such phrases actually refer to? There are many different dialects of both English and German, some so different that it is difficult to consider them the same language. Yet, somehow we all know how to recognize native speakers of our own language, even – in most cases – when they speak dialects radically different from our own. I will define language for our purposes here as "a systematic means of communicating ideas or feelings by the use of conventionalized signs, sounds, gestures, or marks having understood meanings." The "means" of communication in this definition, which comes from the Merriam-Webster dictionary of the English language, is, in my opinion, its grammar, sound system, semantics, and so on, the whole of which makes up a language. However, all members of a society will not use exactly the same grammar, sound system, etc. Ultimately, the concrete language that is shared is an extensional set, a corpus, and the language that is not shared is the individual's internalized habits of interpreting, encoding, and uttering. This is sufficient for our present purposes (see Everett, 2012a, in press, for more discussion and theory of the nature of language). Now let us turn to facts which bear more directly on the issue of attachment among the Pirahã.

Circles of attachment

Sometime in 1985, at about 7 am, a young woman named Xiotaóhoagí [eeowe tao HWA gee] set off from her village with some other women to harvest sweet manioc from her family garden.[2] She carried with her a machete, the common harvesting tool for these roots, as well as a basket woven from palm leaves. The three or four other women with her were similarly equipped. However, what made Xiotaóhoagí stand out was the fact that she was heavily pregnant, clearly due any day. I thought to myself that that was a lot of work for a woman so far along and obviously uncomfortable.

I returned to my work and thought nothing further about this common sight. Around 4 pm, the women returned from the gardens. I saw Xiotaóhoagí pass by my study hut carrying about 40–60 pounds (12–27 kg) of manioc roots packed in her basket, secured by a tumpline across her forehead, the basket hanging to her lower back. Like other Pirahãs, her arms were crossed across her chest, even as she held her machete, much like a scuba diver, in order to take up less space while walking through the thickly jungled, very narrow paths. I started to return to my work when I suddenly realized that she was carrying something else. Looking again, I saw a newborn baby in her arms and that her stomach was much smaller, almost flat. She had given birth and then continued on with her work. The baby was born on the ground by the side of the field. After the birth, the mother continued harvesting and trekked back with the other women, carrying two loads instead of the single load she had intended to carry when the day began.

Not all Pirahã births happen at the side of a field or in the jungle. When women are able to do so, they will often wade into the Maici river up to

---

[2] A Pirahã garden will usually be located within a 30-minute walk from the nearest village. This distance is partly to discourage casual theft from the garden.

their waist, crouch down, and deliver the baby underwater. Very rarely, births may occur on the raised sleeping platform in the woman's hut.

One could, of course, characterize such births among indigenous peoples that do not conform to our Western norms and expectations as little more than ignorance and the absence of modern medical care (though "water birth" has been viewed for years as a healthy alternative to standard forms of delivery at some hospitals). But for our purposes here, it does not matter why the Pirahãs give birth the way they do. We need to understand how this type of birthing's role affects, if at all, the mother-child relationship.

To give birth without pain medication, without a comfortable bed, without the assistance of a physician or midwife, on the jungle floor or crouched in a tropical river with piranhas, electric eels, anacondas, caimans, and so on renders inaccurate any description of the birth event itself as being "safe" or the result of "teamwork." It is the hard, painful effort of a single mother – generally unassisted even by those women who went to the field with her – to bring forth a life. The husband is rarely present. This solitary, painful emission of new life leaves even the very happily married mother a greater sense of the unbuffered immediacy of her biological connection to her child. A Pirahã woman will have a different understanding of the physical and psychological act of giving birth than the suburban American woman. Yet, beyond the stoicism of this or that particular Pirahã woman, what does her different attitude towards birth mean for Pirahã culture?

Well, it means several things. First, the immediately postpartum and subsequent experiences of the newborn, as well as the experience, observations, and expectations about birth of other children, are also important in group-identity formation. Second, it also means that the Pirahãs live in a very different ecological niche, with no access to specialized postpartum care. A Pirahã baby is with its mother, barring her death, from the moment it is born until after it is weaned, a period of at least 3 and more often 5 years. Birth further leads to the formation of a different personal character created in response to the different material and cultural circumstances. Third, it means that Pirahã mothers and children will attach to each other differently than, say, American mothers and children, due to the distinct personal, unmediated (by teachers, doctors, and other professional caregivers) nature of their relationship.

Perhaps an important but not obvious fact is the marital status of the mother in relation to identity formation and attachment. Unlike many Western mothers the Pirahã woman is not concerned with stigma associated with her marital status or age at birth. No one condemns her for children born out of wedlock – the concept of such stigma does not even exist, aside from the economic challenges of a woman alone. And even in the latter case, she will always have family of some sort to care for her. The attachment of the child only optionally includes the biological father.[3]

There are no professional caregivers, nor even the concept of them. The child is completely dependent on its mother, even though it may spend brief times with other Pirahã relatives who smell (of smoke, fish diet, etc.), look (brown, black hair, little body hair, etc), feel (calloused, sinewy), and, especially, talk (Pirahã) nearly the same. The average Pirahã infant (and most other children but with greater variation depending on age) will go to almost any other Pirahãs who stretch their arms out to them.

The Pirahãs are materially poor by Western standards. They occasionally go hungry. They have few material possessions. They have very little access to medical help. They have almost no connection to the economy of the national culture. And so on. Moreover, infant mortality among the Pirahãs is very high, perhaps 60–75% of all children die before the age of 10 years (though this is improving somewhat with the more frequent visits of the Brazilian health agency, FUNASA). In these ways, the Pirahã mothers' circumstances seem similar to those described for Alto do Cruzeiro mothers by Scheper-Hughes (this volume).

Yet their responses are quite different. According to Scheper-Hughes, the Alto do Cruzeiro mothers show a degree of aloofness to their infants, whose "spirits" may leave them unpredictably. These mothers rely on a strong sense of religion to enable them to cope with the tragedy of losing their young at a higher rate than the wealthy Brazilians they see on television or work for in one way or another. However, unlike the Alto do Cruzeiro mothers, Pirahã mothers show no aloofness to their infants, showering them with affection and attention, sobbing long and loud when they die. What might account for this contrast between mothers in materially similar circumstances? I think that there are two potential explanations. First, the Pirahãs, unlike the Alto do Cruzeiro mothers, have no concept of poverty or of alternatives (e.g., the lives of the relatively well-off or even of Americans like me, since nothing I have seems to attract them or interest them a great deal). This absence of a concept of poverty means that the Pirahãs' experience is not filtered through any perception of how life should or could be if only they had better circumstances.

---

[3] Personal character is the sense of being a complex whole that includes the individual's sense of their role in their society, their particular responsibilities and rights, and their inculcated community values – especially all ways in which these values differ from one person to another in the same community.

As far as they are concerned, they live in ideal circumstances and this is just how life is. Second, the Pirahãs have no religion. They believe that you live life as it comes, with no thought of God protecting, killing, or otherwise affecting anything of their daily lives, much less the health of their infants.

The Pirahãs are their only world. This could in turn help explain why their group attachment is to the Pirahãs only. Most infants will turn and scream if a foreigner, especially a bearded, foreign male, tries to take them. Describing the few babies who will reach out to accept my extended hands, their parents usually say, "My child is unafraid."[4] These parents appear to take pride in their babies who prove their braveness by coming to me. Yet the deeper value for their parents is that children will *not* come to me. The parents who might have appeared proud earlier that their children came to me will tell their children to beware of non-Pirahãs (including me) because they will take them away to another jungle. Caregivers will often intentionally scare their small charges by acting like they are going to throw them to me or hand them to me when I am leaving in my boat, etc. This type of caregiver behavior dramatically increases fear of me, and most parents laugh out loud when their children scream at my approach – a valuable lesson from their perspective is being learned (i.e., non-Pirahãs can be dangerous; a lesson based on history). Simultaneously, this sharp delineation between Pirahãs and "others" strengthens the attachment of Pirahã children to Pirahã adults.

Pirahã children are raised to be physically and emotionally reliant only on other Pirahãs, and to avoid imitation of or admiration of foreigners or their ways. Their bond is partially built around the homogeneity of their sensory experiences. Thus, although Pirahãs do not normally talk about the distant future, they do at times, when asked, say something along the lines that their children will be like other Pirahãs.

As is the case with other cultures' infants, Pirahã infants are cared for around the clock. Mothers, nursing or otherwise, are not inseparable from their infants, however. Occasionally, one mother may nurse another mother's baby, allowing the latter to spend more time gathering or engaged in other activities. This depends on the supply of food – that is, how well fed both mothers are – both mothers' health, and the relationship between the mothers (e.g., neighbors in the village, kinship, and so on, mothers' sisters being the most common surrogate milk givers, but not the only ones). Also, older siblings of the infant often care for it between feedings, but even when carrying them about (such as to proudly

---

[4] Toddlers rarely come to me – they look at my beard and say I look like a dog. If I insist, they scream.

Figure 6.1 Pirahã mother breast-feeding a peccary, a small, pig-like mammal (© Daniel Everett, photographer Martin Schoeller).

show them off to the anthropological linguist), the mother is never far away. Others may also carry the infant, but rarely out of earshot of the mother.

Infants are regularly talked to, but without special "baby syntax" or "baby phonology." On the other hand, mothers (and, to a lesser degree, fathers) often use "hum speech" (Everett, 1985, 2005, 2008) with their babies. They also often speak to them in a high-pitched voice, full of laughter and punctuated by kissing, tickling, and playing.

A strong, somewhat paradoxical attachment/identification practice is the nursing of nonhuman mammals. Pirahã mothers not only nurse their own and other mothers' infants, but they also nurse other mammals, as shown in Figure 6.1 (photographer, Martin Schoeller).

I have seen Pirahã women nurse dogs, monkeys, peccaries (as in Figure 6.1), and other animals (even the smaller, tree-dwelling anteater – Tamanduá mirim). Pirahã men joke that women will nurse anything except piranhas (then laugh very loudly and raucously). The Pirahãs are aware (from comments by river traders, government employees, and others) that this is an unusual practice, but they continue it for a couple of reasons.

The first is that all Pirahãs love animals and Pirahã women, in particular, like to raise young animals. They enjoy playing with them, training them, and so on. But the second reason, paradoxically to Western thinking perhaps, is that they raise these pets, nursing them as needed, in order to eat them when they reach adulthood. This does not prevent a close, caring relationship while the animal is moving inexorably towards esculent adulthood. The Pirahã name these animals, raise them with much affection, and take them almost everywhere they go.

Multiple mothers may nurse the mammal or it may be nursed by only one, depending on factors such as perceived ownership (if one woman or her husband makes a strong claim to possession of the animal, other women are less likely to nurse it); who killed or captured the animal's parent; or who has the most breast milk (such as a woman just beginning to wean a toddler but who has no new infant); and so on.

The sharing of human breast milk with animals is observed by children keenly, who seem to find it entertaining. Infants occasionally nurse alongside or immediately following animals. Despite the likelihood that the taste of the animal lingers on the woman's breast, they display no overt reaction.

All of this builds the child's connection to the Pirahã community and to nature – the nursing of other mammals adds a highly peculiar Pirahã sensory experience to the child's development, both conceptually and physically. For example, one remarkable feature of Pirahã children is their almost complete lack of fear of, or repugnance to, animals, even dangerous ones (such as harpy eagles and weasels, which are also raised among them), when in the village. They learn the behavior of many jungle animals from direct observation (even ones that are captured, but not raised, and killed soon after capture, such as caimans). As Pirahã children age, they share not only their mother's milk with animals but solid foods as well, usually sharing their plates with dogs and occasionally other animals, both contentedly eating from the same mound of fish and manioc, etc.

Through their relationship to birthing, animals, and nursing, the Pirahãs establish an immediate and lifelong learning and living connection with nature and their community from the moment they are born. This is a connection that distinguishes them sharply from Brazilians and the rapidly assimilating Parintintin and Tenharim Kawahiv-speaking groups, whose own reservations about the Pirahãs'animal relationships and knowledge underscore the distinctiveness of the latter's community from the river traders, explorers, missionaries, pilots, and others that visit their village from time to time.

These points of group attachment are strengthened during the children's maturation through other natural experiences of community life as the children learn their language, the configuration of their village, and how to sleep on the ground or the rough, uneven platforms made from branches or saplings. As with other children of traditional societies, Pirahã young people experience the biological aspects of life with far less buffering than Western children.

Pirahã children observe their parents' physical activities in ways that children from more buffered societies do not (though in a way often similar to the surrounding cultures just mentioned). They regularly see and hear their parents and other members of the village engage in sex (though Pirahã adults are modest by most standards, there is still only so much privacy available in a world without walls and locked doors), eliminate bodily waste, bathe, die, suffer severe pain (usually without medication), and so on.[5] They know that their parents are like them. Small toddlers walk up to their mothers while they are talking, making a basket, or spinning cotton and pull their breasts out of the top of their dress (Pirahã women use only one dress design for all), and nurse – their mother's body is theirs in this respect.[6] This access to the mother's body is a form of entitlement and strong attachment. However, it is transitory, leading to the huge shock that is produced by the onset of weaning.

At about 4–5 years of age, or much sooner if the mother gives birth to a new infant, the confident, satiated toddler loses access to its mother's milk. The cutoff is sudden and unexpected and exposes the toddler to hunger, work, independence, and an end to the sense of ownership of its mother's body. The transition is always unpleasant for the toddler, who begins to scream and cry most of the night and day, sounding to the unaccustomed ear as though they are suffering horrible pain of some sort (though as one gets to know Pirahã crying patterns, it becomes easy enough to pick out the signs of anger and petulance in the crying).[7]

---

[5] For example, children experience and see others experience toothache on a regular basis. A toothache, where there is no dentist, is agonizing. One must simply tolerate the pain until the nerve dies and the tooth has rotted out.

[6] It does not matter who is around. Mothers are so nonchalant that they often forget to put their breasts back under the dress for periods after the child has finished (breasts are not sexually charged objects for Pirahãs in any case).

[7] I recall one night with a visiting American dentist when a child near where we were sleeping was screaming and crying all night. The dentist asked me "Dan, what is wrong with that baby? It sounds horribly ill and in pain." I replied, "If it were ill, the parents would have already come to us for help. It is just pissed off about something." After about an hour, around 3 am, the dentist said, "Dan, I have had medical training and I know a sick baby when I hear one. We have to go over there now." So I wearily grabbed at my flashlight, slipped on my flip-flops and said halfheartedly, "Let's go." We walked to the small hut near the path that was the source of the siren-like wailing. When we arrived, the parents were feigning sleep, with the toddler sitting up by his father screaming at the top of its lungs. I asked the father "What is wrong with the baby? Is he sick?" The father

During the day, one sees children throwing tantrums as a protest against being hungry, cut off from the mother's milk, and losing the privilege of its mother's arms to a newborn infant. I have seen young children writhing in the dirt screaming, pounding their faces with their fists, deliberately throwing themselves full force on the ground, not infrequently close to or even in the fire (serious burns have occurred), spitting, and carrying on as though they were in the throes of epilepsy. The reaction by the entire village is almost always the same. They are ignored – ignored even though they carry on for hours and occasionally hurt themselves; ignored even though they are in the hot sun, not drinking, seemingly using all of their available energy to the point of exhaustion; ignored even though they are throwing their fit in the main path of the village, forcing everyone to step over or around them. The thrashing little discontent will usually tire, stop throwing fits, and become much more stable within a few weeks. Any long-term psychological effects of this nonritualistic rite of passage are invisible to the external observer. The attachment to the mother has been weakened. In its place now begins the accelerated growth in attachment to the Pirahãs as a group.

This accelerated group identification comes from what I call the "hard-edge" learning phase for weaned toddlers or "scooters."[8] From being pampered and having no work duties at all, the newly weaned child must begin to walk more (to the field, to the river, into the jungle, etc), rather than be carried most of the time; to take on duties, especially carrying small (and always appropriate for its size) loads of firewood, fish, etc.; to go fishing with older children; to watch and carry its younger siblings; and so on. They play with less supervision as well, paddling

---

ignored me, pretending to sleep. I said to the dentist, "They want us to leave and are pretending to be asleep to communicate this." He said, "I am not leaving until the father tells us what is wrong." So I shook the father. He looked at me as though he wanted to tell me to go fug myself but said, "What?" "What is wrong with the baby?" "Nothing. It wants tit." I communicated this to the dentist and said, "Satisfied? Let's go back to bed." The dentist said, "It is hard to believe. I would have sworn that this baby is very ill." As we started to leave, the mother pulled the toddler across the new infant at her side and began to nurse it – clearly to keep us from coming back and to communicate to me that the message had been received. Still, however ignorant of the Pirahãs, the dentist meant well.

[8] Locomotion before walking is mainly scooting. Pirahã infants rarely crawl. Rather, they scoot across the dirt of the village clearing on their bare (and calloused) butts, pulling themselves forward by pulling at the earth with the heels of their feet. Scooting is, of course, found in the development of many babies worldwide. The apparent universal preference for scooting over crawling among Pirahã children is perhaps due to the fact that they usually move on dirt or mud and do not place their hands where there are many parasites, such as chigoe fleas. Yet I have not seen Pirahã mothers discourage their babies from crawling. I am not certain why scooting seems to be so universal. It is possible that closer observation of Pirahã children on different surfaces would reveal more crawling. Perhaps imitation plays a role.

canoes alone. At all stages of life, but especially in this transition to a new independence, the Pirahã child is allowed to take risks. Pirahãs do not generally tell others what to do, not even children. Children run carrying sharp knives, walk near the fire, reach out to touch living, dangerous animals, and otherwise engage in many activities that some Westerners would consider unsafe and unwise practices for children. They get bitten, burned, cut, banged, lost, stung, and hurt in numerous ways during this stage. But they emerge from these traumatic experiences early on (4–6 years of age) with confidence, grace, and pragmatic knowledge. These behaviors are crucial for learning and living in Pirahã culture.

Are Pirahã children innately programmed to carry knives, walk near fires, and be more graceful than Western children? Raising my own children (two girls and a boy) among the Pirahãs and later seeing my grandchildren play in the village, the contrast between the quietness, lack of clumsiness, and common sense and awareness of dangerous things in the environment between the Pirahãs and my own (grand-)children was stark. American children run screaming and talking loudly, fall, get stung by wasps and other insects, bump their heads, fall in the river, fall in the canoe, cannot sit still, and on and on, even into adolescence. Pirahã children show poise and elegance as they move; they are relatively quiet, rarely trip and fall, rarely bump their heads, or get stung or hurt compared to American children. They know how to paddle a canoe and how to sit still for long periods while canoeing. Watching the two sets of young people, one is amazed by how much the Pirahãs have learned already in the first 2 years of their lives. It is often tempting to say that the difference is innate, because it appears so early in development. But observation provides ample evidence that it is learned. The Pirahãs do believe that the contrast between their abilities and ours distinguish us as peoples. Thus, contrasts in skills strengthen their sense of group identity.

The skills are indeed learned early on. For example, one day while talking to a Pirahã man, I felt a sharp poke on my upper back. The man started laughing as I turned to see a small boy, still wobbly on his feet, picking up his blunt, 6-inch (15 cm)-long arrow from the ground where it had fallen after striking me. He was shooting at a mosquito on my shoulder. The child returned my gaze with a serious expression before turning to take aim at a leaf on the ground. My Pirahã interlocutor said that all Pirahã males learn to handle a bow and arrow the same way – trial and error from childhood. By the time they are adolescents, they are good enough to hit just about anything they shoot at.[9]

---

[9] A favorite pastime of preadolescent boys is to shoot small lizards running zigzag more than 5 m away with arrows while holding the bows in their feet.

Sexual behavior is also learned very early among the Pirahãs. A young Pirahã girl of about 5 years came up to me once many years ago as I was working and made crude sexual gestures, holding her genitalia and thrusting them at me repeatedly, laughing hysterically the whole time. The people who saw this behavior gave no sign that they were bothered. Just child behavior, like picking your nose or farting. Not worth commenting about.

But the lesson is not that a child acted in a way that a Western adult might find vulgar. Rather, the lesson, as I looked into this, is that Pirahã children learn a lot more about sex early on, by observation, than most American children. Moreover, their acquisition of carnal knowledge early on is not limited to observation.

A man once introduced me to a 7-year-old girl and presented her as his wife. "But just to play," he quickly added. Pirahã young people begin to engage sexually, though apparently not in full intercourse, from early on. Touching and being touched seem to be common for Pirahã boys and girls from about 7 years of age on. They are all sexually active by puberty, with older men and women frequently initiating younger girls and boys, respectively. There is no evidence that the children then or as adults find this pedophilia the least bit traumatic.

In summary, much of cultural identification and attachment are achieved by nonlinguistic imitation and learning. This type of knowledge is almost exclusively tacit and difficult, if not impossible, to access via questionnaires or other forms of direct elicitation or short-term observation. The tacit knowledge of a community can only – or at least best – be ascertained by the old-fashioned methods of participant observation, note-taking, hermeneutics, conversations, and the interpretations of a variety of behaviors, in order to look for the links between them, whether linguistic or below the threshold of consciousness. This kind of knowledge is what I refer to (Everett, in press) as the "dark matter of the mind." However, a more easily observable form of connection for all circles of attachment is the child's native language.

Pirahã language acquisition

Piaget (1926) and Vygotsky (1978) champion different, apparently incompatible, perspectives on the connection of language and society, such as egocentric language versus language as socialization and socio-cultural development. Piaget's egocentrism appears incompatible with Vygotsky's views as Piaget develops them. However, I believe that the two may in fact be reconciled if we interpret egocentricism as the "formation of identity," at once a deeply personal psychological process that is nonpathological only during socialization in a specific culture. Thus, children learn language to form themselves as autonomous psychological beings, but this autonomy only makes sense in comparison and contrast to others – that is, in a social environment.

Pirahã language acquisition, though I have not studied it experimentally, follows the broad outlines of language acquisition in other cultures. The child begins to learn its language and culture from the womb.

Culturally, the fetus learns its mother's biological rhythms, her diet, her pitch range (modulated by the wet medium the sound waves must cross), and so on. Linguistically, it is exposed to the mother's prosody (tone, stress, and intonation) and other features of (at least) her speech. As soon as the child is born, it is exposed to the clearer and louder linguistic cacophony of its native community.

Pirahã children will be almost immediately exposed to five channels of speech (Everett, 1983, 2008) – hum speech, yell speech, musical speech, whistle speech, and consonant-vowel speech, each of which plays a different but important role in Pirahã culture.

Mothers and other caregivers do not speak "baby talk" or "motherese" to babies. However, many mothers use hum speech more frequently with babies than other channels. Pirahã children thus learn the importance and use of the prosodic complexity of Pirahã at the very outset of their lives, in the womb. And this prosodic complexity is highly distinctive among the Pirahã, setting them apart from any other known group of Brazil. They are also exposed as infants to sounds that occur in no other language of Brazil (one of these sounds occurs in no other known language of the world) – a voiced apico-alveolar laminal double flap (a form of [ɺ]) and a voiced bilabial trill (Everett, 1982).

In addition to sound features of their language, however, Pirahã children must master the structure and meanings of words as well as Pirahã grammar, the range of acceptable story topics, the way stories are told, structures of conversations, and so forth.

Consider first stories. Pirahã children learn the topics that are appropriate in their culture for talking about and discussing – just as American, children, and Sesotho children do. Pirahã children will learn that there is no talk of Creation, God, the end of the world, oral literature about the forest, and so on. They will learn that talk about nature as they have experienced it – hunting, fishing, gathering, unexplained sights and sounds – are the most common topics.

They will learn about their words and that verbs can take up to 65,000 possible forms (Everett, 1983). Perhaps even more important than learning the immensely complex verb structure of Pirahã is learning the evidentiality suffixes that are found at the rightmost end of the verb. Pirahã stories are about immediate experience (Everett, 2005, 2008, 2012a, 2012b), and the function of these suffixes is to communicate that the state or event is reported on the evidence of "hearsay," "deduction," or "direct observation" (Everett, 1983).

Because of their unusual constraints on storytelling and verb structure, as well as the importance of evidence, the Pirahã restrict their sentences to largely single verb frames (Everett, 2012a, 2012b). That is, they lack recursive sentence structures (Everett, 2005, 2012a, 2012b).

The unusual features of discourse topics, the absence of sentential recursion, the prosodic complexity of the language, and the unique sounds – not to mention that Pirahã is a language isolate and that the people are still monolingual (though this is changing) – mean that their language sets the Pirahãs apart from other populations.

Language is the ultimate tool of attachment and group identification for all Pirahãs. If you speak Pirahã natively you are a Pirahã. If you do not, you are not. But what counts as "speaking" is not merely grammatical structure. Mastery of grammar is a necessity for being a Pirahã, in their terms. But ability to use that grammar to tell appropriate stories is the truly crucial skill, blending both language and culture, as discussed in Everett (2005, 2008, 2012a).

Thus, in this view, attachment is a process of defining the self, one's place in society, and the separateness of one's group and culture from others. Theories of attachment, like theories of language and culture, can only benefit from careful descriptive field studies by specialists. Since I am not a specialist, this description of Pirahã can function as a first step, perhaps an indication of empirical riches to be uncovered by such fieldwork.[10]

---

[10] After completing this chapter, I sent a draft to Steve Sheldon, a missionary who lived with his family among the Pirahãs in 1967–76 and learned to speak the language well. Sheldon's comments are given below (email from Sheldon, December 14, 2012):

We felt they preferred to give birth in the river if possible. When Linda was expecting Scott, they kept on us about her having the baby in the river like they did.

We saw some instances where a mother would help her daughter give birth.

One young girl was having a very hard time with a birth and Linda wanted to go "help." The people did not want her to do so, nor would any of them go help. This young girl's mother had died not long before. Normally they would let us do whatever strange things we wanted to do. Not in this case.

When our boys were young and nursing the people did not like them to cry and would say things like: "we cannot dance if they are crying." This in spite of some of their weaned children carrying on just as you described.

Our problem was we were following an American cultural norm of putting the boys to bed and "letting them cry" till they learned.

Once the boys were weaned they could also scream and carry on with no frustration on anyone's part – except ours.

Summary

Pirahã children begin life with an attachment to their mother, developing stronger and closer ties with their community as they age. Mothers are affectionate with their children, from infancy on. Their tenderness with infants superficially contrasts with the hard-edge stage of weaning and the toddler age. But their affection never wavers. They are always ready to come to the aid of their child if it is genuinely and seriously threatened. At the same time, the entire community recognizes the necessity of physical and survival characteristics that do not come easy. In an environment with no doctors, no dentists, no police, no one but yourself, your family, and your fellow Pirahãs to depend on, the imposition of toughness on children is not from machismo but from necessity.

There are no attachment-related discourses that I am aware of developing or explicating the growing relationship between child and mother, child and family, child and village, and so on. There might be some, but I have not observed any. Rather, we see that the growing responsibility of children forces upon them the need to form wider friendships and support within the village and the larger community in order to survive. As with so much of cultural learning, imitation and relationship building are essential and without any special language.

I have often thought that the Pirahãs are among the few people anywhere on earth where just about any member of the society could walk naked into the center of the jungle and emerge well-fed, healthy, clothed (after a fashion), and armed. When I am there, I depend on them and am always grateful for their knowledge, their willingness to instruct me, and their ability to teach me (as I ask questions – that is, at my initiative). Like many traditional peoples around the world, they represent a richness of life and possess a set of solutions to life's problems that can never be recovered if this people or their culture is lost to the world. Unfortunately, they are now under greater threat than ever before.

References

Everett, D. L. (1982). Phonetic rarities in Pirahã. *Journal of the International Phonetics Association, December, 12*(2), 94–6.
     (1983). A Lingua Pirahã e a Teoria da Sintaxe. ScD thesis, Universidade Estadual de Campinas (published as *A Lingua Pirahã e a Teoria da Sintaxe*, Editora da UNICAMP, 1992).
     (1985). *Syllable weight, sloppy phonemes, and channels in Pirahã discourse*. XI Annual Meeting, Berkeley Linguistics Society, University of California, Berkeley, Parasession on Metrical Phonology.

(2005). Cultural constraints on grammar and cognition in Pirahã: another look at the design features of human language. *Current Anthropology*, *76*(4), 621–46.

(2008). *Don't sleep, there are snakes*. New York: Pantheon Books.

(2012a). *Language: the cultural tool*. New York: Pantheon Books.

(2012b). What does Pirahã grammar have to teach us about human language and the mind? *WIREs Cognitive Science*, *3*, 555–63.

(in press). *Dark matter of the mind: how unseen forces shape our words and world*. University of Chicago Press.

Kroeber, A. L., and Kluckhohn, C. (1952). *Culture: a critical review of concepts and definitions*. Harvard University Peabody Museum of American Archeology and Ethnology Papers 47. Cambridge, MA: Peabody Museum.

Kuper, A. (1999). *Culture: the anthropologists' account*. Cambridge, MA, Harvard University Press.

Newson, L., Richerson, P. J., and Boyd, R. (2007). Cultural evolution and the shaping of cultural diversity. In S. Kitayama and D. Cohen (Eds.), *Handbook of cultural psychology* (pp. 454–76). New York: Guilford Press.

Piaget, J. (1926). *The language and thought of the child*. New York: Harcourt, Brace, Jovanovich.

Vygotsky, L. S. (1978). *Mind in society: the development of higher psychological processes*. Cambridge: MA: Harvard University Press.

7 Is it time to detach from attachment theory? Perspectives from the West African rain forest

Alma Gottlieb

Introduction

In the West, strangers have had a problematic profile for some time. In an existential sense, as articulated in moving ways by Camus (1946), strangers challenge the notion of community that, as postmodern, largely urban dwellers, many of us crave – and for which we may nostalgically (though perhaps from a false sense of nostalgia) long.[1] In English, the term itself has decidedly sinister connotations. Strangers are dangerous. They represent a potential threat to our safety, and the safety, especially, of children – *our* children. Via the teachings of parents, teachers, and other authorities, North American and other Western(ized) adults in particular actively socialize children to feel fear at the sight, even the thought, of strangers.

For example, the federally funded initiative, D.A.R.E., which is now administered by local police departments around the USA, takes as its earliest goal the socialization of kindergartners into fearing strangers.[2] Through this program, police officers entering elementary schoolrooms instruct 5-year-old children to shun strangers who might abduct them for unspeakable purposes. "Don't talk to strangers," "Don't get into a

This chapter derives from long-term research I have conducted among the Beng people of Ivory Coast. Because of the continuing conflict in the nation, I have been unable to return to the Beng region since 1993; hence, this chapter depicts conditions before the nation's civil war. The Beng people found themselves on the military front line, and their villages were invaded by both sides of the conflict; the effect on the sorts of community-wide child-rearing practices I report on in this chapter are unknown. Until recently, life in the villages was dramatically disrupted and is only now beginning to return to pre-civil war conditions; for a brief update, see Gottlieb and Graham (2012, epilogue).

[1] On the undeserved nostalgia for an imagined utopic "community" of an earlier America, see, for example, Coontz (1992), May (1988).

[2] The acronym stands for Drug Abuse Resistance Education. According to its website, the program, which was begun in 1983 in Los Angeles, is now active in 75% of schools in the USA. It has also spread well beyond the USA, being present in over forty-four countries internationally (www.dare-america.com).

car with a stranger," "Don't take candy from a stranger" – these lessons become mantras that we hope our young children will memorize and internalize for their own protection. Significantly, D.A.R.E. itself is conceived of first and foremost as an anti-drug-use campaign. Thus, as taught in the program (in quite explicit ways for older students), the category of "stranger" is linked with illegal drug use and drug trafficking, which themselves constitute an undisputed site of evil in the contemporary public imagination. Through initiatives such as D.A.R.E in the USA and other postindustrialized and urbanized societies – coupled with the daily, more informal teachings of parents and other adults – "strangers" have come to represent the epitome of the demonized Other.

Mary Douglas has written convincingly of the broader meanings that danger and risk convey to members of a given society (1966, 1970, 1992; Douglas and Wildavsky, 1982). How a society conceives of dangers – as localized internally or externally, for example, or as sited in tangible or invisible loci – says much about how it imagines the notion of community and relations among neighbors. Accordingly, this constellation of ideas may connect with social networks and the idea of social ties in subtle yet significant ways. Thus, I believe it is not coincidental that the generalized fear of the stranger-as-dangerous-other occurs in contemporary societies in which the bonds of family are themselves often strikingly attenuated. Although some endeavor to maintain active extended family ties, this effort becomes harder and harder to achieve as work demands (and ambitions) separate families across the country, even across the globe, at the same time that a variety of effective birth-control techniques produce ever smaller families.

In post-industrialized societies such as the USA, child development researchers have noted that infants and young children tend to establish a relatively low number of intense relationships, or "attachments" – generally to those in their nuclear family, and especially to their mother. Although the first generation of researchers took this striking pattern as a biologically based model that must be universal (e.g., Bowlby, 1969, 1973, 1980), a more recent generation of researchers sensitive to cross-cultural differences in infant behavior have noticed that the pattern may be a peculiarly Western one resulting from a particular configuration of social, historical and political structures not replicated elsewhere.[3] In this chapter, I aim to contribute to this stimulating and growing literature.

---

[3] For some recent examples, see Neckoway, Brownlee, and Castellan (2007); Rothbaum, Weisz, Pott et al. (2000); Wulff (2006). For an excellent summary of earlier research on attachment theory, see Harwood, Miller, and Irizarry (1995); for an appreciative biography of its creator, see Holmes (1993).

I do so from an anthropological rather than psychological perspective; hence, my approach is somewhat lateral rather than head-on.

I begin by posing the question: Do all societies socialize their youngest members to fear strangers with the goal of defining the very category of "stranger" as socially/symbolically/legally threatening? I explore this question in the context of infant-care practices among the Beng people of Ivory Coast. I then expand this question to look at a set of infant-care practices that, I suggest, promote a large number of "attachments" to a wide variety of people, including relatives as well as unrelated neighbors. I conclude by suggesting some tentative factors that may go some way towards explaining the Beng pattern, which is so distinct from the dominant contemporary Western one.

Strangers in a Beng land[4]

Along the northern edge of the rain forest of Ivory Coast, the Beng term that most easily approximates "stranger" – *tiniŋ* – occupies a strikingly different semantic field from that which it occupies in most urban Western societies. By Beng definition, a *tiniŋ* is neither (intrinsically) morally good nor bad, neither threatening nor protecting. However, far more often than not, *tiniŋ* are seen in a positive light. For most *tiniŋ* who enter a Beng village, "visitor" or "guest" would be a better translation than "stranger." Yet, in some contexts, the English "stranger," with its typically negative connotations, does fit well. In the Beng world, some *tiniŋ* do in the end turn out to be unwelcome, occasionally even threatening. Such is the case of the guest who overstays her welcome, or turns out to be a witch, or humiliates his host with his superior powers of magic, all of which I have seen occur from time to time in Beng villages. But on initial encounters, the benefit of the doubt regarding the character of the *tiniŋ* is routinely given by Beng people. To make an analogy with the US legal system, "strangers" are generally assumed to be innocent until proven guilty.

A *tiniŋ* is immediately *incorporated* into the local social universe as soon as one encounters such a person. In fact, even before entering a new village, a *tiniŋ* usually makes an effort to contact someone who lives in that village so as to forge a social link ahead of time. That new host/ess would then welcome the stranger into the village and introduce him or her to others in the village as *n tiniŋ*, or "my stranger" – or, perhaps we should say, "my guest," because in most social situations in Beng villages, such "strangers" fade into "guests" quite rapidly. This is in effect the

---

[4] For a somewhat general ethnography of Beng society, see Gottlieb (1996). For narratives of fieldwork among the Beng, see Gottlieb and Graham (1994, 2012).

sociological lesson implied by the fact that in the Beng language, only a single word covers both concepts – which are clearly distinguished in Indo-European languages. Indeed, signaling the "ambidextrous" nature of the Beng term *tiniŋ*, those Beng who speak French use the term *étranger(ère)* to translate *tiniŋ* when one might expect the more friendly term *invité(e)* (guest) to be used instead.[5]

That *tiniŋ* often occupy a valued social space in Beng thought is revealed in architectural practice. While building a new house, the home-owner often incorporates one log of a particular tree somewhere in the construction. In Beng, the name of this tree is *gaŋwróŋ*, but it is also referred to as the *tiniŋ yrí*, or "stranger/visitor/guest/tree," because it is said to house benevolent spirits *(bɔŋzɔ)* (see key to phonetic symbols at the end of the chapter) inside it that will attract many strangers/guests to the house. Accordingly, in seeking forest trees to chop down as firewood, women are warned never to cut down *gaŋwróŋ* trees; otherwise, their house will never attract *tiniŋ*.

In short, Beng notions of sociality create a very different set of contours around the notion of "the stranger" than does the dominant contemporary Western understanding of the term. It is not that there is no category whatsoever for "the stranger" (in its negative sense) in Beng-land. Rather, once a person has been placed in the "stranger" category, unspoken rules of politeness demand the abolition of the *potential* threat embodied by the "stranger" rubric as quickly as possible in most ordinary social situations. In other words, a "stranger" is typically transformed into something else almost as soon as his or her "stranger" status has been announced. Through the act of being introduced and greeted, a newcomer – who may indeed at first be a "stranger" in the Western sense – enters into the *moral community* of those whom she or he has just greeted; having already greeted people who are part of their geographical proximity, that geographic space has become in effect a social space, with the possibility of further social interaction now publicly imagined (see Riesman, 1977).

---

[5] In French, the semantic scope of *étranger(ère)* is similar to that of the English "stranger," while *invité(e)* (derived from Latin, *invitare*) corresponds to the English "guest" (derived from German, *Gast*). According to *The New Shorter Oxford English Dictionary* (1993, vol. I, p. 1158), the English term "guest" also denoted what we now term "stranger" for a period, from the mid twelfth through the late sixteenth centuries, but the entry notes that this meaning is now obsolete. It is tempting to speculate that the relatively brief period during which the English term "guest" also meant "stranger" is precisely the late medieval/early modern period leading to the rise of European urbanism – when, increasingly, guests might well have been strangers, and the entire enterprise of urbanization was potentially seen as psychologically threatening. However, I leave it to linguists and historians to pursue this line of inquiry. In any case, my point refers precisely to the modern period, following the late sixteenth century, when the two meanings of the English words "guest" and "stranger" have been, and continue to be, quite disjunct in daily parlance.

And, of course, a member of a moral community is the antithesis of a
"stranger." In this way, the potential danger that "strangers" may in theory represent is almost instantly neutralized in Beng villages, and people
are not continually made anxious by the fear of "strangers" precisely
because in most situations, strangers do not remain "strangers" – in the
dominant, contemporary Western understanding of the term – for more
than a few moments at most.[6]

How are Beng babies taught a worldview in which "strangers" do not
remain "strange" for very long? There are many infant-care practices to
which I can point that begin to teach even the very youngest babies to
treat strangers as welcome. Let us begin at the beginning: the very first
moments of life in "this world," when – according to the Beng model
of reincarnation – the Beng infant has begun the first stages of leaving
the previous life of *wrugbe* behind and has started to enter, however
tentatively, this life (Gottlieb, 1998, 2000).

The first vision the newborn sees is the presence of several people,
typically all women, in the birthing room.[7] Aside from the mother, the
(healthy, alert) baby usually sees/hears a grandmother, often an aunt, and
perhaps one or two other female kin.[8] Of course, at this early stage, the
infant knows nothing about kinship and is unable to distinguish between
kin and nonkin. But very soon the baby will learn that the faces and
voices of those first strangers in the birthing room show up regularly and
begin to seem familiar.

At the same time, the newborn's social circle widens dramatically
almost immediately following the birth. As soon as an infant emerges
from the mother's womb, assuming the baby appears healthy, while one
of the older women present washes the newborn, someone else from
the mother's family walks around the village as a messenger, announcing

---

[6] There is anecdotal and some brief published evidence among scholars that the pattern I
have described may be common in other villages throughout West Africa, and even farther
afield on the continent (e.g., Wall, 2009); comparative research on this issue across the
continent at large is sorely needed.

[7] In the case of a very difficult childbirth in the village, a male healer may be called in
to administer herbal remedies, and a male ritual specialist (commonly referred to as
a "Master of the Earth" across much of West Africa) may enter to offer prayers and
sacrifices.

[8] Naturally, infants vary in their level of alertness during their first few hours, even days
postpartum. However, Western researchers have documented that the sort of "floppy"
(and nonalert) babies one sees increasingly in hospital newborn wards are frequently
explained by the high level of drugs nowadays routinely administered to laboring women
(even more in the case of cesarean-section deliveries, which require anesthesia). In rural
villages such as those I am describing, such drugs are unavailable. As a result, Beng
newborns on the whole are probably more alert than are most newborns born in hospitals.
My own more informal observations in both contexts would support this comparison.

the baby's arrival to members of every village household (Gottlieb, 1995). On hearing the news, people flock to the courtyard to welcome the fresh arrival to the village, and to this life. Within about an hour, a long line forms outside the door of the birthing room. One by one, men and women approach the doorway and address the new mother with a formulaic exchange:

v(isitor): *Na ka kwau* [Mother, good afternoon].
m(other): *Aúúúŋ, mú wiyau* [Good afternoon].
v: *Aúŋ* [Mm-hmm]. *Ka n gba pɔ* [What have you given me]?
m: *Leŋè* [or] *gɔŋè* [A girl (or) A boy].
v: *Ka nuwaliaà* [Thank you].
    (The visitor may then toss small change to the mother.)
m: *Aúŋ* [Mm-hmm].

This exchange is repeated over and over as a representative of every household comes to congratulate the new mother.

During this stream of visitors, the mother lies on mats on the floor with her baby, both keeping warm next to a fire. She is, of course, exhausted, so one of the older attendants, typically her own mother, takes over care of the newborn. This person's primary responsibility is to make sure that the baby stays awake to see the stream of visitors and realize how welcome she or he is to this new life. Depending on the size of the village, the line of guests may take a half-hour or even an hour to complete the greeting series. So within the initial two hours or so of life outside the womb, the newborn is taught his or her first lesson: to be human is to engage in sociable fashion with a large number of new people – and these new people, who at first appear to be strangers, are in fact friendly and indeed welcoming; many, though not all, will turn out to be kin.

This lesson continues well past the ritual welcoming line. Over the next few weeks, the new baby will receive dozens, perhaps hundreds more visits. Some will be from the same people who appeared in that initial welcoming line, some will be from other residents in the village, or from other villages altogether. These visitors will typically enter the room in which the mother and newborn are lying, and will spend some time visiting – anywhere from a few minutes to an hour or two. As hostess, the primary duty of the new mother is to allow each visitor to connect actively with the newborn. A sleeping baby is invariably awakened, and the mother or an attending kinswoman (usually her own mother) addresses the baby directly to introduce him or her to the *tiniŋ*.[9] Indeed, the newborn is

---

[9] The practice of waking a sleeping baby to introduce to visitors has been documented elsewhere in Africa (e.g., Johnson, 2000, on the Fulani) and may indeed be fairly common on the continent.

given early lessons in greeting, which will become so important later in life (Gottlieb and Graham, 1994), when the mother or another woman "speaks for" the baby in encounters with the guest. For example, a visitor may ask the baby her name, and one of the adult women in the room will hold up the newborn and, much as a ventriloquist might speak through a puppet, will answer in the first person as if she were the infant, "My name is so-and-so." This practice is so deeply entrenched that adults may apologize if they fail to engage in it. In one case I observed, a woman who was taking care of a baby failed to respond immediately for the infant when a visitor greeted him; when she did respond after a delay, she did so apologetically, making clear that she had shirked her responsibility of "speaking for" the baby. Through this practice, an infant is in effect taught the value of engaging in social encounters from the first days after birth.

A new child is introduced to visitors not only visually and verbally but also somatically: normally, the infant is handed to the visitor. A visitor may decline the chance to hold the baby, but it is imperative to make the offer. A mother who makes no attempt to awaken her sleeping newborn and hand him or her to a visitor is considered selfish: unwilling to allow her new child to be claimed as owned by the village as a collectivity.

Indeed, Beng villagers extend this principle in a dramatic way. They maintain that, in theory, any young child is eligible to be adopted by anyone else in the village. In practice, this option is typically exercised by close female relatives, especially sisters, or women who call themselves "sisters" (they might be first- or second-degree matrilateral parallel cousins, or even more distantly related clanmates). Nevertheless, the option of adopting any fellow villager's baby exists at the level of local thought, emphasizing the extent to which the bonds of community define any guests and visitors to the household as friendly to the utmost degree.

The somatic lessons of sociality also extend from holding the baby to breast-feeding. During the first few days after birth, it is likely that colostrum has not yet been replaced by milk in the new mother's breasts. Like many women in other parts of the world, Beng women do not consider colostrum substance nourishing.[10] During this period, some Beng mothers give their babies only water to drink; others may look to find another nursing mother who will breast-feed their new child until their own breast milk comes in. The wet nurse may well be the new

---

[10] For some discussions of this issue among several world groups, see Hastrup (1992), Stuart-Macadam (1995, p. 85). Scientific research increasingly points to the nutritional value of colostrum; for overviews, see Uruakpa, Ismond, and Akobundu (2002) and Xu (1996).

mother's own mother, if she herself has a nursing baby at home. If her own mother is unable to serve as a wet nurse, a new mother may find another nursing mother – probably but not always a close relative – to breast-feed her newborn during the first day or two after birth.

Once her milk comes in, a mother will breast-feed her newborn very frequently around the clock (Gottlieb, 2004, ch. 8). Of course, this can well leave a new mother exhausted. In this case, other nursing mothers who live nearby, or who are visiting, may feel sympathy for her. If the newborn cries and the mother is sleeping or worn out, another nursing mother who happens to be in the bedroom may casually pick up the newborn to nurse. Let us observe this scene:

Afwe is a first-time mother of a 2-day-old. Her tiny daughter has been sleeping, nursing, and fussing, generally in 5-minute intervals, for the past hour-and-a-half. At the moment, the baby's paternal grandmother is holding her asleep in her arms. A woman comes into the room and, after greeting and congratulating Afwe, takes the baby out of the grandmother's arms and looks at her. Satisfied at what she has seen, she hands the infant back to her grandmother.

But the baby is unhappy at having been awakened and soon starts to cry hard. Her grandmother speaks softly to her, asking, *"Je'á diŋ – e loà?"* – "Sorry – what's the matter?" The newborn has no reply beyond further crying, and the grandmother offers her a breast. As a nursing mother of a toddler herself, this young grandmother also has milk in her breasts, and the little one nurses happily for 5 minutes before settling back into a comfortable sleep in her grandmother's arms.

Later, when the baby is a little older and the mother has gone back to work, wet nursing may also be a temporary measure to which others resort when they are caring for the baby whose mother is not around. In this case, the momentary wet nurse may be any other nursing mother who may or may not be related to the baby's own mother.[11]

A variation on this theme might be called "dry nursing."[12] Suppose a mother drops off her baby with a friend, neighbor, or relative and goes off

[11] Given women's fertility cycles, this is likely to happen with the first grown daughter or two. The vagaries of demography, of course, increase or decrease the likelihood of a given grandmother being a nursing mother at the same time that her own daughter is also a nursing mother. For example, if a woman has her first child at the age of 18, and that child is a girl, and that daughter likewise bears her first child at the age of 18, there may be another 5–10 years during which mother and daughter are both bearing – and breast-feeding – children at the same time. However, if a woman bears her first child when she is in her twenties and her first or second child is male, this overlap in fertility with a future daughter is less likely to occur.

[12] My use of the term "dry-nursing" differs from conventional usage, which generally refers to the practice of raising an infant on solid foods rather than on any form of milk (whether human or animal) (e.g., Fildes, 1995; Stuart-Macadam, 1995). I find the latter

for some time (perhaps to fetch water or chop wood). In a little while, the baby cries. Perhaps he is hungry, perhaps he misses his mother, perhaps he misses the previous life in *wrugbe* he left behind – no one really knows. The babysitter offers him some water, but he refuses it, or it fails to satisfy him. As long as there's an adult woman around, anyone can offer to "breast-feed" the infant – whether or not there is breast milk available. In effect, such a woman serves as a human pacifier. Consider this scene:

2:30 pm – Tahan decides to fetch water from the pump. On the way back, she will be carrying water on her head, and it would be hard to carry her 6-month-old son Sassandra without spilling the water, plus the two loads together would be quite heavy. She decides to leave Sassandra with her mother, Amenan – a middle-aged woman who had her last child 8 years ago.

As soon as Tahan leaves the compound, Amenan pretends to breast-feed Sassandra. He is happy but not ravenous. Thinking Sassandra is in a mood to play, Amenan asks him, "*ŋo mí sí pɔ?*" – "What's your name?" He does not seem terribly stimulated by the question, and Amenan thinks he might be tired. He has only slept for a few minutes so far today and should be ready for a nap. Amenan says gently to her grandson, "*yilɛ mi delo, nyo mi nyɛ bedà*" – "You're sleepy – nurse, and then go to sleep."

3:05 pm – Sassandra sucks on his grandmother's empty breast until he "nurses" himself to sleep.

3:25 pm – Sassandra awakes, and Amenan sits him up in her lap. She calls over to her 10-year-old daughter, Ajua, to come squeeze her nipple, maybe some milk will come out. Ajua giggles with excitement at the idea of this game. She comes over and playfully tells her nephew to bite his grandmother's nipple. Smiling, Amenan cautions Sassandra not to bite her, but Ajua stuffs her mother's nipple into the baby's mouth, encouraging him to bite it. Afraid he may oblige, Amenan removes her breast and instructs her daughter to carry Sassandra off to his mother at the pump so that he can breast-feed for real.

But Ajua has caught sight of a picture-book I have lying around. She spots a photo of a baby bottle and shows it to Sassandra, telling him, "*a mi!*" – "Drink it!" I find this very funny, but Sassandra does not laugh – never having seen an actual baby bottle, nor having a distinct sense of the difference between two- and three-dimensional objects (DeLoache, Pierroutsakos, Uttal *et al.*, 1998), he clearly does not understand the joke. Besides, he is still sleepy – he is managing to keep himself wake, but not to be very lively.

4:25 pm – Sassandra falls asleep in his grandmother's arms. After a few false starts, he nods off again, and when another young aunt transfers him to a mat on the ground, he manages to sleep for some time.

meaning misleading, however, and prefer the meaning I have indicated in the text as more intuitively flowing from the term.

In this scene, a grandmother's breasts have been used both as a serious pacifier, and as a playful joke. Sassandra is a baby who does not nod off easily, and his grandmother has judged that the only way he will nap – which, she thinks, he needs to do – is via breast-feeding. Since his mother is not around, her own breast should do. Still, Amenan realizes the silliness of the gesture, and she is not offended when her own daughter turns the charade into a joke.

In a communal babysitting setting, even a child may urge a nonnursing woman to pretend-breast-feed an unhappy young charge. Consider the following scene, once again involving my friend Amenan and two more of her daughters:

One afternoon a neighbor drops off her baby Eric for the compound at large to take care of, and the baby gets passed around from person to person. My husband plays for a few minutes with Eric under the coffee trees, and then Amenan's 8-year-old daughter Lucy carries Eric over to her older sister, 13-year-old Esi, who is sitting under the compound's granary. Five minutes later, Eric starts to fuss a bit. Esi brings Eric to her own mother. Having had her last child, Lucy, 8 years ago, Amenan is not a breast-feeding mother and in no position to nurse Eric. But bossy, teenage Esi firmly instructs her mother, "*kà gba nyó!*" – "Give him your breast!" Amenan obliges. Sucking the empty breast, Eric is happy.

These examples all speak to a rather casual attitude towards both wet- and dry-nursing. This casualness is, I suggested, reflected in linguistic usage. It is significant that there is no word in Beng for "wet-nursing," nor for the variation I have termed "dry-nursing." Both are simply called by the same word for breast-feeding: *nyo mialε* (literally, "to drink the breast"). I suggest that this linguistic inattention signals a broader-based inattention. The difference between the breast-feeding biological mother and another woman – whether or not she herself is currently a breast-feeding mother – who might offer a breast to a hungry baby is simply not valorized.

In effect, I suggest that Beng breast-feeding practices produce a particular lactational signature. In the Beng case, this signature is a markedly social one. That is, while there is no doubt that most Beng newborns, like nursing newborns elsewhere, have an especially close relationship with their nursing mothers, the intensity of that relationship – its monogamous nature, as it were – may be significantly mitigated, in part due to the common practice of spontaneous wet- (or dry-)nursing. In the experiences of many Beng babies, any woman's breast – even one that has no milk in it – is potentially a site for pleasurable sucking (if not nourishment). This must lead a baby to create the image of a relatively large pool of people to satisfy two of life's earliest and strongest

Figure 7.1 Often the baby is attached to someone else who is designated as a babysitter (*lɛŋ kuli*) (© and photographer Alma Gottlieb).

desires – the desire to satisfy hunger (by ingesting breast milk) and to relieve stress (by sucking). Perhaps (at least, to the Western mind) ironically, for a Beng baby, learning the value of sociability often begins at the breast.

Somewhere between 2 and 4 months of age, a new baby starts to range out from the household somewhat regularly. It is then that the mother (assuming she has recovered normally from the delivery) starts returning to work in the fields. At first the new mother may go to work just for an hour or two, and maybe just one or two days a week. But by 3–4 months postpartum at the latest, she will be back at her agricultural work full-time. And what of the baby? The little one spends much of the day in a vertical position on someone's back, often napping. Sometimes this back belongs to the baby's mother, but often the baby is attached to someone else who is designated as a babysitter (*lɛŋ kuli*) (Figure 7.1).

Revealingly, the title of such a person translates literally as "baby catcher" or "baby holder," indicating the close physical contact required of the baby's substitute caregiver.

Figure 7.2 A lucky new mother commandeers the babysitting services of a relative (© and photographer Alma Gottlieb).

Doing very demanding physical labor with a baby attached to her back is not considered optimal for a new mother's own health; the Beng acknowledge that it can also seriously reduce her work productivity. For these reasons, the mother often tries to find a regular *lɛŋ kuli* for her infant. A lucky new mother will be able to commandeer the babysitting services of a relative (who is usually but not always female) such as another daughter, a younger sister, a niece, or a young cousin who does not yet have children, or perhaps her own mother or an older sister or older cousin whose children are all grown (Figure 7.2).

Such babysitters may be quite young by Western standards. It is common to see girls as young as 7 or 8 years old carrying around a baby on their back (Figure 7.3).[13]

If there is no such relative available, the new mother may search the village for an unrelated young girl who is willing to provide these services on a fairly regular basis. In all such situations, the baby may become

[13] See Weisner and Gallimore (1977) for a more general discussion of this pattern in non-Western settings.

Figure 7.3 It is common to see girls as young as 7 or 8 years carrying a baby on their back (© and photographer Alma Gottlieb).

quite attached to the young caregiver; in later years, the grown child may point to the now grown woman and indicate with warmth, "She was my *lɛŋ kuli.*" Nevertheless, not all babysitters can be full-time babysitters; especially if they are teenagers or older, they have lives too, perhaps their own fields to farm, their own children to raise. Therefore, many Beng mothers of infants try to have a network of potential *lɛŋ kuli* who can care for their infants while they do their farm and other work.

In order to attract a wide pool of potential babysitters, mothers typically spend an hour or more every morning grooming their babies (male and female) to make them look beautiful (Figure 7.4).

The aim is to make the baby as physically attractive as possible, so as to seduce potential babysitters into offering their caregiving services to the adorable baby. A mother's long, daily routine of beautifying her baby begins with an enema, includes a bath of both skin and jewelry, and ends with the application of makeup, jewelry, and often powder or oil on the very elaborately adorned infant (Figure 7.5) (Gottlieb, 2004, ch. 5).

An especially radiant child may indeed attract a large cohort of potential babysitters.

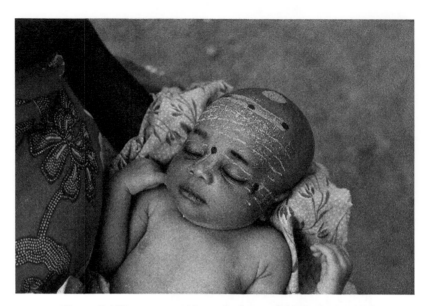

Figure 7.4 To attract a wide pool of potential babysitters, mothers typically spend an hour or more every morning grooming their babies (© and photographer Alma Gottlieb).

Figure 7.5 A mother's long, daily routine of beautifying her baby begins with an enema, includes a bath of both skin and jewelry, and ends with the application of makeup, jewelry, and often powder or oil on the very elaborately adorned infant (© and photographer Alma Gottlieb).

Figure 7.6 Most Beng babies are passed quite often from one back to another on any given day (© and photographer Alma Gottlieb).

In any case, most babies do not spend all of their days attached to the back of a single person – whether their mother or a single babysitter; rather, they tend to be passed quite often from one back to another on any given day (Figure 7.6).

Of course, the younger the child caregiver, the more likely that the baby will not last long on her babysitter's aching back. But older babysitters also have their own reasons to put down their charge after some time – their own lives that demand other kinds of engagements. And the babies may themselves fuss, in ways that are interpreted as a request for a change of carrier. In short, the life of an infant is a sociable one – the young child has abundant social contacts. Frequently, a baby will not spend more than an hour or two with a given person, and a mother may not even know where her baby is at any given time. In such a setting, babies learn to value sociability.[14]

And what about stranger anxiety? Is there a place at all for the concept in Beng understandings of infant development? In fact, the Beng have a

---

[14] Additional factors relating to spiritual considerations account for some of these practices; I explore these elsewhere (Gottlieb, 1998, 2004).

term that might be translated with some accuracy as "stranger anxiety." In referring to some babies, mothers use the term *"gbanɛ,"* which literally means to be clingy and normally refers to the baby's relation to the mother. For example, in explaining to me that none of her children were like this, one mother said proudly, *"ŋo ta sɔŋ klɛ – ŋà gbànɛ"* ("They go with [other] people – they don't cling [to me]"). Clingy Beng infants are very clearly (positively) "attached" to their mothers in the sense meant by child-development researchers. Like many of their Western counterparts, they are happiest when in the company of their mothers and appear noticeably anxious or fearful when confronted with a "stranger." And, like their Western counterparts, they tend to exhibit this quality towards the end of their first year.

One such child often cried in my own presence, for instance. While I did not administer the "strange situation" test in the field to assess the level and nature of his attachment to his mother, as strictly outlined by experimental psychologists, I am certain that if I had, children classified by the Beng as *gbanɛ* would have passed the test with flying colors, crying appropriately when their mothers left the room or courtyard and abandoned them to a stranger. At a *de facto* level, this is indeed what happened when one mother tried to pass such a baby to me to hold, even in her presence – unlike what happened with most other Beng babies of all ages, who usually allowed me to hold them with no qualms, even if the mother left the babies' view (Figure 7.7).

But what is significant in its implications for the attachment literature is that Beng children who are classified as *gbanɛ* are considered by the Beng to be difficult children (*"ŋo sie grégré"* – "Their character is difficult"). Indeed, they are frequently criticized and derided. Their mothers consider themselves unfortunate to have to deal with such clinginess. How will they get their work done?

They will have to keep the baby with them at all times, and for a full-time farmer this is quite physically demanding (Figure 7.8). A Beng baby who exhibits the sort of "stranger anxiety" that was considered healthy by the first generation of attachment theorists is a failure by Beng standards. At best, such a baby is a major nuisance to her mother. In the worst-case scenario, if she hinders her mother's work efforts significantly, the infant may even threaten the food supply of her household, thereby compromising the health of her siblings and others in the compound.[15]

---

[15] For a penetrating discussion of the fully interdependent relations among mothers, infants, and others in the family from the standpoint of the household food supply, see Popkin, Lasky, Spicer *et al.* (1986).

Figure 7.7 Most Beng babies of all ages allowed me to hold them with no qualms, even if the mother left the baby's view. (© Alma Gottlieb, photographer Philip Graham).

Given all I have said so far, what are the circumstances that might produce a "clingy baby" who "does not go to [other] people," including strangers? I was unable to conduct a study of a large number of such babies in Beng-land for one simple reason: there were not many of them at all. Indeed, I identified only one such infant in a very large village (pop. *c.* 1,500). At the time I came to know him, this baby – we will call him Kwame – was 9 months old. In Euro-American babies, this is a classic age for the onset of stranger anxiety, and in the case of Kwame, it had indeed set in with vengeance. Every time he saw me, Kwame crawled anxiously to his mother and stayed firmly in her lap or otherwise clung to her long skirt (*pagne*). Once, I left for a few minutes and returned to the courtyard to see Kwame exhibiting with a rare curiosity in playing with an exotic object – the external microphone of my tape recorder, which I had left on the ground. I decided to seize the opportunity and use the object to see how anxious my presence made him: I moved the microphone on the ground just out of his reach, nearer to me. Now that

Figure 7.8 Mothers of "clingy" children consider themselves unfortunate. How will they get their work done? (© and photographer Alma
Gottlieb).

I was there, Kwame refused to continue indulging his curiosity of a
moment before; he remained steadfastly attached to his mother's *pagne*,
clinging anxiously to her in my presence.

It is of note that Kwame's social biography was marked by quite special
circumstances. As a young girl, his mother – let us call her Au – had a
boyfriend, but her father arranged for her to become the second wife of a
distant cousin from another village, in accord with the complex rules for
arranged marriage that dominate the unions of many Beng villagers even
today (Gottlieb, 1986). Au was deeply unhappy over this development
and made strenuous efforts to resist the arranged polygynous marriage. In
the end, she relented, but her year-long series of rebellions had exacted
a toll on her family, whose level of disputes and alcohol consumption
on the part of several members was raised from what had already been
high.

Soon after she finally settled in with her arranged-marriage husband,
Au gave birth, but the infant died. A second baby died as well. A third
infant survived, but when she was quite young, probably only around

10 years old, this girl was sent off to live with her mother's younger sister who was living on a plantation in the south of the country. Thus, Kwame – the result of Au's fourth pregnancy – was the only living child who was currently residing with his mother.

Under these circumstances, one might expect that Au herself would have reasons to become more intensely attached to Kwame than most Beng mothers would; she had only one child with her, having lost two to the cruelty of death and a third to being foster-raised far away; and she remained unhappily married as a second wife somewhat far from her natal village and her natal family, from whom in any case she remained somewhat estranged. If a mother in these circumstances might be tempted to emotionally "overinvest" (by the standards of her society) in her infant son, it becomes reasonable to expect that in turn the baby might reciprocally "overinvest" in his mother, becoming "clingy" and wary of strangers. In short, examining the contours of Kwame's case identifies a relatively unusual social universe that may produce "stranger anxiety" in a society that routinely discourages – and fairly successfully so – its development.

The (admittedly intriguing) exception of Kwame (and others like him) aside, one striking result of Beng socialization practices is that Beng infants tend to be oriented towards people more than they are towards objects. This became dramatically clear to me in the course of a study I tried to conduct on the ability of infants (aged 7–20 months) to understand the difference between three-dimensional objects and their two-dimensional representations. In conducting the study in a Beng village, I tried to replicate the laboratory study conditions as much as possible of my North American colleagues who had devised the study (DeLoache et al., 1998). To my great frustration, I simply could not get the babies to cooperate in the ways that my colleagues back in Illinois had been able to achieve in their experiments with American babies.

The problem lay in the fact that it was impossible to isolate the babies in a room with just myself and a video camera because that would never have been permitted by the community. In Beng villages, as in much of West Africa, life is normally meant to be lived outside, enveloped by people (Figure 7.9) (Gottlieb and Graham, 1994); experimental social science research is no exception.

Therefore, surrounding the babies whom I seated on the ground of their courtyards were small crowds of interested onlookers – the babies' mothers or "babysitters" plus a host of curious neighbors, both old and young. Inevitably, it was this group of encircling people that intrigued the infants, far more than the object I was trying to show them, or the picture of the object, or even the very alien technology of an exotic video camera. To put it crudely, people won out over objects for Beng babies

Figure 7.9 In Beng villages, life is normally lived outside (© and photographer Alma Gottlieb).

as the most intriguing sites for their attention. Clearly, these infants had effectively internalized the lessons of their upbringing to date.

As Beng babies grow into young children, they tend to exhibit in delightful ways the training they had as infants that strangers are rarely threatening. One sign of the perceived benevolence of strangers is evident in a game that children play. There is an insect in the Beng region, *tiniŋ kaka*, whose name translates as "stranger insect." This insect is a large, flying, beetle-like creature that makes a loud buzzing sound. Normally these insects are absent in the villages. However, on occasion, they show up unexpectedly, usually in groups. Children become very excited at the appearance of these loudly buzzing, sometimes wildly flying bugs. As soon as the insects appear, the children rummage around for a piece of string or a strip of liana, maybe 2–3 feet (61–91 cm) long. Then they run around the courtyard gaily to catch one of the unlucky insects. They tie it to the string or liana and swing it around their heads as the victim protests with its loud buzz and the children chant gleefully, "*Tiniŋ kaka! Tiniŋ kaka!*" – "Stranger insect! Stranger insect!" (Gottlieb and Graham, 1994, pp. 300–1).

The children start looking around the courtyard, and more often than not, just then a real *tiniŋ* – an unexpected guest/visitor/stranger – indeed shows up. Adults in the courtyard smile and, if a visiting anthropologist happens to be present, may explain with some smug satisfaction that their worldview has just been vindicated. "See? The *tiniŋ kaka* was an omen – a *tiniŋ* really has come!" Indeed, in many cases I observed, large groups of *tiniŋ* did show up just then for an unanticipated event, especially a funeral of someone who had died suddenly.

Although funerals, of course, produce grief for those in personal mourning, the village at large may take on a somewhat festive atmosphere during a Beng funeral – the more so, the older was the person who died. If the deceased was quite elderly, the atmosphere becomes genuinely carnivalesque (Gottlieb, 1992; Gottlieb and Graham, 1994). Dances are held, everyone dresses in their finest clothes – colorful, matching outfits for both men and women – food is cooked in abundance, youths may mock the deceased in an elaborate charade and march around shouting teasing sexual insults to each other, distant relatives and friends show up to catch up on gossip, new babies are shown off, and chickens are stolen by funeral guests from other villages as part of a structural joking relationship with members of the host village. In these ways, the sudden arrival of the *tiniŋ kaka* frequently signals the arrival of a large group of human *tiniŋ* . . . which in turn – especially for children – signals the arrival of *fun*. We are a long way here from the dominant vision of the stranger-as-menacing-Other that prevails in so much of contemporary, urban societies.

Interpreting strangers and sociability in Beng villages

What accounts for the distinctive pattern of infant and childcare practices and behaviors we have traced in this chapter? Anthropologists are often wary of posing causal scenarios, aware that social life is far too complex, too messy, too overdetermined to be reduced to a single causal factor. At the same time, as social scientists we cannot entirely abjure the effort to explain. What follows, then, is a tentative set of three ideas – concerning religion, economy, and history – that together may go some way in accounting for the childcare patterns and behaviors we have observed. I do not claim that these three factors add up to a complete explanation, but they are certainly part of an explanation.

First, the pattern of welcoming "strangers" into their midst, and the associated habit of encouraging the creation of a broad variety of social ties and attachments, accords well with Beng religious ideology. As I have mentioned, Beng maintain that all babies come to this life after a previous existence in another life, termed *wrugbe*. Thus, the birth of a baby is not seen as the occasion to receive a strange new creature but rather someone

Figure 7.10 Beng women have sole responsibility for chopping and hauling firewood, fetching water, hand-washing the laundry for a large
family, and doing the vast majority of food preparation – often while
pregnant or breast-feeding (© and photographer Alma Gottlieb).

who has already been here before and then left, to return as a reincarnated
ancestor. I suggest that this ideology provides a template for welcoming
the "stranger" as a friendly guest with social ties to the community.

At another level, the pattern of encouraging children to form multiple
attachments from the earliest days of infancy works well with the demands
of women's labor. As has long been documented for rural Africa at large
(Boserup, 1970), Beng women have enormous labor demands on their
time. In addition to being full-time farmers (growing a large variety of
vegetables as well as rice and corn, clearing the underbrush for and
weeding the yam fields, and gathering wild forest products, as well as
occasionally hunting small game), Beng women have sole responsibility
for chopping and hauling firewood from the forest, fetching water for
the household water supply, hand-washing the laundry for a large family,
and doing the vast majority of food preparation for that family, including
pounding, cooking, and dishwashing (Figure 7.10) – much of this while
pregnant or breast-feeding.

Figure 7.11 It is hard to imagine a woman performing all her demanding work on her own while caring for several small children (including a baby and a toddler) (© and photographer Alma Gottlieb).

It is hard to imagine a woman performing all these tasks continually on her own, day in and day out without relief, while taking full-time care of several small children (including a baby and a toddler) (Figure 7.11).

In order to keep her household running and her share of the family's food supply intact, every mother must arrange either for a single regular babysitter or a network of potential babysitters on whom she can depend for somewhat regular childcare. In this way, the Beng habit of encouraging positive ties to many people, and discouraging the formation of a strong and single attachment to the mother, makes sense in the universe of women's labor.

Finally, there is the obvious question of history. In what sort of historical circumstances would an effort to embrace strangers make sense? Here we are awash in a sea of irony. For at least the brief period for which there is some documented history – barely more than a century – the Beng have appeared to be a relatively remote and insulated group. Surrounded by neighbors speaking languages belonging to different language families (Gottlieb and Murphy, 1995), the Beng have endeavored to maintain some distance from these neighbors. They have a reputation for a certain spiritual fierceness, due to distinctive ritual practices, that makes many neighbors fear them (Gottlieb, 1992, 1996; Gottlieb and Graham, 1994, 2012). The fact that most Beng overall are noticeably shorter than most other Ivoirian populations also lends them a distinctive physiological profile. Moreover, in times of military threat – at least from the nineteenth-century Muslim crusader, Samori, and perhaps from other military threats as well – they have reacted by retreating into the forest to maintain their pacifist stance of passive resistance, rather than actively engaging in combat or other active resistance; more recently, they fled to distant towns and cities to escape occupying rebels trying to topple the government.[16]

At the same time, this apparent isolationism belies a deep engagement with the neighboring world and beyond. The precolonial Beng economy was based in a long-distance trade in kola nuts, which Jula traders from the north (speaking a distantly related Mande language) came regularly to buy from Beng farmers in their villages. To engage in these critical commercial transactions, most Beng were (and still are) bilingual in Jula. Additionally, there appears to be a fair amount of intermixing of cultural practices (such as naming, family structure, and ritual) with Baule and Ando neighbors speaking Akan languages. As a result, most Beng were (and are) also fluent in Baule and/or Ando. Some Beng were (and continue to be) able to speak Jimini (a dialect of Senufo) spoken by their neighbors to the north with whom they also had commercial and ritual links. In short, despite living deep in the rain forest, having a somewhat distinct physiology, and a reputation for singular cultural practices, the Beng were intricately engaged in regional and long-distance networks for both economic and other forms of commerce. In such a setting, welcoming strangers – and training their children to do so from the earliest stages – must have made a certain sort of economic sense. And until the recent civil war and continuing conflict, routes to a wider world were even more open as Beng farmers sold crops to middlemen who came to the villages from Abidjan to buy their harvest, or Beng traveled to town themselves to sell their wares at a greater profit. Before rebels invaded, engaging productively with strangers continued to be critical to their survival.

---

[16] They claim to have no knowledge of the slave trade; contemporary Beng aware of this abysmal epoch of African history speculate that their ancestors must have lived (or retreated?) so deeply in the rain forest that they never encountered (or avoided?) the slave traders' nets. Only recently have the Beng begun to convert to Christianity and Islam. For a brief update on their reaction to the nation's recent political and military upheavals, see Gottlieb and Graham (2012, epilogue).

In short, the set of caregiving practices I have noted in this chapter speak to numerous issues relevant to Beng village life in several different arenas. In looking at the treatment of "strangers" and the nature and extent of "attachments" in Beng social life, we are led in a number of different directions at once. More broadly, beyond the Beng, they suggest for child-development researchers that religion, economy, and history may all turn out to be appropriate loci of relevant factors to consider, as attachment theorists continue to chart the social sense that given patterns of infants' "attachments" to a variety of persons make in particular social and historical settings.

Let us conclude by turning to the title of this chapter. Given the distinctive ways in which Beng promote and value "attachments" in their infants, is it time to detach from "attachment theory" as it has classically been configured by Western and Western-trained researchers? If scholars opt to retain "attachment theory" as a viable model relevant to children beyond the middle-class, Euro-American infants for and among whom the theory was developed, the nature of "attachments" not only to mothers but to all relevant individuals in a child's social universe must be investigated inductively, so as to understand from the local perspective the meanings of "attachment" in culturally relevant contexts. Without such a broadening of conceptual approach, "attachment theory" would remain, in effect, a folk theory relevant to only one of the world's many social systems for raising children.

Acknowledgments

In the field, my greatest debt is to the many Beng babies and their caregivers – mothers, sisters, aunts, and others – who put up with my guest/stranger's ways with far more grace than could be expected. For their continuing interest in this and other research in their villages, I remain grateful to my long-time Beng collaborators and friends, Amenan Véronique Akpoueh and Yacouba Kouadio Bah. During summer 1993, three other Beng assistants were also of enormous help in this research: Bertin Kouadio, Augustin Kouakou, and Dieudonné Kwame Kouassi.

For their support of my work researching among and writing about the Beng over the years, I am beholden to the Guggenheim Foundation, the US National Endowment for the Humanities, the Wenner-Gren Foundation for Anthropological Research, the Social Science Research Council, the US Information Agency, and several units at the University of Illinois (the Center for Advanced Study, the Research Board, and the Center for African Studies).

I presented earlier versions of this chapter to the Department of Anthropology at the University of Chicago; the Annual Meeting of the American Anthropological Association Childhood Interest Group – joint meeting with the Society for Anthropological Sciences and the 39th Annual Meeting of the Society for Cross-Cultural Research (February 17–20, 2010), Albuquerque, New Mexico; the Wenner-Gren Conference on Alloparenting in Human Societies (London); and the Center for African Studies, and the Interdisciplinary Faculty Seminar on the Stranger, both at the University of Illinois at Urbana-Champaign. I am grateful for the stimulating questions and comments I received among all audiences. For helping me orient myself in the attachment literature and productively challenging my reading of it, I am thankful to my colleague and friend, the developmental psychologist Judy DeLoache. Different versions of this chapter appear in print elsewhere (Gottlieb, 2004; and, by permission, Gottlieb, 2009).

At a personal level, I offer my continuing thanks for their emotional support to my husband Philip Graham and our children, Hannah and Nathaniel Gottlieb-Graham, to all of whom I am forever quite firmly attached.

Pronunciation guide to some Beng words:

Transcriptions of some Beng words in this chapter use characters from the International Phonetic Alphabet, which are pronounced as follows:

> ŋ pronounced "ng" as in "sing"
> ɔ pronounced "aw" as in "bawl"
> ɛ pronounced "eh" as in "bet".

References

Ainsworth, M. D. S., Blehar, M. C., Waters, E., and Wall, S. (1978). *Patterns of attachment: a psychological study of the strange situation.* Hillsdale, NJ: Erlbaum.

Boserup, E. (1970). *Woman's role in economic development.* New York: St. Martin's Press.

Bowlby, J. (1969). *Attachment and loss,* vol. I: *Attachment.* New York: Basic Books.

(1973). *Attachment and loss,* vol. II: *Separation: anxiety and anger.* New York: Basic Books.

(1980). *Attachment and loss,* vol. III: *Loss: sadness and depression.* New York: Basic Books.

Camus, A. (1946/1942). *The stranger.* S. Gilbert, trans. New York: Alfred A. Knopf.

Coontz, S. (1992). *The way we never were: American families and the nostalgia trap.* New York: Basic Books.

D.A.R.E. (n.d.). Website for D.A.R.E. (www.dare-america.com).

DeLoache, J. S., Pierroutsakos, S. L., Uttal, D. H., Rosengren, K. S., and Gottlieb, A. (1998). Grasping the nature of pictures. *Psychological Science, 9*(3), 205–10.

Douglas, M. (1966). *Purity and danger.* London: Routledge.

(1970). *Natural symbols.* New York: Pantheon.

(1992). *Risk and blame: essays in cultural theory.* London: Routledge.

Douglas, M., and Wildavsky, A. (1982). *Risk and culture: an essay on the selection of technological and environmental dangers.* Berkeley, CA: University of California Press.

Fildes, V. A. (1995). The culture and biology of breastfeeding: an historical review of Western Europe. In P. Stuart-Macadam and K. A. Dettwyler (Eds.), *Breastfeeding: biocultural perspectives* (pp. 101–26). Hawthorne, NY: Aldine de Gruyter.

Gottlieb, A. (1986). Cousin marriage, birth order, and gender: alliance models among the Beng of Ivory Coast. *Man, 2*(4), 697–722.

(1992). Passion and putrefaction: Beng funerals in disarray. Paper presented at the Eighth Annual Meeting of the Satterthwaite Colloquium on African Ritual and Religion (April 1992), Satterthwaite, UK.

(1995). The anthropologist as mother: reflections on childbirth observed and childbirth experienced. *Anthropology Today, 11*(3), 10–14.

(1996). *Under the kapok tree: identity and difference in Beng thought.* University of Chicago Press.

(1998). Do infants have religion? The spiritual lives of Beng babies. *American Anthropologist, 100*(1), 122–35.

(2000). Luring your child into this life: a Beng path for infant care. In J. S. DeLoache and A. Gottlieb (Eds.), *A world of babies: imagined childcare guides for seven societies* (pp. 55–89). New York: Cambridge University Press.

(2004). *The afterlife is where we come from: the culture of infants in west Africa.* University of Chicago Press.

(2009). Who minds the baby? Beng perspectives on mothers, neighbours, and strangers as caretakers. In G. Bentley and R. Mace (Eds.), *Substitute parents: biological and social perspectives on alloparenting across human societies* (pp. 115–38). Oxford: Bergahn.

Gottlieb, A., and Graham, P. (1994). *Parallel worlds: an anthropologist and a writer encounter Africa.* University of Chicago Press.

(2012). *Braided worlds.* University of Chicago Press.

Gottlieb, A., and Murphy, M. L. (1995). *Beng–English dictionary.* Bloomington, IN: Indiana University Linguistics Club.

Harwood, R. L., Miller, J. G., and Irizarry, N. L. (1995). *Culture and attachment: perceptions of the child in context.* New York: Guilford Press.

Hastrup, K. (1992). A question of reason: breast-feeding patterns in 17th and 18th century Iceland. In V. Maher (Ed.), *The anthropology of breast-feeding* (pp. 91–108). Oxford: Berg Publishers.

Holmes, J. (1993). *John Bowlby and attachment theory.* London: Routledge.

Johnson, M. (2000). The view from the Wuro. In J. S. DeLoache and A. Gottlieb (Eds.), *A world of babies: imagined childcare guides for seven societies* (pp. 171–98). New York: Cambridge University Press.

May, E. T. (1988). *Homeward bound: American families and the Cold War.* New York: Basic Books.

Neckoway, R., Brownlee, K., and Castellan, B. (2007). Is attachment theory consistent with Aboriginal parenting realities? *First Peoples Child and Family Review, 3*(2), 65–74.

Popkin, B., Lasky, T., Spicer, D., and Yamamota, M. E. (1986). *The infant-feeding triad: infant, mother, and household.* New York: Gordon and Breach.

Riesman, P. (1977). *Freedom in Fulani social life.* University of Chicago Press.

Rothbaum, F., Weisz, J., Pott, M., Miyke, K., and Morelli, G. (2000). Attachment and culture: security in the United States and Japan. *American Psychologist, 55*(10), 1093–1104.

Stuart-Macadam, P. (1995). Breastfeeding in prehistory. In P. Stuart-Macadam and K. A. Dettwyler (Eds.), *Breastfeeding: biocultural perspectives* (pp. 75–99). Hawthorne, NY: Aldine de Gruyter.

Uruakpa, F. O., Ismond, M. A. H., and Akobundu, E. N. T. (2002). Colostrum and its benefits: a review. *Nutrition Research, 22*(6), 755–67.

Wall, H. (2009). The parenting and substitute parenting of young children. In G. Bentley and R. Mace (Eds.), *Substitute parents: biological and social perspectives on alloparenting across human societies* (pp. 179–93). Oxford: Bergahn.

Weisner, T. S., and Gallimore, R. (1977). My brother's keeper: child and sibling caretaking. *Current Anthropology, 18*(2), 169–90.

Wulff, D. M. (2006). Commentary: how attached should we be to attachment theory? *International Journal for the Psychology of Religion, 16*(1), 29–36.

Xu, R. J. (1996). Development of the newborn GI tract and its relation to colostrum/milk intake: a review. *Reproduction, Fertility, and Development, 8*(1), 35–48.

8 Don't show your emotions! Emotion regulation and attachment in the Cameroonian Nso

Hiltrud Otto

In 2005, I went to live with a Cameroonian Nso family for half a year and experienced Nso everyday life firsthand: evenings in smoky kitchens while the women prepared dinner, mornings full of noise when children washed dresses and bathed in the courtyard, festive Sundays when everyone dressed up and went for a 3-hour church service. The participation in everyday life provided me with many opportunities to observe expressions of emotion: the laughter of women singing and gossiping, the grief of mourners at a funeral, harsh voices organizing daily work, or angry voices scolding lazy children. But I rarely observed children displaying emotions openly, especially not in the presence of adults. Even infant crying is hardly heard in Nso villages.

Since I had come to the Nso to study the development of attachment relationships in this rural community, I became interested in emotion regulation and the expression of emotions between infants and their primary caregivers. However, identifying their mothers was more difficult than I had expected. The infants in the compounds had a great number of mostly female caregivers. As I found out, it could be an aunt, an older sibling, or a neighbor. From their behavior, it was not obvious that they were not the biological mothers. Though children usually slept in their families' house during the night, it also happened that children from relatives or from neighboring compounds stayed overnight as well – so sleeping arrangements served only as a rough guide for underlying family structures. Yet, the observation of breast-feeding allowed the identification of biological mother–infant pairs, as usually only the biological mothers breast-feed their own infants among the Nso.

Part of this study was supported by a grant from the German Research Foundation (DFG, Grant 772/3). I would like to thank the participating families and my coworkers and colleagues, Dr. Relindis Yovsi and Patience Nsam.

It became quite obvious that before studying emotion regulation and expression in caregiver–infant relationships, I first had to understand the social structure with its norms, values, and beliefs and its function in children's socialization (see Keller, 2007). In this chapter, I will first describe the ecocultural environment of the Nso and the cultural model that is adapted to this environment; I will then illustrate how the cultural norms and beliefs inherent in the cultural model influence Nso socialization strategies; lastly, I will discuss the development of attachment and exemplify emotional expressions in an attachment-arousing situation, the confrontation with a stranger.

The ecocultural environment of the Nso: the basis for relational adaptation

The Nso is the largest chiefdom in the Bamenda Grassfields (Goheen, 1996); with a population of some 250,000 over an area of 2,300 km³, it is a heavily populated, agricultural region (DeLancey, 1989). The capital of the Nso is Kumbo, a city with about 65,000 inhabitants. In the past, the Bamenda Grassfields was a forest zone occupied by hunters (Nkwi and Warnier, 1982). Today the forest has virtually vanished, with only the savannah grass, after which the region is named, remaining as the most distinctive vegetation. The Grassfields is a high lava plateau surrounded by plains and valleys. There are generally a 6-month rainy season from April to September; a cool, dry season from October to December; and a hot, dry season from January to March. Specific ecological relations lead to specific socioeconomic structures to facilitate human survival and striving (Whiting and Whiting, 1975); in the case of the Nso, a subsistence-based farming society evolved, in which successful farm work necessitates cooperation among the members of large extended families. However, as harvests are unstable and seasonal famines occur frequently in the arid north, the larger Nso community is organized as a cohesive union in which members are collaborative and responsible for each other.

Thus, cooperation based on a sense of belonging, solidarity, and protection is crucial. It relies on the strong kin and lineage relations among the Nso, which also involve expectations, obligations, and responsibilities (Fleischer, 2006). Behavioral obligations associated with specific social and gender roles are especially important for the realization of communal goals (Keller and Kärtner, 2013). For example, rich kin are expected to foster children from poorer families, and help with child-rearing costs and education (Eloundou-Enyegue and Shapiro, 2005).

The Nso live in a highly stratified social structure. At the top of the Nso hierarchy is the *fon* ("king"). *Fons* are selected from a group of eligible titleholders to fulfill the role of the traditional ruler. They are the sociopolitical leaders and the chief religious authority in charge of keeping the ancestors satisfied. The *fon* holds large areas of land, with use rights devolving to specific lineages.

Nso society is divided into groups according to lineage, led by a *fai*. Several lineages are grouped together under a *shufai*. In general, Nso societal organization includes hierarchical relations between members of groups with different status, such as royalty and commoners (Nsamenang and Lamb, 1994; Yovsi, 2003). The *fon* has to be treated with utmost respect, excluding any kind of direct interaction. Tradition also prohibits a handshake with *shufais* and *fais*, who are easily recognized by their glass necklaces and walking sticks (Goheen, 1996). Such status differences are also reflected in the housing styles. The wealthiest people have painted, concrete houses surrounded by high walls. The poorest people live in mud houses with thatched or corrugated iron roofs, sparsely furnished with beds and stools.

Nso society is organized patrilineally and patrilocally. People live in extended, multigenerational households with an average household size of eight persons (Goheen, 1996). Men are the authoritative heads of the households. Most households are located within so-called compounds, which consist of houses arranged around open courtyards. Everyday life takes place in these courtyards, where food is prepared, vegetables are laid out to dry, dresses are washed, and news is exchanged. The traditional language of the Nso is Lamnso (Trudell, 2006), an oral language; in recent years, many youths also speak some English and French. Nso families live off subsistence farming, growing maize, potatoes, beans, and other vegetables. Farm work is usually done cooperatively among family members (Goheen, 1996; Keller, 2007). While women are the main laborers in the fields, men perform communal duties, such as attending assemblies and discussing political issues in order to "fully participate in the welfare of the Nso folk" (Yovsi, 2003, p. 8); some are also employed in paid labor. Children have many responsibilities: they are expected to help on the farm, to run errands, and to contribute to housework, with boys mainly being responsible for fetching firewood, and girls helping with household chores and sibling caregiving.

Women in general, and unmarried women in particular, occupy a subordinate status to men and boys. Unmarried women are considered inferior as social persons (Mbaku and Falola, 2005); "in fact they do not exist at all" (Vubo, 2005, p. 168). It is only after marriage that women rise to full status, gaining rights and privileges, besides obligations. Most Nso women belong to *njangis*, women groups that gather every week. Those self-help groups save small amounts of money over the year that can be borrowed in an emergency, and is fairly distributed at the end of the year (Bouman, 1995). The money saved over the course of a year is spent on commodities the women cannot produce themselves and on children's education (Yovsi and Keller, 2003). The functional basis of *njangis* are social relationships and trust (Goheen, 1996). In general, the sharing of food and drink is supposed to demonstrate hospitality and trust and thereby constitutes one of the major ways to cement social relationships. Among the Nso, many social networks are held together with gifts of food, and during our travels in Cameroon, we were often asked to carry huge bags of potatoes, beans, or rice and drop them at a friend's place in a different part of the country.

In Nso everyday life, magic and witchcraft play a very important role. *Jujus*, masked representations of spirits, can be seen regularly on important occasions, such as funerals or the ritual celebrations of secret societies (Goheen, 1996). Indigenous beliefs continue to be an important part of Nso spiritual life, though missionaries have converted approximately 40% of the Cameroonian population to Christianity, while 30% of the Nso population adhere to Islam (*World Fact Book*, 2012).

Thus, Nso society can be said to represent a traditional, non-Western, agrarian society (Keller, 2003, 2007). The specifics of the Nso context led to the development of beliefs and practices focusing on the principles of cooperation, solidarity, and social responsibility. Systems and practices shared by the members of a community are generally referred to as cultural models (D'Andrade, 1981; Holland and Quinn, 1987). Cultural models are developed as specific and adaptive mind-sets that align basic human needs to the structure of the broader ecosocial context (see Keller and Kärtner, 2013). In general, two basic human needs are reflected in cultural models everywhere: the need for autonomy and the need for relatedness. And though every human being longs for the fulfillment of both, the affordances and demands of specific ecocultural contexts define how autonomy and relatedness are conceptualized and expressed. In the case of Nso society, a strong emphasis on relational adaptation is clearly noticeable in the values and practices, instilling obligatory relationships and mandatory roles in members of the society. At the same time, action autonomy is encouraged to put members of the society in the position to perform role-based actions and meet obligations on their own, yet in the service of the community. Thereby, Nso society adheres to a cultural model that clearly differs from the cultural model typical of WEIRD societies (Western, educated, industrialized, rich, and democratic societies; see Henrich, Heine, and Norenzayan, 2010), where psychological autonomy – that is, personal desires, wishes, and intentions – guide individual behaviors, and psychological relatedness – that is, negotiable relations to others – forms the basis of social life (for a comparison of ecocultural contexts and cultural models, see Keller, this volume, 2007; Keller and Kärtner, 2013).

Nso socialization towards relational adaptedness and action autonomy

Cultural models are mind-sets that function in a specific cultural context. They extend to child rearing in the respective contexts (e.g., Sigel, McGillicuddy-DeLisi, and Goodnow, 1992), by defining what is considered good or bad parenting, informing child-rearing practices, and conveying expectations for the onset of developmental achievements, such as the age at which a child is expected to speak or to walk. The ecocultural conditions that children grow up in, together with their caregivers' beliefs and child-rearing customs, are usually referred to as "developmental niches" (Super and Harkness, 1996) or "ecocultural niches" (Weisner, 1984). The developmental niche of Nso children is typical of a traditional and hierarchical, agrarian society with a strong focus on the communal responsibility that is also reflected in the beliefs and practices of child rearing.

Nso mothers believe children to belong to them only as long as they are in the womb. Once born, "a child belongs not to one parent or home" (African proverb); instead "it takes a whole village to raise the child" (African proverb), and this idea is practically realized. Child rearing is a communal activity that, beginning at an early age, aims to initiate a "fledgling" into society through social priming (Nsamenang and Lamb, 1994). For children, this collective approach to child rearing means the availability of a multitude of caregivers, teachers, supervisors, and playmates alike. Thus, children get to know large social networks from early on and become integrated into this community, which helps children to cope without a mother: "If I'm not by her side now or if I maybe die, who will take care of her? She needs to at least love everybody or try to be used to everybody, so that in case I am not around, anybody can take care of her" (Otto, 2008, p. 95). This community also allows mothers to do their daily work: "It is not possible that I can be taking care of him alone. He would be disturbing me most often. It means I will not be able to do any other thing" (Otto, 2008, p. 95). Due to the heavy workload of mothers and the possibility of a premature maternal death, everyone is involved in the task of child rearing: Sibling caregiving is very prevalent, and even children as young as 3 years are responsible for watching younger children (Lamm, 2008). Although females participate most in child-rearing activities, men keep a watchful eye and interfere in case of imminent danger. The communal responsibility for children puts Nso parents at ease. They can allow their infants to explore the whole village area without knowing their whereabouts, because they rely on the caregiving and watchfulness of the community. At the same time, communal caregiving enables children to develop a variety of social bonds with others.

Cultural models also prescribe what children should be trained and taught (Kärtner, Keller, Lamm *et al.*, 2007). Such beliefs and ideas become tangible in the form of ethnotheories when mothers reflect on the desired social behaviors of children (Keller, 2003). Ethnotheories convey precious knowledge about child development that has been passed from one generation to the next. Like cultural models in general, these ideas represent adaptations with respect to child rearing, with the ultimate goal to ensure infant survival in a particular sociocultural context. Nso parents' proximate goals consist of equipping infants with the necessary socioemotional competencies to become competent adults, valued in their cultural community. In the case of the Nso, obedience, conformity, and respect for authority are the most important socialization goals for children. As a Nso mother puts it: "A good child is that one who is obedient, who is ready to listen and ready to act as instructed, not acting his or her own way that pleases her" (Otto, 2008).

The Nso instantiate these socialization goals from very early on, as is apparent when we analyze the discourse of Nso mothers to their 3-month-old infants. The mothers frequently recite social norms and morals. One mother says to her crying baby: "Don't cry again!... We don't cry in Mbah!" (Demuth, 2008, p. 104), conveying the message that crying is socially unacceptable. Another mother uses a rhetorical question to convey the social norm that one should not eat other people's food: "Would you be moving around and eating people's foofoo?" (Demuth, 2008, p. 165). The young Nso child is expected to internalize these explicit lessons on social norms and values as tacit cultural knowledge (Demuth, 2008). During early socialization, Nso mothers focus on the development of a social self in children, in order to raise future community members who have a developed Nso identity and a sense of belonging (Keller, 2007; Nsamenang, 1992).

One important lesson children are taught is that the world does not revolve around them, but instead they have to follow and adapt to the work routines of the community. Caregivers usually do not focus exclusively on the child, but babies are also hardly ever alone. They are integrated into the daily activities, be it cooking, farm work, or – in case of sibling caregiving – playing. Nso babies are almost constantly held on the bodies of their caregivers, mainly in an upright position – in order to grow correctly (Keller, 2003). This position also allows them to observe activities, unless they fall asleep while they are carried around. Even during the night, Nso children remain in close body contact with others as they share a bed with their mothers, siblings, or other children. Presumably, the constant proximity generates feelings of connectedness, belonging, and unity with a variety of significant others in Nso children from early on.

Action autonomy is supported by fostering babies' early motor independence. Besides particular interactional practices of lifting the baby up and down in a vertical position, gross motor skills are also taught in special lessons – babies may be placed upright in buckets or similar containers in order to learn to sit straight for some time. This motor training has to do with the belief that children never learn to sit, stand, or walk if they are not properly taught, since "the bones and the back will be soft and not tightened together" (Keller, Yovsi, and Voelker, 2002, p. 409). In fact, 3-month-old babies can already sit independently for extended periods of time (Lohaus, Keller, Fassbender *et al.*, 2011).

The early motor training is instrumental in the context of sibling caregiving: Young caregivers especially struggle under the additional weight of a sibling on their back and sometimes both caregiver and infant fall while climbing the hillsides. When observing these incidents, my heart would often skip a beat, but usually nothing serious happened. The motor stimulation puts children in the position to contribute to the household from very early on. For example, once the babies are capable of walking, they do their bit in helping in the daily work, and are no longer a burden to others.

During their early social interactions, children develop a sense of self and a sense of self-related-to-others that profoundly affects the ways in which interpersonal relations are experienced (LeVine, 1990). Nso children develop conceptions of themselves as actors in a world full of social commitments and responsibilities in which they are expected to cooperate and contribute their share.

Consequences for emotion regulation and expression in the context of attachment relationships

Socialization towards social cohesion and conformity as valued by the Nso farmers is incompatible with acting out and expressing emotions freely. Especially the display of positive emotionality has been attributed to the instantiation of individuality as valued in the Western world (Shweder and Bourne, 1984). The open expression of emotionality is one characteristic of secure attachment relationships. It can be assumed that the development of Nso emotion regulation and expression does not follow the pathway described by ethological attachment theory (e.g., Ainsworth, Blehar, Waters *et al.*, 1978; Bowlby, 1969), but instead follows the pathway of relational adaptation. Therefore, crucial conceptions of parenting must differ between the assumptions of attachment theory and Nso cultural beliefs and practices.

According to ethological attachment theory, mothers should encourage their children to express their own will and to communicate their emotional states. They should engage babies in conversations about their mental states, their preferences, and their emotions, treating babies as individuals motivated by feeling, thoughts, and intentions. This discourse style was labeled "mind-minded" talk by Meins and Fernyhough (1999), who suggested that mind-mindedness, in addition to sensitive parenting, leads to secure attachments. However, the Nso practice of caregiver–infant discourse occurs in stark contrast to the description given by attachment theory: It is characterized by rhythmic, overlapping vocalizations/verbalizations, which may foster the experience of synchrony between the interaction partners (Keller, Otto, Lamm *et al.*, 2008). Nso mothers project a highly normative-hierarchical discourse, positioning the child to obey and to comply in a hierarchical context (Demuth, 2008). This hierarchical normativity becomes particularly evident when the child behaves in a socially undesirable way. Using a mind-minded style when talking to infants is considered ludicrous by Cameroonian Nso mothers. They perceive small babies as not yet capable of having intentions, preferences, or wishes (Otto and Keller, in press). Moreover, in Nso society, rules often dictate when it is permissible to show emotions, and when not. These rules include a restriction of emotional expressivity towards authorities, as in gaze aversion in interaction with people of higher status. Training starts from early on. When infants try to lock on their mother's gaze during breast-feeding, mothers blow air into their eyes, so they avert their gaze and learn to avoid direct eye contact. In general, Nso mothers expect their children from a very early age to control their emotional expressions (Keller and Otto, 2009), respecting the local display rules. During infants' first year of life, crying is especially considered naughty behavior, and children are scolded harshly for crying without reason.

Emotion regulation in attachment theory is usually assessed with the strange-situation procedure, a laboratory-based sequence of mother–child interactions, encounters with a female stranger, and separation episodes. Attachment theorists defined four attachment patterns representing different emotion-regulation strategies when dealing with stress in this situation: secure, insecure-avoidant, insecure-ambivalent, and disorganized attachment patterns. The entrance of a stranger is supposed to introduce a mild alarm for the child in the presence of the caregiver (Ainsworth, Bell, Stayton et al., 1974, p. 105), but being left alone with the stranger is assumed to heighten the distress enormously (Miller, Bard, Juno et al., 1990; van IJzendoorn, Bard, Bakermans-Kranenburg et al., 2009). Children with a sensitive, mind-minded mother are supposed to communicate their feelings of distress openly, and to calm down once they are reunited with their mother. They have learned that their needs are being met by the caregiver, who helps them to manage their negative emotions. In contrast, insecure-avoidantly attached infants have learned to reveal as little as possible about their inner experiences of negative affect, which is assumed to be a consequence of nonresponsive caregivers (mothers). Infants with an insecure-ambivalent attachment have parents who ignore or misinterpret their infants' emotional signals. Infants therefore overtly display intense negative emotions, as they are never sure whether their needs will be met by their caregiver. Disorganized infants show signs of learned hopelessness or helplessness through either fearful affect generated by the caregiver or fearful affect generated from other sources in the context of emotional unavailability of the caregiver.

However, the application of the strange-situation procedure (SSP) in the Nso villages is impossible; children are never left alone, and definitely not in a closed room. The enforcement of the SSP guidelines would have been really cruel (as it is often for Western children, too). Applying this procedure would have led to the Nso community immediately distrusting my activities, which were otherwise extremely supported. Instead of using the SSP, we induced a quasi-experimental setting in order to observe the children's reactions to a stranger (Keller and Otto, 2009; Otto, 2008): Mothers and infants were visited by a native female stranger, who approached the infant, picked the infant up, and interacted with it for up to 5 minutes, preferably while holding the infant in her arms and moving away from the mother. We video-recorded the interaction and analyzed the children's emotion-regulation strategies in response to the stranger.

Our microanalysis of emotional expressions of 1-year-old infants during the stranger approach revealed three different patterns: the majority of infants did not express any emotional arousal in response to the strangers' approach. This group of 1-year-old infants had already learned to meet the cultural expectations appropriately, presenting a calm and easily handled behavior when interacting with others, including strangers. They had mothers who were married and relied on the support of a large social network. A second group of infants was inexpressive and calm at the beginning of the interaction with the stranger, but displayed negative emotions when the stranger took the child further away from the mother. The moment the infants started to withdraw from the stranger, their mothers became agitated and intervened in the ongoing interaction. They tried to teach the proper behavior by shaking the infant and telling him or her to "stop crying" and to behave properly. Hence, those mothers had not yet completely achieved their socialization goal to have calm and expressionless infants, but were still teaching the child to behave properly. A third group of infants in our sample displayed extreme negative emotions from the very beginning of the stranger's visit, and the demographic data revealed that those children grew up under adverse social conditions, as they had single mothers who reportedly lacked social support.

Due to the culture-specific socialization process during their first year of life, Nso children develop culture-specific emotion regulation and thus attachment patterns representing adaptations to their specific sociocultural conditions. Not surprisingly, our analysis revealed that the optimal attachment pattern found among the Nso differs from the optimal attachment pattern as described by attachment theorists, the "secure" attachment pattern. Under Nso conditions, the optimal strategy is represented by calm and easy children who become attached to many caregivers, relying on a wide social network. As a Nso mother commented: "A calm child is a good child." Moreover, these mothers reported that most often other people besides themselves represent the favorite caregiver of the child. In contrast, the group of Nso children openly displaying negative emotions were faced with an adverse environment, characterized by the lack of social support, including financial support, caused by the mother's pregnancy out of marriage. In the interdependent Nso culture, these contextual determinants can be regarded as detrimental to a mother's and a child's well-being. Since social support is lacking, nobody else may function as a maternal substitute, as in providing additional childcare. Hence, the extremely negative responses of those children may reflect the children's inexperience with other caregivers and indicate the lack of any proper behavioral coping mechanism for such situations.

According to ethological attachment theory, the formation of a close attachment relationship between infant and primary caregiver, mainly the mother, is a universal developmental task. The Nso, however, provide one example that the ontogeny of attachment can deviate from the ethological

attachment theory's assumptions, since Nso mothers are generally neither sensitive nor mind-minded in attachment theory's terms. Moreover,
the assumed normativity of the secure attachment pattern as defined by
ethological attachment theory does not hold true for the cultural context of the Nso. In our sample, the most adaptive emotion-regulation
strategy was represented by the lack of emotional expression. In line
with other chapters in this volume (cf. those of Gottlieb, Keller, Lancy,
and LeVine), a context-informed conception of attachment needs to be
developed since attachment patterns and emotion-regulation strategies
reflect ecocultural and social parameters.

Conclusion

David Zeitlyn, an anthropologist working with the Mambila in Cameroon
since 1985, visited our laboratory last year and showed old photographs
from Cameroonian Mambila photographers, who live in the neighborhood of the Nso. From all these photographs, it became obvious that
Mambila people also presented with neutral facial expressions. Gottlieb
(2004, this volume) reports that calmness and compliance are also highly
valued in Beng infants of Ivory Coast, and Lancy (2008, this volume)
similarly provides evidence that in many cultural contexts mothers swad-
dle their babies to keep them calm. Though, today, calm children are
mostly valued in traditional and agricultural societies with low levels of
formal education, Western families followed the same socialization goals
and taught their children to be calm and obedient until the early decades
of last century.

Cultures are not static entities; they represent dynamic processes. They
change with environmental changes; however, not all environments have
the same pace of change. The Western world underwent big changes
during the last sixty years, and one result is that, in our modern world,
children are not only allowed but also expected to express their wishes,
their preferences, their own ideas – and their emotions. Attachment theory definitely played a key role in the formation of a new image of the
infant, granting children autonomy and individuality; however, attachment theory overlooked the fact that many cultural contexts did not
undergo the same changes. Ethological attachment theory underestimated the power of the varying social and cultural factors that shape
parental thinking and behavior and hence infants' attachment: the cultural meanings of fertility, birth, and death; the mother's assessment of
her economic and social support and her psychological resources; and
maternal belief systems. If cultural and social factors can successfully
be embodied in an attachment-theory framework, this will have serious

consequences for the current debates about healthy child development within different environments. My hope is that such an approach will generate a context-informed, multidisciplinary perspective in which children's needs are assessed and treated with knowledge, respect, and sensitivity to the sociocultural and political contexts in which they occur. This context-informed approach to attachment will have lasting consequences for research, training, and intervention in the area of child development.

References

Ainsworth, M. D., Bell, S. M., Stayton, D. F., and Richards, M. P. (1974). *Infant–mother attachment and social development: socialization as a product of reciprocal responsiveness to signals*. New York: Cambridge University Press.

Ainsworth, M. D., Blehar, M. C., Waters, E., and Wall, S. (1978). *Patterns of attachment: a psychological study of the strange situation*. Oxford: Erlbaum.

Bornstein, M. H., and Bradley, R. H. (2003). *Socioeconomic status, parenting, and child development*. Mahwah, NJ: Erlbaum.

Bouman, F. J. A. (1995). Rotating and accumulating savings and credit associations: a development perspective. *World Development*, *23*(3), 371–84.

Bowlby, J. (1969). *Attachment*. New York: Basic Books.

D'Andrade, R. G. (1981). The cultural part of cognition. *Cognitive Science*, *5*, 179–95.

DeLancey, M. D. W. (1989). *Cameroon: dependence and independence*. Boulder, CO: Westview Press.

Demuth, C. (2008). Talking to infants: how culture is instantiated in early mother–infant interactions: the case of Cameroonian farming Nso and north German middle-class families. Ph.D. thesis, University of Osnabrück, Osnabrück, Germany.

Eloundou-Enyegue, P. M., and Shapiro, D. (2005). Confiage d'enfants et nivelement des inégalités scolaires au Cameroun. *Cahiers Québecois de Démographie*, *34*(1), 47–75.

Fleischer, A. (2006). Family, obligations, and migration: the role of kinship in Cameroon. *MPIDR working paper (WP2006–047)*, 1–32.

(1992). Chiefs, sub-chiefs and local control: negotiations over land, struggles over meaning. *Africa*, *62*(3), 389–412.

Goheen, M. (1996). *Men own the fields, women own the crops: gender and power in the Cameroon grassfields*. Madison, WI: University of Wisconsin Press.

Gottlieb, A. (2004). *The afterlife is where we come from: the culture of infancy in west Africa*. University of Chicago Press.

Henrich, J., Heine, S. J., and Norenzayan, A. (2010). The weirdest people in the world? *Behavioral and Brain Sciences*, *33*(2–3), 1–75.

Holland, D., and Quinn, N. (1987). *Cultural models in language and thought*. Cambridge University Press.

Kärtner, J., Keller, H., Lamm, B., Abels, M., Yovsi, R. D., and Nandita, C. (2007). Manifestations of autonomy and relatedness in mothers' accounts of their ethnotheories regarding child care across five cultural communities. *Journal of Cross-Cultural Psychology*, *38*(5), 613–28.

Keller, H. (2003). Socialization for competence: cultural models of infancy. *Human development*, 46(5), 288–311.

(2007). *Cultures of infancy*. Mahwah, NJ: Erlbaum.

Keller, H., and Kärtner, J. (2013). Development – the cultural solution of universal developmental tasks. In M. Gelfand, C.-Y. Chiu, and Y. Y. Hong (Eds.), *Advances in culture and psychology* (vol. III, pp. 63–116). New York: Oxford Universiy Press.

Keller, H., and Otto, H. (2009). The cultural socialization of emotion regulation during infancy. *Journal of Cross-Cultural Psychology*, 40(6), 996–1011.

Keller, H., Otto, H., Lamm, B., Yovsi, R. D., and Kaertner, J. (2008). The timing of verbal/vocal communications between mothers and their infants: a longitudinal cross-cultural comparison. *Infant Behavior and Development*, 31(2), 217–26.

Keller, H., Yovsi, R. D., and Voelker, S. (2002). The role of motor stimulation in parental ethnotheories: the case of Cameroonian Nso and German women. *Journal of Cross-Cultural Psychology*, 33(4), 398–414.

Lamb, M. E., Bornstein, M. H., and Teti, D. M. (2002). *Development in infancy: an introduction* (4th edn.). Mahwah, NJ: Erlbaum.

Lamb, B. (2008). Children's ideas about infant care: a comparison of rural Nso children from Cameroon and German middle-class children. Ph.D. thesis, University of Osnabrück, Osnabrück, Germany.

Lancy, D. F. (2008). *The anthropology of childhood: cherubs, chattel, changelings*. Cambridge University Press.

LeVine, R. A. (1990). Infant environments in psychoanalysis: a cross-cultural view. In J. W. Stigler, R. A. Shweder, and G. Herdt (Eds.), *Cultural psychology: essays on comparative human development* (pp. 454–74). Cambridge University Press.

LeVine, R. A., and Miller, P. M. (1990). Commentary. *Human Development*, 33, 73–80.

Lewis, M. (2005). The child and its family: the social network model. *Human Development*, 48(1), 8–27.

Lewis, M., and Takahashi, K. (2005). Beyond the dyad: conceptualization of social networks. *Human Development*, 48(1), 5–8.

Lohaus, A., Keller, H., Fassbender, I., Teubert, M., Lamm, B., Vierhaus, M., Freitag, C., et al. (2011). Infant development in two cultural contexts: Cameroonian Nso farmer and German middle class infants. *Journal of Reproductive and Infant Psychology*, 29(2), 148–61.

Mbaku, J. M., and Falola, T. (2005). *Culture and customs of Cameroon*. Westport, CT: Greenwood.

Meins, E., and Fernyhough, C. (1999). Linguistic acquisitional style and mentalising development: the role of maternal mind-mindedness. *Cognitive Development*, 14(3), 363–80.

Miller, L. C., Bard, K. A., Juno, C. J., and Nadler, R. D. (1990). Behavioral responsiveness to strangers in young chimpanzees (*Pan troglodytes*). *Folia Primatologica*, 55(3), 128–42.

Neckoway, R., Brownleea, K., and Castellana, B. (2007). Is attachment theory consistent with Aboriginal parenting realities? *First Peoples Child and Family Review*, 3(2), 65–74.

228   *Hiltrud Otto*

Nkwi, P. N., and Warnier, J. P. (1982). *Elements for a history of the western grass-fields*. Yaoundé, Cameroon: SOPECAM.

Nsamenang, A. B. (1992). Early childhood care and education in Cameroon. In M. E. Lamb, C. Sternberg, C. Hwang, and A. Broberg (Eds.), *Childcare in context: cross-cultural perspectives* (pp. 421–39). Hillsdale, NJ: Erlbaum.

Nsamenang, A. B., and Lamb, M. E. (1994). Socialization of Nso children in the Bamenda Grassfields of northwest Cameroon. In P. M. Greenfield and R. R. Cocking (Eds.), *Cross-cultural roots of minority child development*. (pp. 133–46): Erlbaum.

Otto, H. (2008). Culture-specific attachment strategies in the Cameroonian Nso: cultural solutions to a universal developmental task. Ph.D. thesis, University of Osnabrück, Osnabrück, Germany.

Otto, H., and Keller, H. (in press). Attachment and culture in Africa. In M. Tomlinson, C. Hanlon, L. Swartz, P. Cooper, and A. Sameroff (Eds.), *Infant and child development in Africa: perspectives from the continent*. Cape Town: University of Cape Town Press and United Nations University Press.

Porges, S. W., King, J. A., Ferris, C. F., and Lederhendler, I. I. (2003). Social engagement and attachment: a phylogenetic perspective. *Annals of the New York Academy of Sciences*, *1008*, 31–47.

Rothbaum, F., Weisz, J., Pott, M., Miyake, K., and Morelli, G. (2000). Attachment and culture: security in the United States and Japan. *American Psychologist*, *55*(10), 1093–1104.

Shweder, R. A., and Bourne, E. J. (1984). Does the concept of the person vary cross-culturally? In R. A. Shweder and R. A. LeVine (Eds.), *Culture theory: essays on mind, self, and emotion* (pp. 158–99). Cambridge University Press.

Sigel, I. E., McGillicuddy-DeLisi, A. V., and Goodnow, J. J. (1992). *Parental belief systems: the psychological consequences for children* (2nd edn.). Hillsdale, NJ: Erlbaum.

Super, C. M., and Harkness, S. (1996). *Parents' cultural belief systems*. New York: Guilford Press.

Trudell, B. (2006). Language development and social uses of literacy: a study of literacy practices in Cameroonian minority language communities. *International Journal of Bilingual Education and Bilingualism*, *9*(5), 625–42.

van IJzendoorn, M. H., Bard, K. A., Bakermans-Kranenburg, M., and Ivan, K. (2009). Enhancement of attachment and cognitive development of young nursery-reared chimpanzees in responsive versus standard care. *Developmental Psychobiology*, *51*(2), 173–85.

Vubo, E. Y. (2005). Matriliny and patriliny between cohabitation-equilibrium and modernity in the Cameroon Grassfields. *African Study Monographs*, *26*(3), 145–82.

Weisner, T. S. (1984). Ecocultural niches of middle childhood: a cross-cultural perspective. In W. A. Collins (Ed.), *Development during middle childhood: the years from six to twelve* (pp. 335–69). Washington, DC: National Academies Press.

Whiting, B., and Whiting, J. W. M. (1975). *Children of six cultures: a psycho-cultural analysis*. Cambridge, MA: Harvard University Press.

World Fact Book (2012) (www.cia.gov/library/publications/the-world-factbook/geos/cm.html).

Yovsi, R. D. (2003). *Ethnotheories about breastfeeding and mother–infant interaction: the case of sedentary Nso farmers and nomadic Fulani pastorals with their infants 3–6 months of age in Mbven subdivision of the Northwest Province of Cameroon.* Münster: LIT Verlag.

Yovsi, R. D., Kärtner, J., Keller, H., and Lohaus, A. (2009). Maternal interactional quality in two cultural environments: German middle-class and Cameroonian rural mothers. *Journal of Cross-Cultural Psychology*, *40*(4), 701–7.

Yovsi, R. D., and Keller, H. (2003). Breastfeeding: an adaptive process. *Ethos*, *31*(2), 147–71.

9   Family life as *bricolage* – reflections on intimacy and attachment in *Death Without Weeping*

Nancy Scheper-Hughes

"Today is Father's Day – what a joke!"
> Carolina Maria de Jesus, *Child of the Dark: The Diary of Carolina de Jesus* (1963)

"It has been the fate of mothers throughout history to appear in strange and distorted forms."
> Nancy Scheper-Hughes, *Death Without Weeping* (1992, p. 354)

If infants born on the periphery of the global economy – and that includes parts of the USA – are to be saved, it cannot depend only on their mothers. This was the primary argument launched in my research and writings on mother love, maternal bonding, selective neglect, and infant mortality in northeast Brazil. Motherhood, I argued, is as *social* as fatherhood, and all mothers, like all fathers, are *adoptive* parents. Mother–child and adult–adult attachments are not given – they are socially, historically, and culturally produced. Intimacy, attachment, love, neglect, and social indifference are rarely theorized in anthropological writings. They are assumed to be self-evident. But what does mother love mean to shantytown women who have given birth eleven times and buried nine infants? What does an intimacy and familiarity with premature suffering and early deaths do to other attachments to parents, lovers, spouses, neighbors?

I looked to Winnicott's benevolent concept of the "good-enough" mother (1953) as a likely place to start my analysis of shantytown mothers struggling to stay alive long enough to raise at least two of their many children to adolescence, but in the end I found that Winnicott entertained

I am grateful to the at least four generations of mothers who have shared with me some of their most intimate feelings, sentiments, and practices bearing on maternity. These women have been my most important anthropological teachers, and I hope I have not misjudged or misrepresented what they wanted me to get exactly right. The discussion of mother love and child death draws from Chapters 7, 8, and 9 of my book *Death Without Weeping*. The brief section on "tactics versus strategies" is drawn from Chapter 10 ("A Knack for Life: The Everyday Tactics of Survival") of the same.

an overly optimistic view of the *infant's* adaptiveness (Scheper-Hughes, 1992). Under the murderous economic, environmental, and political conditions of the Alto do Cruzeiro, a hillside slum (*favela*) in the sugar-plantation town (*município*) of Timbauba, especially during the years of military rule (1964–84) and the early and uneven transition to democracy (1985–92), many infants did not survive the first year of life. What were casual and forgivable lapses of maternal attention and care under ordinary, "good-enough" circumstances in the first world, were lethal in the precarious context of shantytown life where hypervigilance of fragile and vulnerable infants was required of mothers who were themselves struggling for survival. Mothers and infants could be rivals for scarce resources. Thus, Alto mothers renounced breast-feeding as impossible, as sapping too much strength from their own "wrecked" bodies. I was once scolded by my Alto neighbor and *comadre*, Dalina: "Why grieve for the death of infants who barely landed in this world, who were not even conscious of their existence? Weep for us, Nanci, for their mothers who are condemned to live in order to care for those who do survive." Obviously, "good-enough mothering" was problematic in a place where, as one woman cited by Marilyn Nations and Linda Anne Rebhun said, "It's easy enough for anyone to die" (Nations and Rebhun, 1988, p. 175 (emphasis added); quoted in Scheper-Hughes, 1992, p. 361).

If mother love is the cultural expression of what many attachment theorists believe to be a bioevolutionary script, what could this script mean to women for whom the repeated experience of infant death has made that love frantic? In my original sample of three generations of mothers living under dire conditions in the sugar-plantation zone of Pernambuco, the average woman had 9.5 pregnancies, 8 births, and 3.5 infant deaths. This was a classic predemographic transition pattern, one in which high fertility was driven by an untamed rate of infant and child mortality. A high expectancy of loss and the normalization of infant death were a powerful shaper of maternal attachments to infants and to the fathers of those infants.

Classic mother–infant attachment (Bowlby, 1969) and maternal bonding (Klaus, Jerauld, Kreger *et al.*, 1972) theories posited essentialist, universal, innate maternal scripts on the basis that the survival of neonates simply depended on it. A bioevolutionary perspective on human attachment predicted the aspects of human life that were most likely to entail innate, unlearned components (see also Johow and Voland, this volume). The more critical the behavior was to "species survival," the more likely that "innate" features would be present. Thus, one would expect that innate factors would play a significant role in reproduction, in courting and mating, and in mother–infant relationships. Because the human

infant is far more immature at birth than other species, intense and prolonged care by mothers is essential to their survival (see also Meehan
and Hawks, this volume). Human mothers, like other higher primates,
are an infant-carrying and prolonged infant-feeding species. Following
his clinical work with traumatized babies in a British hospital at the end
of World War II, John Bowlby, strongly influenced by ethology, argued
that human infants, like other primates, searched for security by clinging, hugging, and sucking. The infant's innate drive for attachment is
the stimulus for mother–infant attachment. Maternal attachment is a
kind of emotional-sensorial call and response, led by the infant. Sarah
Hrdy, whose writings over the years on the bioevolutionary dimensions
of mothering and parenting among humans and other primates, puts this
quite succinctly in an article for *Natural History Magazine*: "We cannot
forget the real protagonist of this story: the baby. From birth, newborns
are powerfully motivated to stay close, to root – even to creep – in quest
of nipples, which they instinctively suck on. But maintaining contact is
harder for little human infants to do than it is for other primates. One
problem is that human mothers are not very hairy, so the mother not
only has to position the baby on her breast but also she has to keep him
there" (2001, p. 3). This is the kind of statement that has raised the hack-
les – that is, the little, residual, primate hairs at the back of the neck –
of traditional (especially French) feminists, from Simone de Beauvoir to
Elizabeth Badinter. Then why do these French feminists not come out of
their intellectual boudoirs to join the fundamentalist Christian creation-
ists in calling for a ban on teaching evolutionary theory to schoolchildren?
If evolution is *not* inclusive of our hairy, hoary legacy and kinship with
other primates, male or female of the species, then why *not* ban it from
our schools as well as from our sensitive feminist consciousness?

What most touched me about the mothers of the Alto do Cruzeiro was
their recognition, without either revulsion or horror, that their scrawny,
little neonates were the missing link – "creatures" (*creaturas*) and "little
animals" (*bichinas*) with their primate prehensile toes, their startled monkey faces, their little mouths rooting with anxiety and hope, their tongues
lapping up milk, breast or bottle, as if it were ambrosia from the gods,
which it is. Cat, reptile, skunk, and monkey are all there on full display
in the human neonate.

Infant–mother attachments are always mediated by different cultures,
individual and collective histories, and environments, but the basic script
was seen as bioevolutionarily hard-wired. In her controversial essay, "A
Biosocial Perspective on Parenting," Alice Rossi, a pioneering feminist and sociologist, famously argued, drawing both on bioevolutionary
theory and anthropological research (especially Melvin Konner – e.g.,

1977 – and Majorie Shostak's – e.g., 1981 – research among San hunter-gatherers of the Kalahari Desert of southern Africa), that "biologically males have only one innate orientation, a sexual one that draws them to women, while women have two such orientations, a sexual one toward men and a reproductive one toward the young. By comparison to the female attachment to an infant, attachment is a socially learned role" (1977, p. 4). Rossi was not arguing for a directly genetic determination of what men and women could do, but rather that biological-hormonal contributions shaped the ease with which the sexes learned certain things. Men showed less ease in infant handling than women, and compensatory training, Rossi argued, would be necessary if more men were being asked – as they were in the second wave of feminism of the 1970s – to care for young infants.

Maternal bonding theory posited an innate sequence of behaviors immediately postpartum. As the infant is handed to the mother, the mother will take the infant in her right arm, and bring it close to her heart to re-create for the newborn the comforting experience of the familiar heartbeat; then she will gingerly touch the infant with her fingertips, next use the palms of her hands, and finally enfold the child. All the while, the mother will adjust her head to engage the infant in face-to-face eye contact. Observations of mothers conducted at the Laboratory of Human Development (Harvard University) in the late 1970s by students of Robert LeVine found that mothers spoke to their infants with their eyes wide open and their eyebrows raised, in high-pitched voices with vowel elongations. New mothers described their infants as "irresistible," and their smell, cooing sounds, and even their huge, misshapen, Humpty-Dumpty heads seemed endearing to their mothers.

This maternal–infant romance, a kind of bioevolutionary love story,[1] flew directly in the face of what I had observed of maternal practice in the

[1] Similar issues are being debated today in a wave of postfeminist books addressing women, work, and bringing up baby; child-rearing manuals; balancing liberation and love; and the latest, chic French, Chinese, and American versions of proper parenting. The trilogy formed by Amy Chua's *Battle Hymn of the Tiger Mother*, Ayelet Waldman's, *Bad Mother: A Chronicle of Maternal Crimes, Minor Calamities, and Occasional Moments of Grace*, and Pamela Druckerman's *Bringing Up Bébé: One American Mother Discovers the Wisdom of French Parenting*, is representative of this new genre of mommy-writing. Elizabeth Badinter's latest postfeminist diatribe in her recently published book, *The Conflict: How Modern Motherhood Undermines the Status of Women*, rails against the ecological, holistic, "deep-mothering" model associated with La Leche League, home birth, midwives and doulas, placenta eaters, co-sleeping, coparenting, baby slings, and skin-on-skin contact. Badinter labels the "attachment" school of baby care a residue of the "essentialist/naturalist" counterculture movement of the 1970s that was, in fact, aimed at reclaiming women's bodies from the medical technocrats. I guess one could suppose that this latest wave of antimaternalism is a backlash against the mother goddesses/Earth mothers

shantytown, beginning in the 1960s – first as a midwife and paramedic, and later as a medical anthropologist. I observed very different sequences of behaviors and practices around birth and early mothering on the Alto do Cruzeiro. Postpartum mothers in the shantytown were often exempt from caring for their infants during an extended period of "lying in" restrictions and prohibitions (*resguadas*) that interfered with holding and nursing the infant. Breast-feeding was discouraged as unhealthy for the mother, sapping her limited strength, and breast milk was devalued as a vehicle of spiritual and medical contagion: original sin and milk-borne diseases. Infants were held on the mothers' lap with their heads resting on her knees all the better to finger-feed the infant its *mingau*, a gruel of manioc flour, sugar, and a dash of powdered milk mixed with contaminated water from a public faucet. Who had the time to boil water on a clay pot fired with sticks collected from the vanishing forests?

Infants were often unnamed for months (they were referred to as baby, *ne-ne*, as *fiapo*, a "little bit of nothing"; for more examples of "delayed personhood," see Lancy, this volume). The infant had a soul, but a restless one, and the chances of that soul escaping the body was high. Therefore, a respectful and self-protective maternal distance was established. The infant was a liminal "creature," a *creatura*, not yet a person or a human and not yet claimed by its mother. There was also some fear that no matter what a mother did, the infant itself might chose to go on its own volition. Some infants were said to have no attachment to the world, that "live or die, it is all the same to them." It struck me that in this environment of material and emotional scarcities – too little food, contaminated water, weak bonds between a woman and her lovers, and far too many infant deaths (the causes and consequences of which almost impossible to unravel) – the classic theory of maternal attachment itself made no bio-evolutionary sense. In a precarious situation where most poor women – and this was true for much of human history – might lose a third or more of their newborns in the first year of life, maternal detachment was a tactic, if not a strategy. The shantytown women were conscious of this, as when I might ask a mother of a failing infant whether the infant was worth fighting for, and she would say, "If the baby were born in a rich household, yes. But not here where this sickly, puny infant will only bring sorrow in the end." A woman who had lost half of her babies said:

a few of the antimaternalists' parents might have identified with. Katha Pollitt, with her usual vim and humor, notes that today's women "are giving up on careers to embrace attachment parenting – breast feeding their kids till age 3 or more; having Baby sleep in your room, if not your bed; and babywearing – carrying your baby in a sling every minute of the day and never, ever letting it cry . . . Turning yourself into a human kangaroo? It's hard to keep up" (*The Nation*, June 4, 2012).

Why are you asking us these questions? Who could bear it, Nanci, if we are mistaken in believing that God takes our infants to save us from pain? If that is not true, then God is a cannibal. And if our little angels [dead infants] are not in heaven flying around the throne of Nossa Senhora [Our Lady], then where are they and who is to blame for their deaths?

If mothers allowed themselves to be deeply attached to all newborns, how could they ever live through their sequential short lives and deaths and still have the stamina to get pregnant and give birth again and again? And they were conscious of this. What I was not saying was that Alto do Cruzeiro mothers did not experience mother love at all. They did and with great intensity, as their children grew in the biblical wisdom and grace. Mother love emerged with the emergence of their children's personalities and as they developed strength and vitality. The apex of mother love was not the image of Mary and her infant son, but a mature Mary grieving the death of her young adult son. The Virgin Mother of the Pietà, not the young mother at the crèche, was the symbol of motherhood and mother love on the Alto do Cruzeiro.

What I found in the shantytowns of northeast Brazil in the 1980s was not very different from what French philosophers and social historians were saying in the mid twentieth century about the flexible nature of childhood in earlier centuries. The French social historian Philippe Ariès (1962), to be followed by Edward Shorter's (1976) *The Making of the Modern Family* and Elizabeth Badinter's (1981) *Mother Love: Myth and Reality*, had already questioned the innate structures of maternal behavior from the perspective of historical demography. Both Shorter and Badinter had looked at the appallingly high rate of infant abandonment and death in eighteenth-century Europe and America attributed to the practice of outsourcing breast-feeding and sending babies to distantly located wet nurses for the first years of life. Peasants as well as aristocrats used the services of wet nurses, despite their seemingly poor outcomes. Shorter argues that parents were not *forced* to abandon their babies, that they simply "did not care and that is why their children vanished in the ghastly slaughter of the innocents that was traditional child rearing" (1976, p. 204). Badinter wondered how mothers could treat their babies in this way, how could they select from among their newborns the ones they would nurse and nurture and the ones they would callously send away to hit-or-miss destinies. Badinter writes: "I am not questioning maternal love, I am questioning maternal *instinct* [italics added]" (1981, p. ix).

That was seventeenth- and eighteenth-century Europe. What about now, today, the contemporary anthropological world? While immersed in writing *Death Without Weeping*, I paused in the mid 1980s to solicit research papers from two dozen anthropological colleagues then working in the field on parenting, attachment and rejection, and infant and child survival in Asia, the Arctic, Africa, the Caribbean, the Middle East, and North and South America. The resulting volume, *Child Survival* (Scheper-Hughes, 1987a), confirmed an ecological model of child survival, one which demonstrated the impact of environmental, political-economic, and sociocultural determinants of parenting practices and child survival.

There were two basic mortality patterns, which I simply labeled "old" and "new," without necessarily seeing these as chronological. The "old" pattern referred to societies where child mortality was so high that infants were often "disposables" in the interests of family, kin, and community survival and solidarity. Reproduction focused on *quantity* –having a great many children in the hope that a few will survive – to make up for, or to cut, the losses. In the "new" mortality pattern, infant mortality was sufficiently tamed, so that reproduction could focus more on the quality of the child, who now occupied a central role in the household and the community. The new morality was linked to a new reproductive pattern – having fewer children and investing heavily in every one of them on the assumption that all will live. The new mortality pattern made infants into scarce commodities of intrinsic value, unless the infant was "deficient" for specific social, psychological, or political reasons. The birth of a baby girl could certainly lead to her "disposability" in rural China under the one-child policy, as described by Potter in the *Child Survival* volume (Scheper-Hughes, 1987a). Once infant mortality was under some human control, mother love could flourish from the start, rather than develop hesitantly, nervously, and gradually once an infant or child showed its mettle.

Nonetheless, a commitment to the idea of "mother love" as a universal sentiment resurfaced in the writings of those cultural feminists who argued for a "poetics" of motherhood – for a specifically female moral voice and sensibility expressed in a maternal ethic of responsiveness, attentiveness, and caring labor. Nancy Chodorow's *The Reproduction of Mothering* (1978) examined the social and psychological conditions that motivate women to assume nurturing, caring, life-preserving social roles. Carol Gilligan (1982) described a distinctive womanly ethos and moral reasoning based on caring and responsibility as opposed to the male ethos based on rights, justice, and autonomy. But it was the feminist philosopher Sara Ruddick (1980) who developed the most cogent statement of "maternal thinking" in her book of that title. Ruddick wrote of certain "universal interests that appear to govern maternal practice throughout the species" so as to make mother love appear altogether natural. Ruddick argued that maternal thinking as a moral and ethical philosophy characteristic of women grows directly from experience, from the practice of nurturing fragile infants and small children. Following Wittgenstein and Habermas, Ruddick argued that specific "ways of seeing and thinking" arise from the work that people engage in. Because of the accident of sex, women, as potential or actual child bearers, are simultaneously thrust into the position of those who will care for the young, and they are predisposed to moral commitments and social values that foster growth, life preservation, and peacekeeping. To protect, to nurture, and to train are the elements of maternal thinking and practice.

Maternal thinking, Ruddick argued, begins in a stance of *protectiveness*, "an attitude governed above all, by the priority of keeping over acquiring, of conserving the fragile, of maintaining whatever is at hand and necessary to the child's life" (1980, p. 80). She was modest in her claims. They were homespun – "made up," she said, through a process of critical introspection and through talking with women who were very much like herself: mostly affluent, middle-class white women living in the USA. Together with Nancy Chodorow and Carol Gilligan, these mid to late twentieth-century cultural feminists were trying to give a voice to women's moral reasoning, to credit a maternal politics of care, nurturing, and peacemaking that could be translated into world making and world repair. However, these celebrations of maternal thinking did not and could not represent the experiences of poor and marginalized women whose behavior and moral visions did not conform to the American feminist paradigm. As a philosopher, not a social scientist, Ruddick was describing a modality of maternity, one that could be applied to men (male mothers) as well as to women. And she invited those who knew rather more about *other mothers* to amend her general theory. And that was precisely what I tried to do in my research and writings on mother love and child death in Brazil.

Letting go – the moral economy of mothering

Ruddick (1980) identified a maternal attitude of "holding" as an essential core of maternal thinking. This implies a metaphysical attitude of *holding on, holding up, holding close, holding dear*. It connotes an image of maternal protectiveness, conserving and valuing what is at hand. But what of mothering in an environment like the Brazilian shantytown where the risks to child survival are legion? There, mothers must concede to a certain humility, even passivity, before a world that is, in so many respects, beyond their control.

Consequently, among the mothers of the shantytown, maternal thinking and practice were often guided by another, and quite opposite, metaphysical stance, one – drawing on the mothers' own choice of metaphors – of *"letting go."* Among the mothers of the shantytown, "letting go" implied an attitude of calm and reasonable resignation to events that cannot easily be changed or overcome. It was a leap of religious faith and trust that was not easy for most shantytown women to achieve. They had to work at it.

Maternal thinking in the shantytown meant knowing when to "let go" of an infant or small child that showed that it "wants" to die. The pragmatics of mothering under extreme poverty required calling on all the strengths and inner resources necessary to help one's mortally weak or sickly infants to die quickly and to die well, with the least trouble. A death without suffering was a death without weeping, an acceptable death.

The good-enough mother versus the good-enough child

There was something consoling in the British child psychiatrist Donald Winnicott's (1973) forgiving notion of the "good-enough" mother – his common-sense faith in ordinary mothers to perform the required tasks necessary to sustain and support new life under ordinary conditions. The good-enough mother was also something of a "holding company," her devotion expressed in holding on and holding up, most of all in protecting the infant from its existential dread of falling off the Earth. Indulging the infant in its basic need to be held, to be reassured, allows the infant to feel secure enough and real enough to develop an autonomous sense of self. Gradually, as mother and infant begin to individuate, as they must, mothers do so by "failing" infants, letting them down, so to speak, by putting them down, leaving them alone. The challenge is how to do this without letting the infant "fall to pieces." Winnicott derived this theory by thinking like an infant. He expressed an acute sensitivity to the infant's dilemma, its woeful state of absolute dependency on its (m)Other.

Were the women of the Alto "good-enough" mothers? Good-enough mothers depend on having an average, expected "good-enough" social and economic environment. Although it is not comfortable to think about this, good-enough mothering may depend on a "good-enough" baby. God knows, Alto mothers were let down and disappointed by their babies often enough, babies who were too soft, too quiet, deathly pale, too little – babies who could never "make it" in context of shantytown life, who did not manifest enough *gusto* (taste) or *jeito* (knack) or a talent for life.

In place of a poetics of motherhood, I refer to the pragmatics of motherhood. For, to paraphrase Marx, these Brazilian shantytown women made choices, but they did not make them just as they pleased, or under circumstances of their making. Consequently, mother love is best bracketed and understood as (m)Other loves.

Basic strangeness: my mother, my Other

In 1964, I moved into a mud hut on the top of the Alto do Cruzeiro with a hugely pregnant Guarani Indian woman from Mato Grosso, Nailza de Araujo, and her Pernambucan husband, José ("Ze") Antonio. There was a deep sadness in the household around the pair's tragic couplings, as Nailza, 32, had miscarried several times. And with her legs, feet, and hands bloated with edema, it was certain that she was en route to yet another fetal rejection. It was as if she were being slowly poisoned by the fetus, or perhaps expressing a violent "allergy" to it. Following this predictable loss, Nailza consulted a local doctor, who examined her and firmly declared that "everything down below was in order," and there was no reason why she could not carry a healthy infant to term. But what has really baffled reproductive scientists for decades is the opposite observation: why Nailza's experience of serial fetal rejections is so rare. How do *any* fetuses manage to survive gestation given that the embryo's tissues are half-foreign. Unlike Nailza and unlike the mismatched organ in a transplant, most human embryos are not rejected. Their strangeness and foreignness are somehow overruled. Some reproductive scientists look to the strength of the placenta as a protective and mediating zone (Munn, Zhou, Attwood et al., 1998).

Some bioevolutionary scientists might suspect that Nailza's serial miscarriages indicate that her immune system was "taking offense" at her choice of a sexual partner. Despite his being a good-looking rake and a meager but dependable wage earner, Ze Antonio's tissues carrying his genes were being immunologically rejected, deselected. If that were the case, Nailza might have done well to discard her sweet husband and look for another sexual partner. But she did not. Instead, Nailza adopted a 2-day-old infant abandoned at the local maternity clinic even though she was warned by a nurse that the infant, whom they named *Marcelinho*, was the rejected infant of a father–daughter seduction or rape. Nailza and Ze Antonio agreed to take in and raise as their own the ultimate outcast in a rural, Catholic peasant society. They courted risk, you might say, and Marcelinho survived the first year of his spindly life, after which Nailza quickly got pregnant by Ze Antonio, and subsequently gave birth to several healthy babies without the help of doctors or genetic counselors, once they returned to live in Nailza's natal home in rural Mato Grosso. I still have a photograph of a broadly smiling Nailza and her brood standing in a circle in a forest clearing. One can come up with various hypotheses to account for Nailza's reproductive turn-about.

Some immunologists would argue that first pregnancies are more sus-ceptible to miscarriage via pre-eclampsia. Previous exposure to a fetus carrying a particular cluster of (initially rejected) paternal genes eventu-ally causes the immune system to "cool down," as it were, and to tolerate the younger fetus-sibling embryos long enough for them to reach full term. Anthropologists might suggest that the real key and solution to Nailza's reproductive impasse was the formation of a female support sys-tem in the matrifocal, matrilocal forest home to which Nailza returned. Another hypothesis might be the positive impact on the mother's immune and hormonal system of her having successfully reared an adopted infant, paving the way for her subsequently successful pregnancy outcomes, all of which is part of contemporary women's folklore, especially among older mothers facing infertility problems. ("Wouldn't you know that after years of reproductive failure, so-and-so adopts a baby from China, and she's pregnant and gives birth to healthy twins within the year!") A recent study of lowered testosterone levels among a large cohort of Philippine fathers who devote hours of daily care to their offspring shows that cultural behavior and human emotions have a decided impact on human biology.

If we revisit the paradox of pregnancy from an embryological per-spective, the question is how the mother–fetus relationship is sustained as nature's most successful graft. Why do autoimmune symptoms sub-side in pregnancy? And why do they *not* subside in the roughly 10% of pregnancies that end in pre-eclampsia, a dangerous and potentially fatal condition of autoimmune toxicity. To this day, biomedical science has never determined and has poorly researched the physiological-hormonal, behavioral-cultural, or climactic factors that trigger the onset of human labor and birth, but one might think of these in terms of immunological rejection.

If human life at the cellular level is dependent on creative risk, gradual incorporation of difference, and misrecognition of self, the mother–fetus relationship is founded on the suppression of rejection for 9 months of pregnancy followed by a dramatic "expulsion" of that same alien material. How might this understanding affect the way we conceptualize "mater-nal thinking" and the politics of peacemaking after the tiny "enemy" is expelled, captured, swaddled, and "adopted" by the stranger, the Other who is also the (m)Other? What if the real challenge for mothers is to straddle the dialectic between rejection and acceptance, between recog-nition and misrecognition, paving the way for an ethic that can accom-modate both "holding on" and "letting go," especially when the survival of mothers and that of their infants are both in the balance.

Donald Winnicott's collected papers (1973), based on his years of clinical experience with mothers and infants, treat a range of maternal emotions, including empathy, love, fear, longing, and even rejection, all of which, taken together, constitutes the ambiguous nature of attachment between two imperfect creatures. Central to maternal care for Donald Winnicott was a mother's basic "holding environment," by which he meant all the tricky "business of picking a baby up ... gathering her together" (1973, pp. 86–7). This was very similar to how Margaret Mead describes and compares mothers' techniques of infant care in India, Japan, France, and Canada with respect to holding, bathing, feeding the baby and toddler, as captured in her classic film, *Four Families* (http://anthrotheorylearning.wordpress.com/2012/02/23/notes-on-four-families-margaret-mead-on-socialization-of-infants./). Winnicott was quite convinced that the child can develop its sense of embodiment as an individual self only by means of his or her experience of being held and thereby secure and secured in a real world.

These are disquieting questions that I have struggled with for many decades. Ruddick (1995, p. 374) writes that "maternal practices begin in love, a love which for most women is as intense, confusing, ambivalent, poignantly sweet as any they will experience." But what if maternal practices begin somewhere else – neither in love nor in hatred (Almond, 2010; Parker, 1995) – but in an existential, immunological, and psychobiological battle of recognition–misrecognition. Maria Piers (1978) referred to "basic strangeness" as the primal scene in mother–infant relations, which I would detach from her psychoanalytic preoccupations. Taken at face value, basic strangeness evokes the elementary trauma of birth, the first encounter between two strangers. One screams, the other is startled, amazed, full of wonder, and perhaps screaming inside herself. Is this creature mine? How did this wrinkled, little waif with a giant head to match its outsized red scrotum ever emerge from *my* body?

While many mothers are surprised by an ecstatic joy in their first face-to-face encounter with the newborn, other women have to be coaxed and coached to accept the little person as an intimate gift rather than as a strange object or an intruder or interloper. Perhaps it is in the creative antagonism between self and Other, between acceptance and rejection, between recognition and misrecognition, that maternal thinking and moral practice begin.

In those parts of the Third World where infectious diseases interact with food shortages to make infant lives particularly fragile, maternal thinking is predicated on a different set of assumptions. On the Alto do Cruzeiro, the high expectancy of death and the ability to face death with stoicism and equanimity produced patterns of infant tending that differentiated infants that were "thrivers" from those thought of as impossible to raise (*difícil de criar*) because of their willingness to die and their fragile hold on life. Thrivers were nurtured, while the "condemned" infants were allowed to die of hunger, dehydration, and neglect. "Good-enough" mothering in a context of hunger, scarcity, and early death requires an ethic of the battlefield, survivor ethics, camp ethics, where triage, thinking in sets, magical replaceability, resignation, and acceptable death predominate.

Under these same conditions, the ethnographer is not always good enough or up to the task of capturing, deciphering, and interpreting the lives of the wretched of the earth and the unlucky – among whom are those who are already dead and whose deaths were not only preventable but whose suffering was utterly and unremittingly absurd and "useless" (Levinas, 1998). In a fraught context such as this, what is the "usefulness" of a critical medical, militant, or barefoot anthropology? For the past two decades, we have been driven by an urgent need to contest and to define "areas of moral clarity" in relation to the suffering of others that makes medical anthropologists more than physicians' *manqués*. Our task is to "[articulate] standards for . . . a moral and an ethical reflection on cultural practices" (Scheper-Hughes, 1992, p. 22).

Extreme ethnography

Good-enough ethnography may not be good enough, but it is a place to start. An "extreme ethnography" is needed in the encounter with people living and dying *in extremis*. Reflecting on my episodes of fieldwork in Timbaúba (the larger *município* that I called with some irony, *Bom Jesus da Mata*, there being very little of Good Jesus there), I recall fevers, nausea, panic, despair, and brief but intense interludes of *animaçao* (intense vitality), intimacy, and hope. In the first anthropological-ethnographic encounter, I realized how much I had failed to see and to understand, two decades earlier, when I first lived and worked on the Alto do Cruzeiro as a door-to-door barefoot doctor, a *visitadora*, for the state health department of Pernambuco.

The first encounter with the cultural Other is like the encounter of the mother with her biological Other, founded on basic strangeness. The limited horizons of understanding, the struggle to pierce the startling opacity of culture, and the profound human differences were slowly expanded through daily dialogues, confrontations, modest successes, and shattering failures. There is no substitute for long-term immersion, many returns to the field, and the anthropologist's constant companion of critical thinking and self-critical reflection.

My call for a "good-enough ethnography" is often questioned by my students. What exactly do I mean by it? It is neither a cop-out nor a competition, but a vote of confidence in good-faith efforts to use our skills, such as they are, in field sites to witness critical events, to face and to recognize suffering, to refuse to legitimate it, and to find our own forms of meaningful work in relation to it. Similarly, the method of *antropologia-pé-no-chão* – anthropology "with its feet on the ground" (barefoot anthropology) – is focused on the here and the now, the being there and being with our chosen others, the need to balance conflicting roles, to take stands and stances in and towards the world. The often-devastating consequences of these all-too-human phenomena – such as ridicule, labeling, scapegoating, benign and malignant forms of neglect, primal scenes of exclusion and rejection, depression, madness, and starvation – are central to *Death Without Weeping*, as they are to my writings on madness in Ireland, on the malignant neglect of the institutionalized mentally deficient during and after the Dirty War in Argentina, and on the homeless mentally ill in Boston and Berkeley.

Death Without Weeping, as the title implies, tried to mediate the disjunctures between "useless" (because unnecessary) suffering, lived experience, and moral thinking and practice against the "weight of the world" bearing down through death-dealing and violent social and political institutions. I still like to think that it is in the "precultural" space of mutual recognition, following Levinas, that we can look for and find the ground of ethics. Each of us has been "thrown" into this world without our consent. Some things are not a question of choice. And not all of those who are thrown into the stew make it, or stay around for very long. My book begins with a trace memory of the trauma of catching a "slippery, blue-gray thing" that was an infant barely alive from a mother's womb and the little "thing's" (*coisinha's*) unheralded demise later that same day.

Good-enough ethnography requires face-to-face and vital engagement with these at-times unfathomable disjunctures as they play out in human lives and communities. *Death Without Weeping* was an experimental ethnography with many subtexts and subplots about the madness of hunger, the violence of death squads, and scarcity and its effects on the ability of women to have and keep faith in the world. A womanly hearted ethnography, *Death Without Weeping* was written through the voices, sentiments, and narratives of women, as was fair enough given that, at the time of my research, shantytown life on the Alto do Cruzeiro was decidedly woman-centered. The harsh political, economic, and social realities of that era – military repression, the decline of sugar production, unchecked infectious diseases, food and water shortages, unstable male agricultural labor, and the chronic state of psychological mortification that forced Alto men to abandon their wives and children for transient relationships with other women and children, themselves also recently abandoned – all contributed to tenuous familial, sexual, and parental attachments.

Bricolage – take what you have and make it into a family

Matrifocality was not a choice, or a symptom, or a culture trait. Matrifocality was what was left after everything else was taken away. Women became *de facto* heads of fragmented and immiserated households. The *mater familias* took possession of the two-room huts built from found or stolen materials, but mostly, like the first two houses of the "The Three Little Pigs," were made of straw, mud, and sticks in the first period of my study (1964–6), and of handmade bricks and mud tiles, with concrete beginning to make its brutal appearance, during the second phase of research (1982–9). The real changes were yet to come in the mid 1990s and in the first decade of 2000. Before that time of political, demographic, and epidemiological transition, existence and individual survival were not assumed; they were the exception rather than the rule. In those days, men and babies were "trafficked" and circulated through female-headed households as if they were transient household guests rather than stable and dependable family members. Babies died in great number, older children frequently ran away to the city, adding to the subterranean population of "abandoned" street children, and Alto men were often more comfortable passing time in the huts of women whose children they did not father, and for whom they did not have to feel any moral responsibility to feed.

The women and men of the shantytown, who worked on temporary, often informal contracts on the outlying sugar plantations and in the homes of the wealthy landowners and sugar barons of "Bom Jesus da Mata," survived by "working the system" vertically through alliances with the rich and powerful, and laterally through what can sometimes appear to be largely instrumental friendships and sexual relationships. Personal loyalties were often shallow and followed a trail of gifts and favors. Love was conflated with favors. "Of course, my mother loves me," a nutritionally dwarfed 9-year-old street kid, Giomar, insisted. An abandoned street child, Giomar sometimes slept in our covered stairwell when it rained. "She *has* to love me," he reasoned with the indisputable logic of the survivor: "I bring her money and food." Similarly, Lourdes described Nelson as her "husband" during the months that he visited her on Saturday nights, bringing her a straw basket of groceries from the open-air market. When the groceries ended, so did the relationship.

The people of the Alto do Cruzeiro formed households and families through an inventive *bricolage*, fashioning and "making up" relations as they went along, following a kind of Bourdieuian structured improvisation. Women did sometimes fashion husbands from weekend visitors, just as they might later replace their own mortally neglected and dead infants with *filhos de criação*, foster children rescued from younger women unable to rear, as they once were, a living child. On the Alto, a mother and her surviving children formed the stable core of the household, while fragile infants, casual husbands, and weekend fathers were best thought of as detachable, exchangeable, and circulating units. Alto men often engaged in an informal practice of polygyny, referring to two (or more) women and offspring as their "wife and children," while married to neither woman, and were often not the biological father of any of their children. Biu de Caboclos, the winsome and charismatic head of an organized "samba school" preparing for the annual carnival celebrations on the Alto do Cruzeiro, managed to keep the secret of his second wife and children from me for a very long time, until the day I was told the secret by a group of men drinking beer and playing dominoes on a lazy Sunday afternoon. "Your good friend, Biu de Caboclos, has a *mulher branca* [a white woman] but also a little *neguinha* [a black sweetheart] who lives along the Rua dos Indios."

"Who told you?" Seu Biu replied, when I tracked him down to his second little hut and family on the Alto that same afternoon. "Well, it is true," Biu continued. "I have had three wives in my life, but I never intended to live with more than one woman. I am a good Catholic. I lived with my first woman for ten years, but she died before I had a chance to marry her as we had intended. We never had any children. She had a terrible sickness that wasted her flesh and made her old, old. Just before she died, I arranged a little *neguinha* on the side. It was a small consolation for me, and it meant a great deal to her, for the poor woman had a gang of hungry kids. No, not by me, not any one of them! But I felt sorry for her and her children, and I began to visit her and help her out. I never intended to live with her, because the woman didn't come free, she came burdened with all those children."

So as soon as he had a chance [after his first "wife" died], Biu said that he got together with his little *galega* (blonde) Gabriela. "She was just a kid of 14, a virgin, and she came to me from the *mata* (forest) innocent and free! We've had had eight children in nine years together. But I couldn't just walk out on the other woman. She depended on me, and her children knew just *me* as their father. They called me *paiinho* ("little papa"). I have such pity for them! But Gabriela is a jealous woman. She resents every little thing I give to them. She begrudges even the crusts of bread I put in their mouths." "But, Seu Biu," I protested, "*how* can you divide your earnings [about $9.50 week] among so many mouths?" "Well, I can't! If I were to *divide* what I earn, *everyone* would starve. So I give every penny of my earnings to Gabriela. She has no reason to complain. What I manage to give to the 'other' woman is only what I can arrange on the side: the little bit I win from gambling, or a few bucks I borrow from friends, or a package of pasta or a box of powdered milk that I can buy on credit. She is grateful for whatever little I bring into her hut."

These loose and improvisational families and attachments are sustained only as long as they are useful or gratifying. Women will readily rid themselves of an alcoholic or unemployed "husband" with sentiments of good riddance. And Alto men will, when forced, choose among their wives and households and are capable of walking out on a woman and her young children with chilling words that their relationship was only a temporary arrangement, a bit of *malandragem* ("naughtiness") on the side. Oscar used words similar to these when walking out on Biu, although his conjugal situation was complicated by the fact that he had fathered children by *both* women so that each could claim him as their "legitimate" spouse. In the Alto context, "legitimacy" refers to biological paternity, with or without marriage, as distinguished from more voluntary (I would not say fictive) social relations, as, for example, when Biu de Caboclos chooses to treat his sweetheart's children by other men as his own.

There is a parallel in the often fragile relations between women and their informally "adopted" foster children, *filhos de criação*. Although grandmothers on the Alto frequently rear their daughters' children for indefinite periods of informal fosterage, many of the older women are explicit about the ground rules. "I will keep them only as long as they are virgins," is a common stipulation. Almost as quickly as one woman will cast off a disappointing husband or a "spoiled" adult daughter or granddaughter, other *moradores* (residents) will come forward to claim them and bring them into their own household for an indefinite period of time. Flexibility is a prerequisite of Alto life.

So is the ability to dance, spitefully, in the face of death. In concluding the account of her life history, Biu refused to let it end on a sorrowful or a desperate note. She came close up to my face, so close I could smell the faint aftertaste of dried fish and *cilantro*, as salty and bitter as tears. But Biu would not have it that way: "No, Nanci, I *won't* cry," she said. "And I won't waste my life thinking about it from morning to night. My life is hard enough. One husband hanged himself and another walked out on me. I work hard all day in the cane fields. What good would it do me to lie awake at night crying about my fate? Can I argue with God about the state that I'm in? No! So I'll dance and I'll jump and I'll play *carnaval!* And yes, I'll laugh and people will wonder at a *pobre* (wretch) like me who can have such a good time. But if I don't enjoy myself, if I can't amuse myself a little bit, well then I would rather be dead."

Meanwhile, we all tried to ignore the hacking, convulsive coughing of Biu's miserable 3-year-old daughter, Mercea. As Biu and I made plans to meet up again later that evening in the *praça* to greet the first carnival dancers, Mercea whined pitifully. Her breathing was shallow and rapid, and her tiny, bony chest jumped along with the fast beat of the *frevo* music that blasted from every transistor radio on the Alto. "And, what will be *your* carnival costume?" I bent down to ask Mercea, trying to divert her attention. But as I touched the child she whined more loudly and crawled away from me, dragging her wasted legs behind. Her skin was hot and as dry as parchment. The excitement was too much for the sick little girl; she began to cough violently and she threw up into the eroded and rocky ravine that separated the two sides of her hillside niche. An older sister, Pelzinha, was asked to mind Mercea during the first night of carnival, but Pelzinha, carefully painting her toenails and smiling quietly to herself, did not look like a very likely babysitter.

I never did meet up with Biu, and I soon got swallowed up in the crush of bodies. The next time we met, carnival was over and we were hurriedly assembled at the home of Antonieta to prepare little Mercea's body for burial. Mercea had died early the previous evening, alone and unattended. Everyone within her network had left the house. Mercea's father, Oscar, was at the home of his second woman. Xoxa, Mercea's sister and usual babysitter had gone off to a plantation to earn some money during the holiday period. Pelzinha had deceived Biu in promising to stay with Mercea as she planned that very evening to elope to the countryside with her 15-year-old boyfriend, Joao. Biu, like me – the little girl's godmother – was dancing in the streets. Many similar family calamities occur on the Alto do Cruzeiro – affecting adults as well as children – because the net of collective responsibility and reciprocity, while cast very wide, is neither very strong nor very deep.

"Babies are like birds," Biu's neighbor Juliana offered, philosophically by way of consolation, "here today, gone tomorrow, babies don't have that certain 'attachment' to life of the older child or the adult." "But men, too, are like birds," I thought, "here today, gone tomorrow, and without that certain 'attachment' to the women they bed or to the infants and toddlers they father." Although disappointment is a theme that runs through the lives of Alto women, who speak of being deceived and disappointed by children who collapse and die on them, by bad bosses who exploit them, and by men who fool them, they continue to hold out the possibility that next time they will be rescued by a "good boss" or a "good man," both described in nurturing terms as a man or a boss who will "be like a mother" to me and to my children. Scarcity and want produce a noose of dysfunctional dependencies and attachments. The patron–client relation that governed survival on the Alto do Cruzeiro was a form of Stockholm syndrome or the dependency of a battered wife on her batterer. When extreme need and poverty meet the system of *clientismo* (bossism), dependency is a drug or an addiction. The dependent sugar-cane field workers or the domestic servants in the *casa grande* (the "big house") of the plantation owner are locked into intimate and destructive attachments to their bosses just as the women of the Alto are locked into serial relations with the various fathers of their children, but these are survival tactics that often backfire.

Jeitos and malandragem – getting by and making do

Although I have used the word "strategy" with reference to the daily practices of the women and men of the Alto, perhaps it is best to disown the term with all its biological *and* militaristic overtones. The people of the Alto do not really "strategize," though they do imagine, invent, dream, and play. Michel de Certeau made a useful distinction between "strategy" and "tactic" that I shall take up here. The strategic metaphor (see de Certeau, 1984, pp. 35–9) implies that people are consciously organized and prepared for action. It suggests that they have a clear-sighted vision of the lay of the land, a certain knowledge of the "enemy," that they can look (optimistically) to the future, and can plan for an upset victory. But this is not the reality in which the *residents* of the Alto do Cruzeiro find themselves. Their daily lives are circumscribed by an immensely powerful state and by local economic and political interests that are openly hostile to them. The power that constrains them is so encompassing, so globalizing that it has obscured their field of vision.

A strategy implies a base, a starting point, a specific location, one that is also a *locus* of power. None of these were available to the *moradores* of the shantytown, who live, instead, with the shadow of the death squads falling across their doorstep, so that even speech is suppressed, for fear of being "overheard" and thereby marked. Suspicion is rampant: "No one is innocent here" is a popular expression of general mistrust. It is too much to expect the people of the Alto to organize collectively when chronic scarcity makes individually negotiated relations of dependency on a myriad of political and personal "bosses" in town a necessary survival tactic.

Following Michel de Certeau, we saw "tactics" rather than "strat-egy" as a better description of the everyday, oppositional, survival-driven morality, ethics, and practices of the poor. Tactics are not autonomous and they are defined in the absence of real power:

> The space of a tactic is the space of the other. It must play on and with a terrain imposed on it . . . It does not have the means to keep to itself, at a distance, in a position of withdrawal, foresight, and self-collection: it is a maneuver 'within the enemy's field of vision' . . . and within enemy territory . . . It operates in isolated actions, blow by blow. It takes advantage of opportunities and depends on them, being without any base where it could stockpile its winnings, build up its own position, and plan raids. What it wins, it cannot keep . . . In short, a tactic is an art of the weak. (de Certeau, 1984, p. 37)

Tactics are defensive and individual, not aggressive and collective practices; they are not to be confused with "resistance." While tactics may temporarily divert the more organized power plays of the *patrão* and planter class of northeast Brazil, they do not challenge the definition of the political and economic situation. When the residents of the Alto refer to finding a *"jeito"* or a *"jeitinha,"* a quick solution to a problem or a way out of a dilemma, they are speaking the language of tactics. *Jeitos* entail all the mundane tricks for getting by and making do within the linear, time-constrained, everyday, uphill struggle along the suffering *caminho,* the path of life. The Brazilian *jeitoso* is an ideal personality type, denoting one who is attractive, cunning, deft, handy, and smooth. When the word *jeito* is invoked to imply a sort of "getting away with murder" or a "taking advantage" of a situation at someone else's expense, it is closely related to *malandragem,* a term without an English equivalent, although the behavior of the scoundrel comes close. *Malandragem* is the art of the scoundrel and the rascal: a "badness" that entails an enviable display of strength, charm, sexual allure, charisma, street smarts, and wit.

The *malandro* (the rake) and the *jeitosa* (one who manages to elude the law and who lives by her wits) are products of the clash of competing realities and social ethics in contemporary Brazil. In part they are culturally derived defenses against the rigidity of the Brazilian race-class system, the complexity of Brazilian laws, and the corruptions of state bureaucracy. My research was concerned with the necessary daily improvisations and sleights of hand used by the poor of the Alto to stay alive at all.

Although *malandragem* among middle-class Brazilians is a characteristically male, sex-linked trait, in the rougher context of shantytown life, women, too, can survive as rakes and scoundrels. Staying alive in the shantytown demanded a certain selfishness, what Brazilians call *egoismo,* that pits individuals against each other and rewards those who take advantage of those weaker than themselves. They admire toughness and strength, and they point with pride to those, babies or grownups, who show a real knack for life. The infant or toddler that was angry, wild, and savage (*brabo*) was preferred to the quiet and obedient. Men and women with seductive charm who have a way with words that can move, motivate, and fool others are better off than those who are less manipulative. And everyone pities those who are *sem jeito* – hopeless, lacking the right stuff – graceless and deficient beings, like some of their hopeless infants.

False rescues – oral rehydration therapy

A UNICEF program initiated free distribution of ORT (oral rehydration therapy) sachets in poor communities in northeast Brazil where infant mortality was sometimes the solution rather than the problem of besieged households. The distribution of ORT was based on the assumption that parents everywhere share a common set of nurturing goals in which equal value is given to the survival and health of every child born. It was widely held that once a dehydrated baby is snatched from the jaws of death by a simple, cheap solution, the normal maternal practices of caring and preserving would resume. But where infant death is viewed as a highly probable, expected, and even acceptable feature of everyday life, mothers are sometimes unwilling to take back into the family an infant that was already perceived as "giving up" and therefore as "given up on."

I observed scores of shantytown babies who were rescued with ORT and with antibiotics several times during the first year of their lives only to die of chronic diarrhea, slow starvation, and respiratory ailments. The distribution of ORT sachets does not take into account polluted water supplies or anticipate local perceptions of the salts as a powerful medicinal infant "food" that requires little supplementation. Babies raised on ORT, like babies raised on manioc gruel, will often die on the diet. ORT is no substitute for breast milk, clean water, attentive nurturing, adequate housing, fair wages, a decent system of public education, and sexual equality, all of them prerequisites for child survival. In contexts like these is ORT less a life-affirming than a death-prolonging intervention?

Over the years that I observed Biu and her family, Mercea received ORT on several occasions. She was brought to clinics and immunized against most communicable diseases. She was treated for worms. The apparent pneumonia from which Mercea died in acute distress – the "acute infantile suffering" listed in the death certificates of the civil registry office now begin to take on a human face – was perhaps, as Biu eventually came to see it, a blessing in disguise. Mercea's escape from chronic hunger and sickness would require far more than any "technological fix" could possibly offer. The child's rescue could not be accomplished without the simultaneous rescue of her mother and other siblings. And the rescue of Biu and her other children depended, in part, on the rescue of her alienated husband, Oscar, whose state of permanent economic humiliation kept him running from household to household in shame. Oscar's poverty made him a promiscuous father and a deadbeat husband. The rescue of Oscar and all the other descendants of plantation slaves in northeast Brazil, where the mythology of racial democracy hides the legacies of ruined sexual relations, destroyed families, and deadly forms of dependency on bad bosses, requires a Brazilian Truth Commission on race relations, accompanied by a realignment of north–south relations and the redistribution of wealth within the national and the global economy. (Today these are both in process.)

Father's milk and infant death

The well-documented studies of mothers and infants in contemporary hunter-gatherer societies is characterized by close physical contact and virtually continuous nursing with long-term lactation for up to 4–5 years (see Meehan and Hawks, this volume). Maternal attachment theory is rooted in the conception that breast-feeding triggers what we call mother love, maternal bonding, and what others may simply call the art and practice of mothering. There is no doubt that in the poor world, infant survival is strongly correlated with breast-feeding and infant death with bottle-feeding. The promotion of breast-feeding was always one of the pillars of international child-survival campaigns, complicated in recent years by the spread of the HIV-AIDS epidemic with all the public-health caveats that follow from that tragedy, including strictures against breast-feeding.

Unfortunately, it has been well documented that every new generation of mothers in the Third World is less likely to nurse their offspring than the previous generation. *The Lancet* (Black, Allen, Bhutta *et al.*, 2008) reported that, worldwide, 43% of newborns were breast-fed within the first hour after birth, and just 30% were breast-fed exclusively for the crucial months of life. In northeast Brazil, breast-feeding is largely symbolic and has been so since the last decades of the twentieth century. While in the 1950s the percentage of babies breast-fed for any period of time was 96%, by 1983 it had dropped to under 40%. This decline in breast-feeding was especially marked among rural migrants to urban areas since wage labor, whether in the field or the factory, is incompatible with breast-feeding and puts a barrier between mother and infant and between infant and breast. A public-health study of breast-feeding (Marques, Lira, Lima *et al.*, 2001) sponsored by the Department of Maternal and Child Health at the Federal University of Pernambuco,

Recife, Brazil, was discouraging. The team followed 364 women at birth and during the first year of life in four small towns in northeast Brazil. While the mothers were extraordinarily positive immediately postpartum, and 99% breast-fed their new infant while in the hospital, they had no intention of breast-feeding their babies exclusively. The median duration of *exclusive* breast-feeding was zero days. The custom of giving water, tea, pacifiers, and, before long, milk formulas and *mingau and papas*, immediately interrupted breast-feeding. Breast milk was the occasional and largely symbolic substitute for Nestlé infant formula and its generic alternatives. The median duration of any breast-feeding for mothers who used supplementary bottles was 2 months before bottle and pacifier won out. The staple food for the infants of women working for wages is reconstituted, powdered milk extended with a starch filler and sweetened with sugar. Most poor women on the Alto do Cruzeiro cannot afford sufficient quantities of commercial powdered milk to satisfy their baby's hunger. The solution was to increase the starch, sugar, and water, until times of acute economic crisis, when they would eliminate the expensive powdered milk entirely and feed their infants *papa d'agua,* a water pudding. Babies readily sicken and die on it.

Why is this practice maintained in the face of such graphic failure? Why did poor women so readily give up the breast for bottle and powdered milk? How were they turned into consumers of a product that they do not need, which they cannot afford, and which contributes so directly to the death of their infants? Survey research, including an early WHO-sponsored study of infant-feeding patterns in nine countries by Gussler and Briesemeister (1980), indicated that the most common explanation given worldwide by women for discontinuing breast-feeding was "insufficient milk." This finding led to many unfounded arguments about the biological fragility of breast-feeding as a practice (including height-weight measure of body fat and other nutritional correlates of successful breast-feeding). In fact, breast-feeding is bioevolutionarily "protected," and even very skinny and malnourished women – not to mention famished women – can adequately breast-feed a young infant. Saying this does not, however, require a lack of empathy for the individual bodies of women.

One thing is certain. Mother's milk assumes new cultural and symbolic meanings wherever subsistence economies have been replaced by wage labor. The "culture of breast-feeding" was lost over a very rapid period in modern sugar-plantation workers' life in northeast Brazil. What changed radically was poor women's belief in the essential "goodness" of what comes out of their own (now seen as) "dirty," "disorganized," and "diseased" bodies as compared to what comes out of "clean," "healthy," "modern" objects, such as cans of Nestlé infant formula, clinic hypodermic needles, and rehydration tubes.

Moreover, in terms of attachment theory and the *bricolage* that governs family formation in the shantytowns of Brazil, the ritual that creates social fatherhood today relocates baby's milk from mother's breasts – disdained by responsible, loving women – to the pretty cans of powdered milk formula (bearing corporate and state warnings about the dangers of the product that these illiterate women cannot read) which are carried into the shacks and shanties of the Brazilian *favela* by responsible, loving men. Paternity is transacted today through the gift of "male milk" – Nestlé powdered milk. Father's milk, not his semen, is a poor man's means of conferring paternity and of symbolically establishing the legitimacy of the child. And so, a new mother on the Alto do Cruzeiro will delightedly say, when her common-law husband appears on her doorstep carrying the weekly requisite can of powdered milk: "Clap your hands, baby! Clap your hands! Your milk has arrived!" Conversely, the woman whose breasts flow with milk and who sustains her infant from them is, symbolically speaking, the rejected and abandoned woman, the woman whose baby has no father. For a woman to declare that she has no milk, or that she has very little milk, or that her milk is weak and watery may be a proud assertion that both she and her baby have been claimed and are being nurtured by a protective male mother, a milk-giving father. All the UNICEF-sponsored posters and ads promoting the obvious benefits of maternal breast-feeding cannot turn around an entrenched practice, which has transformed gender and generativity in such profoundly complicated ways.

Witnessing

At the heart of anthropological method is the practice of "witnessing," which requires an engaged immersion, in so far as possible, in the lived, phenomenological worlds of anthropology's "subjects." Looking, touching, seeing, feeling, and reflecting with people on the key experiences and moral dilemmas of their lives – and our own lives with them – as these are happening in the field constitute the hard to categorize and harder still to teach method of participant observation. This flawed, human encounter demands that the researcher take stands, make mistakes, move in, pull back, and move in again.

In northeast Brazil, witnessing meant living with and absorbing the protective guise of "indifference" to hunger and death until I could not stand it any more and I allowed the repressed horror to return. Witnessing means taking people at their word and second-guessing them at other times. It means keeping an open dialogue with women and men, mothers and fathers, who were, by turns, as morally conflicted and challenged as I was. Witnessing means refusing to stand above and outside the fray, coolly observing and recording data and turning these into scientific models or grand theoretical arguments. Against this little tradition and minor practice of engaged ethnography are arrayed the temptations of abstract philosophy, on the one hand, and the quagmire of quantitative scientific research, on the other hand. We do not want to dance theoretical pirouettes over the bodies of the dead. I am inclined to say, data, yes (in moderation); theory, good, but less is best.

We are so accustomed today to thinking that official and government policies can be based only on "hard data" – an accumulation of "neutral" and objective "facts" – and statistical figures and flow charts that we can scarcely imagine public policies emerging from in-depth, carefully described case studies, interpretive analyses, or morally and politically inflected arguments. But until very recently in most parts of the world, public policies were argued and decisions were reached on the basis of historical, ethical, and philosophical arguments, while statistically based "facts" and figures were used only as supporting evidence. Quantitative data were not expected – as they are today – to form the final argument.

Critically interpretive research begins with a series of *negative* questions. What is being hidden from view in the official statistics? Whose economic or political interests are reflected in the kinds of records kept? How are records kept? What events are kept track of? What events are thought hardly worth counting at all? And what can all this tell us about the collective invisibility of certain groups and classes of people – women and small children in particular? Only a paradigm shift towards a theoretically driven and critically interpretive work can open new areas of knowledge about the relationship between the way people live and the way they die.

In writing about poverty and its devastating effects on family life and the political economy of the emotions, I have tried to suggest a middle ground. It is important to acknowledge the destructive signature of poverty and oppression on the individual and the social bodies which contributes, as in the shantytowns of Brazil, to a culture of silence and complicity that does, indeed, make public executioners of many. The tactics of *bricolage*, a bowdlerization and carnivalization of family life, the tragicomedy of human intimacy and attachments that, in the end, fail more often than rescue, nonetheless makes human existence (*in extremis*) possible within the cramped and hostile space of the shantytown seen as permanent transit camp. Existence is in and of itself good-enough grounds for celebration.

Epilogue – the day that change came along

So how has the situation changed for mothers and infants in the Alto
do Cruzeiro in the ensuing years and especially since the coming to
power of President Enrique Cardoso (aided by his formidable wife,
the anthropologist and women's advocate, Ruth Cardoso); President
Comapnheiro "Lula" da Silva; and, since 2011, President Dilma Rouss-
eff? The advantage of long-term ethnographic research is that one can
see history in the making and also in the unmaking, the undoing. I
began my engagements with the people of the Alto in 1964 at the start
of twenty years of military rule, a ruthless political-economic regime
that produced widespread impoverishment among those excluded populations living in dense urban slums (*favelas*) and in peripheral rural
communities. The scarcities and insecurities of that era contributed to
the death of infants and small babies. By the time I had completed my
ethnographic study of mother love and child death in the early 1990s,
Brazil was well on its way to democratization, which ushered in many
important changes, most notably a free, public, national healthcare system (SUS). The latter guaranteed poor women adequate prenatal care,
hospital delivery, and basic maternal infant care during the first years of
life.

By the late 1990s, Brazil had experienced what population experts call
the demographic or epidemiological transition (see Carvalho and Brito,
2005; Victora, Aquino, do Carmo Leal *et al.*, 2011). The nation accomplished in three decades a dramatic fall in fertility that took Europe a
few centuries to achieve. The overall annual fertility fell from 5.8 to 2.3.
Sterilization among Brazilian married women rose from 27% to 40% in
the period 1986–96 (BEMFAM, 1997). While sterilization was the primary form of contraception among Alto women in the 1960s to 1970s,
women resorted to it *after* they had experienced multiple infants' deaths
and only when they had raised two or three offspring to early adolescence. As infant deaths declined, women could begin to trust that their
newborns would survive. The old stance of maternal "watchful waiting,"
accompanied by maternal "deselections" of infants viewed as having no
"taste" or "talent" for life, was replaced by a maternal ethos of "holding
dear" each infant now seen as capable of survival. Sterilizations were
requested by young women who had no desire to experience multiple
pregnancies.

Today, young women of the Alto can expect to give birth to two or
three infants, to greet the births with confidence, and to "shut down
the [baby] factory" (*fechar a fabrica*) as quickly as possible. With the
factory closed, mothers had the energy to devote themselves to each of

their infants, to enjoy them, and to allow themselves to love them, as individuated, precious, and irreplaceable beings. This is not the same as Elizabeth Badinter's savage critique of the privileged class in France, who enthrone their child as *le roi*, the king of the household. Not at all.

Many fortuitous social-economic and cultural factors came together in producing this amazing reproductive transition in Brazil. The great engines of the Brazilian economic-industrial tiger turned Brazil in a short period into a modern, industrialized state, urban and urbane. The new teachings of liberation theology eventually dislodged the folk Catholicism that saw God and the saints as "authorizing" infant death by "calling" the infants to themselves. Women began to think of themselves as capable of deciding how many pregnancies they would have, whether or not their husbands or the priests liked it. The ready availability, over or "under" the counter, of the drug Cytotec, as an effective but risky "morning-after" pill, provided an easy means of birth spacing. President Fernando Henrique Cardoso (1995–2003) reinforced the national healthcare system (Serviço Único de Saúde) with a program of local health agents, the "barefoot doctors," who visit poor households door to door, identifying those at risk and rescuing a great many vulnerable infants, toddlers, and old people from premature death. President Lula's "Zero Hunger" campaign supplied basic foodstuffs (*cestas basicas*) to the most vulnerable groups. His policy of dispensing monthly stipends (called student grants) to poor and single mothers for keeping their children in school made pupils into valuable household "workers," and literacy increased for both the children and their mothers, who often studied alongside their children as they completed their homework. Women's literacy remains one of the best predictors of lowered birthrates and reduced infant mortality, but the journalist and author Cynthia Gorney (2011) puts her money on the impact of television and Brazil's production of steamy *telenovelas* ("soap operas"), which reached urban *favela* homes before decent schooling became available to the poor and working classes.

Brazilian "soaps" produced by the influential Globo TV network, which are popular throughout Latin America, feature strong, leading female characters who are single, have complex relationships, face paternity mysteries, consider abortion, get divorced, and long for more glamorous lives. A sociological study (La Ferreira, Chong, and Duryea, 2008) prepared for the Inter-American Development Bank found that the rate of marriage breakup rose and the number of children born fell quickly in areas that began to receive the Globo TV signal. Over the two decades that were studied, the researchers estimated that some 3 million fewer Brazilian babies were born than would have been born if *telenovelas* had not been broadcast.

While Brazil's army of demographers and epidemiologists will squabble forever about the multiple factors that combined to bring this radical transition about so abruptly – women's literacy and education, and the amazing growth of Brazil's economy, the relatively free access to cheap, morning-after drugs, and the independence of Brazilian women who will not be lectured to by Catholic priests or bishops when it comes to their bodies ("What do priests know about women's bodies?") – I am fairly certain that on the Alto do Cruzeiro the primary cause of the sharp decline in the rate of infant mortality was the result of a "simple" municipal program, the installation of water pipes bringing sufficient, clean water to almost all the homes in the shantytown. Water = life! It is amazing to observe how "culture," beliefs, "maternal thinking," and infant and childcare practices are radically transformed, revolutionized, by changes in the material conditions, and therefore the possibilities, of everyday life.

Maternal thinking and attachments are embedded in a constellation of embodied practices responding to the requirements and limitations of the political economy that determines the food people eat or do not eat, the water they drink or do not drink, the shoes they wear or do not wear, the books they read or cannot read, the homes whether made of mud and sticks or of bricks and tiles.

In *Death Without Weeping*, I referred to the "political economy of the emotions." I might have taken it further to refer to the moral economy of mother–infant attachment. Yes, Badinter was correct in seeing "mother love" as a petit-bourgeois value. The sick poor, the marginalized, and the excluded are not in a position to lavish loving attention on their newborns. The elite classes, for whom Badinter writes, can outsource their infants and children to elite nurseries and nannies. It is the emerging class of young, petit-bourgeois mothers on the Alto do Cruzeiro who are suddenly given the freedom to love, to attach, to trust, to have faith in their infants.

There are other problems now faced by the people of the Alto do Cruzeiro today. Since the publication of *Death Without Weeping*, drugs and gangs have left their ugly mark on the community, as have new disease epidemics. The community was devastated by a cholera epidemic that carried away hundreds of residents, needlessly. Gang "death squads" and "extermination groups" have grown and spread, so that, by the first decade of 2000, these groups and their hit men (and women) had become, for all practical purposes, the agents of law and order (or disorder) and the shadow "government" of the municipality – its legislative, executive, and judicial branches combined. These new features of antisocial life in Bom Jesus da Mata (the *municipio* of Timbauba) take some of the pleasure away, as one now sees that the young boys of the

Alto do Cruzeiro survived that dangerous first year of life only to be cut down by bullets and knives at the age of 15 or 17 by local gangs, *bandidos,* or local police in almost equal measure.

Biu lost her favorite son to a death squad in 2000, and she herself died, so unfairly, in 2004, of drug-resistant tuberculosis, slow starvation, and ovarian cancer. On my last visit to the Alto do Cruzeiro, a few months before she died, Biu was thin as a rail but cheerful and upbeat. It pleased her to know that many readers from all over have frequently asked about her and wished her well. I took Biu to the local clinic and then to a public hospital in Recife. It was too late for her, and I grieved deeply at her loss and the realization that health agents, activists, and *visitadoras* (as I had been) can catch certain problems, but neither they nor anthropologists are physicians, and sometimes our job, though fundamentally inadequate, nowhere near "good enough," remains what it is, an attempt to listen, to record as accurately as we can, and to hold dear the rough beginnings, and often even rougher ends, of those who have taken us in and instructed us in the diverse ways of being in the world, and the graceful forms of exiting it, often by surrendering to the things that could not be changed in their lifetimes.

References

Almond, B. (2010). *The monster within: the hidden side of motherhood.* Berkeley, CA: University of California Press.
Ariès, P. (1962). *Centuries of childhood.* New York: Vintage Books.
Badinter, E. (1981). *Mother love: myth and reality: motherhood in modern history.* New York: Macmillian.
    (2012). *The conflict: how modern motherhood undermines the status of women.* New York: Henry Holt.
BEMFAM (Sociedade Civil Bem-Estar Familiar no Brasil) (1997). Pesquisa Nacional Sobre Demografia e Saude, 1996. Rio de Janeiro.
Black, R. E., Allen, L. H., Bhutta, Z. A., Caulfield, L. E., de Onis, M., Ezzati, M., Mathers, C., *et al.*, for the Maternal and Child Undernutrition Study Group (2008). Maternal and child undernutrition: global and regional exposures and health consequences. *Lancet, 371,* 243–60.
Bowlby, J. (1969). *Attachment.* New York: Basic Books.
Carolina Maria de Jesus (1963). *Child of the dark: the diary of Carolina Maria de Jesus.* New York: Signet Books.
Carvalho, J. A. Magno de, and Brito, F. (2005). Brazilian demography and the fall in fertility in Brazil: contributions, mistakes and silences. *Revista Brasileira de Estudos de População, 22*(2), 351–69.
Chodorow, N. (1978). *The reproduction of mothering: psychoanalysis and the psychology of gender.* Berkeley, CA: University of California Press.
Chua, A. (2001). *Battle hymn of the tiger mother.* New York: Penguin.

de Certeau, M. (1984). *The practice of everyday life*. Berkeley, CA: University of California Press.

Druckerman, P. (2011). *Bringing up bébé: One American mother discovers the wisdom of French parenting*. New York: Penguin Press.

Gilligan, C. (1982). *In a different voice: psychological theory and women's development*. Cambridge, MA: Harvard University Press.

Gorney, C. (2011). *Machisma*: how a mix of female empowerment and steamy soap operas helped bring down Brazil's fertility rate. *National Geographic Magazine* (September) (http://ngm.nationalgeographic.com/print/2011/09/girl-power/gorney-text).

Gussler, J., and Briesemeister, L. H. (1980). The insufficient milk syndrome: a biocultural explanation. *Medical Anthropology*, *4*(2), 45–74.

Hrdy, S. B. (2001). Mothers and others: from queen bees to elephant matriarchs, many animal mothers are assisted by others in rearing offspring. *Natural History Magazine*, May (www.naturalhistorymag.com/picks-from-the-past/11440/mothers-and-others).

Klaus, M. H., Jerauld, R., Kreger, N., McAlpine, W., Steffa, M., and Kennell, J. H. (1972). Maternal attachment: importance of the first postpartum days. *New England Journal of Medicine*, *286*, 460–3.

Konner, M. J. (1977). Infancy among the Kalahari Desert San. In P. H. Leiderman, S. R. Tulkin, and A. Rosenfeld (Eds.), *Culture and infancy: Variations in the human experience* (pp. 287–328). New York: Academic Press.

La Ferreira, E., Chong, A., and Duryea, S. (2008). Soap operas and fertility: evidence from Brazil. *BREAD Working Paper*, *172* (March).

Levinas, E. (1998). Useless suffering. In *Entre nous: on thinking-of-the-Other*, trans. M. B. Smith and B. Harshav, pp. 78–97. New York: Columbia University Press.

Marques, N. M., Lira, P. I., Lima, M. C., da Silva, N. L., Filho, M. B., Huttly, S. R., and Ashworth, A. (2001). Breast feeding and early weaning practices in northeast Brazil: a longitudinal study. *Pediatrics*, *108*(4), E66.

Munn, D. H., Zhou, M., Attwood, J. T., Bondarev, I., Conway, S. J., Marshall, B., Brown, C., *et al.* (1998). Prevention of allogeneic fetal rejection by tryptophan catabolism. *Science*, *281*(5380), 1191–3.

Nations, M., and Rebhun, L.-A. (1988). Angels with wet wings can't fly: maternal sentiment in Brazil and the image of neglect. *Culture, Medicine and Psychiatry*, *12*(2), 141–200.

Parker, R. (1995). *Mother love/mother hate: the power of maternal ambivalence*. New York: Basic Books.

Piers, M. W. (1978). *Infanticide*. New York: Norton.

Rossi, A. S. (1977). A bio-social perspective on parenting. *Daedalus*, *106*(2), 1–31.

Ruddick, S. (1980/1995). *Maternal thinking: towards a politics of peace*. Boston: Beacon.

Scheper-Hughes, N. (Ed.) (1987a). *Child survival: anthropological perspectives on the treatment and maltreatment of children*. Dordricht: Reidel.

    (1987b). Basic strangeness: maternal estrangement and infant death: a critique of bonding theory. In C. Super (Ed.), *The role of culture in developmental disorder* (pp. 131–51). New York: Academic Press.

(1992). *Death without weeping: the violence of everyday life in Brazil.* Berkeley, CA: University of California Press.

(1996). Maternal thinking and the politics of war. *Peace Review: A Journal of Social Justice, 8*(3), 353–8.

Shorter, E. (1976). *The making of the modern family.* London: Collins.

Shostak, M. (1981). *Nisa: the life and words of a !Kung woman.* Cambridge, MA: Harvard University Press.

Victora, C. G., Aquino, E. M. L., do Carmo Leal, M., Monteiro, C. A., Barros, F. C., and Szwarcwald, C. L. (2011). Maternal and child health in Brazil: progress and challenges. *Lancet, 377,* 1863–76.

Waldman, A. (2009). *Bad mother: a chronicle of maternal crimes, minor calamities, and occasional moments of grace.* New York: Random House.

Winnicott, D. W. (1953). Transitional objects and transitional phenomena. *International Journal of Psychoanalysis, 34,* 89–97.

(1973). *The child, the family, and the outside world.* London: Penguin Books.

Zelizer, V. A. (1985). *Pricing the priceless child: the changing social value of children.* New York: Basic Books.

Part III

Looking into the future and implications for policy development

10   The socialization of trust: plural caregiving and diverse pathways in human development across cultures

Thomas S. Weisner

The universal socialization task for cultures regarding attachment concerns the learning of trust, not ensuring the "secure" attachment of an individual child to a single caregiver in a dyadic relationship. The question that is important for many, if not most, parents and communities is not, "Is [this individual] child 'securely attached'?", but rather, "How can I ensure that my child knows whom to trust and how to show appropriate social connections to others? How can I be sure my child is with others and in situations where he or she will be safe?" Parents are concerned that the child learns culturally appropriate social behaviors that display proper social and emotional comportment and also shows trust in appropriate other people.

I lived with children in Kenya and other communities in Africa with the most remarkable focus, social awareness, politeness, and memory for names and people at the youngest ages. Children routinely sat quietly for long periods observing – as well as periods of boisterous running and soccer playing, joking, and teasing. I did not fully appreciate when I first lived and worked with the Abaluyia in Kenya that this was more than respect and deference to hierarchy. These children were both having the appropriate calm and emotional display and showing a desired form of social relationship to others. As a number of other chapters in this volume and evidence from many communities around the world show, this emotional profile and socialization practice are very widespread (Keller, 2007).

The cultural problem of attachment might be thought of as the lifelong, complex, and varied answers to the infant's initial separation distress at 9 months of age (as well as earlier and subsequent relationship-formation experiences). The baby can be thought of as "saying" to its intimate, as yet small, social world at that point: "Whom can I trust? How will I know the signs that other people and situations are safe and secure when I experience them? What will help me survive?"

I explore three themes in this chapter regarding the holistic understanding of the socialization of trust. First, the emotional attachment
mechanisms afforded by evolution are universal and important. The
emphasis on diversity and pluralism in attachment and trust socialization is the focus of this chapter, but this evolved capacity is important. The maturationally sensitive period around 9–11 months of age is
when infants orient to specific others, approach and seek comfort and
soothing from them, feel fear when with strangers, and experience distress at the absence of those specific others. (The age of resolution of
this initial separation distress is much more variable and takes much
longer – up to 3 years and more.) These processes influence neurological development, and entrain many other evolved capacities. Attachment
mechanisms evolved to assist in ensuring close, protective relationships,
and in turn to ensure the acquisition of knowledge about the environment the child is growing up in. Siegel (2012), for example, describes
this and its importance for development and for clinical interventions:

> "Attachment" is an inborn system in the brain that evolves in ways that influence
> and organize motivational, emotional, and memory processes with respect to
> significant caregiving functions . . . The emotional transactions of secure attach-
> ment involve a parent's emotionally sensitive responses to a child's signals.
> (p. 91)

However, there are many other evolved capacities to acquire culture and
be sensitive to people and environmental information – not only the
attachment mechanism. These processes are described in many chapters in this volume and in summary form in *The Evolution of Childhood*
(Konner, 2010). Evolution has prepared children and their caregivers to
seek out information from the environment in all its many forms, both
cultural and noncultural. There is no question that despite the remarkable variation in parenting and children's learning environments around
the world, children and adults alike are prepared by evolution to embody
what Konner (2010) has called "culture acquisition devices" (CADs).
Thinking of children as uniquely prepared by our evolutionary past to
respond to and learn from the environment is a useful way to think
about the continual interactions between our genetic inheritance and the
importance of the cultural learning environments. Konner (2010, p. 720)
outlines twenty of these CADs, or putative mechanisms that evolved
to acquire cultural knowledge. These are divided into four broad categories of these learning mechanisms that are involved in the acquisition of

culture (see p. 266 below): (1) reactive processes in the cultural surround; (2) social learning; (3) emotional/affective learning processes; and (4) symbolic processes.

Good parenting for trust and attachment includes practices that ensure that the child will be exposed to the full social world they need to connect with and be able to adapt to – not only practices to protect the child from that environment. But many other mechanisms other than the attachment emotional system evolved to do this (nineteen other important evolved capacities by Konner's account!). Attachment is but one of many, and the privileging of this mechanism over all others does not seem, based on cross-cultural evidence and theory, to be justified (Chisholm, 1995). The connections between attachment mechanisms and all the others is very understudied, though it is clearly an essential topic in cross-cultural research.

The second theme is that the study of the *cultural* beliefs and practices regarding attachment and trust are very understudied and undertheorized, compared to the psychometrically defined attachment categories putatively proposed to apply around the world. Cultural communities offer different, pluralistic solutions to this universal problem of trust and security around the world (LeVine and Norman, 2001). Keller also points to fundamental differences in the socialization of affect and expressions of fear in different cultural environments and to the neurobiological pathways for the regulation of attachment in early development – not only to the behavioral, observed differences commonly used (Keller and Otto, 2009).

Third, monomatric attachment to the mother certainly is not the sole sign, or even the primary sign, of secure attachment in many communities around the world. This evidence is recognized within the attachment field itself, as well as in other fields (Heinecke, 1995; van Ijzendoorn, Bakermans-Kranenburg, and Sagi-Schwartz, 2006). Rather, socially distributed, polymatric, plural trusting relationships with a network of caregivers is a social sign of appropriate, developmentally optimal social-emotional attachment. One example of culturally variable beliefs and practices regarding caregiving concerns multiple caregiving by siblings and other children as well as by adults other than the parents. How do children learn whom to trust and how to display and recognize trust in communities with socially distributed, or multiple caregiving of children, given that such caregiving systems are so common cross-culturally, and given that this form of shared care and trust may have evolved with the capacity for intersubjective awareness itself (Hrdy, 2009)?

Many capacities evolved for acquiring information from the cultural learning environment, including, but not limited to, attachment mechanisms

Attachment research from the time of Bowlby includes the assumption that attachment mechanisms are evolutionary adaptations and thus have a particularly important standing. It is therefore remarkable how far removed conventional attachment theory and measures seem to be from evolutionary theory regarding the acquisition of cultural-relational knowledge. If attachment emotional responses have been selected to enhance survival, then so have many other human (child and caregiver) adaptations that do the same. We are prepared for sociocultural learning in many ways in addition to attachment mechanisms. Attachment mechanisms should be neither more nor less privileged than others, in the absence of evidence showing that the attachment mechanism supersedes all the others in signaling, producing, and sustaining security or trust. How and why attachment mechanisms, important as they are, interact with all the other mechanisms should be at the forefront of theory and methods in this field.

Consider the list of twenty putative evolved mechanisms that lead to preparedness for the acquisition of social and cultural knowledge proposed by Melvin Konner (2010, p. 720, Table 29.3). He presents four broad categories of evolved learning, attentional, and emotional/motivational characteristics that are involved in the acquisition of culture (culture-acquisition devices): (1) *reactive processes in the cultural surround* (such as classical conditioning, or social facilitation due to reduced inhibition, or instrumental or intentional conditioning); (2) *social learning* (such as scaffolding, mimicry, imitation, and direct instruction); (3) *emotional/affective learning processes* (attachment appears here, along with positive or negative identification, or emotional management through rituals and scripts); and (4) *symbolic processes* (cognitive modeling, schema learning, and narrative and thematic meaning systems). The behavioral expression of security and trust in relationships and in community context are influenced by all twenty of these – including, but not dominated by, attachment processes.

Konner asks a basic evolutionary and sociocultural question: through what mechanisms are we preadapted to acquire culture, to enculturate? All children enculturate to the local world of their caregivers, families, and communities. Evolution has ensured that this will happen through multiple mechanisms in many different ways – not by relying exclusively or primarily on only one mechanism such as attachment responsiveness (Super and Harkness, 1999). The emotional processes of attachment, seen as an evolved mechanism to recruit the child and the caregiver into the socialization of trust and security, is in conversation with all the other mechanisms in Konner's framework. How do these processes form a choir in each local cultural community and in each family situation, a choir with many different songs and lyrics in many different and wonderful idioms, all contributing to the goals and moral directions for life desired, with varying scripts for producing a secure and sufficiently trusting person? This surely is an understudied and undertheorized question in the field of attachment.

As shown in chapters throughout this volume and in cross-cultural socialization research, this acquisition process depends substantially on all these CADs mechanisms. Yet, how can it be that attachment, as but one of a putative twenty such evolved mechanisms for enculturation, is so disproportionately foregrounded, when so many other mechanisms have certainly also evolved to ensure socialization and child survival in the context of social relationships? Furthermore, what evidence is there that, of all these nineteen other mechanisms, early attachment-sensitive periods and child and caregiver preparedness would be uniquely efficacious, compared to all the others? It is highly unlikely that evolution relies on just one of these twenty mechanisms over and above all the others for ensuring a sense of security and social relatedness.

It is also clearly untrue that cultural groups overwhelmingly respond to and emphasize the dyadic emotional attachment relationship to a single caregiver over all other ways of socializing emotional security and trust. The research question should rather be framed as follows: How do these twenty CADs interrelate to produce a sense of relational trust and security in children in diverse cultural learning environments around the world? Socialization and enculturation activities are organized around multiple goals, buffeted by resource and family pressures and constraints, and influenced by many socialization processes other than the attachment mechanism and other than the mother as primary caregiver. The concept of the "sensitivity" of caregiver behavior itself, or attunement, one of the components of attachment security, is now recognized as only a part of a wide-ranging set of conditions that influence attachment – only one part of a nurturing ecocultural *environment*. Leaving aside chaotic or pathological circumstances, "sensitivity" is not a single set of behaviors by caregivers, but rather a blend of contextually sensitive and behaviorally appropriate practices. And, like measures claiming to assess children who are "secure," scales claiming to assess sensitive or attuned caretaking have their unidimensional opposite: insensitive. This places communities with different ways of ensuring trust and social and emotional sensitivity as inherently lesser along whatever scales or assessment systems are used to define those other socialization patterns and the parents who follow them. Some chapters in this volume (such as that by LeVine) critique directly the explicit moral/evaluative claim being made by arraying societies or mothers along a unilinear scale where the labels "insecure" or "insensitive" anchor one end of the scale.

Quinn (2006) recently proposed a set of socialization processes that would distinguish culturally marked, normatively significant socialization processes from all the rest of the everyday bits of information and requests and so forth that make up a child's activities. She identifies four such patterned practices: constancy of learning around key lessons; associating emotional arousal with those key cultural lessons; generalizing and marking evaluations of the child as culturally significant, and emotional priming of the child to attend to such key messages and associated situations. Quinn's list, of course, presumes the presence of many of the CADs from Konner's (2010) review. Socialization for trust and security is no exception to the overall pluralism in socialization processes in cultures, and the marking of some practices as culturally significant, not only individually so.

Cultural communities offer diverse solutions to this universal problem of trust and security around the world

Measuring and assessing attachment and trust depend on bracketing context in, not bracketing it out. The developmental pathways for children are not linear, and their early experiences are not additive, nor are they defined (barring true pathology in parenting circumstances, or disability or illness) by a particular cultural definition of "sensitivity" or caregiver security. As Carlson and Harwood (this volume) put it in their chapter:

[T]he precursors of healthy attachment relationships are not specific, individual behaviors on the part of isolated caregivers, but rather systems of supports that nurture the development of caregivers who are able to successfully protect and socialize their children. (p. 297, this volume)

It has been shown repeatedly that indigenous perceptions of desirable and undesirable "attachment behaviors" do not necessarily fit the labels and definitions given by conventional attachment theory. For example, Harwood, Miller, and Irizarry (1995) showed that "Anglo mothers preferred that toddlers balance autonomy and relatedness, and they disliked clinginess; [and] Puerto Rican mothers preferred that toddlers display respectfulness, and they disliked highly active or avoidant behaviors" (p. 65).

I have described some US parents observing their child through a one-way mirror in situations where the child would be classified as "avoidant" in the attachment classification system. These parents were proud of their child's being "independent" and able to play alone during separation (Weisner, 2005, p. 89). Many middle-class US parents experience the ambivalence and multiple and conflicting goals that result from combining the press towards the child's being independent, exploratory, and autonomous, with the goal of being a good "attachment parent" so that the child feels secure. This "dependency conflict" does not signal "poor attachment," but rather the expectable balancing of cultural goals that are inconsistent or in conflict (Weisner, 2001). The goal of being a successful "attachment parent" can become the primary goal (and concern) of some US parents, "synonymous with good, correct child rearing" (Lancy, this volume). In these situations, the mother is not ambivalent, but instead is more or less in continuous pursuit of an unreachable goal of true, full, unconflicted attachment for their children.

Learning about trust and security in many communities includes socialization for respecting hierarchy, showing deference, and training children *not* to expect parental responsiveness and warmth. Many communities are concerned about the potential for relationship fragility in such overdependence, as Jannette Mageo has shown for Samoan family life, for example (Mageo, 1998). Mageo describes Samoa as a community that is hierarchical and controlled and has an emotional climate with a great deal of suppressed tension and anger. The achievement of group trust and attachment is not merely a positive feeling of security. It is, instead, often ambivalent, a mix of anger and avoidance, along with trust, acceptance within the group, and support. Dominance or obedience, compliance, and nurturance are intertwined in these kinds of societies. Similarly, managing anger and accepting or expecting only intermittent maternal attention are believed to be the appropriate training for learning how to anticipate and deal with security among the Murik of Papua New Guinea (Barlow, 2004). The Murik combine early, mother-specific, attachment socialization closely tied to nursing and the provision of food, followed by diffusion of emotional relations outwards to other caregivers (other siblings and kin), who are harsher and who discipline the young child. The cultural intention is to complement the one with the other kind of care. The cultural message? Both intimate care and nurturance, as well as harsh discipline and learning the hierarchy and peer worlds, are needed for true emotional security in the Murik world. Both patterns are what Murik will face in life; both are "sensitive" to the ecology and social worlds children will live in. Hence the two patterns each are emphasized and defined as good mothering and secure attachment. To be *situation-centered*, not only person-centered or dyadic-relationship-centered, is an important component of the socialization for security in these and many communities.

Another example of the importance of understanding social context and the intentions of parents and community is a common West and East African socialization pattern of intentionally practiced dampening of emotional engagement. A study by Walter Goldschmidt, who lived with the Sebei pastoralist/farmers in northern Uganda, illustrates this. He and others took hundreds of photos, including photos of mothers nursing or just sitting with young children. He noticed something as he looked at the photos upon returning from the field – the otherwise very responsive and attentive Sebei mothers would sit with their children but not look directly at them. The photos showed them looking away and orienting the children outwards in these photos. The photos were not taken with the idea of documenting this or some other socioemotional pattern at the time. The cultural goals of this pattern for socializing emotional comportment and social trust include low affect, calmness, and an outward sociocentric orientation, clearly visible in the photos (Goldschmidt, 1975).

For good *analytic* reasons, it can, of course, be of scientific value to bracket context out – to isolate specific behaviors in an experimental design to understand the attachment system, measured in an interview or questionnaire paradigm. But this does not actually separate out context, since the experiment itself, or the items on the questionnaire, carry some historical and contextual meaning. To then claim that the results can be interpreted without equivalent scientific attention to diverse cultural contexts misses the value of the analytic approach and methods, which is to find key mechanisms and then re-place them in context.

These diverse schema for relationships probably have their origins in the varied environments parents faced in the past as well as today. James Chisholm (1999) summarized this idea by using life-history theory, which proposes that stability and variability in past environments are visible in variations in contemporary responses to separation and emotional attachment patterns (Chisholm, 1996). The idea that humans are prepared to recognize signs of positive emotional support as well as negative signals appears to be true during maturation nearly everywhere, but this does not lead to one pattern of adaptive security, as is proposed in the standard attachment classification of "secure." This is because cultural learning environments (CLEs) throughout both evolutionary and contemporary time scales are highly variable with regard to their resources, ecology, and social circumstances. Are children and caregivers facing environmental, economic, and social situations that are relatively harsh or easy? Are the environments stable or unpredictable and variable? Is there high or low parental and other caregiver mortality? Are only a few or many caregivers available?

Do mothers need to leave their children due to heavy subsistence workloads or other reasons or are they remaining nearby? Every one of these conditions varied throughout our evolutionary past and vary widely today. The reason that there appear to be different behavioral profiles of responses seen in the strange-situation procedure today, and the reason that communities vary in how they socialize for trust, is that different profiles were more adaptive to varied environments in the past and so have survived to the present (Lamb, Thompson, Gardner *et al.*, 1984). Such variations continue to exist today in contemporary CLE and family situations, and so children and caregivers continue to be socialized differently in response. As Johow and Voland (this volume, p. 40) put this in their chapter on evolutionary anthropology,

> If the child has to cope with varying conditions, then conditional development strategies that are able to react to the respective ecological conditions are superior to an inflexible behavior pattern.

This is where attachment research meets evolutionary life-history theory.

There is further support for this prediction of heterogeneous patterns of "secure" or "adaptive" behavioral profiles for children and parenting strategies when we consider models of family conflict. Kin both share genes and compete for attention, resources, and responsive relationship security – the very behavioral systems of attachment. Hence, from the perspectives of alloparenting/cooperative breeding and kin competition theory,

> a uniformly optimal solution to the attachment problem for all socioeconomic living situations is very unlikely. This would contradict the functional logic of an adaptive system. Family constellations can have diverse influences and either enable a very close mother–child attachment and extended breast-feeding periods or open up productive or other reproductive opportunities for the mother, by having the offspring be cared for by allomothers at an early age. (Johow and Voland, this volume, p. 45)

The same significance of a contextual understanding of what is sensitive or attuned between caregivers and children is true for the definitions of what "sensitive" parenting or attunement is. Close attention to modulating the caregiver response to what the child "needs" at that moment is an important component of attunement – being warm or cuddly or actively stimulating the child all the time, for example, would not be sensitive parenting, since that would not be contingently responsive to the child that moment:

Attunement, or sensitivity, requires that the caregiver perceive, make sense of, and respond in a timely and effective manner to the actual moment-to-moment signals sent by the child. (Sroufe and Siegel, 2011, p. 2)

But this is not only true moment-to-moment, at the scale of microinteraction. Such differences are crystallized in shared community and cultural patterns when the environment consistently calls for one or another kind of care. Hence, sensitivity and attunement behaviors (caregivers and children alike) will appear and be experienced differently depending on the cultural goals for development. For example, some cultural communities want young children to show emotional and behavioral calmness and attentional focus when around kin other than their mother, and even around strangers, as Keller and Otto (this volume) describe for the Nso. Thus, the cultural goals are for children to be calm among the Nso; socially active and accepting of many other people and caregivers among the Beng; quiet, respectful, and close to sibling caregivers among the Gusii (LeVine, LeVine, Dixon *et al.*, 1994); lively and "vivace" among Italian families (Axia and Weisner, 2002); displaying symbiotic harmony in relationships with anticipatory empathy and relational understanding of others in Japan (Rothbaum, Pott, Azuma *et al.*, 2000); displaying shared care with multiple and deep emotional attachments to joint family households in north India (Seymour, 1999, 2004), and verbal, outgoing, responsive, "independent," and "exploratory" (among the goals that describe parental "concerted cultivation" of the child) for many US middle-class families (Lareau, 2003). This means that good, appropriate parenting – attuned and sensitive parenting – is not attuned only to the child at hand and that child's moment-to-moment needs. Good, sensitive, trust- and security-enhancing parenting is attuned to the cultural expectations and cultural world as well.

Socially distributed care and multiple attachment are normative and may well have been selected for along with attachment mechanisms themselves

Socially distributed care and cultural relationship models assume that caregiving and close relationships will include siblings, cousins, and others, along with parents. They emphasize less intense affective and maternal ties in favor of relationship nets spread among many people. Learning how to get and give support in such relational networks is part of learning how to survive in often harsh, uncertain, and impoverished circumstances for children around the world today and certainly in the past.

Sibling caregiving, a common feature of socially distributed care (Serpell, Sonnenschein, Baker et al., 2002), is a very common context for understanding attachment, trust and security for children throughout most of the world (Lancy, this volume; Weisner, 1996; Whiting and Edwards, 1988). Sibling care promotes what Margaret Mead long ago called "pivot roles" in childhood, in which developmental pathways afford the child the roles of being taken care of and then being the caregiver of other children younger in age. This is an expectable and culturally valorized experience during development in many communities. Children learn all sides of receiving and providing nurturance, dominance, and responsibility tasks and roles while young. They recognize that the intimate attachments of caregiving can and will extend to noncare contexts and that such reciprocity is at the center of "socially distributed support" within a wide network of relationships. Children become adults with relational and attachment security different from, but no less competent and healthy than, what might be a working model of a single secure base, which is then to be generalized to others.

There are several chapters in this volume with extended examples of socially distributed caregiving. For example, Gottlieb describes the world of the Beng in which strangers are not to be feared, and training across a wide range of social mechanisms is directed at the cultural goal of encouraging sociality and multiple caregiving and the moral goal of valorizing community and extended kin ties. Religious beliefs, economic trade, and cultural history all influence how and why the Beng think about strangers, caregiving, and "trust" in these ways, and hence what attachment means in their world.

If scholars opt to retain "attachment theory" as a viable model relevant to children beyond the middle-class, Euro-American infants for and among whom the theory was developed, the nature of "attachments" not only to mothers but also to all relevant individuals in a child's social universe must be investigated inductively, so as to understand from the local perspective the meanings of "attachment" in culturally relevant contexts. Without such a broadening of conceptual approach, "attachment theory" would remain, in effect, a folk theory relevant to only one of the world's many social systems for raising children. (Gottlieb, this volume, p. 211)

Early language socialization also has a sociocentric pattern of practice and belief and a cultural goal similar to multiple caregiving systems. For example, Ochs and Izquierdo (2009) describe early socialization practices that orient the child outwards towards others, in order to read social cues, and have appropriate social awareness through anticipation of the needs of others. Sociolinguistically, polyvocal language socialization or multiparty speaking contexts are very widespread and, in many communities, practically the only language-learning environment children will experience Hence, in many African, Meso-American, and Pacific societies, children learn at an early age their place in a complex social network, in which adults orient the child about how and when to respond appropriately. Conversational skills, social positioning and referencing, and prompting are key, early sociolinguistic routines closely tied to sociocentric social developmental training (Weisner, 2011).

Rabain-Jamin (2001) found in her study of 2-year-olds, 4+-year-olds, and mothers, that "Appropriate phrases and structures are presented to the learning child in the form of prompts, which the child is expected to try to repeat. Discourse devices that require the involvement of other persons broaden the mother–child relationship and force the child to take part in multi-party dialogues [often directed at siblings and sibling caretakers]" (p. 380). Older siblings participate sociolinguistically to manage a sequence of acts that must be accomplished. These are culturally framed as positive for the children; they bring younger children into the community activity and recognize the child's active learning role, though not directly through the mother. A Wolof mother's speech to her 2-year-old, for example, is primarily directed "to get her child to carry out socially appropriate actions [rather than] teaching the baby to describe the state of the world by means of assertions" (Rabain-Jamin, 2001, p. 378).

All of these practices depend on the fundamental human cognitive ability to grasp the fact that others' minds and intentions are like our own – that is, the human capacity for intersubjective awareness of other minds and intentions, joint attention, and engagement with others. Neither trust nor sociality itself would exist, nor would any form of socially mediated attachment or sense of social security, without these abilities. Hrdy (2009) proposes that this capacity itself evolved along with joint care and alloparenting of offspring during human evolution. To share care of children in a primate group requires this capacity. Hence, it is likely that multiple attachments and shared caregiving evolved along with the capacity for intersubjective understanding and social awareness itself. Security itself, therefore, may have been achieved not exclusively through dyadic attachment to a primary caregiver, but signaled and socialized through sharing of care and joint attention within a trusted social group.

Conclusion

Consider the attachment system in the context of all the many other evolved capacities for the acquisition of cultural-environmental information, including language, prepared learning patterns, and other mechanisms. Recognize the importance of socially distributed caregiving and networks of connections. Appreciate the pluralism and multiple pathways that exist around the world for the attainment of security, confidence, and social trust. Integrate qualitative and quantitative methods, and experimental and naturalistic research designs, to describe and understand attachment and social trust. Sample as widely as possible diverse cultures and contexts. Improve our measures to provide biosocial, individual, and social-contextual measures, so that assessments of trust and security can better inform theory as well as policy and practice. As a result, our scientific understanding and holistic appreciation of what matters for trust and well-being will be richer and more inclusive.

References

Axia, V. D., and Weisner, T. S. (2002). Infant stress reactivity and home cultural ecology of Italian infants and families. *Infant Behavior and Development, 140,* 1–14.

Barlow, K. (2004). Critiquing the "good enough" mother: a perspective based on the Murik of Papua New Guinea. *Ethos* (Special Issue: *Contributions to a feminist psychological anthropology*), *32*(4), 514–37.

Chisholm, J. S. (1995). The evolutionary ecology of attachment organization. *Human Nature, 7*(1), 1–38.

  (1996). *Navajo infancy: an ethological study of child development.* New York: Aldine de Gruyter.

  (1999). *Death, hope and sex: steps to an evolutionary ecology of mind and morality.* New York: Cambridge University Press.

Goldschmidt, W. (1975). Absent eyes and idle hands: socialization for low affect among the Sebei. *Ethos, 3*(2):157–63.

Harwood, R. L., Miller, J. G., and Irizarry, N. L. (1995). *Culture and attachment: perceptions of the child in context.* New York: Guilford Press.

Heinicke, C. M. (1995). Expanding the study of the formation of the child's relationships. *Monographs of the Society for Research in Child Development, 60*(2–3), 300–9.

Hrdy, S. B. (2009). *Mothers and others: the evolutionary origins of mutual understanding.* Cambridge, MA: Harvard Press.

Keller, H. (2007). *Cultures of infancy.* Mahwah, NJ: Erlbaum.

Keller, H., and Otto, H. (2009). The cultural socialization of emotion regulation during infancy. *Journal of Cross-Cultural Psychology, 40*(6), 996–1011.

Konner, M. (2010). *The evolution of childhood: relationships, emotion and mind.* Cambridge, MA: Belknap Press of Harvard University Press.

Lamb, M. E., Thompson, R. A., Gardner, W. P., Charnov, E. L., and Estes, D. 1984. Security of infantile attachment as assessed in the "strange situation": its study and biological interpretation. *Behavioral and Brain Sciences, 7*(1), 127–47.

Lareau, A. (2003). *Unequal childhoods: class, race, and family life.* Berkeley, CA: University of California Press.

LeVine, R. A., LeVine, S., Dixon, S., Richman, A., Leiderman, P. H., and Keefer, C. (1994). *Child care and culture: lessons from Africa.* Cambridge University Press.

LeVine, R. A., and Norman, K. (2001). The infant's acquisition of culture: early attachment reexamined in anthropological perspective. In C. C. Moore and H. F. Mathews (Eds.), *The psychology of cultural experience* (pp. 83–104). New York: Cambridge University Press.

Mageo, J. (1998). *Theorizing self in Samoa: emotions, genders, and sexualities.* Ann Arbor, MI: University of Michigan Press.

Ochs, E., and Izquierdo, C. (2009). Responsibility in childhood: three developmental trajectories. *Ethos,* 37(4), 391–413.

Quinn, N. (2006). Universals of child rearing. *Anthropological Theory,* 5(4), 475–514.

Rabain-Jamin, J. (2001). Language use in mother–child and young sibling interactions in Senegal. *First Language,* 21(63), 357–85.

Rothbaum, F., Pott, M., Azuma, H., Miyake, K., and Weisz, J. (2000). The development of close relationships in Japan and the United States: paths of symbiotic harmony and generative tension. *Child Development,* 71(5), 1121–42.

Serpell, R., Sonnenschein, S., Baker, L., and Ganapathy, H. (2002). Intimate culture of families in the early socialization of literacy. *Journal of Family Psychology,* 16(4), 391–405.

Seymour, S. (1999). *Women, family and child care in India.* New York: Cambridge University Press.

(2004). Multiple caretaking of infants and young children: an area in critical need of a feminist psychological anthropology. *Ethos,* 32(4), 538–56.

Siegel, D. J. (2012). *The developing mind: how relationships and the brain interact to shape who we are* (2nd edn.). New York: Guilford Press.

Sroufe, A., and Siegel, D. (2011). The verdict is in: the case for attachment theory. *Psychotherapy Networker,* 35 (www.psychotherapynetworker.org/recentissues/1271-the-verdict-is-in).

Super, C. M., and Harkness, S. (1999). The environment as culture in developmental research. In S. L. Friedman and T. D. Wachs (Eds.), *Measuring environment across the life span: emerging methods and concepts* (pp. 279–323). Washington, DC: American Psychological Association.

van Ijzendoorn, M. H, Bakermans-Kranenburg, M. J., and Sagi-Schwartz, A. (2006). Attachment across diverse sociocultural contexts: the limits of universality. In K. H. Rubin and O. B. Chung (Eds.), *Parenting beliefs, behaviors, and parent–child relations: a cross-cultural perspective* (pp. 107–42). New York: Psychology Press.

Weisner, T. S. (1996). The 5–7 transition as an ecocultural project. In A. J. Sameroff and M. M. Haith (Eds.), *The five to seven year shift: the age of reason and responsibility* (pp. 295–326). University of Chicago Press.

(2001). The American dependency conflict: continuities and discontinuities in behavior and values of countercultural parents and their children. *Ethos,* 29(3), 271–95.

(2005). Attachment as a cultural and ecological problem with pluralistic solutions. *Human Development*, *48*(1–2), 89–94.

(2011). Culture. In M.K. Underwood and L.H. Rosen (Eds.), *Social development: relationships in infancy, childhood, and adolescence* (pp. 372–99). New York: Guilford Press.

Whiting, B., and Edwards, C. P. (1988). *Children of different worlds: the formation of social behavior*. Cambridge, MA: Harvard University Press.

11   The precursors of attachment security: behavioral systems and culture

Vivian J. Carlson and Robin L. Harwood

Attachment theory predicts that sensitive, responsive maternal care is a precursor to the development of secure attachment relationships and subsequent socioemotional competence (Ainsworth, Blehar, Waters *et al.*, 1978; Bowlby, 1969). Bowlby summarized the ideally sensitive mother as "being readily available, sensitive to her child's signals, and lovingly responsive when he or she seeks protection and/or comfort and/or assistance" (Bowlby, 1988, p. 4). Ainsworth found the sensitivity variable to be pivotal – mothers rated high in sensitivity were rated high in acceptance versus rejection, cooperation versus interference, and accessibility versus ignoring; whereas mothers rated low in any one other dimension were also rated low in sensitivity (Ainsworth, Bell, and Stayton, 1974). This finding led Ainsworth and many subsequent researchers to focus on maternal sensitivity as the key predictor variable or precursor to secure attachment relationships, and to virtually abandon investigations of the other three dimensions. In a meta-analysis of sensitivity and attachment, De Wolff and van IJzendoorn (1997) found that more than half of the included studies that measured maternal sensitivity used Ainsworth's standard definition and rating scales. These studies are a tribute to the enduring appeal of Ainsworth's conceptualization of maternal sensitivity as an individual characteristic manifested in caregiving behaviors, with maternal sensitivity a predictor of or precursor to the child's development of a secure attachment relationship.

Despite Ainsworth's painstaking efforts to operationalize the concept of sensitivity, interpretation of maternal sensitivity necessitates observer judgments based upon a variety of cultural beliefs and environmental contexts. Moreover, the hypothesis that sensitive, responsive maternal care is the single most important precursor of secure attachment relationships and subsequent socioemotional competence (Ainsworth *et al.*, 1974, 1978; Bowlby, 1969) has been tested in meta-analyses that find only weak to moderate relationships between maternal sensitivity and security of attachment. The studies included in these meta-analyses measure sensitivity by Ainsworth's or other rating systems based upon discrete maternal behaviors (De Wolff and van IJzendoorn, 1997; Goldsmith and Alansky, 1987). These effect sizes for maternal sensitivity are much smaller than would have been predicted by Ainsworth's early attachment work. Such meta-analytic findings are more compatible with a hypothesis in which maternal sensitivity is one of several important precursors of secure attachment instead of the single, primary precursor. Indeed, DeWolff and van IJzendoorn (1997) conclude that efforts to understand the specific contributions of sensitivity should be abandoned in favor of a multidimensional approach to investigating the antecedents of quality of attachment. In particular, the role of multiple contextual influences, considered simultaneously, is highlighted as an area in need of further investigation in studies of attachment antecedents (Belsky and Pasco Fearon, 2008).

The most comprehensive effort to reframe the definition of sensitivity is presented by George and Solomon (2008). In his theoretical work, Bowlby proposed that the infant's developing attachment behavioral system is supported by the attachment figure's organized caregiving behavioral system (Bowlby, 1969). Bowlby's work, however, remained focused on the infant attachment system, and little or no investigation of the caregiving system was undertaken. George and Solomon suggest that the effort to define sensitivity in terms of discrete behaviors or behavioral patterns be abandoned in favor of the same behavioral systems approach to caregiving as Bowlby used to describe the attachment system.

Consistent with the concept of evolutionary adaptedness that framed Bowlby's theory, the immediate goal of the caregiving behavioral system is the protection of the infant from danger in order to secure survival (see Röttger-Rössler, this volume). However, it might be useful to note that Bowlby differentiated among three different meanings of adaptedness:

First, there is the level of evolutionary adaptation; this meaning exists at the level of the species and is generally viewed as universal among humans. According to this perspective, children's attachment relationships, and the maternal caregiving system which works in concert with those relationships, work together to promote survival (Johow and Voland, this volume) of the species; examples include protection from predators and other dangers, as well as the provision of basic survival-promoting necessities, such as food and shelter. Very young children who move towards a caregiver for protection when a survival threat is detected are more likely to survive than those who do not; in turn, caregivers who provide health-promoting care and protection are more likely to have children who survive and reproduce successfully than those who do not. Thus far, secure attachments have been modal in all populations, Western and non-Western, studied thus far, suggesting that, from an evolutionary perspective, secure attachment relationships have successfully worked to promote child survival and reproductive success in the next generation; however, a sizable minority of insecure attachments exist across world populations, suggesting that diversity in attachment relationships has also served a survival purpose among humans.

Second, Bowlby describes an ontogenetic level of adaptation, which reflects the child's individual adaptation over time to his or her own unique environmental and family circumstances. In this case, different types of attachment relationships represent the child's adaptation to his or her caregiving environment, and the mother's own caregiving system similarly reflects her own life experiences. For example, van IJzendoorn and Bakermans-Kranenburg (2010) conclude that the overrepresentation of dismissing attachments among low-SES (socioeconomic status) adolescent mothers reflects a prediction of life-history theory that, in harsh environments, individuals may adopt a quantity-oriented reproductive strategy together with a dismissive view of the importance of attachment relationships. Such a mother has adapted to her own life circumstances, and is likely to engage in caregiving behaviors with her children that lead to avoidant attachments, thus completing the generational cycle.

The third meaning of adaptation that Bowlby discusses is at the level of the child's social and psychological health – that is, from the standpoint of attachment theory, some individual adaptations are viewed as *socially and psychologically healthier* than others. Although this could affect reproductive success (for example, a person's dismissive or preoccupied attachment style could lead to a decreased likelihood of finding mates, reproducing, and then successfully rearing those children to reproductive success of their own), the primary concern here is not so much with survival of the species, but with culturally defined models of normative social and emotional competence, and the extent to which specific types of attachment relationships and their associated caregiving systems promote culturally defined parameters of social and emotional health.

It is in this third, mental-health meaning of adaptation that much of the keen interest in Bowlby and Ainsworth's work exists; it is also in this level that cultural meanings are most evident (Lancy, this volume). That is, just as culture shapes the concept of mental health, so it shapes the extent to which different attachment types – and their corresponding caregiving systems – are viewed as leading to healthy versus unhealthy child development. As Weisner (2005) notes, "The cultural meaning of relationships affects attachment because cultural communities are interested in socializing children for appropriate trust in particular local cultural and social contexts" (p. 89; see also Weisner, this volume).

The caregiving system, like the child's attachment system, is associated with strong emotions. For example, the majority of caregivers are negatively aroused when their protective efforts are unsuccessful. The caregiving system is activated or terminated by infant cues, caregiver internal processes, and environmental events. Cultural definitions of optimal caregiving are similarly organized by caregiver cognitive processes, and incorporate complex transactions between biological, individual, and cultural factors. Biologically, child survival is more likely when caregivers seek to protect and children seek protection by their caregivers when faced with dangerous or life-threatening circumstances. Experientially, a caregiver's own personal history (ontogenetic adaptation and life circumstances) comes to bear on the environment he or she provides for an infant. Culturally, different reference groups place different values on different behaviors, and "sensitive parenting" may take somewhat different form in different cultural settings, just as "socioemotional competence" does.

The organization of a caregiving system includes infant participation in the feedback loops which activate and terminate the system, the caregiver's own mental representations (ontogenetic history) of attachment experiences, a variety of contexts that directly and indirectly influence the parent–child relationship (e.g., family, socioeconomic, and community influences), and the broader context of societal structures and cultural beliefs and values. Whereas Ainsworth's definition of sensitivity views caregiving behavior only from the child's perspective, George and Solomon (2008) challenge us to examine caregiving from the perspectives of both the caregiver and the child, using the behavioral systems approach which forms the foundation of attachment theory.

Investigation of caregiving systems across cultural contexts necessitates a broader conception of the identities of primary caregivers (Keller, this volume). Attachment research has focused on mothers as primary caregivers. This maternal focus fails to encompass the variety and complexity of family structures and caregiving strategies employed in both contemporary and traditional contexts. Fathers, grandparents, extended family members, and nonfamilial caregivers may all serve as primary caregivers, singly or in tribal or group contexts. The following discussion of the precursors of attachment will thus use "caregiver" or "caregivers" to indicate the adult or adults most concerned with the protection and care of an infant.

Attachment and caregiving systems

Investigations of the development of attachment relationships have only recently begun to attend to the caregiving system from the same control-systems perspective used in attachment theory. The caregiving system, investigated from the perspective of the caregiver, includes the infant contributions to dyadic interactions, parental internal models and cognitions, and the effects of the family and larger social systems on the caregiver (George and Solomon, 2008). Cultural researchers are now calling for a more integrative approach to the study of the interactions among caregiving, the broader cultural context of the family and community, and children's social and emotional development (e.g., Harwood, Miller, and Irizarry, 1995; Kağitçibaşi, 2007; Posada, Gao, Wu *et al.*, 1995; van IJzendoorn and Sagi-Schwartz, 2008).

A behavioral system includes biologically based adaptive behaviors that are activated by environmental and internal cues and regulated by long-term goals (George and Solomon, 2008). Bowlby (1969) conceptualized the caregiving system as the reciprocal counterpart to the attachment system, with the provision of protection as its primary evolutionary function. The caregiving system is activated by any perceived threats to the infant's well-being, and it is terminated by the infant's safety and comfort. The caregiving behavioral system, like the attachment system, is goal-corrected. Thus, the activated caregiving system will respond flexibly according to the caregiver's understanding of the child's needs and perceptions (Weisner, this volume) of environmental cues regarding the level of threat in each particular context. In addition, caregiving behaviors are also the product of interactions among the caregiver's competing behavioral systems (George and Solomon, 2008). Flexible responsiveness to the child's need for protection may also require the caregiver to integrate simultaneous competing demands such as her own need for protection or another child's need for care. Caregivers who are consistently able to organize these multiple sources of information into flexibly responsive behaviors that comfort and protect the child are likely to have positive internal working models of attachment and to develop positive representations of themselves as competent, effective caregivers (George and Solomon, 2008). Since the caregiving system is regulated by both immediate cues and long-term goals, the caregiver's ability to respond flexibly to the infant's cues by behaviors that are culturally valued and consistent with long-term socialization goals would be expected to arouse feelings of competence and joy in the caregiving relationship. Flexible responsiveness is also a hallmark of an integrated caregiving system and would thus be expected to contribute to secure attachment relationships.

Tronick and Beeghly (2011) focus on "meaning-making" in the context of interactions between infants and their caregivers. The mutual regulation required to achieve these shared meanings is necessary for the development of attachment relationships. The infant and the caregiver must share "meanings, intentions, and relational goals" in order to achieve a "dyadic state of consciousness" (Tronick and Beeghly, 2011, p. 111). Furthermore, these dyadic interactions inevitably encounter mistakes, misunderstandings, and mismatches in communicative interactions. For example, expression of infant happiness that includes loud vocalizations would constitute a misstep in emotionally reserved cultures. The manner in which these interactive missteps are repaired, or not, reflects the flexibility of the infant and caregiver communicative systems. The ability of the caregiver to shape infant behavior flexibly and responsively in order to conform with culturally appropriate behaviors by responding selectively and repairing infant cultural missteps contributes to both the caregiver's and the infant's sense of competence, thus promoting shared meaning and positive affect in interactions. For example, the culturally appropriate use of eye gaze or expression of emotions in interactions is thus learned gradually, across time in multiple positive interactions.

From the perspective of contemporary attachment theory, this history of successful meaning sharing builds trust between caregiver and child in understanding that communicative mismatches will be repaired and harmonious relationships will prevail, leading to secure attachment relationships. Secure attachment relationships thus develop in the context of trust and confidence on the part of the infant that the caregiver will provide comfort and protection when needed. Likewise, caregivers are confident in their ability to provide comfort and protection whenever infants are frightened or stressed (Tronick and Beeghly, 2011).

In contrast to the development of a secure attachment, cross-cultural research provides evidence that insecure avoidant and ambivalent attachment relationships develop in the context of a history of limited, inconsistent, or ineffective efforts to comfort or protect the infant on the part of the caregiver or caregivers. Insecure attachment relationships have been found in a variety of industrialized cultural settings to predict nonoptimal adaptation from a mental-health perspective, including poorer emotional and behavioral regulation, as well as the development of internal working models of the world as unpredictable and the self as undeserving of care (Weinfield, Sroufe, Egeland et al., 2008). Although insecure avoidant and ambivalent relationships predict suboptimal emotional and social development in a variety of industrialized cultures, they are considered "good enough" in that they are organized and predictable, and are not found to be associated with pathological outcomes (George and Solomon, 2008). In addition, it is likely that there are some environmental settings where avoidant or ambivalent attachment relationships could confer a survival advantage by reducing a young child's expectations that nurturing adults will be available to help in a life-threatening circumstance (see also Keller, and Johow and Voland, this volume).

A caregiving system characterized by active abuse or neglect increases the likelihood of what is known as a disorganized attachment relationship (Main and Solomon, 1990). Disorganized attachment relationships are associated with caregiving systems that are dysregulated by a caregiver's helplessness, fear, rage, or distress, or constricted by a caregiver's perception of the child as the more competent caregiver (George and Solomon, 2008). These dysfunctional caregiving systems are associated with a history of childhood maltreatment (Cicchetti, Rogosch, and Toth, 2006), unresolved trauma and loss, and significant caregiver psychopathology (Lyons-Ruth and Jacobvitz, 2008).

Cultural meaning systems

Long-term socialization goals are based on ideal developmental end-points that are shared by members of particular cultural groups. These long-term goals are instantiated in daily caregiving routines and practices that are imbued with cultural meanings (Harwood, Schoelmerich, Schulze *et al.*, 1999; Harwood, Schoelmerich, Ventura-Cook *et al.*, 1996). Experiences that contradict or fail to promote culturally desired outcomes thus pose a threat to the child's competent participation in the cultural group and would be expected to activate the caregiving system.

Cultural meanings represent our understanding of the world, help us interpret events and experiences, direct behavior, and evoke particular feelings (D'Andrade, 1984). The cultural meaning systems of caregivers could thus be expected to include mental representations of ideal parent and child behaviors and desirable child developmental endpoints, as well as to direct daily caregiving behaviors, and evoke strong emotions in relation to child-rearing beliefs and practices. Adults use their understandings of these cultural meaning systems to construct long-term child-rearing goals. Caregivers use long-term socialization goals to guide their participation in social networks, to shape their expectations for attainment of developmental milestones, and to define their parenting practices in the context of everyday life (Harwood, Miller, Carlson *et al.*, 2002; Harwood *et al.*, 1999).

A number of researchers (e.g., Bornstein, Haynes, Azuma *et al.*, 1998; Stevenson-Hinde, 1998; Harkness and Super, 2002; Thompson and Virmani, 2010) have proposed conceptual frameworks for cultural research that take the functions of meaning systems into account. These frameworks utilize research designs that include parental self-evaluations and attributions, caregiving practices and parenting style (along with other family system characteristics), child outcomes, and considera-tion of the broader social and physical environments. The use of such frameworks enable investigations of the ways in which cultural mean-ing systems interact with development and necessitate the inclusion of methodology which supports emic (using the point of view of the par-ticipants) as well as etic (using the point of view of the researchers) perspectives.

Behavioral systems and cross-cultural studies

Research has found evidence that cultural meanings are differentially assigned to attachment behaviors and caregiving responses among a vari-ety of diverse cultures (Carlson and Harwood, 2003b; Jackson, 1986; Keller, 2007; LeVine, 2004; Posada *et al.*, 1995; Rogoff, 2003; Roth-baum, Pott, Azuma *et al.*, 2000; Thompson and Virmani, 2010). In particular, cultural groups that value different developmental endpoints demonstrate significant differences in caregiving behaviors, patterns of attachment classifications, and child outcomes. Such differing cultural meanings lead to differences in agreements about what constitutes sen-sitive, responsive caregiving and optimal child outcomes.

A number of investigations find evidence that caregiving practices are clearly related to long-term socialization goals. Among caregivers who emphasize obedience, respect, and fulfillment of familial roles, child behaviors are carefully monitored and directed. Caregivers who hope to encourage participation in traditional cultures also closely monitor their children, but tend to follow the child's lead more responsively and gently shape the child's motivations to match traditional values. Care-givers who strongly value the development of individual agency allow and encourage autonomous activity on the part of the child and reward creativity and the violation of norms (Ipsa, Fine, Thornburg *et al.*, 2001; Martini, 2001; Pauls, Choudhury, Leppanen *et al.*, 2001; Rao, McHale, and Pearson, 2003).

These studies lend support to the hypothesis that caregivers use cultur-ally defined socialization goals to direct their daily caregiving interactions in meaningful ways. Caregiving strategies may thus reflect caregivers' efforts to encourage the development of culturally valued traits in their children. Caregiving as a goal-corrected system includes the immediate, evolutionary goal of providing protection, and the long-term, mental-health goal of promoting the development of competent participants in the surrounding culture. Thus, caregiving strategies which are markedly discrepant from those endorsed by the larger cultural group (for example, physical-control strategies among middle-class Euro-Americans who highly value caregiving systems that promote individual agency) may be associated with lower levels of culturally defined social and emotional competence (Carlson and Harwood, 2003a). Caregivers who are encouraging behaviors that do not match cultural expectations may become anxious or defensive as extended family and community members express disapproval. The inability to consistently promote culturally valued behaviors may thus contribute to a pattern of ineffective efforts to protect the infant from cultural missteps and could thus increase the likelihood of an insecure attachment relationship.

The following paragraph is a description of data obtained for an investigation of the ways in which the differential cultural patterning of early mother–infant interactions may affect the developing mother–child relationship among low-risk, middle-class Puerto Rican and Anglo mother–infant pairs (Carlson and Harwood, 2003b). Mother–infant pairs were videotaped in five everyday home settings when the infants were 4, 8, and 12 months old. Trained, ethnically matched graduate assistants, blind to the study hypotheses, rated maternal use of physical control, emotional expression, and maternal sensitivity. In addition, standardized, laboratory-based, strange-situation procedures at 12 months were coded by expert outside coders (Carlson and Harwood, 2003b).

The following is a brief description of one home-based observation from this study. A Puerto Rican mother is videotaped for a study of parenting and attachment while engaging in social play with her 12-month-old infant. She uses gestures and simple language to request that her child give her a kiss on the cheek, wave at the camera, touch his head, and shake hands. She is very persistent in her requests, consistently pulling the child back into position to focus on her directions, using intervals of tickling and kisses to maintain his attention to her.

Anglo Americans who view this 10-minute segment of maternal–infant interaction during research presentations quickly become uncomfortable and often state that the mother should "just let him go." They find this mother to be overly controlling and are distressed by her failure to follow the child's lead when he tries to wriggle out of her grasp. Puerto Rican viewers usually smile and talk about what a good mother this is and often comment that this is how they played with their own children (Carlson and Harwood, 2003a).

These differential responses indicate widely disparate cultural meanings regarding mental representations of ideal parent and child behaviors, desirable child developmental endpoints, and daily caregiving behaviors. The Anglo American viewers are likely to value parental promotion of autonomous child behaviors in the context of daily caregiving, whereas Puerto Rican viewers are likely to value parental promotion of attention to the needs of others, respect, and obedience in the context of daily caregiving (Carlson and Harwood, 2003b; Harwood and Miller, 1991). Thus, the caregiving systems of the Anglo American viewers are negatively aroused by maternal behavior which is perceived as a threat to the development of the child as an autonomous individual. The caregiving systems of the Puerto Rican viewers are positively aroused as this mother is perceived to be promoting the development of a respectful, considerate, well-behaved child. Indeed, research findings indicate that the caregiving behaviors exhibited by this Puerto Rican mother are associated with a secure attachment relationship with her child and that similar behavior patterns among Anglo American mothers are associated with insecure attachment relationships (Carlson and Harwood, 2003b). Thus, the caregiving system that includes culturally valued relational behaviors and promotes culturally consonant developmental outcomes appears most associated with secure infant–caregiver attachment relationships.

Cultural definitions of appropriate systems of care not only vary widely across cultures but also are so deeply embedded in cultural meaning systems that cross-cultural comparisons by individuals from widely disparate groups are likely to result in very negative judgments about the caregiving of the "other" (Keller, 2007). For example, Saraswathi and Ganapathy (2002) report that, in the traditional Hindu culture, maternal caregiving systems are deeply embedded in spiritual and familial beliefs and practices that include intense physical closeness with breastfeeding as a sacred duty (as cited in Keller, 2007). These mother–infant interactions are designed to foster a mutually dependent mother–infant relationship in the context of the extended family system. In contrast, most educated members of Western cultures value caregiving systems that view the infant as a separate individual, capable of asserting its own will. These caregivers interact with infants as equals and value caregiving practices that promote infant expressiveness, confidence, and assertiveness. Such caregiving systems are carefully attentive to the perceived needs and desires of the infant as a means of optimizing the development of an autonomous individual (Keller, 2007; see Keller, this volume). Traditional Hindu mothers would undoubtedly find the Western caregiver to be cold, distant, and seriously lacking in the knowledge and skills required for both proper infant development and the development of appropriate mother–child relationships. The Western caregiver would probably accuse the Hindu mother of "infantilizing" her growing infant and obstructing the child's individual development. These views of the "Other" are based on observations of specific caregiving behaviors and do not represent a systemic view of caregiving as embedded in sociocultural contexts.

These findings call into question the specific conceptualization of what constitutes sensitive, responsive parenting behaviors developed by Ainsworth *et al.* (1974, 1978) and widely accepted in attachment research paradigms. Indeed, the emphasis on caregiving that seeks to view the world from the infant's perspective as a means of promoting individual autonomy and self-direction is so engrained in Western thought and ideology that the promotion of interdependence may be viewed as indicative of a pathological caregiver–child relationship (Keller, 2007). Such instinctive negative judgments pose one of the fundamental challenges for human-service professionals in our increasingly diverse world. Thus, non-Western cultures that value a focus on the needs of the group, careful attention to appropriate social behavior, and the development of an embedded self require different conceptualizations of optimal caregiving. If caregiving is viewed as a behavioral system as opposed to a collection of discrete behaviors or behavioral patterns, then the antecedents to secure attachment will vary in systematic ways according to culturally valued developmental outcomes, caregiver's internal working models, and environmental and experiential factors that encompass the complexity of human development in context.

Systemic influences of the sociocultural context

The environments and experiences of daily life inevitably include stressors and risks combined with supports and protective factors. Evaluations examining the impact of the sociocultural context on caregiving–attachment relationships must attend to these factors simultaneously, just as they are experienced simultaneously in the daily lives of caregivers and their children (Belsky, 1996; Belsky and Jaffee, 2006). A key consideration in exploring the influence of the sociocultural context on the caregiving and attachment systems is the relative balance of stressors and risks versus supports and protective factors. The ontogenetic evidence suggests that in urban settings, risks balanced by protective factors are more likely to result in secure attachment relationships than cumulative risks and stressors that are not balanced by strengths and protective factors (Belsky and Pasco Fearon, 2008). For example, a caregiver in the

USA who experiences poor partner relationship quality, low SES, high workplace stress, and low social support is significantly more likely to develop an insecure attachment relationship with his or her infant (Belsky, 1996) as compared to a caregiver coping with fewer risks and a more supportive environment.

An even more problematic outcome of cumulative risks in the caregiving system is disorganized attachment relationships. Among developed countries, disorganized attachment classification is perhaps the strongest known infant-level predictor of significant developmental disruption and psychopathology lasting into adulthood. The links between disorganization, trauma, violence, maltreatment, and fear-inducing situations for the caregiver and infant disorganization are well established in developed countries (George and Solomon, 2008), though less studied in developing and traditional societies. Infants from social contexts that include high rates of poverty, violence, domestic abuse, substance abuse, maltreatment, and mental illness are found to have incidences of disorganized attachment ranging from 19% in a low-income group with no history of maltreatment (Carlson, Cicchetti, Barnett et al., 1989) to 90% among maltreated children (Cicchetti, Rogosch, Toth et al., 2006). Disorganized infants in developed countries are more likely to exhibit psychopathology and emotional and behavioral problems (Carlson, 1998; Main, Hesse, and Kaplan, 2005) and are thus less likely to become competent adult participants in their cultural communities.

The challenge for practitioners seeking to understand and serve caregivers from widely diverse cultural and experiential contexts lies in teasing out the network of factors that enhance or limit the development of culturally consonant, flexibly responsive, balanced, and integrated caregiving behavioral systems.

Socioeconomic status (SES)

Poverty presents persistent challenges to the development of positive, mutually regulated caregiving and attachment systems. Evidence of the effects of poverty on attachment were found by De Wolff and van IJzendorn's (1997) meta-analysis, in which the association between sensitivity and security of attachment was lower among caregivers living in poverty. Research among low-income populations is often confounded by multiple additional risk factors, such as chronic depression and exposure to violence, that increase variability within the group (Diener, Nievar, and Wright, 2003). Persistent poverty is more damaging to development than transient poverty (McLoyd, 1990), and infants and young children are the most vulnerable age group (Duncan and Magnuson, 2003; Elder, 1985, 1995).

Food insecurity, defined as the inability to provide sufficient food to support a healthy, active lifestyle, affects 14.5% of US households (US Department of Agriculture, 2011). Food insecurity undermines caregivers' ability to consistently protect their children from the effects of poor nutrition and is associated with caregiver depression as well as increases in hostile and disengaged caregiver–infant interactions (Bronte-Tinkew, Zaslow, Capps *et al.*, 2007; Lovejoy, Graczyk, O'Hare *et al.*, 2000). Food insecurity during the first year of life is found to negatively influence health, attachment quality, and mental proficiency in toddlers (Bronte-Tinkew *et al.*, 2007; Zaslow, Bronte-Tinkew, Capps *et al.*, 2009).

Barriers to effective caregiving in the form of chronic economic and social stress tend to exacerbate caregiver vulnerabilities, making the formation of attachment relationships that support survival, health, and sociocultural competence less likely (Valenzuela, 1997). However, some caregivers who experience multiple stressors resulting from long-term poverty and lack of social support are nonetheless able to provide the basic protection and nurturance required for infant survival and adequate growth (Valenzuela, 1997). Despite high levels of external stress, these resilient caregivers are able to provide "environments of evolutionary adaptedness" (Bowlby, 1969, p. 85) that ensure the survival and growth of their offspring. Remarkable caregiver resilience has also been highlighted in the context of extreme urban poverty in South Africa by Tomlinson, Cooper, and Murray (2005). This longitudinal study found secure attachments among nearly two-thirds of the 147 participating mother–infant pairs. The motivational intensity of the caregiving system when child survival is threatened is evident in the tenacity with which some caregivers in very resource-poor settings struggle to provide care and protection for their offspring. In an interview with the first author, one Guyanese mother of nine children recalled, "Sometimes, when they were growing up, we had nothing to cook... we had to make 'tea' out of the ashes of newspapers – we called it coal tea. It was better than nothing" (Carlson, 2014, manuscript in preparation). In this case, the arousal of the caregiving system by desperately hungry children is so compelling that the mother continues to "cook," and offer sustenance to her family even when no food is available. This also serves as an illustration of the exaggeration principle in systems theory in which systems under severe stress tend to increase their efforts to maintain habitual behaviors as a means of reducing stress (Day, 2010).

On the other hand, the cumulative stresses of poverty may lead to a poorly integrated, rigid caregiving system, chronically unable to offer consistent care and protection. The caregiver who is enmeshed in violent relationships and suffers from mental illness or addiction in addition to the stresses of poverty may sometimes organize caregiving behaviors that are responsive to infant survival and attachment cues, but is also frequently unable to do so. Indeed, this caregiver is likely to resort to neglect or maltreatment when infant needs conflict with the caregiver's efforts to maintain emotional equilibrium amidst the chaos of conflicting severe stressors. It is this type of unpredictable and sharply contradictory responsiveness that leads to disorganized relationships.

War, famine, prolonged social trauma, and caregiving systems

In extreme situations the underlying universal need to protect one's off-spring may be abdicated such that the traumatized caregiving system is disabled. Although rare in the contexts of the developed world, an adaptive response to extreme poverty or a toxic social environment may include a disabled caregiving system that accepts infant death or abandonment as necessary for the survival of the caregiver and other family members (Hrdy, 1999). Disabling of the caregiving system requires extreme social and ecological conditions that overwhelm the typical response capacities that govern human interactions. Genocide, systematic rape, multiple generations of living in desperate poverty, war, family and community violence, exploitation of children as soldiers, and sex trafficking are among the horrors that may either slowly or precipitously destroy the ability of caregivers to organize adequate nurturing responses to ensure the viability of their offspring.

In Scheper-Hughes' comprehensive ethnography of family life in a Brazilian shantytown, a complex system of parental ethnotheories, cultural beliefs, and environmental contingencies are revealed as primary influences on maternal caregiving (1992). Many generations of experience with high infant mortality rates in desperately poor communities has led these mothers to believe that a quick death is preferable to prolonging the life of a child perceived at birth as lacking adequate desire to live. Thus, children who appeared weak, underweight, too small, or otherwise impaired at birth were thought of as mere "visitors" as opposed to members of the family. This sense of calm resignation in the face of multiple, overwhelming, lifelong trauma that is beyond individual control is enhanced by religious traditions that encourage "holy resignation" and belief in young infants' easy ability to return to heaven as angels (Scheper-Hughes, 1992, p. 363). Interestingly, mothers whose caregiving systems are thus disabled express one common fear: that their weak infants will not become little angels quickly, but will suffer a lingering, prolonged death. From a caregiving systems perspective, this outcome would indicate that maintaining a disabled caregiving system in the face of persistent, if weak, attachment cues from an infant in desperate need of care and protection would become increasingly difficult and emotionally painful for the mother over time.

A systems perspective that includes the sociocultural and physical contexts of development, the infant interactive contributions, and the internal working models of the caregiver enables understanding of behaviors that are morally abhorrent to most observers. The goal of such understanding should be the development of systematic solutions that address complex human interactions and behaviors in the full context of toxic social and physical environments.

Child disability, chronic health problems, and gender

Caregivers faced with infants with special healthcare needs (that is, children who have, or are at increased risk of, a chronic physical, developmental, behavioral, or emotional condition, and who also require healthcare and related services beyond those typically required by children), as well as infants of a nonpreferred gender, often experience challenges affecting the emotional integration of their caregiving systems. Activation of the caregiving system when presented with an unexpected infant who exhibits differences that may be frightening or may limit the infant's ability to generate typical attachment cues may be more or less difficult according to the cultural meanings and parental ethnotheories associated with the particular difference, as well as on the social and economic resources available to a parent to meet the infant's needs. For example, epilepsy is considered evidence of possession by evil spirits or witchcraft among a variety of traditional cultures. These beliefs then contribute to caregiver fear, shame, stigma, and neglect of the affected individuals (Carod-Artal and Vázquez-Cabrera, 2007; Scheper-Hughes, 1992). The challenges faced by caregivers of an infant with early-onset epilepsy in the developed world are less likely to involve stigma or shame and more likely to involve the mobilization of intensive medical and developmental interventions.

The Brazilian mothers quoted by Scheper-Hughes (1992) describe deformity, a lack of vitality, or "fits" in a newborn as a stigma and tend to view the infant as immediately excluded, not truly human, and without feelings. Stigma and exclusion generally lead to neglect and often result in the death of helplessly dependent infants in the developing world. There are many anthropological reports of traditional societies that dispose of infants seen as deformed or defective (i.e., Eberly, 1988; Sargent, 1987; Scheper-Hughes, 1979). The practice of infanticide in such cases is usually supported by cultural beliefs regarding the necessity of returning these less than human creatures to the spirit world or to the earth, water, or sky.

In more industrialized societies, significant special healthcare also represents challenges to the biobehavioral foundation of the caregiving system. In these cases the caregiver is unable to completely protect the child from difficulties associated with the diagnosed condition. The intense emotions accompanying this fundamental negation of the primary goal of caregiving are typically exacerbated by a host of other challenges associated with having a child with special healthcare needs. These challenges may include navigating a complex medical system; responding to insensitive comments by friends, family, and even strangers; and the emotional and financial burdens that are often associated with the intensive caretaking that children with special healthcare needs may require. It is important to note here that immigrant caregivers may also have greater difficulty receiving a timely diagnosis after the birth of a child with significant special healthcare needs, especially if they lack the cultural knowledge (such as language, understanding of healthcare systems, and understanding of disability) to access community resources or to navigate healthcare systems effectively. The competing demands of such an overwhelming and unexpected situation contribute to the finding that many caregivers continue to offer confused or incoherent descriptions of the diagnostic experience when their child is in preschool (Pianta, Marvin, Britner et al., 1996). Findings also indicate that caregiver emotional and cognitive integration of the child's diagnosis has a strong relationship to security of attachment (Pianta et al., 1996; Oppenheim, Dolev, Koren-Karie et al., 2007; Walsh, 2003). This association between difficult caregiver experiences with the diagnosis of special healthcare needs and insecure attachment may persist beyond the preschool years. A current study finds that adolescents who were born extremely prematurely have higher levels of insecure attachment as compared to a full-term peer group (Hallin, Bengtsson, Frostell et al., 2012). In contrast, recent research finds that positive maternal–child interactions, characterized by sensitivity, dyadic pleasure, and effective scaffolding, promote resilience and adaptive competence among preschoolers with intellectual disabilities (Fenning and Baker, 2012). Until medical and early intervention systems are able to offer care that systematically addresses the potentially challenging effects of infant special healthcare needs on caregivers and supports the reorganization of integrated caregiving systems, families of children with special healthcare needs may continue to struggle in their efforts to establish secure, flexible, and mutually positive relationships with their children.

Traditional cultural beliefs in the superiority of male versus female offspring continue to result in higher infant and early childhood mortality and lower birthrates for girls in many regions of the world (Hvistendahl, 2011). Discrimination against girls and discriminatory practices against women who give birth to girls may lead to disabled caregiving similar to that offered to infants with disabilities in some traditional societies. The caregiver's disappointment at bearing a girl would thus result in the female infant being offered only minimal food, less healthcare, and fewer caregiving interactions than a male infant. This type of neglect inevitably results in a higher mortality rate for female infants and young children (Joshi and Tiwari, 2011).

In the context of many industrialized societies, education and modern medicine have combined to produce both a desire for fewer children and the ability to select the sex of a fetus long before birth. Although India outlawed sex-selective abortion in 1994, the 2011 census documents a declining ratio of girls as compared to boys under 6 years of age (Hvistendahl, 2011). In the USA, fertility clinics use preimplantation genetic diagnosis to screen embryos prior to implantation in the uterus. As many as 70% of wealthy fertility clinic clients are reported to seek *in vitro* fertilization specifically for the purpose of selecting the sex of their child. Two of the leading US clinics report that 75-80% of parents select female embryos (Hvistendahl, 2011). The author of a popular guide to infant sex selection speaks of "family balancing" and discusses the longing and pain resulting from giving birth to a child of the nonpreferred sex (Weiss, 2007). These examples illustrate the ways in which both deeply held traditional cultural values and modern ethnotheories regarding gender preference may affect the psychology of the caregiver and thus affect the development of responsive caregiving behavioral systems.

Social policy

Global investigations of infant development and infant mortality are highlighting the fact that positive caregiver–infant dyadic interactions are necessary not only for healthy growth and development but also for infant survival, especially in resource-poor settings (McCall, Groark, Groza *et al.*, 2012; Richter, 2004). For example, social policies that promote foster, adoptive, and family care options for orphaned or abandoned infants will help to avoid the insecure, disorganized attachment systems, psychosocial growth failure, and neurobiological deficiencies found among children exposed to globally depriving institutional care during the first

2 years of life (McCall *et al.*, 2012). The integration of support for positive caregiver–child interactions into existing programs may increase the
effectiveness of services designed to support child survival, health, and
development (Richter, 2004). In particular, the integration of support
for caregiver–infant relationships into maternal and child health, nutrition, childcare, parenting, orphan care, and violence-prevention initiatives would be expected to increase the long-term effectiveness of these
programs.

The potential long-term negative and multiplicative effects of environmental risk factors on early development are mediated by caregivers in
the context of family systems (Kağitçibaşi, 2007). For example, the single risk factor of food insecurity, as mediated by maternal mental health
and parenting, is linked to insecure attachment and lower cognitive proficiency in toddlers (Zaslow *et al.*, 2009). Given the finding that food
insecurity affects over 10% of homes with infants in the USA (Zaslow
et al., 2009), the long-term importance of programs that promote access
to such basic necessities as adequate nutrition for all families is highlighted. From a systems perspective, amelioration of chronic caregiver
distress based on the persistent inability to protect their child(ren) from
hunger, illness, low-quality childcare, etc., would be expected to result
in a greater sense of competence and positive affect in caregiver–child
interactions. It then follows that more shared positive affect in dyadic
caregiver–child interactions would promote more flexible, integrated, and
secure attachments and socioemotional outcomes. This internal core of
positive affect also promotes child resilience and enables more effective
learning.

Efforts to integrate caregiver–infant relationship support into programs
that address family, health, and environmental risk reduction will necessarily involve holistic, contextual strategies. Such approaches may best
be conceptualized by behavioral systems theory to elucidate the multiple
embedded relationships within and between caregivers, families, communities, cultural meaning systems, and social services.

Conclusion

The universal and biobehavioral nature of the complementary caregiving
and attachment systems is fundamental to the survival of helpless human
infants. Although adults are biologically programmed to respond to the
attachment cues of their infants, these response strategies vary in systematic ways across cultural communities and environmental contexts.
Survival strategies for both adults and children vary widely according to
available resources, cultural values and beliefs, individual characteristics,

and the constraints of the broader social system. Identifying and understanding diverse cultural patterns requires a lifelong effort to understand one's own cultural heritage and actively seek the perspective of others while studying the fluid connections and patterns that underlie our similarities and differences. This nested complexity is succinctly captured in the following statement: "Humans develop through their changing participation in the socio-cultural activities of their communities, which also change" (Rogoff, 2003, p. 11).

The ways in which communities manage the resources and challenges of their local environments directly affect the ways in which caregivers establish relationships with their infants (Rogoff, 2003; Scheper-Hughes, 1992). As previously discussed, very resource-poor environments with high infant, child, and adult mortality rates necessitate cultural and caregiving systems that favor high birthrates and selective investment in only those infants judged to be likely to survive (Eberly, 1988; Rogoff, 2003; Sargent, 1987; Scheper-Hughes, 1992). On the other hand, the resource-rich environment of the developed world often includes many conflicting practices and expectations regarding the roles of caregivers *vis-à-vis* infants who require intensive interventions in order to survive and thrive. It is also important to note that very resource-poor communities and areas of extreme poverty are not limited to the industrialized world, but also exist in the USA (Bishaw, 2011). Indeed, more than one in every five children in the USA now lives in poverty (Macartney, 2011).

When attachment research attends to the complementary caregiving system, it avoids the need to describe caregivers according to discrete behaviors and characteristics, instead embracing a holistic view of the individual who struggles to integrate competing internal and external systems (George and Solomon, 2008). Expanding this systemic thinking to the macrosystem and exosystem levels, Biglan, Flay, Embry et al. (2012) call on us to work towards a "nurturing environments" paradigm that avoids the separation of multiple, and potentially conflicting, research, intervention, and prevention efforts directed at particular developmental, social, and environmental concerns. Instead, we are asked to undertake a paradigm shift and consider a broadly focused interdisciplinary initiative aimed at uniting the key components of support for positive developmental outcomes across families, schools, neighborhoods, healthcare systems, communities, and the broader social context (Biglan et al., 2012). A systemic approach that attempts to eliminate toxic physical and psychological environments, actively promote the behaviors and skills necessary for culturally competent adulthood, limit opportunities for negative behaviors, and teach mindful, values-based psychological flexibility has the potential to address many of the significant challenges to healthy caregiving systems discussed in this chapter. Halfon and his colleagues (Halfon and Hochstein, 2002; Halfon, Inkelas, and Hochstein, 2000) also argue for a systemic, population-based approach to child-health promotion that capitalizes on the plasticity of early development to enhance health across the life span. This life course health development framework emphasizes the role of individual, family, and community relationships and contexts in health promotion, and advocates population-wide public health initiatives that include particular attention to the amelioration of risk factors in early development (Halfon et al., 2000). Although it is often easier to target assistance or intervention to one particular aspect of the environment – providing access to clean water, abating lead paint, providing nutritional supplements, supporting breast-feeding, etc. – the fact is that no single intervention is sufficient to overcome the persistent stress that negatively affects the development of nurturing, protective relationships. Indeed, the precursors of healthy attachment relationships are not specific, individual behaviors on the part of isolated caregivers, but rather systems of support that nurture the development of caregivers who are able to successfully protect and socialize their children.

Recommendations for future research

Attachment theory posits that attachment relationships are formed in the context of reciprocal, goal-corrected caregiving and attachment behavioral systems (Bowlby, 1969).

Examining the precursors of attachment from the perspectives of both the caregiver and the child by a behavioral-systems approach enables a more comprehensive understanding of the complex interplay of universal, cultural, and contextual influences (George and Solomon, 2008).

The ways in which infant and caregiver behavioral systems interact as well as the interactions among the caregiver's different behavioral systems remain largely unexplored. Few investigations of fathers' caregiving systems or caregiving during middle childhood and adolescence have been undertaken (George and Solomon, 2008). Little is known about the development of the caregiving system across the life span, beginning with early empathic behaviors among toddlers and ending with elders' caregiving roles in families and communities.

Finally, resilience among caregivers faced with a variety of environmental, psychological, and sociocultural challenges has received little attention from a caregiving-systems perspective.

Britner, Marvin, and Pianta (2005) have developed a preliminary measurement tool that evaluates the caregiving system in the context of the laboratory-based strange situation with preschool children and their mothers. This work confirms the expected relationships between the caregiving and attachment systems, but requires further validation in home and community contexts. It is also limited to the preschool age level and maternal relationships. Clearly, investigations of caregiving and attachment relationships as embedded in family, community, and cultural systems will require multimethod, complex studies.

References

Ainsworth, M. D. S., Bell, S. M., and Stayton, D. J. (1974). Infant–mother attachment and social development: socialisation as a product of reciprocal responsiveness to signals. In M. J. M. Richards (Ed.), *The integration of a child into a social world* (pp. 99–135). London: Cambridge University Press.

Ainsworth, M. D. S., Blehar, M. C., Waters, E., and Wall, S. (1978). *Patterns of attachment: a psychological study of the strange situation*. Hillsdale, NJ: Erlbaum.

Belsky, J. (1996). Parent, infant, and social-contextual determinants of attachment security. *Developmental Psychology, 32*, 905–14.

Belsky, J., and Jaffee, S. (2006). The multiple determinants of parenting. In D. Cicchetti and D. Cohen (Eds.), *Developmental psychopathology*, vol. III: *Risk, disorder, and adaptation* (2nd edn., pp. 38–85). Hoboken, NJ: Wiley.

Belsky, J., and Pasco Fearon, R. M. (2008). Precursors of attachment security. In J. Cassidy and P. R. Shaver (Eds.), *Handbook of attachment: Theory, research, and clinical applications* (2nd edn., pp. 295–316). New York: Guilford Press.

Biglan, A., Flay, B. R., Embry, D. D., and Sandler, I. N. (2012) The critical role of nurturing environments for promoting human well-being. *American Psychologist, 67*, 257–71.

Bishaw, A. (2011) Areas with concentrated poverty: 2006–2010. *American Community Survey Briefs*. US Census Bureau, December (www.census.gov/hhes/www/poverty/).

Bornstein, M. H., Haynes, O. M., Azuma, H., Galperin, C., Maital, S., Ogino, M., Painter, K., *et al.* (1998). A cross-national study of self-evaluations and attributions in parenting: Argentina, Belgium, France, Israel, Italy, Japan, and the United States. *Developmental Psychology, 34*, 662–76.

Bowlby, J. (1969). *Attachment*. New York: Basic Books.

    (1988). Developmental psychiatry comes of age. *American Journal of Psychiatry, 145*, 1–10.

Britner, P. A., Marvin, R. S., and Pianta, R. C. (2005). Development and preliminary validation of the caregiving behavior system: association with child attachment classification in the preschool strange situation. *Attachment and Human Development, 7*, 83–102.

Bronte-Tinkew, J., Zaslow, M., Capps, R., Horowitz, A., and McNamara, M. (2007). Food insecurity works through depression, parenting and infant feeding to influence overweight and health in toddlers. *Journal of Nutrition, 137*(9), 2160–5.

Carlson, E. A. (1998). A prospective longitudinal study of attachment disorganization/disorientation. *Child Development, 69*, 1107–28.

Carlson, V., Cicchetti, D., Barnett, D., and Braunwald, K. (1989). Disorganized/disoriented attachment relationships in maltreated infants. *Developmental Psychology, 25*, 525–31.

Carlson, V. J. (manuscript in preparation, 2014). Women in leadership: a cross-cultural exploration of strategies and visions for women in resource-poor communities.

Carlson, V. J., and Harwood, R. L. (2003a). Alternate pathways to competence: culture and early attachment relationships. In S. M. Johnson and V. Whiffen (Eds.), *Attachment processes in couple and family therapy* (pp. 85–99). New York: Guilford Press.

  (2003b). Attachment, culture, and the caregiving system: the cultural patterning of everyday experiences among Anglo and Puerto Rican mother–infant pairs. *Infant Mental Health Journal, 24*, 53–73.

Carod-Artal, F. J., and Vázquez-Cabrera, C. B. (2007). An anthropological study about epilepsy in native tribes from Central and South America. *Epilepsia, 48*, 886–93.

Cicchetti, D., Rogosch, F. A., and Toth, S. L. (2006). Fostering secure attachment in infants in maltreating families through preventative interventions. *Development and Psychopathology, 18*, 623–49.

D'Andrade, R. G. (1984). Cultural meaning systems. In R. Shweder and R. LeVine (Eds.), *Culture theory: essays on mind, self, and emotion* (pp. 88–117). New York: Cambridge University Press.

Day, R. D. (2010). *Introduction to family processes* (5th edn.). New York: Routledge.

De Wolff, M. S., and van IJzendoorn, M. H. (1997). Sensitivity and attachment: a meta-analysis on parental antecedents of infant attachment. *Child Development, 68*(4), 571–91.

Diener, M. L., Nievar, M. A., and Wright, C. (2003). Attachment security between mothers and their young children living in poverty: associations with maternal, child and contextual characteristics. *Merrill-Palmer Quarterly, 49*, 154–82.

Duncan, G., and Magnuson, K. A. (2003). Off with Hollingshead: socioeconomic resources, parenting, and child development. In M. H. Bornstein and R. H. Bradley (Eds.), *Socioeconomic status, parenting, and child development* (pp. 83–107). Mahwah, NJ: Erlbaum.

Eberly, S. S. (1988). Fairies and the folklore of disability: changelings, hybrids and the solitary fairy. *Folklore, 99*, 59–77.

Elder, G. H., Jr. (1985). The life course as developmental theory. *Child Development, 69*, 1–12.

  (1995). Life trajectories in changing societies. In A. Bandura (Ed.), *Self-efficacy in changing societies* (pp. 46–57). New York: Cambridge University Press.

Fenning, R. M., and Baker, J. K. (2012). Mother–child interaction and resilience in children with early developmental risk. *Journal of Family Psychology, 26*(3), 411–20.

George, C., and Solomon, J. (2008). The caregiving system: a behavioral approach to parenting. In J. Cassidy and P. R. Shaver (Eds.), *Handbook of attachment: theory, research, and clinical applications* (2nd edn., pp. 383–416). New York: Guilford Press.

Goldsmith, H. H., and Alansky, J. A. (1987). Maternal and infant predictors of attachment: a meta-analytic review. *Journal of Consulting and Clinical Psychology*, *55*, 805–16.

Halfon, N. N., and Hochstein, M. M. (2002). Life course health development: an integrated framework for developing health, policy, and research. *Milbank Quarterly*, *80*(3), 433–79.

Halfon, N., Inkelas, M., and Hochstein, M. (2000). The health development organization: an organizational approach to achieving child health. *Milbank Quarterly*, *78*(3), 447–97.

Hallin, A. L., Bengtsson, H. H., Frostell, A. S., and Stjernqvist, K. K. (2012). The effect of extremely preterm birth on attachment organization in late adolescence. *Child: Care, Health and Development*, *38*(2), 196–203.

Harkness, S., and Super, C. M. (2002). Culture and parenting. In M. H. Bornstein (Ed.), *Handbook of parenting*, vol. II: *Biology and ecology of parenting* (2nd edn., pp. 253–80). Mahwah, NJ: Erlbaum.

Harwood, R. L., and Miller, A. M. (1991). Perceptions of attachment behavior: a comparison of Anglo and Puerto Rican mothers. *Merrill Palmer Quarterly*, *37*, 583–99.

Harwood, R. L., Miller, A. M., Carlson, V. J., and Leyendecker, B. (2002). Parenting beliefs and practices among middle-class Puerto Rican mother–infant pairs. In J. M. Contreras, K. A. Kerns, and A. M. Neal-Barnett (Eds.), *Latino children and families in the United States* (pp. 133–54). Westport, CT: Praeger.

Harwood, R. L., Miller, J. G., and Irizarry, N. L. (1995). *Culture and attachment: perceptions of the child in context.* New York: Guilford Press.

Harwood, R. L., Schoelmerich, A., Schulze, P. A., and Gonzalez, Z. (1999). Cultural differences in maternal beliefs and behaviors: a study of middle-class Anglo and Puerto Rican mother–infant pairs in four everyday situations. *Child Development*, *70*(4), 1005–16.

Harwood, R. L., Schoelmerich, A., Ventura-Cook, E., Schulze, P., and Wilson, S. P. (1996). Culture and class influences on Anglo and Puerto Rican mothers' beliefs regarding long-term socialization goals and child behavior. *Child Development*, *67*, 2446–61.

Hrdy, S. B. (1999). *Mother nature: history of mothers, infants, and natural selection.* New York: Random House.

Hvistendahl, M. (2011). Unnatural selection. *Psychology Today*, *July/August*, 81–7.

Ipsa, J., Fine, M., Thornburg, K., and Sharp, E. (2001). Maternal childrearing goals: consistency and correlates. Poster presented at the biennial meeting of the Society for Research in Child Development, Minneapolis, MN, USA.

Jackson, J. F. (1986). Characteristics of black infant attachment behaviors. *American Journal of Social Psychiatry*, *6*(1), 32–5.

Joshi, A., and Tiwari, N. (2011). Sex ratio in India – embarrassing to be honest. *Current Science*, *101*, 1006–8.

Kağitçibaşi, C. (2007). *Family, self, and human development across cultures: theory and applications* (2nd edn.). Mahwah, NJ: Erlbaum.

Keller, H. (2007). *Cultures of infancy*. Mahwah, NJ: Erlbaum.

LeVine, R. A. (2004). Challenging expert knowledge: findings from an African study of infant care and development. In U. P. Gielen and J. L. Roopnarine (Eds.), *Childhood and adolescence: cross-cultural perspectives and applications* (pp. 149–65). Westport, CT: Praeger/Greenwood.

Lovejoy, M. C., Graczyk, P. A., O'Hare E., and Neuman, G. (2000). Maternal depression and parenting behavior: a meta-analytic review. *Clinical Psychology Review*, 20(5), 561–92.

Lyons-Ruth, K., and Jacobvitz, D. (2008). Attachment disorganization: genetic factors, parenting contexts, and developmental transformation from infancy to adulthood. In J. Cassidy and P. R. Shaver (Eds.), *Handbook of attachment: theory, research, and clinical applications* (2nd edn., pp. 666–97). New York: Guilford Press.

Macartney, S. (2011). Child poverty in the United States 2009 and 2010: selected race groups and Hispanic origin. *American Community Survey Briefs*. US Census Bureau, November (www.census.gov/hhes/www/poverty/).

Main, M., Hesse, E., and Kaplan, N. (2005). Predictability of attachment behavior and representational processes at 1, 6, and 18 years of age: the Berkeley longitudinal study. In K. E. Grossmann, K. Grossmann, and E. Waters (Eds.), *Attachment from infancy to adulthood* (pp. 245–304). New York: Guilford Press.

Main, M., and Solomon, J. (1990). Procedures for identifying infants as disorganized/disoriented during the Ainsworth Strange Situation. In M.T. Greenberg, D. Cicchetti, and E. M. Cummings (Eds.), *Attachment in the preschool years: theory, research, and intervention* (pp. 121–60). University of Chicago Press.

Martini, M. (2001). Parents' goals and methods of shaping infant intentionality in four cultural groups. Poster presented at the biennial meeting of the Society for Research in Child Development, Minneapolis, MN, USA.

McCall, R. B., Groark, C. J., Groza, V., Juffer, F., van IJzendoorn, M. H., and Vorria, P. (2012). The development and care of institutionally reared children. *Child Development Perspectives*, 6, 174–80.

McLoyd, V. C. (1990). The impact of economic hardship on Black families and children: psychological distress, parenting, and socioemotional development. *Child Development*, 61, 311–46.

Oppenheim, D., Dolev, S., Koren-Karie, N., Sher-Censor, E., Yirmiya, N., and Salomon, S. (2007). Parental resolution of the child's diagnosis and the parent–child relationship: insights from the Reaction to Diagnosis Interview. In D. Oppenheim and D. F. Goldsmith (Eds.), *Attachment theory in clinical work with children: bridging the gap between research and practice* (pp. 109–36). New York: Guilford Press.

Pauls, C. D., Choudhury, N., Leppanen, P. H. T., and Benasich, A. A. (2001). *The relationship among maternal knowledge and beliefs about infant development, infant temperament, and mother–infant interaction*. Poster presented at the biennial meeting of the Society for Research in Child Development, Minneapolis, MN, USA.

Pianta, R. C., Marvin, R. S., Britner, P. A., and Borowitz, K. C. (1996). Mothers' resolution of their children's diagnosis: organized patterns of caregiving representations. *Infant Mental Health Journal, 17,* 239–56.

Posada, G., Gao, Y., Wu, F., Posada, R., Tascon, M., Schoelmerich, A., Sagi, A., *et al.* (1995). The secure-base phenomenon across cultures: children's behavior, mothers' preferences, and experts' concepts. *Monographs of the Society for Research in Child Development, 60*(2–3), 27–48.

Rao, N., McHale, J., and Pearson, E., (2003). Links between socialization goals and child-rearing practices in Chinese and Indian mothers. *Infant and Child Development, 12,* 475–92.

Richter, L. (2004). *The importance of caregiver–child interactions for the survival and healthy development of young children: a review.* Geneva: World Health Organization.

Rogoff, B. (2003). *The cultural nature of human development.* New York: Oxford.

Rothbaum, F., Pott, M., Azuma, H., Miyake, K., and Weisz, J. (2000). The development of close relationships in Japan and the United States: paths of symbiotic harmony and generative tension. *Child Development, 71,* 1121–42.

Saraswathi, T. S., and Ganapathy, H. (2002) Indian parents' ethnotheories as reflections of the Hindu scheme of child and human development. In H. Keller, Y. Poortinga, and A. Schölmerich (Eds.), *Between culture and biology* (pp. 79–88). Cambridge University Press.

Sargent, C. F. (1987). Born to die: the fate of extraordinary children in Bariba culture. *Ethnology, 23,* 79–96.

Scheper-Hughes, N. (1979). *Saints, scholars and schizophrenics: mental illness in rural Ireland.* Berkeley, CA: University of California Press.

(1992). *Death without weeping: the violence of everyday life in Brazil.* Berkeley, CA: University of California Press.

Stevenson-Hinde, J. (1998). Parenting in different cultures: time to focus. *Developmental Psychology, 34*(4), 698–700.

Thompson, R., and Virmani, E. A. (2010). Self and personality. In M. H. Bornstein (Ed.), *Handbook of cultural developmental science* (pp. 195–207). New York: Psychology Press.

Tomlinson, M., Cooper, P., and Murray, L. (2005). The mother–infant relationship and infant attachment in a South African peri-urban settlement. *Child Development, 76,* 1044–54.

Tronick, E., and Beeghly, M. (2011). Infants' meaning-making and the development of mental health problems. *American Psychologist, 66,* 107–19.

US Department of Agriculture (2011). *Food security in the U.S.: key statistics and graphics.* US Department of Agriculture (www.ers.usda.gov/topics/food-nutrition-assistance/food-security-in-the-us/key-statistics-graphics.aspx).

Valenzuela, M. (1997). Maternal sensitivity in a developing society: the context of urban poverty and infant chronic undernutrition. *Developmental Psychology, 33,* 845–55.

van IJzendoorn, M. H., and Bakermans-Kranenburg, M. J. (2010). Invariance of adult attachment across gender, age, culture, and socioeconomic status? *Journal of Social and Personal Relationships, 27,* 200–8.

van IJzendoorn, M. H., and Sagi-Schwartz (2008). Cross-cultural patterns of attachment: universal and contextual dimensions. In J. Cassidy and P. R. Shaver (Eds.), *Handbook of attachment: theory, research, and clinical applications* (2nd edn., pp. 880–905). New York: Guilford Press.

Walsh, A. (2003). Representations of attachment and caregiving: the disruptive effects of loss and trauma. *Dissertation Abstracts International, 64.*

Weinfield, N. S., Sroufe, L. A., Egeland, B., and Carlson, E. (2008). Individual differences in infant–caregiver attachment: conceptual and empirical aspects of security. In J. Cassidy and P. R. Shaver (Eds.), *Handbook of attachment: theory, research, and clinical applications* (2nd edn., pp. 78–101). New York: Guilford Press.

Weisner, T. S. (2005). Attachment as a cultural and ecological problem with pluralistic solutions. *Human Development, 48*(1–2), 89–94.

Weiss, R. E. (2007). *Guarantee the sex of your baby.* Berkeley, CA: Ulysses Press.

Zaslow, M., Bronte-Tinkew, J., Capps, R., Horowitz, A., Moore, K. A., and Weinstein, D. (2009). Food security during infancy: implications for attachment and mental proficiency in toddlerhood. *Journal of Maternal and Child Health, 13,* 66–80.

Zeanah, C. (Ed.). (2009). *Handbook of infant mental health* (3rd edn.). New York: Guilford Press.

Part IV

Conclusion

12   Epilogue: the future of attachment

Heidi Keller and Hiltrud Otto

The aim of this book is to situate attachment theory and research as a culturally informed conception of socialization and child development. All chapters in this book concur that developing attachment with responsible caretakers is an evolved necessity for infant survival, thriving, and development. All chapters also concur that the mainstream attachment theory as developed by John Bowlby and Mary Ainsworth has not adequately accommodated existing and emerging knowledge that was not available or accessible to the founders. There is no doubt that attachment is a basic human need, a pancultural motivation that babies carry in their genes when entering this world. However, this world is not a uniform environment with one adaptive ideology of parenting, with one conception of good parenting, and one view on valued developmental achievements. Current attachment theory has concentrated on the universal aspects of the necessity of attachment relationships. The context that is taken into consideration is the social environment, mainly the mother, without situating the mother also into a social and physical context that obviously affects her parenting style and children's developmental outcomes.

The need for "cross-national studies on early attachment" has been stated recently by Causadias and Posada (2013). However, their claim is mainly to include more diversity in terms of stressful life circumstances like poverty and war. They also want to see more studies assessing differences in values and parenting preferences, yet they feel that "research on parental preferences . . . does not entirely address the issue of cultural specificity" (p. 18). The position that is exemplified in this volume, however, is that contextual and thus cultural variation cannot be reduced to situations of affluence or adversity, but that culture is expressed in the everyday life of practices and beliefs over the entire life span. Infancy is a cultural lens, as Alma Gottlieb (2004) has put it, that magnifies cultural preferences, values, and practices. As we have shown in our own research program, caregivers respond substantially differently to the same infant signals from the first days on (Keller and Kärtner, 2013).

Interestingly, the cultural variation that has been noticed because of its obvious evidence has been downplayed by attachment researchers, so that the conclusions unanimously attest to the confirmation of attachment theory's assumptions (e.g., the examples in Sagi, van IJzendoorn, and Koren-Karie, 1991). Seemingly, there are contradictions in attachment theory itself, when – on the one hand – contextual dependency is acknowledged and – on the other hand – cultural variation is ignored. The present volume demonstrates that cultural variation cannot be ignored, since if contextual dependency is acknowledged, different contexts with different experiences cannot be seen to lead to the same developmental results (for more details on culture-specific developmental pathways in general, see Keller and Kärtner, 2013). We hope that the collection of cultural and cross-cultural chapters in this volume will help to substantiate the argument that contextual variation is nontrivial and will necessarily imply different social systems and different conceptions of relationships with different developmental results.

The present volume puts forward an important argument regarding cultural variation. So far, multiple caregiving, alloparenting, distributed caregiving, and other common denominators of nonmonotropic mother–child relationships have been discussed as an alternative to monotropic mother–child bonds. The chapters in the present volume make a strong case that all children grow up in multiple social arrangements, yet these may differ in various respects, composition, hierarchy, and meaning. Most of the world's children do not grow up just with their mothers. Rather, this represents even an adverse condition in many cultural environments, since it is often associated with economic problems, poverty, and low social rank. Humankind would not even have survived if this had been the social scenario of our ancestors, as Sarah Hrdy has argued with her cooperative breeding model, which puts a special emphasis on the role of grandmothers (Hrdy, 1999). However, the special configuration of caregivers and their responsibilities and roles in the lives of infants varies substantially. The Western model of monotropic relational development includes the father, whose active role is more and more emphasized (see, e.g., Shwalb, Shwalb, and Lamb, 2013). However, the father does not participate actively in infant care in subsistence farming communities like that of the Cameroonian Nso. This does not mean that babies are less important for fathers and fathers less important for babies. It indicates that parenting and parental love is differently defined, whether as an emotional bond or provision of economic security to mother and children. Yet, also in the lives of Western, middle-class babies, grandparents – mainly grandmothers – other relatives, and babysitters play a role. Western, middle-class babies attend day care earlier than babies from lower socioeconomic family backgrounds, so that day-care professionals also belong to their social world.

Nonmonotropic caregiving arrangements represent a universe on their own. This volume presents an array of arrangements and responsibilities of caregivers during children's first years – the mother being the primary caregiver within a network of others (as among the Aka); the mother being the primary caregiver for a short period of time (as in the Beng community) and then complemented and replaced by other caregivers; the mother being a primary caregiver who holds intensive caregiving relationships also with other infants and even animals (as among the Pirahã); and distributed caregiving arrangements with the mother not being necessarily the primary caregiver (as in the Brazilian *favelas* and the Cameroonian Nso). This collection is in some respects random, because the study sites were not identified with respect to the study of attachment relationships, so that many other arrangements are conceivable. Related to the caregiving arrangement is the pattern of meaning that relationships in general and particular caregiver–infant bonds carry. As outlined in the Introduction, two major relational models can be identified, that of the child-centered and mind-minded psychological bond and that of permanent physical availability. Both models aim at describing and explaining children's development of trust in others as well as trust in their own agency. Again, the selection of cultural environments that allow us to infer ideas about the nature of this development of trust is restricted, so that systematic research programs need to be developed. The conception of relationships is embedded in the conception of the person or the self that is embodied in the relational networks. Moreover, the chapters in this volume allow thinking about other realities beyond the autonomous infant in Western, middle-class ideology. In his chapter, Lancy offers the conception of "delayed personhood," in which the infant receives the human condition not automatically with birth or earlier, but after days, weeks, or months postnatally. The reasons for this include the need to cope with a high infant-mortality rate, mothers' vulnerabilities, and dysfunctional families (see also Scheper-Hughes, this volume). Each of these conditions leads to different folk psychologies of what babies are and how parenting should be organized.

The acknowledgment of multiple caregiving arrangements should also lead to de-emphasizing the mother as the primary influence on children's developmental outcomes in all cultural environments. The sole consideration of the mother may not do justice to the complexity of children's developmental pathways. Meehan and Hawks' chapter in this volume offers some evidence that allomothers' caregiving style influences not only child behaviors but also early childhood developmental outcomes.

Here dynamics must also be taken into consideration – alloparenting influences not only children and their development but also mothers and their caregiving. In their chapter, Meehan and Hawks also report on concordances and discordances among mothers and other caregivers, factors which have not been adequately addressed in the literature so far. This is not only a topic of traditional family-based parenting, but also reaches out to the relationship between the family and day-care institution in Western, middle-class milieus. We know that the family usually has a larger impact on children's developmental outcomes (European Child Care and Education (ECCE) Study Group, 1999), but we do not know much about the effects of matching and mismatching care ideologies between institution and family. In fact, we know very little about the social embeddedness of caregiving, the internal organization, and the consequences in general. In particular we do not know very much about intracultural variation beyond the WEIRD world. Hiltrud Otto offers in her chapter some interesting insights on this topic, which is grossly understudied.

A topic that we excluded from this volume is the neurophysiological and psychobiological bases of attachment relationships. In recent decades, there has been an increasing interest, combined with research, in the understanding of the (neuro-)physiological underpinnings of attachment relationships. So far, different physiological measures have been assessed in terms of attachment regulation, mainly in response to encounters with strangers (for a summary, see Ellis-Davies, 2013; Fox and Hane, 2008):

(1) *Heart rate (HR)*: securely attached infants' HR seems to recover faster after HR increases during separation from the mother than insecurely attached infants; nevertheless, the results are not unequivocal across studies, and there seems to be an interaction with temperament and other personality descriptors.

(2) *Cortisol*: salivary cortisol reactivity is a very common measure due to its noninvasiveness. Nevertheless, results differ with different assessment modalities. In general, it may be tentatively argued that stress during the strange situation is reflected in increases in cortisol levels – here interactions with temperament and other psychological measures are also reported (Gunnar, Mangelsdorf, Larson et al., 1991).

(3) *Oxytocin*: the role of oxytocin in facilitating reciprocity and bonding is another recent area of intensive research (Feldman, Zagoory-Sharon, Weisman et al., 2012).

Attachment theorists mainly follow Schore (2001) as well as others who concentrate in their neurological analyses on the dyadic interactional exchange, especially in the face-to-face mode between infant and mother. In particular, the mother's emotionally expressive face is considered to attract the infant's gaze and engage the infant in periods of intense

mutual gaze. Through the interactional exchange, an interpersonal chan-
nel is created that is assumed to be directly linked to brain development.
However, there is ample evidence that face-to-face contact is not the
primary mode of exchange between infants and their caregivers in many
cultural environments, as the chapters in this volume impressively document. The neurobiological development of attachment in proximal channels is still unknown.

Moreover, there is an exciting emerging field of cultural neuroscience
that has documented the first evidence that brain functioning and development are also culture-specific (e.g., Chiao, 2009; Panksepp, 1998).

The chapters in this volume demonstrate that we already have substantial information about different faces of attachment. What is needed now
are systematic research programs to study intra- and intercultural variation in order to predict children's future developmental achievements.
The implementation of cultural conceptions of attachment will be crucial for the success of prevention and intervention programs and should
inform practitioners as well as policymakers.

A study program to investigate attachment as a biocultural construct
should comprise the following phases.

First, conceptions of attachment and caregiver–child relationships
should be reconstructed from indigenous perspectives in focus-group
discussions and qualitative and semistructured interviews. Second, following from the Baltimore study of Ainsworth, Blehar, Waters *et al.*
(1978), children and their families should be observed in their natural
social environments longitudinally over the first year of life by an array
of methods in order to document and analyze infants' social experiences.
Third, the indigenous conceptions of attachment and their different qualities should be assessed in terms of behavioral and neurophysiological
measures when children are 1 year of age. A research program like this
can only be realized through a cooperative network of scholars coming
from different disciplines and having access to the cultural groups that are
to be specified by socioecological parameters. However, such a research
program is necessary in order to comprehend attachment as an evolutionary adaptation. We hope to have instigated with the present volume
some moves in this direction.

References

Ainsworth, M. D. S., Blehar, M. C., Waters, E., and Wall, S. (1978). *Patterns of attachment: a psychological study of the strange situation.* Hillsdale, NJ:
Erlbaum.

Causadias, J. M., and Posada, G. (2013). The relevance of cross-cultural studies on early attachment: research advances in Latin America. *Bulletin of the International Society for the Study of Behavioural Development*, *1*(63), 18–21.

Chiao, J. Y. (2009). Cultural neuroscience: a once and future discipline. *Progress in Brain Research*, *178*, 287–304.

Ellis-Davies, K. (2013). Early attachment research: new and recurring themes. *ISSBD Bulletin*, *63*(1), 33–8.

European Child Care and Education (ECCE) Study Group (1999). Final Report, submitted to the European Union DG XII: Science, Research and Development, RTD Action. *Targeted socio-economic research* (www.uni-bamberg. de/fileadmin/uni/fakultaeten/ppp_lehrstuehle/elementarpaedagogik/Team/ Rossbach/Ecce_Study_Group.pdf).

Feldman, R., Zagoory-Sharon, O., Weisman, O., Schneiderman, I., Gordon, I., Maoz, R., and Ebstein, R. P. (2012). Sensitive parenting is associated with plasma oxytocin and polymorphisms in the *OXTR* and *CD38* genes. *Biological Psychiatry*, *72*(3), 175–81.

Fox, N. A., and Hane, A. A. (2008). Studying the biology of human attachment. In P. Shaver and J. Cassidy (Eds.), *Handbook of attachment* (2nd edn., pp. 217–40). New York: Guilford Press.

Gottlieb, A. (2004). *The afterlife is where we come from*. University of Chicago Press.

Gunnar, M. R., Mangelsdorf, S., Larson, M., and Hertsgaard, L. (1991). *Attachment, temperament, and adrenocortical activity in infancy: a study of psychoendocrine regulation*. Philadelphia: Brunner/Mazel.

Hrdy, S. B. (1999). *Mother nature: a history of mothers, infants, and natural selection*. New York: Pantheon.

Keller, H., and Kärtner, J. (2013). Development – the culture-specific solution of universal developmental tasks. In M. L. Gelfand, C.-Y. Chiu, and Y. Y. Hong (Eds.), *Advances in culture and psychology* (vol.III , pp. 63–116). Oxford University Press.

Panksepp, J. (1998). *Affective neuroscience: the foundations of human and animal emotions*. New York: Oxford University Press.

Sagi, A., van IJzendoorn, H. M., and Koren-Karie, N. (1991). Primary appraisal of the strange situation: a cross-cultural analysis of preseparation episodes. *Developmental Psychology*, *27*(4), 587–96.

Schore, A. N. (2001). The effects of a secure attachment relationship on right brain development, affect regulation, and infant mental health. *Infant Mental Health Journal*, *22*, 7–66.

Shwalb, D. B., Shwalb, B. J., and Lamb, M. E. (Eds.) (2013). *Fathers in cultural context*. New York: Routledge.

Index